RESISTANCE AND REFORM IN TIBET

Resistance and Reform in Tibet

edited by

ROBERT BARNETT

General editor
SHIRIN AKINER

INDIANA UNIVERSITY PRESS
BLOOMINGTON AND INDIANAPOLIS

Manufactured in Hong Kong

Library of Congress Cataloging-in-Publication Data

Resistance and reform in Tibet / Robert Barnett and Shirin Akiner
    [editors].
        p.   cm.
    Includes bibliographical references.
    ISBN 0-253-31131-4
    1. Tibet (China) — Congresses.   I. Barnett, Robert,
    II. Akiner, Shirin.
    DS785.A1R47   1993
    951'.5 — dc20   93-3072

1 2 3 4 5   98 97 96 95 94

CONTENTS

Contents

Part IV. RESISTANCE IN TIBET, 1987–1990

MAPS

ILLUSTRATIONS

PREFACE AND ACKNOWLEDGEMENTS

On first visiting Tibet some five years ago I was vaguely aware that what I was seeing did not fit the pictures familiar from the writings of the two parties in the political debate. Tibet was neither a cultural mausoleum nor a replica of modern China. Back in Europe, where I took to writing about this subject, it became clearer that this new Tibet was a society with its own distinctive character and evolution, matching neither the descriptions of new China provided by sinologists nor the studies of earlier Tibetologists. There was little I could find in Western academic literature which sought to describe that society as it was then developing.

At the time of that visit there was much journalistic interest in Tibet because of the upsurge of demonstrations, but for the most part the journalists seemed to go from one to another asking hopefully if anyone knew someone who knew about the subject. There were numerous China-scholars, Buddhologists and experts on the Himalayas, not to mention travellers and adventurers, but apart from isolated scholars like Goldstein and Clarke there was no pool of independent experts who could speak from experience about the country.

This book is offered as a response to that dearth of studies on contemporary Tibet. For both 'general readers' and scholars it offers perhaps the first description in a Western language of Tibet over the four decades since 1950. In October of that year the Chinese army had begun its advance into Central Tibet, bringing to an end three centuries of rule by the Dalai Lamas. Although Tibet was completely isolated from the outside world for much of the next thirty years, during which the Chinese authorities attempted to erase Tibetan culture, the visit of Hu Yaobang to Lhasa in 1980 led to a policy of reform and liberalisation. It was a dramatic change, but seven years later, in October 1987, when police opened fire on Tibetans demonstrating in the central square of Lhasa, that policy of reform had to be set against the reality of passionate resistance to Chinese rule. The spate of protests and unrest that followed, which led to the imposition of martial law in March 1989, threw the credibility of those reforms into disarray, and raised into high profile once again the question of Tibetan nationhood and the country's contemporary identity: what is it that has survived the thirty years of isolation, and what will it become?

In seeking answers to these questions, the book embraces a wide range of subjects, most of them not previously approached outside

China or Tibet. Others have been tackled previously only in the context of polemical debate or without the benefit of scholarly research. To procure these studies meant asking scholars to venture into what was for most of them a new and uncharted area, a task I approached with some trepidation. A leading sinologist and expert on modern China had no doubts: Tibet, he said, was 'peripheral and of no significance', and he refused to write on the subject.

Tsering Shakya and Robert Mayer, who first initiated this project, had greater vision and perseverance, and were instrumental in turning our attention to the classical field. If I had imagined classical Tibetologists as a desk-bound species who would be reluctant to venture into the broad light of modernity, I was wrong, for there was an enthusiastic response to our request for studies on the four decades since 1950. Some of the contributors to the volume had previously written purely on classical Tibetan studies; others, particularly exile Tibetan scholars, had been interested in modern studies, but had been hampered by the difficulties of access to the region.

The academics working on Tibet seemed able to shift their focus with ease, and had, I suspect, been waiting only for an opportunity to write about a Tibet that was evolving rather than one which had perished; it was as if no one in the West had bothered to ask them before. The facility with which Western classicists also adapted their disciplines to deal with a modern and greatly changed Tibet was also instructive: it seemed a reflection of the continuity between the old and the modern. It is this continuity which, in part, defines Tibet as a distinct society, rather than as a regional variant of the Chinese conglomerate.

This continuity reflects other things too, and one which is of prime importance in such an aggravated field: the value of scholarly discipline. Academic restraint may be considered in some quarters an outmoded virtue, but in the study of modern Tibet at least it is indispensable. Here we invited social scientists in particular to apply their techniques to the study of modern Tibet, much as they would to any other evolving society. We were aware that modern, and in fact earlier, writing in both China and the West had tended to depict Tibetans either as passive participants or as victims in a larger process. But the Tibetans we had encountered in person or through their own writings were creative agents in whatever situation they found themselves, and the social sciences seemed to offer a more expressive and more dignified language with which to describe them than that of either hagiography or martyrology.

Journalistic and popular writing on Tibet has clearly been hampered in its range and credibility by the lack of a literature based on detailed contemporary research. By promoting the study of modern Tibet we sought to remedy that omission, and above all raise the level of discourse. To be academic is not to be impartial, and it does not bring with it any entitlement to claim truth; the studies in this volume are essentially interpretive, but they are founded on verifiable research and on adherence to certain principles of analysis and description which, we believe, provide a foundation for further discussion.

It will be for others to judge whether this collection of studies achieves any of those ideals. But if it encourages the perception of Tibet as an evolving and distinctive society, if it leads to further research and informed discussion of modern Tibetan society, and if it brings about more involvement in that discussion by Tibetans and Chinese themselves, it will have served its purpose well.

Many of the studies presented here were first prepared as papers for the conference 'Forty Years On: Tibet 1950–90', held at the School of Oriental and African Studies in London in April 1990, under the chairmanship of Tsering Shakya and of Dr Shirin Akiner of the Central Asian Studies Association.

Special thanks are due to Patricia Carley for her dedicated work, and to the British Council, the Universities' China Committee in London, the Morton Charitable Fund and the David Montefiore Trust for their assistance with travel grants for scholars from China and India. Special gratitude is also due to Per Kvaerne for his advice and patience, and to John Rowley and other volunteers for their assistance. Picture research was by Jane Moore of the Tibet Image Bank, London, and the Royal Geographic Society. Anders Anderson and Jirina Simajchlova all contributed valuable photographs. Special thanks are due to Christophe Besuchet of Atelier Golok, Geneva, for the maps.

Tibetan studies are beset by the difficulties of arriving at a standard orthography, and this book is no exception. Formal transliterations have been given according to the Turrell Wylie system, but authors have been allowed to retain their own preferences with regard to capitalisation. These will be of little value for non-specialists, so after most transliterations a phonetic rendering, or sometimes an alternative spelling, is added in brackets.

The phonetic approximations of Tibetan names and places have been standardised in a form which we hope will aid non-specialist readers, although this has sometimes meant ignoring the wishes of the writers, all of whom have their own practice in this matter.

For Chinese words the *pinyin* system is used, except for certain pre-Revolution names which are more easily recognised as rendered in the Wade-Giles system. Thus Peking and Mao Tse-tung have become Beijing and Mao Zedong, but Chiang Kai-shek has been allowed to remain in his traditional form, as he would certainly have preferred.

I would like to thank Tsering Shakya for his untiring assistance and scholarship in helping prepare the manuscript and inspiring the enterprise, all the authors for their patience and generosity in contributing to this collection, and above all the people in Tibet who made it possible and who continue to make it possible to talk about a modern Tibet.

London   ROBERT BARNETT
August 1994

THE CO-AUTHORS

PREMEN ADDY is the author of *Tibet on the Imperial Chessboard*, an account of early 20th-century Tibeto-British politics. He is an editor of the London-based journal *India Weekly* and lectures on modern Asian history and politics at Rewley House, Oxford.

ROBERT BARNETT is a researcher and writer specialising in Tibetan and Chinese affairs. He founded and directs the Tibet Information Network, an independent monitoring organisation based in London.

MELVYN C. GOLDSTEIN is the John Harkness Reynolds Professor of Anthropology at Case Western Reserve University in Cleveland, Ohio, where he is also Director of the University's Center for Research on Tibet. He was the first Western scholar to be allowed to undertake extensive research in Tibet, and his numerous works on the country include a *Dictionary of Modern Tibetan* and his *History of the Modern Tibetan State*.

HANNA HAVNEVIK is the author of *Tibetan Buddhist Nuns: History, Cultural Norms and Social Reality*. She gained her MA in the history of religion at the University of Oslo, and acts as an adviser on refugees to the Norwegian government.

SAMTEN KARMAY is Head of Research at the Centre National de la Recherche Scientifique and a member of the Laboratoire d'Ethnologie et de Sociologie Comparative at the University of Paris X. His books include *The Great Perfection*, *Secret Visions of the Fifth Dalai Lama* and *A Tibetan History of Bon*.

PER KVAERNE is Professor of the History of Religions at the University of Oslo, and has been a Research Professor at the Nordic Institute of Asian Studies. He is the author of *An Anthology of Buddhist Tantric Songs: A Study of the Caryagiti*, and has written studies of the pre-Buddhist Bonpo religion.

JAMYANG NORBU is a leading Tibetan writer, novelist and commentator. He was Director of the Tibetan Institute for Performing Arts (TIPA) in Dharamsala until 1987. He was himself a member of the Tibetan Guerrilla Force which operated from Nepal until 1974. His books include *Horseman in the Snow* and *Illusion and Reality*.

RONALD D. SCHWARTZ is Head of the Department of Sociology at Memorial University, St John's (Nfld), Canada. He is the author of 'Reform and Repression in Tibet' in *Telos* (Summer 1989), and of *Circle of Protest: Political Ritual in the Tibetan Uprising* (1994). One of the few Tibetan-speaking sociologists, he spent eight months in Tibet between 1987 and 1989.

TSERING W. SHAKYA, a graduate of the School of Oriental and African Studies in London, is a leading Tibetan historian. He is currently working on a major history of modern Tibet from 1949 to 1990.

WARREN W. SMITH, Director of the Tibet Project of Cultural Survival, is a graduate of the Fletcher School of Law and Diplomacy in Boston, Mass.

ELLIOT SPERLING is Professor of Tibetan Studies at Indiana University, Bloomington, and recently held the same position at Harvard University. He is the author of numerous articles on Sino-Tibetan and Sino-Mongolian relations.

HEATHER STODDARD is Head of the Tibetan Department at the Institut National des Langues et Civilisations Orientales at the University of Paris III. Her books include *Early Sino-Tibetan Art* and *Le Mendiant d'Amdo: A Biography of dGe.'dun Chos.'phel.*

TSERING WANGYAL is the Editor of *Tibetan Review*, the monthly journal of Tibetan affairs. He studied history at the University of Bristol.

WANG XIAOQIANG, currently a research scholar at Cambridge University, was Deputy Director of the Institute for Economic Structure Reform in Beijing and Vice-President of the Beijing Young Economists' Society. He is a co-author of *The Poverty of Plenty*, a study of China's economic policies towards its western region.

WANG YAO is a leading Tibetologist and a senior member of the Tibetan Department of the National Institute of Minority Nationalities in Beijing. He was Hu Yaobang's translator during Hu's visit to Tibet in May 1980. His academic work includes *Influence of Lamaism on Tibetan Culture* and *A Collection of Documents about Ancient Tibetan History from the Dunhuang Caves.*

CHRONOLOGY

1902. Rumours reach the Viceroy of India, Lord Curzon, that the Russians have signed a secret treaty with the Tibetans. Preparations begin for a British military invasion of Tibet.

1903–4. Colonel Francis Younghusband marches with 3,000 British troops to Gyantse. The 13th Dalai Lama flees from their approach and shelters in Mongolia and in China. The British withdraw after signing the Anglo-Tibetan Convention which allows them to have trade agents at Gyantse and at Gartok in Western Tibet.

1909. The Dalai Lama returns from exile. Chinese troops occupy parts of Kham (Eastern Tibet) and the Dalai Lama appeals to Britain for assistance.

1910. A Chinese army, led by Zhao Erfeng (Chao Erh-feng), invades Tibet and enters Lhasa. The Dalai Lama flees to India.

1911. In Beijing the Manchu (Qing) Dynasty is overthrown and the Republic of China is established under Yuan Shikai (Yuan Shih-k'ai), who declares Tibet, Xinjiang (East Turkestan) and Mongolia to be provinces of China

1912. Throughout the country Tibetans rise up against the Chinese. *August 12.* The Chinese sign a Surrender Agreement with the Tibetans, and are obliged to return to China via India.

1913. The Dalai Lama returns to Lhasa and issues a formal Proclamation of Independence in conjunction with Mongolia.

1914. Tibet, Britain and China attend the Simla Convention as equal powers and initial an agreement, never ratified by China, to settle the Sino-Tibetan border dispute.

1918. Tibetan troops advance to the east and defeat the Chinese; the Treaty of Rongbatsa is brokered by Eric Teichman.

1920. Sir Charles Bell is sent to Lhasa as British representative to reassure the Tibetans of British support for its self-rule and self-defence.

1923. The Panchen Lama, long distrusted for his close relations with the Chinese, disputes his tax liability to the Tibetan Government and flees to China.

1933. Choekyi Gyaltsen, the 13th Dalai Lama, dies in Lhasa aged 58.

continued on page xviii

TIBET

xvi

© Atelier Golok, 1993

 Tibet Autonomous Region (TAR) or Western Tibet	Areas with Tibetan autonomous status under Qinghai, Gansu, Sichuan and Yunnan provinces
Territory claimed by the Tibetan Government in exile	

1937. The 6th Panchen Lama (9th by the Chinese count) dies in Jyekundo (Chinese: Yushu) on the Chinese border.

1940. Tenzin Gyatso, the 14th Dalai Lama, enthroned at Lhasa.

1941–4. Tibet remains neutral during the Second World War and refuses permission for the Americans or the Chinese nationalists to transport military supplies through Tibetan territory.

1947. Tibet sends a delegation to discuss trade and to open formal relations abroad, to India, China, Britain and America.

Tibet is nearly plunged into civil war when Retring, the former regent, supported by the monks of Sera, attempts a *coup d'état*.

1949. In China the People's Liberation Army overcomes the Nationalists (KMT) and on October 1 Mao Zedong proclaims the People's Republic of China. The 10th Panchen Lama, then eleven years old, telegrams Mao Zedong asking him to 'unify the motherland'. The PLA announces its intention to 'liberate Tibet from foreign imperialists'.

1950. The 14th Dalai Lama, then fifteen years old, takes over the running of the Government.

October 7. The Chinese cross the upper Yangtse River into Eastern Tibet and destroy the small garrison force at Chamdo in Kham. The Tibetan Government and the Dalai Lama move to Yarlung and send appeals for help to the United Nations. The British and the Indian delegates there persuade the General Assembly not to discuss the matter.

1951. May 23. The Tibetans, led by Ngapo Ngawang Jigme, sign the Seventeen Point Agreement with the Chinese, which promises cultural and political autonomy to Tibet but relinquishes independence. *October 24*. The agreement is ratified by the Dalai Lama and the National Assembly.

1954. April 29. India and China sign a treaty enunciating the 'Five Principles of Peaceful Co-existence', and recognising China's claim to Tibet.

Revolt grows in Eastern Tibet when the Chinese begin destroying monasteries and imposing collectivisation. Birth of the Tibetan resistance movement and of the Voluntary National Defence Army.

December 25. The Chinese declare open the Qinghai–Tibet and the Xikang–Tibet highways.

1955. Preparatory Committee for the Tibet Autonomous Region

(PCART) set up with the Dalai Lama as chairman and the Panchen Lama and Zhang Guohua as deputy chairmen.

1956. The Dalai Lama goes to India for the Buddha Jayanti celebrations and tells Nehru he wants to stay; after Zhou Enlai and Mao promise that there will be no forced reforms, he returns to Lhasa.

1959. March 10. Thousands of Tibetans take to the streets in Lhasa. *March 17.* The Dalai Lama flees to India; 80,000 Tibetans follow him. *March 19.* Tibetan troops join the uprising against the Chinese. *March 23.* Uprising suppressed. The Chinese dissolve the Tibetan local government and impose a military government, fronted by the Panchen Lama, and in April begin 'democratic reforms'. Thousands of Tibetans are executed, imprisoned or sent to labour camps. Destruction of monasteries in Central Tibet begins.

1959–61. The Great Leap Forward leads to widespread famine, with up to 30 million believed to have died in China and many thousands in Tibet.

1962. October 20. War between China and India over disputed border claims in Tibet.

1965. September 9. The TAR is formally established.

The Cultural Revolution begins, destroying 90 per cent of the remaining monasteries and outlawing most Tibetan cultural customs and religious practices.

The United Nations passes a resolution supporting the Tibetan people's right to self-determination.

1971. The PRC is admitted to the UN.

1972. US President Nixon visits China.

1976. The Cultural Revolution ends with the death of Mao. The Chinese acknowledge 'past mistakes in Tibet', and blame them on the Cultural Revolution and on the ultra-leftist policies of the Gang of Four.

1979. Deng Xiaoping initiates a policy of opening up to the outside world. The Chinese invite the Dalai Lama to return from exile, on condition he remains in Beijing. He is allowed to send a fact-finding mission to Tibet. The delegates are greeted by demonstrations calling for independence and the return of the Dalai Lama; many demonstrators are imprisoned.

1980. Party Secretary Hu Yaobang visits Tibet and initiates liberalisations that allow some private trade, outward display of religious activities and the recall of several thousand Chinese cadres.

1983. The Tibetan economy is recentred on tourism. The Dalai Lama sends negotiating teams to Beijing, but talks collapse in 1984.

1987. The Dalai Lama proposes the Five Point Peace Plan during a visit to the US Congress in Washington.
  September 27. Pro-independence demonstration led by twenty-one monks in Lhasa; all are arrested. *October 1.* Police open fire on crowd of 2–3,000 demonstrators. Foreign journalists and tourists expelled.

1988. March 5. Major demonstration on last day of the *Monlam Chenmo* festival in Lhasa; hundreds of arrests follow. One Chinese policeman and at least 8 Tibetans killed.
  June 15. The Dalai Lama puts forward the Strasbourg Proposal, offering the Chinese control of Tibetan foreign policy and defence in return for full internal autonomy. The Chinese promise to negotiate with him in any place he chooses.
  December. Hu Jintao replaces Wu Jinghua as Party Secretary of the TAR.
  December 10. Police shoot dead two monks carrying the Tibetan national flag in a demonstration in Lhasa.

1989. January 28. The Panchen Lama dies while visiting Shigatse.
  March 5. Police open fire and kill a group of demonstrators in Lhasa. Demonstrations spread.
  March 7. Martial law is declared in Lhasa. The PLA takes over the city; all foreign tourists, journalists and diplomats are expelled. Up to 200 people believed killed by security forces; thousands arrested.
  October 5. The Dalai Lama is awarded the Nobel Peace Prize.

1990. April. Expulsion of politically suspect monks and nuns from monasteries.
  May 1. Martial law is lifted. Varying restrictions on foreign visitors and journalists remain in force. Small demonstrations continue in the capital but most are dealt with rapidly by increased presence of armed police. The Dalai Lama is officially received by Swedish, Dutch and French Governments, and privately by Czech and German presidents.
  October. First foreign official is allowed to visit a Tibetan prison.

1992. March. Chen Kuiyuan arrives in Lhasa to prepare to take over as First Party Secretary of the TAR from Hu Jintao, who has returned to Beijing. *May.* Chinese authorities announce preparations for creation of a 'Special Economic Zone' in Lhasa.

July. Regulations are declared which offer substantial incentives for investment from inland China and abroad.

GLOSSARY

Amban. Political commissioner representing the Chinese Emperor during the Manchu (*Qing*) dynasty. The post was created in 1727 and disbanded by the Thirteenth Dalai Lama in 1913.

Amdo (Tibetan *a-mdo*). One of the three provinces or regions (*chol-kha-gsum*) traditionally considered to constitute Tibet. The area is now largely within the Chinese province of Qinghai. Before 1949, it was divided into semi-independent principalities, not ruled by Lhasa. Tibetans from the area have distinctive dialect and cultural traditions and are known as Amdowas.

a-ni (Tibetan). Nun.

Anquan Bu (Chinese). Ministry of State Security. Tibetan: *rgyal-khab dbe-'jags las-khung* (gyalkhab denjak lekhung).

Barkor (Tibetan *bar-skor*). 'Middle circuit'; the road or alleyway used for circumambulation around the Jokhang temple in Lhasa, and the main site for *korwa* (*q.v.*) there.

Bodhisattva (Sanskrit). Person who has the 'mind of Enlightenment' and who is set on becoming a Buddha; usually refers to a form of Buddha or enlightened being, including Jampeyang (Manjushri) and Chenrezig (Avalokiteshvara), and thus the Dalai Lama. Tibetan: *byang-chub sems-dpa'* (changchub sempa).

Bonpo (Tibetan). Traditional animist, pre-Buddhist religion of Tibet; still practised in many areas.

Bourgeois Liberalisation. Party expression for certain Western or capitalist ideas with special reference to the Western notion of freedom and democracy; subject of a campaign (or purge) in 1987. Tibetan: *'byor-ldan gral-rim rang-mos can-du 'gyur-ba* (chorden drelrim rangmoe chendu gyurwa). Chinese: *zichan jieji ziyou hua*.

Cadre see *ganbu*.

Cardinal Principles. Party term for the fundamental dogmas of the Chinese state: the supremacy of the Socialist system, the dictatorship of the proletariat, the leadership of the Party, and the supremacy of Marxist–Leninist–Mao Zedong Thought. Chinese: *jiben zhengce*.

CCP – Chinese Communist Party. Chinese: *Zhongguo gongchan dang*; in Tibetan the term is rendered phonetically as *krung-go gung bran tang*. Founded in Shanghai, July 1921.

cheng guan qu (Chinese). Administrative term for the inner urban area within a municipality (Chinese: *shi*) which is administered by the town or city, a level of government below the municipality. Tibetan: *tran gong chu* or similar.

counter-revolutionary. Legal/political term for an enemy of the state or for any act 'committed with the goal of overthrowing the political power of the dictatorship of the proletariat and the socialist system' (Chinese Criminal Code, 1980, Article 90). Chinese: *fan geming*. Tibetan: *gsar-brjer ngo-rgol* (sar-je ngo-gol).

CPPCC – Chinese People's Political Consultative Conference. First convened in 1949, the CPPCC is an institution consisting of representatives of non-Party organisations which support the Party. In minority nationality areas it includes leading religious figures and former aristocrats ('patriotic upper strata') who support the Party. It is the main public organ for the United Front (*q.v.*) and meets regularly to express support and sometimes comment on Party policies. Tibetan: *Krung-go mi-dmangs chab-srid gros mol tshogs-'du*, or, more simply, *chab-srid gros* (chab si droe).

Cultural Revolution. Campaign initiated by Mao Zedong to regain control of the Party by ordering the youth to 'bombard the head-quarters' (purge opponents within the Party) and to eradicate 'the four olds' (old ideas, old culture, old customs, old habits). The Chinese authorities now describe it as 'the Ten Bad Years', referring to the period 1966–76. In Tibet it is sometimes considered to have continued until 1979. Tibetan: *rigs-nas gsar-brje* (rigne sar-je).

dang'an (Chinese). File or archive containing information held by the state on each individual's social and political history, usually retained in the security section (Chinese: *baoweike*) of each individual's work unit. Tibetan: *yig-tshag*.

danwei (Chinese). Work unit; the basic-level unit of administration which controls the allocation of housing, food rations, permission to marry and bear children, change employment, etc. Work units now cover only people working in government organisations and state enterprises. Tibetans use a variety of terms including *las-khung*, which also means office, or the term for unit, *ru-khag*.

Democratic Reforms. Party term for the implementation of radical reforms, particularly land distribution; initiated from the early 1950s in Kham and Amdo and from March 1959 in the TAR, where it followed the March 1959 Uprising. Chinese: *minzhu gaige*; Tibetan: *dmangs-gtso'i bcus-sgyur* (mangtso chugyur).

Dharamsala. Hill station in Himachal Pradesh, Northern India, currently the seat of the Dalai Lama and of the exile Tibetan Government.

Dharma (Sanskrit). Religion or truth; can also refer to the nature of reality. Used as a synonym for Buddhism or for Buddhist teachings. Tibetan: *chos* (choe).

dratsang (Tibetan *grwa-tshang*). College within a major monastery or monastic university, usually composed of *khamtsen* (*khang-mtshan*), units accommodating monks from one area.

ganbu (Chinese). Cadre; usually refers to any member of the Party who holds a responsible position, but technically also a non-Party member who holds a responsible position in the government. Tibetan: *las byed-pa* (le che pa).

Gelugpa (Tibetan *dge-lugs-pa*). Dominant school of Tibetan Buddhism, sometimes called the 'Yellow hat' school. Founded in the 15th century by Tsongkhapa, and led since the 17th century by the Dalai Lamas.

geshe (Tibetan *dge-bshes*). Monk or lama who has completed the highest course in metaphysics and other academic monastic studies in the Gelugpa school; similar to a doctor of theology.

Gong'an Ju (Chinese). Public Security Bureau (PSB); local-level police force. Tibetan: *sbyi sde chu* (chi de chu).

gonpa (Tibetan *dgon-pa*). Monastery.

gyama (Tibetan). Measure of weight, equivalent to half a kilo. The Chinese equivalent is the *jin*.

Han (Chinese). Originally a term for a Chinese imperial dynasty (206 BC-AD 220), applied in Communist Party jargon to the ethnic Chinese to distinguish them from other ethnic groups regarded by them as Chinese.

Hui (Chinese). Chinese Muslims, regarded officially as one of the 55 'minority nationalities' in China.

hukou (Chinese; Tibetan *them-mtho*). Residence permit. Also used for ration permit.

Jokhang (Tibetan *jo-khang*). Most sacred temple in Tibet, situated in the Tibetan quarter or Old City of Lhasa; usually referred to in Tibetan as the Tsuglakhang (*gtsug-lag-khang*).

Kagyupa (Tibetan *bka'-rgyud-pa*). School of Buddhism originating in the 11th century, and now led by the Karmapa, whose traditional seat is at Tsurphu, fifty miles west of Lhasa.

kalon (Tibetan *bka'-blon*). Minister in the Kashag (*q.v.*).

kanshousuo (Chinese). Detention centre. See also *laogai* and *shourongsuo*.

Kashag (Tibetan *bka'-shags*). Cabinet of the Tibetan Government before 1959 and currently in exile based in Dharamsala (*q.v.*).

Kham (Tibetan *khams*). Eastern province of Tibet as traditionally conceived, ruled mainly by local rulers rather than by Lhasa. Currently divided between Sichuan and Yunnan provinces and the TAR. Tibetans from the area have their own dialect and customs and are known as Khambas.

korwa (Tibetan *skor-ba*). 'Circuit'; form of religious practice which involves walking around a Buddhist temple or religious site in a clockwise direction.

Kuomintang (Chinese; *Guomindang* in pinyin). Nationalist Party, which ruled China under Chiang Kai-shek until 1949, and has since ruled Taiwan. Often referred to as the KMT.

kusho (Tibetan *sku-bzhogs, sku-zhabs*). Term of respect for a learned or distinguished person; similar to English 'sir'.

labrang (Tibetan *bla-brang*). Residence or estate of a *tulku* (*q.v.*) or lama, and the patrimony inherited by his successors. Also the name of the town (Xiahe or Labuleng in Chinese) surrounding the Gelugpa monastery of Labrang Tashikyiel in Amdo, in present-day Gansu Province.

laogai (Chinese). Reform through labour (camp); equivalent to a prison. Holds more serious prisoners than a *laojiao*, a reform through education (camp) which houses detainees usually for up to four years. See also *kanshousuo* and *shourongsuo*.

le che pa (*las byed-pa*). See *ganbu*.

ledun rukha (*las-don ru-khag*). 'Work team'; temporary unit of Tibetan Party members specially formed to conduct investigations or give political re-education in a particular institution or locality. Chinese: *gongzuo dui*.

lonchen (Tibetan *blon-chen*). Chief minister in the traditional Tibetan Government between 1904 and 1959.

Monlam (Tibetan *Smon-lam*). 'Prayer'; short form of Monlam Chenmo, the Great Prayer Festival, held traditionally during the third week of the Tibetan New Year at the Jokhang temple in Lhasa. It was banned by the Chinese in 1966, reinstated in 1986, and banned again as a public ceremony in 1989.

mu (Chinese). Measure of land area, equal to 1/15th (0.0667) of a hectare, or 67 square metres (i.e. 1,500 *mu* = 1 sq. km.).

neighbourhood committee. See *u-yon lhan-khang*.

paichusuo (Chinese). Police substation.

Panch Shila (Sanskrit). 'Five rules'; the five principles, guidelines or slogans defining 'peaceful co-existence' and 'mutual benefit', the CCP's basis for foreign relations, enunciated in the 1954 Indo-Chinese 'Agreement on Trade and Intercourse'.

PAP – People's Armed Police. Chinese: *Wu Jing* (*q.v.*).

PCC – Party Central Committee. Chinese: *Dang-zhongyang*; Tibetan: *tang krung yang*.

peaceful evolution. Party term for a Western strategy to undermine Communism by gradually introducing Western ideas; often attributed to John Foster Dulles. Chinese: *heping yanbian*; Tibetan: *zhi-wa'i rim 'gyur* (shiwei rim gyur).

peaceful liberation. Party term for the PLA's entry into what is now termed the Tibet Autonomous Region in 1950. Chinese; *heping jiefang*; Tibetan: *zhi-wa'i bcings-bkrol* (shiwei ching drol).

ponpo (Tibetan *dpon-po*). Local chief; official in the traditional Tibetan Government, usually at local level; officer in the Tibetan Army before 1959.

prefecture. Administrative area below the level of a province or region and above the level of a county. Chinese: *diqu* or *zhou*. The TAR is divided into seven prefectures, each of which is divided into seven or more counties. A 'Tibetan autonomous prefecture' (Chinese: *Xizang zizhizhou*) is a prefecture outside the TAR but still considered to include a predominantly Tibetan population.

procuracy. Chinese governmental organisation responsible for investigating and prosecuting criminal cases. Chinese: *jiancha*; Tibetan: *zhib chu*.

PSB – Public Security Bureau. See *Gong'an Ju*.

pundit (Sanskrit). Scholar; in particular, the Indian scholars, agents and cartographers, including Sarat Chandra Das, sent clandestinely into Tibet by the British authorities in India to collect information in the late nineteenth century.

qu (Chinese). District; an administrative area smaller than a prefecture (*zhou*) and a county (*xian*), but larger than a *xiang*. Tibetan: *chu*. Also refers sometimes to a region, which is an area larger than a prefecture.

reactionary. Thinking which is backward or resistant to correct political ideas. Chinese: *fandong pai*; Tibetan: *log spyod-pa* (lok choe pa).

reform and opening up. Guiding policy of the Party which was initiated by Deng Xiaoping in 1978 to allow the development of the 'household responsibility system' and the 'socialist market economy', but not to encourage political liberalisation. Chinese: *gaige kaifang*; Tibetan: *'gyur-bcos sgo-bye srid chus* (gyur choe go-che si chu).

Rinpoche (Tibetan *rin-po-che*). 'Precious'; a term of respect added to a lama's name.

shourongsuo (Chinese). Shelter and investigation centre; a local prison for holding short-term offenders or vagrants. See also *kanshousuo*.

Sikang (Chinese *Xikang*). Province created by the Chinese nationalists in 1939 to describe Kham (q.v.). In 1955 the province was disbanded and the area absorbed into Sichuan.

splittism. Party term for the movement for Tibetan independence or any secessionist movement. Tibetan: *kha-bral ring-lugs* (khadrel ringluk).

TAR – Tibet Autonomous Region. The Tibetan area west of the Yangtse and south of the Kanlun mountains. This is the only area recognised by modern-day China as 'Tibet'. It was formally constituted as an 'autonomous region' in 1965. Chinese: Xizang zizhiqu; Tibetan: *Bod rang-skyong ljongs*.

thangka (Tibetan *thang-ka*) – religious painting depicting Buddhist deity, usually hung as a scroll on canvas with silk backing.

them tho. See *hu kou*.

ting (Chinese). Government department or office at the level of a province or autonomous region; below a *bu* (ministry, at state level; Tibetan: *pu'u*) and above a *ju* (local office or department; Tibetan: *chu*). Tibetan: *thing*.

tsampa (Tibetan _rtsam-pa_). Roasted barley flour; the staple food-stuff in Tibet and the national dish. The Chinese refer to it as _qingke_.

tsepon or _tsipon_ (Tibetan _rtsis-dpon_). Minister in the Tsigang or finance/taxation office of the Tibetan Government before 1959.

tulku (Tibetan _sprul-sku_). 'Manifestation body'; an incarnate lama, i.e. a person who has achieved a level of spiritual ability which allows him to choose to be reborn as a human in order to help others. The Chinese translate the term as 'living Buddha'.

turing (Tibetan _kru-ring_). Modern Tibetan loan term for the appointed foreman or leader of a committee; Chinese: _zhuren_.

United Front. Organ of the Party devoted to forming broad 'alliances' with non-Party and often with non-Chinese sectors, particularly by co-opting 'patriotic upper strata' to get them to acknowledge the supremacy of the Party. See also CPPCC. Chinese: _tong zhan bu_; Tibetan: _'thab-phyogs gcig-sgyur_ (_thab-chog chig-gyur_).

U-Tsang (Tibetan _dbus-gtsang_). Traditional name for the two areas of Central Tibet, including Lhasa, and Shigatse.

u-yon lhan-khang (Tibetan). Committee, based on the Chinese term _hui yuan_. Sometimes used as a short form of _sa-ngas u-yon lhan-khang_ (sa-nge u-yon lhan-khang), the neighbourhood committee (the grassroots-level administrative unit for local residents who are not members of a work unit). In a monastery, for example, it is used to refer to the 'Democratic Management Committee'.

work unit. See _danwei_.

Wu Jing (Chinese). People's Armed Police, a paramilitary unit formed in 1983.

xian (Chinese). County, the middle-level administrative unit. Tibetan: _shen_ or _dzong_.

xiang (Chinese). Lower-level administrative unit that formerly covered a township, but in rural areas covers a group of villages. Tibetan: _shang_.

Xikang. See Sikang.

Xizang (Chinese). Term for Tibet that refers only to the area now covered by the TAR.

Zang (Chinese). Term for the Tibetan race.

Sha-pe (Tibetan *zhabs-pad*). Term for the four ministers in the *kashag* (*q.v.*) of the Tibetan government before 1959.

zhang (Chinese). Head or leader (of committee). Tibetan: *drang*, *krang* or *go-'khrid* (*go-tri*). For example, Tibetan *shang-drang* is the head of a *xiang*, *pu'u-krang* (*bu-drang*, from the Chinese *buzhang*) is a minister (in the Chinese Government).

Zhou. See prefecture.

zhuxi (Chinese). Chairman or (Party) Secretary. Tibetan: *hru-chi*.

ABBREVIATIONS

CCP	Chinese Communist Party
CPPCC	Chinese People's Political Consultative Conference
FBIS	Foreign Broadcast Information Service
NCNA	New China News Agency (Xinhua)
NPC	National People's Congress
PAP	People's Armed Police
PCART	Preparatory Committee for the Tibet Autonomous Region
PCC	Party Central Committee
PLA	People's Liberation Army
PRC	People's Republic of China
PSB	Public Security Bureau
RAB	Religious Affairs Bureau
SWB	BBC Summary of World Broadcasts
TAR	Tibet Autonomous Region
TASS	Tibet Academy of Social Sciences (Tibetan branch of the Chinese Academy of Social Sciences)
TIN	Tibet Information Network

THE DEVELOPMENT OF MODERN TIBETAN STUDIES

Tsering Shakya

On September 27, 1987, a small group of monks staged a demonstration in Lhasa which once again drew the attention of the world to Tibet. In the following eighteen months, thirty or more such incidents occurred in different parts of the region, leading to the imposition of martial law in Lhasa in March 1989. This was the first time that the government of the People's Republic of China had formally imposed martial law on any part of the territories under its control. These events propelled Tibet into the headlines of the international press for the first time in thirty years.

Martial law was still in place in Lhasa when, in April 1990, a number of scholars gathered in London to examine the context in which the above events had occurred. This volume is the result of that gathering. The conference, 'Forty Years On: Tibet 1950–90', was held at the School of Oriental and African Studies in the University of London. Its specific aim was to look at developments in Tibet over the past four decades. But the conference intended also to establish the study of modern Tibet as a subject in its own right. In this, it was breaking with tradition. The Western, Tibetan and Chinese scholars who met in London that April to initiate the academic discussion of contemporary conditions and changes in Tibet were opening a new chapter in the history of Tibetan studies.

The field of Tibetan studies had not previously dealt with Tibet as an evolving and contemporary society. Although there had been great interest in Tibet in the West since at least the early 19th century, academic studies of Tibetan in Western universities began in earnest only in 1959. In that year the Dalai Lama and some 80,000 followers fled to India, and soon after the Rockefeller Foundation made funds available for university courses in Tibetan studies. Since then, many Western universities have developed courses in Tibetan language and culture.

Even with the establishment of Tibetan studies in universities, Western studies of Tibet and debates on the subject have tended to reflect the perceptions current among popular writers as well as scholars. It is to these current perceptions that we must turn to

1

explain the absence of serious study of contemporary Tibetan society and its politics.

John K. Fairbank, in his introduction to the *Cambridge History of China*, described four aspects of the Western approach to the study of China. 'These phases of understanding may be characterised as missionary, diplomatic, journalistic and social scientific,' he wrote.[1] To some extent we can apply these 'phases' to Tibetan studies, although in the study of Tibet these descriptions represent not discrete historical phenomena, but the overlapping and ongoing interpretations of Tibet among Western writers. In the case of Tibet we can add to Fairbank's list the category of the travelogue, which has become the dominant and most accessible mode of interpreting Tibet for the Western public.

The Missionary View

The first Westerners to penetrate Tibet were Jesuits who, in 1624, arrived from India to establish a mission in Tsaparang, then the cultural centre of Western Tibet. By the beginning of the 18th century, however, Tibet had been granted as an area of missionary activity by the Papal See to the Capuchins, who reached Lhasa in 1707 to establish a mission there. The reluctance of the Jesuits to depart from Tibet led to conflict and, in 1745, to the collapse of the entire missionary effort.

Both China and British India, however, were to benefit greatly from the material gathered by the Jesuit missionaries. When, in 1774, the British decided to expand their interests beyond the foothills of the Himalayas and sent George Bogle to Shigatse, their prime source of information was a map of Tibet which the missionary D'Anvill, then based in Beijing, had drawn ten years earlier for the Manchu (Qing) Emperor Kangxi. The material for D'Anvill's map had been provided by his co-religionists.

In 1762 the Augustin friar Antonio Giorgi, using information supplied by the Capuchin missionaries, published in Rome the *Alphabetum Thibetanum*, which introduced the Tibetan script to the West. The last of the Jesuit missionaries, Ippolito Desideri, left an important record of his sojourn in Tibet, which included a valuable account of the Dzungar (Mongol) invasion. This account was not published in English until 1904, but was influential in clerical circles from earlier times. Although Desideri mastered the Tibetan language and studied the culture, he did so not because his studies were the subject of academic exploration but in order to 'arm myself to launch a war'. He was impelled by a desire to refute Tibetan religious ideas and beliefs, and thus to propagate Christianity.

The dominant feature of the missionaries' study of Tibet was their view of the country as particularly fertile ground for conversion. They saw what they took to be the prominent role of religion in that country as an indicator that Tibetans were well suited to conversion to the Christian faith.

The Moravians, the most successful of all missionary groups working among Tibetan-speaking peoples, with a settlement established in Leh in 1885, shared Desideri's motivation. In 1881 in the introduction to his Tibetan–English dictionary (originally produced in German), the well-known scholar-missionary Jaeschke explained that 'the chief motive of all our exertions lay always in the desire to facilitate and to hasten the spread of the Christian religion and of Christian civilisation among millions of Buddhists who inhabit Central Asia, and who speak and read in Tibetan idioms.'[2] Nevertheless, the missionaries developed in their writings a highly scholarly approach which stemmed from their efforts to translate the Bible. Between 1891 and 1931, Jaeschke's colleagues, A.H. Francke and K. Marx, produced a corpus of historical and ethnological studies on Ladakh which remains unsurpassed.

Although the missionary approach introduced an important mode of the Western interpretation of Tibet, its significance has since become primarily historical. Today Tibet is still seen as prime territory for conversion by Christian missionaries, but their contribution to scholarly studies in the modern era has never equalled that of the pioneer figures; viewing Tibetan society mainly as degenerate, modern missionaries have attached little importance to studying its culture.

The missionaries shared with later scholars a common focus on Tibetan religious systems and institutions as the primary subject of inquiry. They looked to Tibetan religion essentially in terms of the vocabulary it could provide for the translation and description of Christian concepts. The focus on the religious aspect of Tibetan society has dominated Western views and studies of Tibet ever since the first missionary writings.

The Traveller's View

Among the earlier missionaries were figures such as Desideri and Abbé Huc, whose accounts of their travels were widely read in late-19th century Europe. These accounts provided inspiration for a generation of Westerners who viewed the Tibetan region in terms

of its potential for exploration and adventure. Those who realised
the dream of travel in Tibet, motivated by what Alexandra David-
Neel described as a 'desire to explore beyond the garden gate',
regarded the act of chronicling their wanderings as an essential part
of the traveller's experience.[3]

A small number of travel writers sought to describe the social
milieu they encountered. Spencer Chapman's story of his life in
Lhasa in the late 1930s provides interesting insights into the daily
lives of people in the capital, and Heinrich Harrer too sought to
provide a description of the city's inhabitants in the 1930s and
1940s. More recently, Catriona Bass has given a detailed impression of people's attitudes towards their daily experience, in an
account based on her work in Tibet as a teacher in the mid-1980s.
To these writers, all of whom worked and lived in Lhasa, the focus
was on the people they met rather than on the process of
exploration.

But they were the exceptions in the travel-writing genre. From
Walter Savage Landor onwards the majority of Western travel
writers have sought to emphasise the difficulties of their journey
and the uniqueness of their encounter with the Tibetan environment. What struck these writers was a combination of their personal fortitude and the exclusivity of their experience. When they
wrote about the context of these exploits, it was to stress the 'other-
ness' and exotic nature of the culture of Tibet, a place which they
often characterised as sacred and mystical.

These travellers were struck primarily by the landscape, frequently referring to the harshness of the environment and the
splendour of the mountains. This landscape they saw reflected in
the essential nature of the Tibetan character and philosophy. 'Up
here we are in a realm of ice and clarity, of ultimate and primordial
purity', wrote Fosco Mariani, the Italian explorer-writer.[4] The
combined perception of Tibet as landscape and mystique was aptly
summed up by Marco Pallis in the title of his travelogue, *Of Peaks
and Lamas.*[5]

The traveller's perception of Tibet has contributed little to our
understanding of Tibetan culture, but its influence has far out-
weighed its significance; it has sustained a popular and continuing
perception of Tibet as the 'hidden kingdom' and as a land of adventure and mystique. Tibet continues to excite Western travellers in
this way, irrespective of the development of other literary presenta-
tions of it. The opening of Tibet to Western tourists in the 1980s
saw the publication of numerous accounts of travellers' experiences
in there. These accounts still focussed on the singularity of the
authors' experience much as their Edwardian forebears had done,

even though foreign tourists visiting Lhasa each year peaked at 40,000 in 1986-7.

The Diplomatic View

Britain's desire to expand its political and trade interests into Central Asia led to the need to establish contact with Tibet. The missions of Bogle and Samuel Turner opened the diplomatic chapter in the Western encounter with Tibet. Turner's account, *An Account of an Embassy to the Court of the Teshoo Lama in Tibet*, published about 1800, was the first book in the English language on Tibet. Its publication reflected the increasing dominance of the British in the region, a role that was to be mirrored by their subsequent literary output on the country.

The primary concern of the British was the attempt to define the territorial limits of Tibet, the political authority of its rulers and its relations with neighbouring states. To accumulate the information needed for this exercise the British state provided patronage for an entire generation of scholars. Csoma de Körös, the great Hungarian researcher and linguist, was commissioned by the government of Bengal in the 1830s to compile a Tibetan dictionary; Sarat Chandra Das, a pioneer of Tibetan studies, was employed by the Survey Department of the British government of India as one of the Pundits, specially trained Indian agents sent by the British to Tibet to gather information about the region.

Writings motivated by Britain's strategic interests reached their high point around the time of the 1903 Younghusband invasion. Eight books were published by senior members of that expedition, including the detailed description of Lhasa provided by Perceval Landon, the correspondent for *The Times* attached to the mission. Younghusband's medical officer, L.A. Waddell, later went on to become the first university professor of Tibetan in Britain.

The political nature of their encounter with Tibet radically changed the perception of it as remote and isolated, at least for the diplomats and officers concerned. To them, Tibet was a country of strategic importance with whose leaders European governments now sought to enter into formal correspondence. To support the attempt to define its status and its boundaries, there was an urgent need for information about its economy, geography and political system, all of which was seen in terms of the possibilities it offered to British interests in the region. William Moorcroft was looking for the best place to buy horses for the Indian army, F.M. Bailey was sent to find the sources of the major rivers, and others looked into the possibility of using Tibet as a market for Indian tea.

Hodgson, later to become a prolific writer on the area, even wrote a paper on the suitability of the southern Himalayas for European settlement.

Younghusband, Bell, O'Connor, MacDonald, Gould and other writers on Tibet, most of whom served the British administration in one capacity or another, tended to see Tibetan history within the context of rivalries between the major regional powers: China, Britain, and to some extent Russia. Consequently, scholarly writings on the history of Tibet in the late 19th and 20th centuries by writers such as Mehra, Lamb, Kaur Singh and Addy concentrate on the territorial limits and definition of Tibet. These writers have invariably depended on primary sources in British archives, thus seeing the history of the period against the backdrop of what Kipling christened the 'Great Game'. This view of Tibet has been heightened by the establishment of Chinese control in Tibet since 1950, which is based on the much disputed territorial claim that Tibet was part of China. Leading to detailed and contentious study of the status of Tibet, this view has been further encouraged since 1962 by the Sino-Indian disputes over the former Tibetan borders.

The Journalistic Approach

The first extensive reports on Tibet to emerge in the Western press were the dispatches submitted by journalists who, like Perceval Landon, travelled into Tibet with the Younghusband mission. It was with Edmund Candler, the *Daily Mail* reporter who accompanied the expedition, that the distinctively journalistic view of Tibet emerged. His reports from the battlefront at Khampa Dzong near Gyantse were to have a significant impact on British public opinion, and he was largely responsible for the popular disdain with which Curzon's cavalier approach to Tibet came to be regarded. But his work was unique: until the 1950s what little journalistic coverage there was remained indistinguishable from the travel book.

The Chinese invasion in 1950 initiated widespread interest in Tibet. It came at the same time as the Korean war, when the Cold War was at its height. Anti-Chinese feeling was thus seen as an automatic extension of anti-Communist fervour in the West, and there was a tendency to view the Tibetan situation as an example of the Communists' desire for world domination. The flight of the Dalai Lama to India in 1959 initiated a flood of popular writing on the course of the Tibetan rebellion and its consequences by writers such as Barber, Patterson, Moraes and Peissel. Their accounts were driven by both a sense of mission and a taste for high drama. For example, in 1959 Lowell Thomas, introducing his epic record of the Chinese invasion, wrote: 'This tragic sequel . . . is not an adventure story. It is not a pleasant story. But it is a true story. And we of the free world ought to know more about it.'

By its nature the journalistic perception shared by these writers focussed on those events that were seen to be of major significance at the time: the uprising, the 'flight into exile' and so on. The exploits of the protagonists were described as adventures or as acts of individual heroism, but the causes of the events which engendered them were generally not examined beyond their role in provoking people into action. The nature of the society that produced or was changed by these incidents was not within the purview of these writers.

The writers who were close to the Chinese point of view, such as Felix Greene, Gelder, Han Suyin and Israel Epstein, did attempt to describe traditional Tibetan society, but they were dedicated to eulogising the social improvements that China had brought to Tibet and were therefore committed to stressing the backwardness of pre-1950 conditions. Where they talked about the present, it was to emphasise what they saw as the economic advancement of Tibetan society and its progression towards a Chinese-defined notion of modernity.

Sympathetic accounts of the Tibetan exile movement, later to be dominated by John F. Avedon's work, have stressed the role of Tibetans as essentially passive victims suffering under Chinese rule. Within these works the interpretation of Tibet has been an essentially journalistic experience, further heightened by the events of 1987, which were witnessed by both Tibetans and Westerners. A literature of reportage emerged that ranged from the chronicling of events to exercises in sensationalism: 'the first-ever eyewitness account of Chinese oppression in Tibet', as one author described their book in 1990. This genre chose rarely to explore questions of social change or of the diversity of political interest groups in Tibet. Journalistic literature on Tibet has remained limited to exploring the traditional dramatisation of the issue as a conflict between two protagonists.

The Emergence of a Social Scientific Approach

Today, the study of Tibet has become a distinct academic discipline, as that notion is understood within the Western tradition of studying the Orient. Both Tibet's cultural homogeneity and its geographical location have allowed Western scholars to accede to the Tibetans' definition of their culture as a discrete tradition in its own right.

Western studies on Tibet are rooted in the historical encounter between the West and Tibet, some aspects of which we have discussed earlier. These studies remain defined by their origins in, on the one hand, the intellectual encounter with Tibetan Buddhism and, on the other hand, the expansion of Western political interests across the Himalayas.

More recently the field of Tibetan studies has become largely institutionalised with a network of international conferences, university posts and regular contributions to scholarly journals devoted to it. There is an accepted corpus of scholarly literature, a standard system of transliteration and broad consensus on the area of studies. The founding fathers of Tibetan studies operated under the aegis of Western imperial or religious administrations; modern Tibetan studies are now legitimised by their presence within the institutions of Western *academia*.

Two parallel traditions of scholarship are discernible in academic Tibetan studies, one of which is the continuation of the tradition of textual analysis. The knowledge acquired by the scholar-missionaries had, by the end of the 19th century, allowed scholars of Sanskrit to extend their studies to the Tibetan Buddhist canon, and thus focus on the historical origins of the Tibetan texts and their relation to the Sanskritic tradition. These scholars tended to perceive the Tibetan religious system as a degenerate form of Buddhism, which they sometimes referred to in a pejorative sense as Lamaism.

The tradition of textual analysis, focussing primarily on Buddhist literature and its exegesis, has continued in the modern era. But it is characterised now by a widespread recognition of the Tibetan contribution to and development of Buddhist philosophy and practice. The wider concerns of modern textual scholars – like Tibetan scholars themselves – have been the history of Buddhism and Buddhist thought in Tibet. In addition the primary interest of the scholars in earlier Tibet, the period in which much of Buddhist literature was produced, has also led to the study of Bon, the indigenous religion of Tibet. Within this tradition the study of texts was accorded more importance than the study of the social conditions under which they were produced.

The second strand of academic Tibetan studies applied Western social science methodologies to the study of Tibetan culture and society. For these scholars the primary focus is the people and the society. However, in the 1950s, when this tradition emerged, Tibet was still closed to Westerners and there was virtually no opportunity for first-hand research on these subjects. This situation persisted until the mid-1980s.

The influx of refugees into Northern India enabled social scientists to conduct research on Tibetan society using the exiles as informants. A number of scholars, such as Aziz, Goldstein, Eva Dargyay and Franz Michael, made an effort to reconstruct a description of the traditional social system in Tibet based on retrospective interviews within the exile community.

While these scholars concentrated on the reconstruction of the traditional society, other social scientists carried out first-hand field-work among the Tibetan-speaking peoples of the Himalayan region, which provided primary material for comparative analysis of traditional Tibetan social systems. However, while there were studies by Chinese scholars, which remained largely unknown outside the People's Republic, no research was carried out within Tibet itself in this period by Western scholars.

Behind both these approaches, one dealing with reconstructions and the other with parallels, lay the concept of a traditional Tibetan society, which the scholars sought to describe. There were, however, a small number of social scientists, such as Novak, Saklani and Palakshappa, who made studies of social adaptation and change among the refugee community. These studies reflected the emergence of new ideologies and identities following the experience of exile.

But developments within Tibet since 1950 were not examined by Western scholars. While this was partly because those areas remained inaccessible to foreigners, there was also a residual sense that there was nothing worthy of study in post-1950 Tibet; as if the apparent demise of traditional society rendered further studies valueless and uninteresting. This attitude appears to have been widespread among scholars in the Tibetan field, so that, for example, contemporary language and literature have received little attention or analysis.

This absence of scholarly interest in contemporary developments in Tibet has tended to allow the field to be dominated by polemical writings from both sides. On the one hand, the Tibetans and their sympathisers have accused the Chinese of cultural genocide, implying that there has been no development in Tibetan culture. The Chinese have argued, on the other hand, that over the past forty years Tibet has marched forward into a progressive and civilised socialist society.

This antagonistic and often ferocious debate has to some extent obfuscated the real issues concerning the development of Tibetan society today. For the past forty years the imposition of

Communist ideology has directly challenged the traditional Tibetan worldview and undoubtedly influenced traditional Tibetan culture and its social system. But even the economic changes in Tibet have remained largely unobserved by foreign scholars. For example, the 22,000 kilometres of roads that have been built in the Tibet Autonomous Region since 1950 must have dramatically altered the social and economic relations of Tibetan communities. It is clear that Chinese rule in Tibet has affected Tibetan society in a major way, not merely as the destructive agent that dominates popular Western writings on the subject, but as an instrument of change of other kinds. Some of these changes have been discussed within the polemical debate, but as social phenomena they remain undocumented, indeed undescribed, in Western academic literature.

While the West, hampered by difficulties of access, has been slow to extend its interest into the study of modern Tibet, the Chinese have established a series of institutions to facilitate Tibetan studies. In the 1950s, a large number of leading Chinese social scientists were sent to Tibet to investigate conditions there, but the literature resulting from these studies remains largely unknown outside the People's Republic. The Chinese have also set up a network of institutes for the 'national minorities', as they call the non-Chinese peoples. Since the liberalisations of 1979, these institutes have developed into significant centres of studies.

The period of liberalisation has led to a further growth of academic institutions, including the founding of the University of Tibet in 1985 and the Chinese Institute of Tibetology in Beijing in 1986. The Tibetan Branch of the Chinese Academy of Social Sciences was formally established in Lhasa in 1985.

Perhaps more important has been the expansion of Tibetan-language publishing houses in Beijing, Lhasa and in Tibetan areas outside the Tibet Autonomous Region. They have republished numerous religious texts and have sponsored the translation of Chinese books, and even some English texts, into Tibetan. This minor renaissance of Tibetan publications was epitomised by the publication in 1984 of the three-volume *Great Tibetan–Chinese Dictionary*, the *Bod-rGya Tsig-mDzod Chen-mo*.

These institutions represent the emergence in Tibet itself of Tibetological research using Western academic methods. This process can be seen, for example, in the study by Dung-dkar bLob-zang 'Phrin-las (Dungkar Lobsang Thrinley), *Bod-kyi Chos-srid Zung-'brelskor bShad-pa* (*The Merging of Religious and Secular Rule in Tibet*), which applies Western social science methods to the social origins of the Tibetan political system. Following traditions established in the West, these scholars have focussed on the study of texts, inscriptions and ancient history, in preference to contemporary studies. The methodologies adopted by contemporary scholars in Tibet are, of course, influenced and constrained by the theoretical and political demands of the Chinese state.

It was to initiate the study of the contemporary situation that the conference 'Forty Years On: Tibet 1950–90' was convened at the School of Oriental and African Studies in London in April 1990. Taking as its subject the development of Tibetan society over the previous forty years, the conference brought together those scholars who have begun in recent years to study contemporary Tibet. In addition, a number of scholars renowned for their work on earlier periods took the opportunity to apply those skills to the modern era. It was envisaged that academic discussion at the highest level could only help to promote deeper understanding of the complex and critical issues which surround the current situation in Tibet.

As organisers of the conference we sought to establish a tradition of looking at what had been contentious issues in dispassionate and rigorous ways, and to encourage a shift from the populist debate to the relatively disinterested examination of the phenomena of social change in Tibet. As had been hoped, the contributors examined aspects of social change in Tibet in this way, and by doing so opened a tradition for serious study in this field. But it was noticeable that almost all the papers continued to place their observations in the context of the larger political debate concerning the 'Tibetan Question'.

The historical origins of that question are examined by Premen Addy in his study of the role of Tibet within British and Indian strategic concepts. Dr Addy describes the British and Russian manoeuvres along the borders of their empires, which left Tibet's own status indeterminate; a legacy which has been passed on to today's regional powers. In his paper he sees the roots of the current Sino-Indian dispute as being found in the earlier years of this century, thus demonstrating the continuing role of Tibet as a major issue in regional rivalries.

Warren Smith's paper deals with the Chinese attempt to interpret the Tibetan issue as a question of a minority group within the context of a multi-national state. He analyses the varying attempts to apply Marxist nationality theory to the Tibetan problem and the consequences of Mao's decision to abrogate his 1931 commitment to the right of national self-determination.

After the death of Mao and the toppling of the Gang of Four, Chinese policy focussed on economic reform and liberalisation. Melvyn Goldstein analyses the effectiveness of this reform policy in Tibet for a nomadic group among whom he conducted research, together with Cynthia Beall, from 1987 to 1989. He finds within the nomadic community evidence of a widespread revitalisation process that has accompanied the reform policies.

A major issue in Tibetan social studies is the question of how Tibetans in the modern era define themselves and express their identity as a distinctive group; Melvyn Goldstein deals with a historical aspect of this question in the introduction to his paper. In an essay reflecting an ethnological approach to this question, Samten Karmay discusses the central role of geography, and of the mountain cult in particular, in the definition of Tibet as a distinctive entity. He goes on to argue that Buddhism, now serving as an expression of national identity among Tibetans, had in earlier times actually dissipated that sense of national unity.

Heather Stoddard's paper looks at the role of literature in fostering a contemporary Tibetan identity, and documents the extent of Tibetan-language publications in Tibet since 1979; she raises the question of whether a distinctive Tibetan identity is more likely to evolve and survive in Tibet or in the exile community.

Per Kvaerne and Tsering Shakya both consider in different ways the post-1950 use of, respectively, symbols and language, in earlier times part of an intrinsically Tibetan cultural identity, to convey secular messages of modernity and of Marxist ideology.

The Tibetans' response to the imposition of the Communist system and its ideology in 1950 has been marked by two contrasting characteristics: diplomacy and resistance. Jamyang Norbu discusses the genesis of the Tibetan armed opposition to the Chinese advance and questions the popular presentation of non-violence as the dominant characteristic of the Tibetan political response. By contrast, Tsering Wangyal dates diplomatic initiatives by the exile Tibetan government as beginning from as early as 1972, and goes on to describe the subsequent response of the exile community, which now primarily takes the form of diplomatic dialogue between Beijing and Dharamsala.

The demonstrations that began in Lhasa in 1987 implied on the surface that China's reform policies had failed as a political strategy. The actual course of the protests is charted in some detail by Ronald Schwartz and Robert Barnett in their studies. Schwartz goes on to examine the role of the United Front in the Chinese response to the protest movement, and suggests that its attempts at political re-education may have served to consolidate Tibetans' political consciousness. Barnett describes the evolution of a shared symbolism by Tibetan protestors as they developed rituals of defiance which served to reinterpret and invalidate successive Chinese responses.

Hanna Havnevik looks at the prominent role played by nuns in the recent protest movement, a role which can be seen as a process of revitalisation. She argues that the nuns are prompted by the desire to overcome the double discrimination they face as Tibetans under the Chinese rule and as women in a patriarchal society. The decision to become a nun in Tibet today is, she suggests, not only a religious commitment but in itself an expression of dissent and of commitment to the survival of Tibetan culture.

Elliot Sperling's paper applies scholarly methods to examine contemporary political documents circulated by the pro-independence movement in Tibet. He argues that the growing sense of national identity that these documents reflect is in some ways a consequence of the importation of Marxist-Leninist ideology, which itself has served as a vehicle for European political ideas of nationhood, rights and individuality.

The two contributions made by Chinese scholars to the conference have been brought together as a postscript and offer an insight into Chinese academic perceptions of the Tibetan issue. Wang Yao and Wang Xiaoqiang were both themselves deeply involved in the evolution of China's post-1979 reform policies: Wang Yao, as a member of Hu Yaobang's pivotal 'inspection team' in Tibet; and Wang Xiaoqiang, as an adviser to Hu's successor, Zhao Ziyang.

It was during the visit of Hu Yaobang to Lhasa in May 1980 that the key policy statement of China's effort at reform in Tibet was made. Wang Yao was not able to travel to London to deliver his paper in person at the 1990 SOAS conference, but the attention drawn in his paper, at a time when the reform movement in China was in disarray, to the pivotal role of Hu Yaobang in the transformation of Chinese policy towards Tibet excited considerable interest in the press as well as in academic circles.

Wang Xiaoqiang, one of the leading reform economists sent by the Beijing authorities to Tibet in 1983 to assess the progress of Hu's reforms, addresses in his paper opportunities for future prospects for development and co-operation. Arguing that economic and political progress cannot advance without religious reforms by Tibetans, Wang's paper criticises some of Beijing's Tibet policies, in particular its stand on religion, its replacement of Wu Jinghua and its failure to advance beyond policies already proposed in the 1950s.

There was unanimity among the scholars at the London

conference about the need to develop the field of modern Tibetan studies. It is apparent from the papers collected here that there exists a wide range of contemporary issues that are worthy of academic debate and of detailed documentation. We hope that the papers reproduced in this collection will serve as a starting-point for the development of a scholarly discourse on modern Tibet.

NOTES

1. John K. Fairbank, *The Cambridge History of China*, Cambridge University Press, 1987, vol. 14, part I, p. 1.
2. H. Jaeschke, *A Tibetan–English Dictionary*, London: Routledge and Kegan Paul, 1965, p. iii.
3. Alexandra David-Neel, *My Journey to Lhasa*, London: Heinemann, 1927, p. ix.
4. Fosco Maraini, *Secret Tibet*, London: Hutchinson, 1954, p. 46.
5. Marco Pallis, *Of Peaks and Lamas*, London: Cassell, 1946.

Part I

HISTORY: ECONOMICS AND IDEOLOGY

BRITISH AND INDIAN STRATEGIC PERCEPTIONS OF TIBET

Premen Addy

At the start of the 20th century Britain was still the world's foremost power, albeit by then the first among equals. It was the possession of India which had given the British their global reach in both economic and military terms. Meanwhile, the governance of India and the protection of its frontiers had grown into an enormous enterprise, leading the men who ruled India to insist that British imperial policy give due weight to Indian strategic concerns. The men in Whitehall were, on the other hand, convinced that a true appreciation of imperial problems was only possible when these were placed on the widest political canvas. They were conscious of the breadth of their own outlook in contrast to what they perceived as the tunnel vision of their colleagues in India. As the Indian tunnel was of a continental scale, however, the question of India's frontier security was of a dimension to match.

Despite his great intellectual gifts, Lord Morley, during his tenure in Whitehall as Secretary of State for India, failed to grasp this elementary truth. Determined to avoid the confusion and potential disaster of two imperial policies, which he claimed had existed at the time of Lord Curzon's regime in India, he helped draw up a single policy, which also was to prove disastrous. Indian considerations were brushed aside with almost cavalier unconcern.

The fallout from these political conflicts was that, while the Curzon-inspired Younghusband expedition to Lhasa ended in the humiliation of Tibet, Morley's incorrect perceptions of the situation and subsequent stubborn inaction in the face of expert warnings of the dangers, presented the victim to China on a plate. Later, independent India was to compound British errors with those of its own. But it was during the first decade and a half of this century that the seeds of the present Tibetan tragedy were sown.

15

The Legacy of the British Raj

From 1774 to 1900 and beyond, Anglo-Tibetan relations operated under a set of multiple influences. While they represented the uncomplicated interplay between the economic needs of British India to gain access to the trans-Himalaya and the Tibetan resolve to deny it entry, they also reflected the pressures of Tibet's ambiguous relationship with China, its historic ties with the Mongols and the Manchus, as well as its shadowy links to – and Britain's rivalry with – the Tsarist government in St Petersburg. Furthermore, by the time Anglo-Tibetan relations were moving to their climax at the turn of the 20th century, considerations of European *realpolitik* had become a principal determinant in the politics of Asia.

Thus, as the perspectives of Lord Curzon (1899–1905) would differ from those of Warren Hastings (1772–85), so too would their diplomatic methods. The first British Governor-General of India had represented a nascent power in the camouflage of a trading company; his viceregal successor personified the high noon of imperial authority. By the time Curzon grew to maturity British India had already set its sights beyond the engirdling ranges of the Hindu Kush and the Karakorum, deep into Central Asia. It contested Russia's right to dominate its markets or to bend its political direction to the Tsar's will. The spoils were rich and tempting, for China's Manchu (Qing) Empire, apart from an occasional spasm, appeared inert and moribund.

This, then, was the 'Great Game', in which Cayley, Shaw, Forsyth and Younghusband exemplified the values of an ascendant bourgeoisie in search of fresh imperial outlets, where the explorer was soldier, surveyor, political agent, commercial prospector, linguist and diplomat. But the Russian advance, aided by geographical contiguity and railway development, proved inexorable. Slowly British India's dream dissolved; thwarted, it turned its attention to pastures new.

In the Himalayas an equally inspiring tradition of Tibetan and trans-frontier exploration had taken root. Bogle, Turner, Manning and Moorcroft in the late 18th and early 19th centuries were followed some fifty years later by the Pundits, a group of Indian secret agents of whom the best known was Sarat Chandra Das, a Tibetan scholar of the first rank. In their footsteps went Younghusband, O'Connor, Bell, Bailey, Williamson, Gould and Richardson.

The question for British India was how, in the wider interests of strategy, to establish diplomatic and commercial relations, and to foster border trade with a Lhasa government equally determined to protect its cherished isolationism.

'We seem, in fact, in respect of our policy towards Tibet,' wrote Curzon to Hamilton, the Secretary of State for India, 'to be moving in a vicious circle. If we apply to Tibet, we either receive no reply, or are referred to the Chinese Resident. If we apply to the latter, he excuses his failure by his inability to put pressure on Tibet. As a policy this appears to be unproductive and inglorious.'[1]

When all efforts to induce a positive response from Lhasa had failed, the Viceroy turned his thoughts to other methods. If trade could not lead, the flag, naturally, could not follow. The order had now to be reversed. 'It is, indeed, the most extraordinary anachronism', observed Curzon in high dudgeon, 'that there should exist within 300 miles of the borders of British India, a State and a government with whom political relations do not so much as exist and with whom it is impossible even to exchange a written communication. But it seems desirable that it should be brought to an end with as little commotion as possible since there are factors that might at a later date invest the breaking down of these unnatural barriers with a wider and more serious significance.'[2]

Chief among these 'factors', with its 'wider and more serious significance', was the possibility of Russian intrigue in the region. Already, through a Buriat Mongol named Dorjieff, the Dalai Lama was seeking the patronage of the Tsar. Tibetan missions were being received with ceremony at St Petersburg. Was this the prelude to something more sinister?

Writing to Hamilton, the Viceroy pointed out: 'Tibet is not necessary to Russia; it has no relations, commercial or otherwise, with Russia; its independent existence implies no menace to Russia. On the other hand, a Russian protectorate there would be a distinct menace and a positive source of danger to ourselves. I hope no Government at home would quietly acquiesce in such a surrender.'[3] In Curzon's view, Russia would have as much right to object if Britain planned similarly to reduce Manchuria. A Russian presence in Lhasa, he warned, would be a 'source of possible intrigue between Russia and Nepal . . .'[4] And Nepal, as the India Office in London noted, was the key to the Tibetan problem.

Be that as it may, Hamilton cautioned Curzon about the 'reluctance on the part of the Cabinet to acquiesce in your scheme for asserting our political influence in Tibet'. Warming to this theme a few months later, he continued: 'The truth is, my dear George, that if there were two more of you in other parts of the British Empire occupying big posts, the machine would not be

manageable. You are a big Proconsul in India, Milner is a big but
lesser Proconsul in South Africa. We let him push things to
extremities, and we know the result . . . we cannot afford, looking
to the dispersed nature of our interests, and to the manner in which
we cross the aspirations of every great European power, to adopt
a truculent tone upon every difference which may arise.'[5]

Despite Hamilton's cautionary words and the Cabinet's reluctance to sanction the enterprise, Curzon pressed ahead with the
Younghusband mission. Younghusband's column left Indian territory in October 1903 and, having overcome Tibetan resistance at
Guru, where the primitively equipped Lhasa forces were slaughtered, encountered a more wearing obstacle in the Tibetan refusal
to negotiate until the intruders returned whence they had come.

Younghusband and his party eventually reached the fabled
Tibetan capital on August 3, 1904, and discovered no trace of any
Russian presence. The Dalai Lama had fled the country for
Mongolia but the Tibetan Regent, who remained in his stead, signed
a treaty with the British envoy. Known as the Lhasa Convention, it
was dated September 7, 1904.

The convention imposed a heavy indemnity on the Tibetans; it
allowed a permanent British diplomatic and commercial presence
at Gyantse, including the right of a British representative there to
visit Lhasa whenever it was considered necessary for him to do
so. These critical clauses of the Convention were substantially modified by Younghusband's superiors in London. The indemnity was
drastically reduced and the timetable for its payment significantly
shortened. There were to be no British visits to Lhasa as of right,
and the British trade presence was restricted to a number of outposts
within easy reach of the Indian frontier. It constituted a snub for
Curzon and a repudiation of his Tibetan policy.

What caused the Home Government to turn its back on the
Viceroy? The searing effect of the Boer war and Milner's role in
starting it was one reason; the memory of the Kabul disaster of 1879
was another; third was the spectre of Germany which was pushing
Whitehall towards a diplomatic understanding with France and,
through that country, with Russia as well. Younghusband's arrival
in Lhasa had provoked a flurry of protests from the United States,
Russia and, to the chagrin of the British Foreign Office, the Kaiser's
Germany, which had no conceivable interests in the region. Britain
was criticised for violating the territorial integrity of China which
was synonymous with the farthest reaches of what China considered
to be its empire. Such was the substance of a famous note of 1900
by Hay, the US Secretary of State, regarding the open-door policy
in China.

Curzon had strenuously argued that India's own strategic impera-
tives deserved to be given due weight; that it was wrong for India
to be simply treated as an imperial drudge. He had explained his
overall view to Hamilton during his first year in office. Writing
then about the Persian Gulf he said: 'When you say that I look at
the question from the Indian point of view, I do not see in that
any reproach, since it appears to me to be the main point of view
from which it in any case must be regarded. We have got to provide
for the safety of the Indian Empire. That duty is of course
ex-hypothesi an Indian interest; but being an Indian interest it is
equally an Imperial interest. All that falls within the radius of our
political influence in India must inevitably be looked at from the
Indian point of view, and any statesman who looks at it from any
other point of view will not only have no knowledge of its real
proportions, but will also do an injustice to the wider Imperial
interests, of which Indian interests form a part . . .'[6]

When Curzon returned to London on furlough in April 1904,
with Younghusband still on his way to Lhasa, he exploded with
scorn at the spectacle which awaited him: 'Each Cabinet Minister
admits to me in private that the Cabinet have been wrong but
shelters behind the collective ignorance and timidity of the whole:
while Lansdowne, who declared six months ago that the Russians
had no voice in the matter, has now made a bargain with them on
Egypt in connection with Tibet! Good God! Such is the wisdom
with which we are ruled.'[7]

Having won Russian assent to the Khedivial Decree in Egypt, the
Home Government promised in return to withdraw from Tibet and
leave the country to its own devices. This in effect meant the revival
of Chinese power there, for Lhasa, militarily weakened by its
encounter with Younghusband's expeditionary force, had become
vulnerable to the expansionism of its eastern neighbour.

The Chinese laid claims to Tibet which the Tibetans had refused
to recognise. Nevertheless, Tibet was perceived internationally to
be a constituent of the Chinese empire, whose territorial integrity
the Great Powers, foremost among which was the United States,
were committed by treaty to uphold. China wished to extend its
nebulous position in Tibet with the aid of another treaty bearing
the British signature. Britain was keen to get Beijing's seal to an
agreement which would salvage the residue of Younghusband's
Lhasa Convention, and also earn the Tsar's trust for the sought-
after Anglo-Russian accord.

The Anglo-Chinese conference opened in Calcutta in March
1905. Contrary to the inclinations of his colleagues in London,
Curzon was tenacious in his rejection of the Chinese claims to Tibet

Premen Addy

British troops march through the western gate of Lhasa below the Potala Palace, 1904. (*Royal Geographical Society*)

Tibetan Cabinet ministers visit Younghusband's camp, August 1904. (*Royal Geographical Society*)

Younghusband with his officers in Tibet, May 1904. Standing: Ray, Major O'Connor, Dunlop, Major Iggulden, Colonel Hogge, Waddell; sitting: Walsh, Younghusband, General MacDonald, Bretherton. (*Royal Geographical Society*)

advanced by Beijing's delegation. He had previously scoffed at the 'so-called suzerainty of China over Tibet as a constitutional fiction'; he had stated that 'for the first time for nearly a century that country [Tibet] is under the rule of a young man, some twenty-eight years of age, who, having successfully escaped from the vicissitudes of childhood, is believed to exercise a greater personal authority than his predecessors, and to be *de facto* as well as *de jure* sovereign of the country. In other words, there is for the first time in modern history a ruler in Tibet with whom it is possible to deal instead of an obscure *junta* masked by the Chinese Amban.'[8]

These perceptions were based on the valuable intelligence gathered by Sarat Chandra Das who had noted on his clandestine journeys to Tibet that lay elements in the upper echelons of Tibetan society were curious about the outside world and were prepared to welcome greater contacts with it. A Tibetan official, Lonchen Paljor Dorje Shatra, impressed by the power of the Raj during his stay in Darjeeling and convinced that it had no ulterior designs on Tibet, favoured an approach from Lhasa to British India but fell foul of the ignorant, all-powerful Tibetan clergy. His time would come later in 1913–14 at the Simla Conference – a high point in

Anglo-Tibetan relations – where his charm and negotiating skills
drew praise from seasoned diplomats such as Hardinge and
McMahon.

Meanwhile, the Anglo-Chinese talks in Calcutta dragged on.
Curzon gave vent to his feelings with characteristic bluntness: 'I
would not budge a single inch, and would personally sacrifice all
hope of a convention with China – to which I attach the minimum
of importance – than yield.'[9]

The Home Government preferred to sacrifice Curzon rather than
hope of a convention with China. Curzon resigned over another
issue and left India in November 1905. In the ensuing general
election in Britain the Liberals came to power with a thumping
majority. Campbell-Bannerman was Prime Minister, Grey Foreign
Secretary and Morley Secretary of State for India. The new government's prime objective in the diplomatic field was to reach an
accommodation with Russia over Asia in the interests of a common
front against a possible German threat in Europe.

Working in tandem with Grey, Morley was determined to do
everything in his power to rein in British Indian officials who from
long tradition viewed Russia with suspicion. Guardians of the
Indian Empire, they were sensitive to potential dangers along its
frontiers. They had no which to see Tibet pass under Chinese
control.

For the Home Government an Anglo-Chinese agreement, which
met Russia's objections to the Lhasa Convention, was to be the
stepping-stone to the ultimate goal: an Anglo-Russian accord. To
start with, the stalled Anglo-Chinese conference was resumed not
in Calcutta, but in Beijing, where Indian officials would be unable
to bring their obstructive influence to bear on the outcome.

The Anglo-Chinese convention was signed in Beijing on April 27,
1906. British commercial rights and privileges were confirmed in
Tibet, but Britain was committed to a policy of strict non-
interference in Tibetan affairs. Henceforward, journeys to Tibet
from India for purposes of commerce, science, pleasure or even
diplomatic courtesy were to be frowned upon, and any official
trangressing these rules would earn a stinging rebuke from the
Secretary of State in London.

For Britain, the Beijing convention was a self-denying ordinance;
for China, it was a licence to transform her *de jure* suzerainty into
de facto sovereignty. Chinese officials, in a carefully planned and
subtle campaign, undermined the remaining British rights in Tibet,
reduced the authority of local British trade officials and increased
their own power over ordinary Tibetans, gradually isolating their
subjects for the final kill. When the British trade agent at Gyantse

or his subordinates protested at this harassment, they received scant encouragement from Whitehall.

Younghusband was driven to complain bitterly in a private letter to Curzon. 'I really do not know', he said, 'how a Home Government can expect us again to serve them at all, for after all we have to go through immense risks to carry out a policy and then all we do is thrown aside. Mr Morley thinks he is avoiding risks by closing Tibet. I say he is *running* risks [Younghusband's emphasis]. The way to avoid them was to keep a gentle friendly touch. I had hoped that in giving up so much in Tibet they might have got something substantial in exchange elsewhere, but I have not seen any sign of it.'[10]

Further afield, the Dalai Lama, after his wandering in Mongolia and north-west China, finally found himself in Beijing. The American Minister to China, W.W. Rockhill, a distinguished traveller and acknowledged authority on Tibet, sent a report to the American Government on the Tibetan pontiff's predicament. His President, Theodore Roosevelt, made the document available to the British Ambassador in Washington, Lord Bryce.

Having read it, Bryce wrote to Grey: 'There is a sort of tragic interest in observing how the Chinese Government, like a huge anaconda, has enwrapped the unfortunate Dalai Lama in its coils, tightening them upon him until complete submission has been extorted . . . The history of the whole transaction enforces once more the moral which seems the natural one to be drawn from the British expedition into Tibet. The chief result of that expedition has been to immensely strengthen the hold of China on Tibet, making it now almost a province of the Chinese Empire, and therewith to give British India upon the northern border instead of the feeble and half-barbarous Tibetans, a strong, watchful, and tenacious neighbour which may one day become a formidable military Power.'[11]

The Chinese, having consolidated their authority in Tibet, began to display an equally bold hand in the Himalayan borderlands which were long-established spheres of British Indian influence. The Chinese Commissioner at Lhasa, Chang Yin-tang, wrote: 'China, Nepal, Tibet, Bhutan and Sikkim might be compared to the five colours, *viz.* yellow, red, blue, black and green. A skilful painter may so arrange the colours as to produce a number of beautiful designs or effects.'[12] With China soon laying claim to Nepal and Bhutan, it became clear that there was no Chinese Morley in Beijing.

Nepal issued a firm rebuttal of Chinese claims, and had the necessary military strength to defend its sovereignty. Moreover, it was certain of full British support in the event of armed aggression from China. Sikkim had been a British protectorate from 1890, and any Chinese move against it would have meant war with Britain. Bhutan was the weak link in this chain of Himalayan states.

The Tongsa Penlop, Ugyen Wangchuck, one of the most powerful of the Bhutanese chiefs who had assisted Younghusband on his journey to Lhasa and helped bring the Tibetans to the negotiating table, was recognised as the country's maharaja by the British. An official British delegation attended his coronation. The new maharaja was granted a British subsidy and, in exchange for a British undertaking of non-interference in Bhutan's internal affairs, he allowed Britain control of his country's external relations. The Anglo-Bhutan treaty was signed on January 8, 1910.

In Beijing, the exiled Dalai Lama met the British Minister to China, Sir John Jordan, with whom he had a friendly conversation. Reports reaching the Tibetan dignitary from Lhasa had indicated his misjudgement of the British, who showed no desire to occupy or hold Tibet. When he returned to Lhasa in 1909, his attempts to rid the country of its Chinese fetters brought Beijing's wrath upon him. Zhao Erfeng, among the most capable generals in the Chinese army, was dispatched to Tibet.

A month after the signature of the Anglo-Bhutan treaty, units of Zhao Erfeng's force entered Lhasa and the Dalai Lama fled his country for a second time, this time to the sanctuary of India. The *Morning Post* in London on February 25, 1910 reflected sombrely: '. . . a great Empire, the future military strength of which no man can foresee, has suddenly appeared on the North-East Frontier of India. The problem of the North-West Frontier thus bids fair to be duplicated in the long run, and a double pressure placed on the defensive resources of the Indian Empire. The men who advocated the retention of Lhasa have proved not so far wrong, whatever the reasons for giving the advice. The evacuation of the Chumbi Valley has certainly proved a blunder. The strategic line has been lost, and a heavy price may be exacted for the mistake. China, in a word, has come to the gates of India, and the fact has to be reckoned with.'[13]

Some two years before, W.F. O'Connor, one of the Indian Government's foremost Tibetan experts, had described the Chumbi Valley, dividing Sikkim from Bhutan, as a wedge of territory 'thrust down to the south of the Himalayas into the middle of States friendly or subject to us'. He had argued strongly for its retention on strategic grounds, but the Anglo-Russian Convention, signed on August 31, 1907, and the Anglo-Chinese Convention of April 27, 1906, required that the Chumbi Valley be returned to the

Lhasa authorities where, O'Connor feared, it would become a possible centre for Chinese intrigues on the Indian frontier.

The pliant Lord Minto retired as Viceroy of India at the end of 1910 and was succeeded by Sir Charles Hardinge, the Permanent Under Secretary of State at the Foreign Office. He had been one of the principal architects of the Anglo-French and Anglo-Russian accords, experience which, it was felt, would enable him to co-ordinate Indian policy with that of Whitehall.

In an early letter from India to Sir Arthur Nicolson, his friend and successor at the Foreign Office, Hardinge had remarked confidently: 'People in England and elsewhere talk and write a good deal of the danger we are in here of being enveloped by China on our North-East frontier. I assure you it is all moonshine. We have the good fortune to have on that side an almost impenetrable jungle for some hundreds of miles where there is neither food nor water, and where the risk of invasion by as many as 1,000 Chinese is nil. So long as we are on our present terms of friendship with Russia we have no external danger to fear.'[14]

But the disquieting evidence of Chinese probes along the Assam Himalaya was impossible to ignore. It was a course in imperial education the lessons of which Hardinge was not slow to learn. To start with, he permitted a comprehensive survey and exploration of the region between 1911 and 1914 through a series of missions in a bid to secure a sound frontier along the Indo-Burmese divide with Tibet.

With the new Chinese military presence in Tibet, Beijing's irredentist claims to other crucial areas along the Himalayas could no longer be brushed aside as just the eccentric manifestations of an age-old ethnocentric conceit. A member of the British Embassy in St Petersburg reported a conversation with W.W. Rockhill, the new American Ambassador to the Tsarist court, who 'wondered how we could watch with equanimity the manner in which the Chinese were over-running Tibet and trying to extend their influence over Nepal, Bhutan and other principalities on our frontiers'.[15]

Within a year of these admonishing words, Hardinge perceived an opportunity to recast British policy towards Tibet and correct the errors of the past. In November 1911, the Manchu Dynasty in China collapsed. So, inevitably, did its power in the outlying dependencies of Mongolia and Tibet, sister nations whose destinies had first been crossed with that of China by the Mongol Emperor Kublai Khan in the 13th century, then recrossed to an altered political design in the late 17th and 18th centuries by the Manchus Kangxi and Qianlong.

The disappearing spectre of Chinese authority encouraged the Dalai Lama to return to Lhasa from his exile in Darjeeling. He had grown to trust the British, and Hardinge planned to make this confidence the foundation of a new Anglo-Tibetan relationship. Hardinge wished to send a representative to the Tibetan capital as a responsive gesture to the Dalai Lama's goodwill, and also to set up a valuable listening post. However, the Home Government in London, with Morley in the lead, opposed the move on the ground that it would violate the Anglo-Russian Convention, and Hardinge's envoy was recalled half-way on his journey to Lhasa.

The view Morley held of India's role in the making of imperial policy was the precise opposite of that held by Curzon. Morley had once scolded Minto for concerning himself with a 'host of under-lying matters in Tibet, Persia, the Gulf, etc., which only secon-darily and indirectly concern you'. The Secretary of State went on to tell the Viceroy that, 'notwithstanding all you say about the Man on the Spot, I humbly reply that this is just what the Government of India is not.'[16]

Morley's latest obstructiveness caused Valentine Chirol, the influential Foreign Editor of *The Times* and an old confidant of Hardinge's, to lament: 'I am afraid the F.O. [Foreign Office] is inclined to listen exclusively to the Hong Kong and Shanghai Bank.'[17] In a second letter to the Viceroy, Chirol wrote of the need to present the interests of India to the Home Government in the uncompromising manner of the White Dominions. 'Now it is clear to me', he concluded, 'that the Government of India does not possess that authority. You know better than I do how often it is over-ruled from Whitehall in deference to the narrow interests of these islands or the still narrower interests of the party in office. It is this that will have to be modified in any readjustments of rela-tions between the component members of the Empire if, in the long run, we are to preserve India to the Empire.'[18]

Hardinge, in a sense, was hoist with his own petard. Many years earlier, as a senior member of the Foreign Office, he had taken a line similar to that of Morley, and had wanted the Indian Govern-ment's wings, especially during Curzon's regime, to be clipped. Now, as head of that very same government, he was able to appre-ciate fully the true responsibilities of that office.

Curzon at the time had pointed to the flaws in the popularly acclaimed Anglo-Russian Convention of August 1907 because in his eyes it took insufficient account of Indian interests when the Convention covered Persia, Afghanistan and Tibet, with each of which India shared a frontier. The convention was designed to protect India's strategic zone but failed to address itself directly to Indian concerns.

There was a moment in the talks preceding the convention when the Russian Foreign Minister Izvolsky had broached the idea of a *quid pro quo*: for Russia's recognition of Britain's special interests in Tibet, Britain would view with equal favour Russia's interests in Mongolia. Grey, Nicolson and Hardinge turned down the proposal. Russia, having already made inroads into Mongolia, sealed a bargain with Japan in the secret Russo-Japanese convention of July 31, 1907 and July 4, 1910, under which Outer Mongolia fell within the Russian sphere of influence and Inner Mongolia fell to the Japanese.[19]

The British rejection of the Russian scheme stemmed from the fear that Britain's commercial interests in China would become hostage to the rising force of Chinese nationalism. As Viceroy, Hardinge was to note sourly that Russia's territorial ambitions at China's expense had not appeared to harm Russian commercial interests in China.

It was from India that Hardinge attempted to reopen with Russia the possibility of an arrangement he had helped foreclose as a senior Foreign Office adviser. At his prompting, Whitehall put out a feeler to the visiting Russian Foreign Minister Sazanof in 1913 about a possible trade-off on Mongolia and Tibet.

For Russia it was too little too late. Outer Mongolia was firmly under its grip, hence Sazanof argued that Mongolia and Tibet were not *in pari materia* since only the latter was the subject of a convention with Britain. For a revision of the 1907 Convention 'sterilising' Tibet, and for Russia's recognition of Britain's special interests there, the British would have to make similar concessions to Russia in northern Afghanistan. The British were peeved by this hard bargaining, but the First World War intervened before the discussions could proceed further.

It became painfully clear to Hardinge and his colleagues that the Anglo-Russian Convention was neither immaculately conceived nor immaculately applied. Morley, too, eventually saw the light, for in a private letter to Curzon after the war he confessed sadly: 'It had crossed my mind many a time in these days that you were right and Grey and I were wrong about the Anglo-Russian Convention.'[20]

The Simla Convention

The British exploration of the Assam Himalaya, Whitehall's approaches to Russia about a possible revision of the convention

on Tibet and the expulsion of the Chinese garrison in Lhasa pro-
vided the backcloth to a conference between British India, Tibet
and China held at the Indian hill resort of Simla in October 1913.
Sir Henry McMahon represented the Indian Government, Lonchen
Paljor Dorje Shatra was Tibet's plenipotentiary and Ivan Chen
(Chen I-fan) spoke for China.

Like Mongolia, Tibet was placed under Chinese suzerainty and
divided into Inner and Outer zones. The former comprised the area
contiguous to China where the Chinese were given a free hand.
Outer Tibet consisted of the provinces nearest India and included
Lhasa, the capital. This latter region, although under Chinese
suzerainty, was designed to function as a quasi-independent polity
under the Dalai Lama's direct control.

Ostensibly the major point on which no side could concur at
Simla was the demarcation of the Sino-Tibetan border: neither
Lonchen Shatra nor Ivan Chen was willing to make concessions.
Beyond this, however, Chen repeated the traditional Chinese position that Tibet had been part of China for centuries; he also made
it clear that Beijing was not ready to accede to an arrangement that
would lead to a diminution of its sovereign rights.

In March 1914, McMahon and Lonchen Shatra, in secret bilateral
discussions, arrived at an agreement on the delimitation of the
Indo-Burma-Tibet divide to which McMahon lent his name. They
further agreed that China would be deprived of the benefits
accruing from the confidential Anglo-Tibetan understanding unless
it accepted the purposes for which the Simla conference had been
convened.

Tibet ceded to India the valuable Tawang tract on the apparent
presumption, it would appear, of British support for Tibetan
border claims against China in the east. Sir Charles Bell, the principal British adviser on Tibet, pointing to the generosity of the
Tibetan gift, emphasised the boon a friendly Tibet was for the
security of 1,500 miles of exposed Indian frontier.

The Simla conference, which drew to a formal close on July 3,
1914, was a failure. Ivan Chen had initialled the conference settlement but his action was repudiated by his government. Beijing
refused to proceed to full signature. The validity of the Simla Convention in international law is at best questionable, at worst null
and void.

The Chinese attacked Tibet in the spring of 1917 but were repulsed
and then driven back from a considerable swathe of Tibetan
territory which they had controlled under the terms of the Simla
Convention. Peace was eventually restored between the two sides
in the Treaty of Rongbatsa of August 19, 1918, thanks to the good

offices of Eric Teichman who, having served as British Vice-Consul in Tibetan-populated Tachienlu, knew the area well.

Indeed it was Teichman who had earlier warned his government of China's ultimate goal in Tibet on the basis of a document submitted to the government in Beijing by the Chinese Frontier Commissioner, Yin Ch'ang-cheng (Yin Changcheng), to which he had gained access. In it was outlined an ambitious military and political reorganisation of China's frontier region which would facilitate Tibet's subjugation.

The fighting had thus come as no surprise to Teichman. When his name was put forward by Britain as a possible mediator, the Tibetans, who had always desired a higher British profile in their dealings with China, welcomed the suggestion. The Chinese were keen to eliminate any British role in their relations with Tibet and were lukewarm in their response. But in view of their military reverses they went along reluctantly with the Tibetans to whom they would otherwise have been in danger of losing even more territory.

This again highlighted the need to achieve an enduring settlement of the Tibetan issue. Bell had repeatedly impressed on his superiors in India and In Britain the advantages to India and to Britain of Tibetan goodwill; he reminded them of Tibet's territorial and trade concessions to India; he argued for the supply of arms to Lhasa on the scale requested and warned of the perils of listening too closely to the anti-Tibetan grievances of Nepal or of siding with Kathmandu in its quarrel with Lhasa.

The Indian Government of Lord Hardinge had refused a Tibetan request for arms on the ground that this would offend the Nepalese Durbar to which it was clearly partial. Gurkha troops were, after all, in the forefront of the Allied war effort against Germany.

Hardinge left India in April 1916. His successor as Viceroy, Lord Chelmsford, faithfully followed his predecessor's policy. He even turned down a Tibetan request that arms purchased abroad be permitted due passage through India. However, as a sop the new Viceroy offered Tibet 200,000 rounds of .303 ammunition provided no machine-guns were on the list.

The British Legation in Beijing, in its September 1916 *Memorandum on the Tibetan Question* (it arrived in London towards the end of May 1917 by which time much water had flowed down the Yangtse), proposed another conference on the subject but cautioned that further concession to China would be necessary before Beijing would agree to attend. In short, the Simla Convention would require serious revision involving the abrogation of the previous Sino-Tibetan frontier and of Tibet's division into Inner

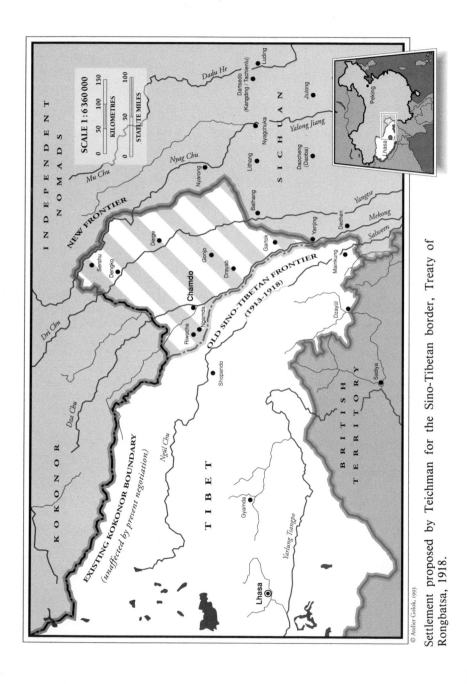

Settlement proposed by Teichman for the Sino-Tibetan border, Treaty of Rongbatsa, 1918.

© Atelier Golok, 1993

and Outer zones. According to the Memorandum, the matter needed urgent attention as it was feared that the Chinese would soon attack Tibet and that Tibetan resistance would crumble under the onslaught. China did attack, but it was China that was humbled.

As the Tibetans prepared for further confrontation, Lhasa asked the Indian Government for a million rounds of ammunition and, following their capture of Chamdo, of artillery as well, in case the Chinese attempted a counter-attack. Bell recommended that these requests be granted but to no avail. Tibet's goal of regaining all Tibetan territory under China's control was effectively thwarted. The Teichman-designed Treaty of Rongbatsa made the Yangtse–Mekong watershed the boundary between the warring parties. China lived to fight another day.

The sight of Tibetan forces more than holding their own against Chinese aggression made the Indian Government a little more sympathetic to the Tibetan position from the middle of 1917. Bell was told to inform Lhasa that, while its request for machine-guns could not be immediately met, these would be made available once the war in Europe was over. Also, there was an offer to train batches of Tibetan soldiers in drill and musketry, and to educate Tibetan mechanics in the simple manufacture and repair of weapons at Indian ordinance factories.

With the war over, Tibet wanted Britain to redeem its promise. The Indian Government, with the approval of the Secretary of State for India, Edwin Montagu, in London, suggested the dispatch of two machine-guns and 50,000 rounds of ammunition to Lhasa. But even this derisory offer was vetoed by the Foreign Office on the plea that it would violate the Paris Arms Traffic Convention of September 1919 which was designed ostensibly to restrict the flow of arms to sensitive areas of the world, and to promote international peace and stability. In fact, its principal aim was to limit the export of Japanese armaments to China as a means of controlling Tokyo's influence in the country.

Beilby Alston, Jordan's successor as British Ambassador to Beijing, and Eric Teichman, who had returned to his desk at the Foreign Office, strongly opposed such tardiness and supported Bell. A slow thaw in Whitehall attitudes followed. Fresh developments on the ground accelerated this change. The Indian Government, alarmed at the arrival in Lhasa in January 1920 of China's Kansu Mission, called Bell back from retirement and instructed him to resume his watching brief.

A few years before, the Dalai Lama had invited Bell to Lhasa, but his superiors had opined that the invitation, if accepted, would contravene the Anglo-Russian Convention and it thus had had to be shelved. The advent of the Bolsheviks in Moscow and Russia's withdrawal from the struggle against the Kaiser's Germany led to British nullification of the convention at the earliest opportunity after the war. The moment had now arrived to take the Dalai Lama's invitation off the shelf.

Bell left for Lhasa in November 1920 and remained there for almost a year. For Tibetan trust to be restored, Britain, he wrote, must supply Lhasa with its military needs which he itemised as follows: 10 mountain-guns; 20 machine-guns; 10,000 rifles; 1,000,000 rounds of small-arms ammunition to be re-supplied annually; help in training the Tibetan army; and two British mechanics to teach Tibetans how to make gunpowder and rifles.

'By barring Tibet from buying munitions in India', Bell continued, 'we are breaking promises which were made to her in the name of His Majesty's Government, we are undermining her hard-won freedom and we are jeopardising the security of the northern frontier of India.'

Bell felt that Britain 'should wait no longer for a China that does not intend to negotiate until she finds it definitely in her interest to do so . . . Finally, we should recognise India's vital interest in this problem and the dangers that threaten her in the present policy of inaction.'

He ended on a high note of warning: 'China is pressing, Japan has begun to press. We cannot bury our heads in the sand, like the ostrich, trying to prevent dangers by ignoring them. Our only chance of keeping out Japan and China is by establishing our influence in the country [Tibet] first. Government have an exceptional, possibly an unique opportunity, of settling this question now, while I am in Lhasa.'

Influence, as Bell made clear, implied no British domination over Tibet. By allowing Lhasa to draw supplies from India or Britain, the Tibetans would be 'economically and militarily dependent on us to just that extent that is desirable, and they will promote our interests by promoting their own.'[21]

Bell's list of military supplies for Tibet was accepted and the basis of trust in Anglo-Tibetan relations was established. But for this trust to endure, complementary political and diplomatic measures from Britain would be required to guarantee Tibet's freedom from China.

Montagu was in accord with Bell, but he pointed to difficulties 'arising mainly from the fact that Tibet is – or has been hitherto – recognised as a part of Chinese territory'. He was in favour of 'more active measures to help the Tibetans' and could not help 'wondering whether it would not be wise – and entirely justifiable, in view of Chinese procrastination, and of the existing disorganisation in China and *de facto* position as between China and Tibet – to take the bold line of recognising Tibetan independence – not perhaps formally, but at any rate for practical purposes – without much ado'.[22]

Alston was for opening Tibet to the outside world as an insurance against its possible reconquest by China. In the mean time, the bilateral ties between British India and Tibet should be strengthened.

On May 30, 1919, China submitted draft proposals, some of which modified or altered key sections of the Simla Convention to its advantage, for a fresh tripartite conference on Tibet. Lhasa expressed its suspicions about the document, which it saw as old wine in a new bottle. In any case, informal preliminary talks between the British and Chinese had scarcely got under way before Beijing called off the venture for the stated reason that it feared strong domestic opposition to the projected settlement. China, at the time, was swamped by a tide of nationalism, and any perceived retreat from the old imperial borders, under pressure from the British, was anathema to Chinese nationalists.

By the middle of 1921, despite much interdepartmental parleying in Whitehall and frequent representations to Beijing, there was no movement from China on the desired conference on Tibet. When the Chinese Minister to London, Dr Wellington Koo, called on the British Foreign Secretary with a fanciful story of British troops marching into Tibet, Lord Curzon – the old viceregal fires burning within – gave him a severe dressing down.

He handed Koo a Foreign Office memorandum which reviewed the unsatisfactory course of Anglo-Chinese negotiations over Tibet. It was two years since these had lapsed, the note pointed out, yet it was the Chinese Government which, having initiated them, had brought them to an abrupt end and created the present stalemate. Curzon then told his visitor 'that the delay in dealing with the matter had become almost a scandal . . . that unless the Chinese Government were willing to resume negotiations for a Tripartite settlement without further delay, say, written or non-written, we should be compelled to proceed alone. In that case, we should regard ourselves at liberty to deal with Tibet, if necessary, without again referring to China; to enter into closer relations with the Tibetans; to send an agent to Lhasa from time to time to consult the Tibetan Government; to open up increased trading intercourse between India and Tibet – and to give the Tibetans any reasonable assistance they might require in the development and protection of their country . . .'[23]

Curzon felt that Koo had realised that 'His Majesty's Government were in earnest and that the game of shilly-shally could no longer be pursued'. There were echoes of Simla and the high noon of the Raj in all this, but times had changed and the month passed without a tremor in Beijing.

Koo had defended his government's dilatoriness with the plea that it was preoccupied with the forthcoming Washington Conference, which excuse Curzon refused to accept since the conference had nothing whatever to do with Tibet. He was naturally riled when he discovered that the Foreign Office had acceded to Koo's request that discussion of Tibet be postponed. Only three weeks ago, Curzon complained, 'the Department urged me to send for Mr Koo and bring the matter to a head by giving a sort of ultimatum to China. I did so in language the emphasis of which was unmistakable. Now because the Chinese whine, as they are bound to do, it is proposed that we should back down . . .'[24]

The new reality of a weakened post-war British Empire meant that the Foreign Office had to tread warily, as American opinion was sensitive to any supposed violation of China's rights. Chinese diplomats and politicians played cleverly to the American gallery from time to time.

The evolving Anglo-American relationship, in order to retain its special character, required that Britain fall in with American wishes when called upon to do so by Washington. Even the prized Anglo-Japanese Alliance, which had been one of Britain's principal diplomatic anchors since its signing in January 1902, was terminated in December 1921 in response to American pressure. It was a decision much regretted later by Churchill in his memoirs and by Vansittart.

As the prospects of a Tibetan settlement disappeared in the labyrinth of post-Washington Conference diplomacy, relations between Britain and Tibet cooled. Bell had left India. His personal standing with the Dalai Lama had been unique and his departure was a considerable loss to Anglo-Tibetan understanding.

The impact of these developments on Tibet's internal politics was also far-reaching. British support for Tibet, of the sort envisaged by Bell, might have strengthened the modernising Young Tibet Party headed by Tsarong Dzasa, who had led the heroic rearguard action of 1910 that had enabled the Dalai Lama to escape the Chinese dragnet and reach India. Tsarong's programme of political and economic change and his hopes for the creation of a modern army for Tibet were thwarted by the reactionary clergy who eventually won the day.

In the 1930s, visiting Chinese and British missions to Lhasa kept jealous watch over each other. China, through its instrument the Panchen Lama, had a foot in the Tibetan door. Tibetan drift and confusion deepened with the death of the 13th Dalai Lama in December 1933. As one of the most remarkable holders of his office, he incarnated the spirit of Tibetan independence. Following his demise, the Tibetan Government, such as it was, appeared oblivious of the need for national reform to prepare for the challenges ahead.

In these intervening years the substance of the Simla Convention lay almost forgotten until the arrival of Olaf Caroe at the Indian Foreign and Political Department in 1938. With a new international war looming ever larger, he proceeded to reactivate the McMahon Line by sending to the Tawang tract, in the summer of that year, Captain Lightfoot and a party of his Assam Rifles.

As the conditions underlying Tawang's cession to India remained unfulfilled, Tibetan tax collectors had returned to levy Lhasa's traditional revenues. Lightfoot proceeded to expel them and Tawang became a bone of contention between the Tibetan authorities and the Indian Government. Eventually, India expressed willingness to consider a territorial compromise provided Tibet agreed to a comprehensive settlement. No solution had been reached when the British withdrew from India on August 15, 1947.

The 14th Dalai Lama's enthronement in Lhasa in February 1940 was witnessed by a British delegation headed by Basil Gould. There were other dignitaries from China, Nepal and Bhutan. Gould and Caroe may have wished to chart a new course for Anglo-Tibetan relations in the context of a rapidly changing world. However, for this to become official policy would have required Whitehall's seal of approval, but wartime preoccupations, the struggle against Germany and Japan, and the need to keep China happy, meant that such assent was unlikely. The United States, in keeping with past policy, and also with an eye to its ally Chiang Kai-shek's claims, underwrote Chinese authority over Tibet.

It was perhaps no accident that British officialdom turned lukewarm on Tibet as the prospect of a self-governing India loomed larger on the political horizon with the announcement of the Montagu-Chelmsford Declaration. Bell opined that the Himalayan border states and Tibet would gravitate towards China once Britain had withdrawn from India.[25]

In sum, there was no fundamental alteration in Anglo-Tibetan relations from the conclusion of the Simla Convention in July 1914

to Indian independence in August 1947. The ambiguities and contradictions in British policy, pointed out as long ago as August 1907
by Sir John Jordan, British Minister in China, remained to the
bitter end. Jordan had complained in his dispatch: 'The present
position is anomalous. One day we treat some Tibetan question,
scientific missions for example, with China exclusively without any
reference to Tibet, and the next time we insist that, so far as the
1904 Convention is concerned, the co-operation of Tibet is essential
to give Chinese action due validity. It is very much as if the United
States had made, say, a Fishery Convention independently with
Newfoundland and insisted that while Great Britain was at liberty
to regulate the other foreign relations of the Island as she pleased,
she must be associated with the Colonial Authorities in seeing that
the terms of the particular Convention were duly fulfilled.'[26] This,
then, was the legacy of the Raj.

The Emergence of an Indian View of Tibet

India and China as independent nation-states came face to face for
the first time in their history in the aftermath of the Second World
War. Previously, contacts between Indian and Chinese civilisations
had consisted largely of a one-way traffic of Buddhist monks from
China, a millennium and more ago, visiting India in search of scriptural wisdom. Indians and Chinese as a whole knew very little
about each other. However, if there was no friendship between
them, there was no enmity either.

Separated by desert and mountain, the Indian and Chinese worlds
remained strangers till the Western intrusion into the Orient in the
19th century. In the preceding centuries each of these worlds had
shrunk under military and political pressures from Central Asia.
The difference, however, was that while India traditionally had
been a constellation of competing polities, the miracle of China's
unification had occurred under the Qin Emperor Shi Huangdi as
far back as 221 BC.

China's world-view was incubated in political and cultural isolation, as was its statecraft. Its institutional manifestation was the
tributary system in which 'barbarian' kingdoms kowtowed to the
Son of Heaven in Beijing. This Confucian world order was a
parody of international relations, as British and other foreign gun-
boats kept reminding China's rulers throughout the nineteenth
century.

Tradition and psychology are, however, slow to alter. C.P. Fitzgerald, the noted historian of China, observes that 'the Chinese
view of the world has not fundamentally changed: it has been

adapted to take account of the modern world, but only so far as to permit China to occupy, still, the central place in the picture.'[27]

Irrespective of differences of political ideology, this sinocentricism was a common bond between China's two principal adversaries. Chiang Kai-shek, in his book *China's Destiny*, called for the restoration of what he considered to be his country's lost territories. His rival Mao Zedong, unlike Lenin or Karakhan, was no Marxist knight errant advocating the return of China's imperial possessions to its subject peoples. He lamented: 'After having inflicted defeats on China, the imperialist countries forcibly took from her a large number of states tributary to China, as well as parts. Japan appropriated Korea, Taiwan, the Ryuku Islands, the Pescadores; England took Burma, Bhutan, Nepal, and Hong Kong; France seized Annam; even a miserable little country like Portugal took Macao from us.'[28]

China and India had emerged from their encounters with the West with different political visions. There was a strong totalitarian strain in modern Chinese nationalism, whether Kuomintang or Communist. It perceived Western science and technology as useful instruments that could strengthen China at home and project its power abroad; there was less interest in Western liberal values and democratic institutions. In contrast, the most refined grain in Indian political and cultural nationalism, as embodied in Tagore, Gandhi and Nehru, was an amalgam of much that was best in the indigenous philosophical tradition and the enlightenment of the West.

Asian figures in the 19th and 20th centuries were mostly critical of the West's political and economic imperialism without necessarily having a common view of the self-determining societies they wished to create in the future. They often spoke of Asian solidarity but were at odds on its possible meaning and application. Despite Tagore's early admiration for Japan (in keeping with other Asians), he was prompt to denounce its depredations in China in the 1930s in a letter to the Japanese poet Noguchi Yonejiro. While reaffirming his faith in the 'message of Asia', Tagore said, 'I never dreamed that this message could be identified with deeds which might rejoice the heart of Tamerlane.'[29]

Nor was Tagore's love and admiration of China and Chinese civilisation reciprocated by the bulk of radical Chinese; during his visit to their country in 1924, they had denounced him as a pro-British reactionary.[30]

Jawaharlal Nehru, who shared much of Tagore's world-view, was present at the Brussels Congress of Oppressed Nationalities in February 1927, when the Indian and Chinese delegations in a joint declaration stated: 'British imperialism, which in the past has kept us apart and done so much injury, is now the very force that is uniting us in a common endeavour to overthrow it.'[31] The Indian National Congress had earlier criticised British policies in China and the dispatch of the Younghusband mission to Tibet, and had repeatedly denounced the use of Indian troops abroad in the interests of British imperialism.

When General Zhu De, the leader of the Chinese Red Army, wrote to Nehru from Yan'an on November 26, 1937, appealing for help against the invading Fascist Japanese, the Indian National Congress, at Nehru's prompting, sent a medical mission to the Communist-administered area of China under Dr M. Atal and including Dwarkanath Kotnis.

The Kuomintang Government of Chiang Kai-shek also had close and friendly links with Congress leaders. Both he and his wife pleaded the cause of Indian independence in the wartime counsels of the Allied powers. For his part, Mahatma Gandhi assured the Generalissimo that Congress's Quit India movement of 1942 was in no way designed to weaken China's struggle against Japan.

As the Second World War drew to its end, Nehru outlined his thoughts on the international order of the future. The pre-eminence of the United States and the Soviet Union would be unchallenged, but China, even a Communist China, would be too big and proud ever to become a Soviet satellite. In this he was to be vindicated, as he was also in his support of the Chinese Government's right to its seat at the United Nations following the collapse of Chiang Kai-shek's regime and his flight from the Chinese mainland to the island-sanctuary of Taiwan. By contrast, the Truman Administration's chief spokesman on the Far East, Dean Rusk, was to argue that China, after Mao's accession to power, had been reduced to a 'Slavic Manchukuo' and thus did not qualify for UN membership.

Nehru's vision of India's world role was a sort of bridge between East and West: '. . . an Asian state, traditionally friendly to China, without any legacy of conflict with Russia, yet friendly to the West and following a middle way in its programme of economic and social change'.[32]

The Chinese civil war had reached a critical stage in the middle of 1947 when India attained independence, and Nehru, as Prime Minister, couched his instructions to his Ambassador in Nanjing, K.P.S. Menon, with great care. They read: 'In China the situation is difficult because the civil war is going on. I have been on very friendly terms with the Chiang Kai-sheks and we hold each other in esteem. I have been friendly also with some of the prominent Communist leaders of the North-West, though I have not met them. It would appear from American reports that neither party in the Chinese dispute is free from blame. If American statesmen say so in spite of their violent dislike of everything communistic, then it seems clear that the Chinese Communists have no bad case. Our Ambassador in China, while maintaining close and friendly relations with Chiang Kai-shek's Government, should not himself become partisan in the civil conflict. Nor should he say anything disparaging to either side. Some words I have used or written have been exploited by the Chinese Government as against the North-West Communist Government. If our Ambassador in China has any opportunity, without causing ill-will to the Chinese Government, to visit the North-West areas, he should seize it and explain to the Chinese leaders there our general policy of friendship and non-interference.'[33]

Menon was succeeded half-way through 1948 by K.M. Panikkar, who was to write later: 'It did not take me long to discover that the Kuomintang attitude towards India, while genuinely friendly, was inclined to be a little patronising. It was the attitude of an elder brother who was prepared to give advice to a younger brother struggling to make his way. Independence of India was welcome, but of course it was understood that China as the recognised Great Power in the East after the war expected India to know her place . . . soon I realised that even in regard to America the attitude of China was one of patronising condescension . . . To the Kuomintang, which had inherited the mantle of the Son of Heaven, America was no more than the great barbarian for whose dollars and equipment she had immediate need, but for whose culture she had no great admiration. Chiang himself was in no sense a pro-American, while those around him like Chen Pu-li and Chen Li-fu were aggressive Confucians who believed in the racial superiority of the Chinese.'[34]

But whatever the problems arising from the divergences of historical and political outlook, Sino-Indian relations would scarcely have plummeted in so dramatic a fashion in the late 1950s and early 1960s without the developments in Tibet. The forcible incorporation of a *de facto* independent Tibet into Maoist China by the People's Liberation Army in October 1950; the subsequent Chinese military build-up in a strategically placed country which had no armed forces of its own in any modern sense and was thus a peaceful buffer; the reactivation of a dormant Himalayan frontier and continuous Tibetan unrest in the face of Chinese repression together produced an explosive brew which transformed an avowed friendship between India and China into one of dangerous enmity.

A Chinese note to India on May 11, 1962, was to state: 'If one respects the objective historical facts, one cannot but acknowledge that there has been a dark side to Sino-Indian relations since their beginning . . . Obviously the Indian Government is not reconciled to the fact that the Chinese Government is exercising its sovereignty over Tibet.'[35]

The Kuomintang Government had already fired a shot across India's bows at the Asian Relations Conference in Delhi in March 1947, where Tibet was admitted as an independent member-state. Since 1911, at least, Tibet had fulfilled all the requirements of sovereignty: it had a government in control of a settled and well-defined territory, which was represented abroad by its own plenipotentiaries and issued a national currency.

With Mao Zedong the victor in China's civil war and his new People's Republic firmly in place on October 1, 1949, the Tibetan Minister, W.D. Shakabpa, visited Delhi and solicited Nehru's support. He warned that the destruction of Tibet as a buffer would imperil India's future security. But weakened by the surgery of partition and engaged in a military exercise in Kashmir against Pakistan, the Indian Government was reluctant to embark on a quarrel with China which would embroil the Soviet Union, at the time a close ally of Beijing. Nehru hoped that a peaceful settlement could be reached between the Lhasa authorities and Beijing, which would allow loose Chinese control over Tibet, involving perhaps maximum autonomy for the Tibetans in exchange for China's regulation of Tibet's external relations and defence.

India had begun quietly to place its own strategic markers for a defensive line along the Himalayas through a series of treaties from 1949 to 1951 with Bhutan, Nepal and Sikkim. The administration of India's North East Frontier Agency (known today as the state of Arunachal Pradesh) east of Bhutan was simultaneously strengthened. It seemed a throwback to Morley's policy earlier in the century and had even less chance of success. Instead of a weak Manchu government there was now a strong, militarised regime in Beijing determined to rewrite what generations of Chinese nationalists considered to be the 'unequal treaties' of the past.

Whatever Nehru's hopes for a peaceful solution to the Tibetan problem, he received short shrift in the Chinese press. One paper called him 'a rebel against the movement for national independence, a blackguard who undermines the progress of the people's liberation movement, a loyal slave of imperialism. Into his slavish and bourgeois reactionary nature has now been instilled the beastly ambition of aggression.'[36]

The Chinese army had started moving into the eastern Tibetan border area of Kham in the final months of 1949. Having established satisfactory lines of communications, it attacked and invaded the Tibetan heartland in October 1950. India's mild protests at this development were dismissed brusquely in Beijing.

Tibet appealed in vain to the United Nations for help on November 11, 1950. However, New Delhi was informed by Beijing, in its note of November 16, that a peaceful outcome to the Tibetan question was still possible. This note may have led the Indian Government to prompt the world body to keep the subject pending in the likelihood of further talks between Tibet and China rather than press for firm action against a China formally branded as an aggressor. There was, undoubtedly, also an element of Indian wishfulness in this approach

It was sufficiently evident for Sardar Vallabbhai Patel, India's Home Minister and Nehru's most senior colleague in government and in the Indian National Congress, to issue a letter of warning to Nehru on December 7, 1950, a fortnight before his sudden death:

My Dear Jawaharlal,
Ever since my return from Ahmedabad . . . I have been anxiously thinking about the problem of Tibet and I thought I should share with you what is passing through my mind.

I have carefully gone through the correspondence between the External Affairs Ministry and our Ambassador [K.M. Panikkar] in Peking and through him the Chinese Government. I have tried to peruse this correspondence as favourably as possible, but I regret to say that neither of them comes out well as a result of this study.

The Chinese Government have tried to delude us by professions of peaceful intentions. My own feeling is that at a crucial period they managed to instil into our Ambassador a false sense of confidence in their so-called desire to settle the Tibetan problem by peaceful means.

There can be no doubt that, during the period covered by this correspondence, the Chinese must have been concentrating for an onslaught on Tibet. The final action of the Chinese, in my judgement, is little short of perfidy.

The tragedy of it is that the Tibetans put faith in us; they chose to be guided by us; and we have been unable to get them out of the meshes of Chinese diplomacy or Chinese malevolence . . .

Our Ambassador has been at great pains to find an explanation or justification for Chinese policy and actions. As the External Affairs Ministry remarked in one of their telegrams, there was a lack of firmness and unnecessary apology in one or two of our representations that he made to the Chinese Government on our behalf. It is impossible to imagine any sensible person believing in the so-called threat to China from Anglo-American machinations in Tibet. Therefore, if the Chinese put faith in this, they must have distrusted us so completely as to have taken us as tools and stooges of Anglo-American diplomacy or strategy. This feeling, if genuinely entertained by the Chinese in spite of your direct approaches to them, indicates that, even though we regard ourselves as the friends of China, the Chinese do not regard us as their friends.

Outside the Soviet Bloc, continued Patel, India was virtually alone in championing the cause of Chinese entry into the United Nations and 'in securing from the Americans assurances on the question of Formosa'. He doubted that 'we can go any further than we have done already to convince China of our good intentions, friendliness and goodwill. In Peking we have an Ambassador who is eminently suitable for putting across the friendly point of view. Even he seems to have failed to convert the Chinese. Their last telegram to us is an act of gross discourtesy not only in the summary way it disposes of our protest against the entry of Chinese forces into Tibet but also in the wild insinuations that our attitude is determined by foreign influences. It looks as though it is not a friend speaking in that language but a potential enemy.'

Against this background, Patel suggested that 'we have to consider what new situation now faces us as a result of the disappearance of Tibet as we know it, and the expansion of China up to our gates. Throughout history, we have seldom been worried about our impenetrable barrier . . . We had a friendly Tibet which gave us no trouble.'

Continuing in this prophetic vein, he noted: 'Chinese irredentism and Communist imperialism are different from the expansionism and imperialism of the Western powers. The former has a cloak of ideology which makes it ten times more dangerous. In the guise of ideological expansion lie concealed racial, national and historical claims . . . While our western and north-western threats to security are still as prominent as before: a new threat has developed from the north and north-east. Thus, for the first time, after centuries, India's defence has to concentrate itself on two fronts simultaneously. Our defence measures have so far been based on the calculations of a superiority over Pakistan.'[37]

This is a remarkable document. If its author had lived a few years longer, India's unfolding China policy might have carried a stronger seasoning of realism. Mired in the exhausting Korean war with the United States and its allies, who fought collectively under United Nations colours, China especially needed India's goodwill in the early 1950s as a bridge to the non-Communist world from which it had been largely isolated by Washington.

It was an opportune time for India to have pressed China to place its seal on a Himalayan border settlement based on existing realities. Instead, New Delhi formally conceded every inch of

Beijing's claim to Tibet in the Sino-Indian Treaty of April 29, 1954, without any territorial *quid pro quo*.

The treaty referred to Tibet as the 'Tibet region of China' and it included an Indian undertaking to 'voluntarily renounce all the extra-territorial rights enjoyed by Britain in Tibet'. This exercise, in Nehru's view, was a reaffirmation of India's anti-imperialist credentials as well as a wise investment in the future well-being of Sino-Indian relations. Premiers Nehru and Zhou Enlai announced that the *Panch Shila*, the 'Five Principles of Peaceful Co-existence', would be the framework of Sino-Indian relations and would provide a model for other states in Asia in their dealings with China.

Zhou Enlai claimed that the McMahon Line was a legacy of British imperialism but, because it was an accomplished fact and in the light of the friendly relations existing between India and China, he was prepared to accord provisional recognition to the Line. The Chinese Government had not yet consulted the Tibetan authorities about it but proposed soon to do so. Nehru was assured that Tibetan autonomy would be respected.

While the bulk of the Indian media hailed the Sino-Indian accord as another feather in Nehru's cap as world statesman, there were a number of discordant voices as well. *The Pioneer* of May 1, 1954, for instance, described China's action in Tibet as a 'violation of the peace of the most peaceful nation in the world'. The paper charged that China had never exercised 'effective control' over Tibet and that it would have been in 'everybody's interest if the delicate balance of power in Tibet had not been disturbed'.

The right-wing *Organiser* of May 10, 1954, said: 'Tibet was a useful – and natural – buffer between our two States. By letting China do what it will with Tibet, we have exposed ourselves to potentially serious infiltration, and Tibet to a rule to which it has given no consent. It is strange that there should have been no Tibetan representative at a conference whose sole agenda was Tibet.'

The next few years were to mark the high noon of official Sino-Indian friendship. It was the period when Indians and Chinese were informed by their respective governments that they were brothers; in India under the intoxicating slogan *Hindi-Chini bhai bhai*. The intoxicant appeared, however, to have a greater effect on the Indian leadership than it did on the Chinese. A number of Indian newspapers pointed to the continuing publication of irredentist Chinese maps which, apart from including areas of India, took in Bhutan and Nepal as well. To gentle remonstrances from New Delhi about their continued publication, Beijing blandly replied that these were old Kuomintang issues which it had not had the time to examine or rectify, but it would do so in due course.

Professor Meghnad Saha, the eminent Indian physicist and a member of the Upper House of India's Parliament, raised the subject at question time but was unable to elicit a satisfactory response from the government benches. Later Nehru was to tell Parliament that 'map or no map' India stood by the McMahon Line, a statement which betrayed his unawareness of the lack of a Chinese signature to the settlement. With the disappearance of Tibet as an independent entity, the juridical validity of the McMahon Line was now open to question. Having swallowed the camel of China's occupation of Tibet, the Indian Prime Minister was straining at a gnat bearing the name of a British civil servant. The appearance in Beijing in 1954 of Liu Peihua's book, *A Brief History of China*, with its accompanying maps of China's lost territories, was a portent of things to come.

At the Bandung Conference of April 1955, when Sino-Indian relations were supposedly at a peak of cordiality and goodwill, Premier Zhou Enlai made a quiet approach to his Pakistani counterpart, Mohammed Ali, for a diplomatic understanding, despite Pakistan's membership of the American-sponsored anti-Communist, anti-Chinese SEATO pact. Zhou told Ali that a conflict of national interests would soon undermine Sino-Indian friendship.[38]

Meanwhile, China's militarisation of Tibet continued apace. The young Dalai Lama, on a visit to India in June 1956 for the Buddha Jayanti celebrations, expressed a desire to remain in the country but was persuaded by Nehru to return to Tibet following his conversations with Zhou Enlai in Delhi and the latter's assurances that Chinese 'reforms' would be relaxed. In early 1957, Chairman Mao announced a token withdrawal of Chinese troops from Tibet and a slowdown in the pace of 'reforms' there.

The Dalai Lama, during his stay in India, had issued an invitation to Nehru to visit Lhasa. It was formally routed through Beijing at Nehru's request and was accepted. He was due to make his visit in the summer of 1958, but it was cancelled by the Chinese Government on the plea that it could not guarantee his safety in the disturbed conditions prevailing in Tibet. That there was serious unrest in Tibet was for the first time openly admitted by Beijing; nevertheless, the excuse to cancel the visit on the grounds that it would be dangerous for Nehru struck him as specious, as he made clear in a conversation with the French author Amaury de Riencourt. It was Zhou Enlai who was likely to be in danger in Lhasa, Nehru said, not himself.[39]

In March 1959, the unrest in Tibet flared into a major rebellion against Chinese rule, and the Dalai Lama made a dramatic flight to the sanctuary of India, where he was received with honour and granted asylum. The effect of this on Indian public opinion and on Nehru himself was indeed deep. Equally deep was the Chinese Government's resentment of the cordiality of India's welcome to the Tibetan dignitary.

Later in the summer that year, Chinese troops opened fire on an Indian border patrol at Longju, east of Bhutan, killing and wounding a number of Indian soldiers. The shock to Indian opinion intensified with Beijing's first formal declaration that the demarcation of the frontier alignment between India and Tibet, negotiated during the period of the British Raj, was null and void as it had been thrust upon a weak China. It was packaged in an 'unequal treaty' whose validity no government in China had ever accepted. Alarmingly, Beijing also questioned the propriety of India's relations with Bhutan, Sikkim and Nepal.

The Sino-Indian relationship revealed another conundrum when it emerged that New Delhi and Beijing had been exchanging confidential protest notes over an older stretch of disputed territory in the Aksai Chin area of India's Ladakh, through which China was building a road linking Xinjiang with Tibet. There had also been occasional skirmishes between Indian and Chinese military units in this region.

In April 1960, Zhou Enlai visited New Delhi in an ostensible bid to stem the slide in Sino-Indian relations. He offered Nehru a package under which China would forgo its claims to Arunachal Pradesh in India's north-east and broadly accept the McMahon Line, while expecting India to do likewise over the Aksai Chin plateau in the western sector.

A year earlier, Beijing, in its note to New Delhi, had stressed that America remained its principal adversary and that China, therefore, had no wish to open a second front against India. With an eye to India's troubled relations with Pakistan, Beijing warned: 'It seems that you too cannot have two fronts.'[40]

Nehru arranged a series of meetings between his Cabinet colleagues and Zhou Enlai so that he could gauge for himself the strength of Indian feeling on what was perceived as Chinese aggressiveness and duplicity, and the reluctance to make further concessions to China. The Indian Prime Minister had been the principal, if not the sole architect of his country's China policy, against the better judgement of some of his colleagues, like Patel, and political opponents such as Jayaprakash Narayan and J.B. Kripalani. He was no longer prepared to put his name singly to a second mortgage on Chinese goodwill. Any new Sino-Indian arrangement this time would have to bear the collective signature of his ministers; without this there would be no deal. Zhou Enlai went home empty-handed. The decision to allow officials from either side to compile historical evidence on the disputed border was merely a face-saver which has in the intervening years brought a solution no nearer. This could only be achieved at the highest political level.

Beijing's claim-line in the disputed frontier continued to expand and serious clashes occurred in 1961 between Indian and Chinese border patrols in the western sector, leading to some loss of life. Yet, with all this, there was a lack of urgency in the higher echelons of the Indian Government and thus a conspicuous absence of the necessary co-ordination between the civil and military wings of the administration.

Military development had not been high on the list of Nehru's priorities in the 1950s, and recent political interference had demo-ralised the Indian Army. Nehru's mistaken calculation, despite clear evidence to the contrary, that China would resist the tempta-tion to use *force majeure* scarcely helped matters; nor did his loose statement in September 1962, made entirely for domestic consump-tion, that he had ordered his forces to throw the Chinese out of disputed territory. With its cotton armour, inadequate weaponry and lack of training or planning for high-altitude warfare, the Indian border patrol was in no position to carry out such orders.[41] But Nehru's words were grist to the mills of China's propaganda, enabling Beijing to claim that India had launched an attack to which China was simply responding defensively.

As massive Chinese forces overwhelmed India's penny-packet defences, Nehru, in a moment of great personal anguish, confessed in Parliament in October 1962 that his China policy had been framed in 'an artificial atmosphere of our own creation'. It had much in common with the policy of the Morley years, as did China's response in using its free hand in Tibet to try eventually to under-mine India's position in the Himalayan borderlands. The Chinese strategic calculus proved that passive defence along the Himalayas was no more a guarantee of Indian security than the Maginot Line had been for France in 1940.[42] The Chinese had also reduced the vaunted *Panch Shila* – the Five Principles of Peaceful Co-existence – to a licence to impose their will on Tibet without fear of Indian protest or response. In effect, the Five Principles became five shrouds for a dying Tibet.

Conclusion

The differing territorial fortunes of the Ottoman and Manchu empires present an illuminating parallel: each was in possession of polities held under the title of suzerainty, and in their declining years each came to rely on Great Power *realpolitik* for its existence. However, the Ottoman dominions, by the end of the First World War, had shrunk to the Anatolian plateau of Turkey, while those of China incorporated the farthest Manchu outposts, save that of the Mongolian People's Republic. And Mongolia was prised from China's imperial grip only because Mongol nationalists were supported by the Tsar and his Bolshevik successors.

To point these out is not to argue for contemporary China's dissolution. The legacies of empire can not simply be wished away; they have to be redesigned, with reason and common sense, into the political fabric of present-day realities. Otherwise stable international life would cease to exist as the consequent confusion and anarchy become breeding grounds for fresh cycles of conflict.

In the case of Tibet, however, China's massive nuclear and non-nuclear military presence in Tibet has had a destabilising impact on the regional politics of South Asia and beyond. The high Tibetan plateau occupies a location of unique significance: Chinese missiles point from there in the direction of India and the territories of the former Soviet Union, and governments in New Delhi and the latter cannot disregard their possible use in the event of rising tension.

The Dalai Lama's Five Point Peace Plan, put forward at the European Parliament in Strasbourg in 1988, called for the demilitarisation of Tibet, while expressing willingness to accept Chinese sovereignty over his country in lieu of the full Tibetan independence demanded previously. In making this climb-down he disappointed, even angered, a large number of his compatriots.

Beijing dismissed his plan, and refused even to consider it as a basis for possible discussion with Tibetan representatives. Clearly, China's view of its sovereign rights in Tibet is not confined to juridical or political definitions.

China has had border disputes and conflicts with three of its principal continental neighbours: the former Soviet Union, India and Vietnam, each of which once boasted close and friendly ties with Beijing. In each instance, the border dispute became a refracting prism of deeper rivalries and suspicions. When China attacked Vietnam in February 1979, its paramount leader, Deng Xiaoping, with a touch of Prussian arrogance, informed the world that Vietnam was being taught a lesson just as India had been in 1962.

India's Foreign Minister under the Janata Government, A.B.
Vajpayee, having just arrived in Beijing on an amateurish fence-
mending exercise, felt so humiliated that he took the first available
flight home. The projected great leap forward in Indian diplomacy
became a disastrous great leap backwards. The irony was that, as
an opposition member of Parliament, Vajpayee had been a tren-
chant critic of Nehru's policies on China and Tibet.

The Chinese aggression against Vietnam had been closely preceded by an official visit to Washington by Deng Xiaoping, which
underlined the new understanding between the two sides since the
summer of 1971 following two decades of intense mutual antagonism. They kept in step in the Asia-Pacific region in defence of their
'parallel strategic interests', to quote then US Secretary of Defense,
Harold Brown.

In December 1971, this Sino-American understanding worked
against the people of East Bengal and the Indian Government in
their war with the Pakistani military regime of Yahya Khan. It
prompted I.F. Stone, the well-known American radical writer and
columnist, to remark that 'the world has seen strange bedfellows
before but never in a stranger and bloodier bed'.[43]

To ensure that Chinese threats of possible military intervention
from Tibet, first renewed against India during the latter's conflict
with Pakistan in September 1965, remained at the level of verbal
broadsides, India signed a Treaty of Peace and Friendship with the
Soviet Union on August 9, 1971. It was a diplomatic riposte to the
Sino-American entente; New Delhi and Moscow discovered that
they, too, had 'parallel strategic interests' in the region. The issue
of Tibet is thus caught in a web of conflicting international
interests.

The 1980s were characterised by a slow thaw in Sino-Indian relations, but the undercurrent of uncertainty surfaced dramatically in
the summer of 1987 when the Chinese and Indian armies, jockeying
for favourable positions along the eastern sector of the Indo-
Tibetan border, came perilously close to another war.

Local measures have since been undertaken by both sides to
avoid the sort of misunderstanding that could spark off a con-
flagration. The Sino-Indian dialogue on a border settlement pro-
ceeds in a more relaxed atmosphere. But, just as Beijing had once
made the withdrawal of Soviet forces from Mongolia one of three
pre-conditions for a fresh chapter in improved Sino-Soviet relations, India would be well advised to stress the necessity for Tibet's
transformation into a demilitarised, democratic zone of peace as
the *sine qua non* of a fruitful and enduring relationship with China.

NOTES

1. India Office Records (IOR), L/PS/7/148, Curzon to Hamilton, February 13, 1902.
2. Ibid.
3. IOR, Hamilton Papers, D510/8, Curzon to Hamilton, July 10, 1901.
4. IOR, Hamilton Papers, F123/76, Curzon to Hamilton, February 12, 1903.
5. IOR, Hamilton Papers, F123/1, Hamilton to Curzon, July 9, 1903.
6. IOR, Hamilton Papers, F123/76, Curzon to Hamilton, January 4, 1900.
7. IOR, Ampthill Papers, E233/37, Curzon to Ampthill, June 23, 1904.
8. IOR, L/PS/7/151, Curzon to Hamilton, January 8, 1903.
9. IOR, Curzon Papers, F111/345, Minute by Curzon, May 13, 1905.
10. IOR, Curzon Papers, F111/15, Younghusband to Curzon, April 20, 1908.
11. Public Record Office (PRO), FO 535/12, No. 3, Bryce to Grey, December 17, 1908. Enclosure to No. 3, Rockhill to Roosevelt, November 8, 1908.
12. IOR, L/PS/10/149, No. 654, Bailey to Bell, February 11, 1909.
13. IOR, L/PS/10/147, No. 341, extract from *Morning Post*, February 28, 1910.
14. PRO, Nicolson Papers, FO 800/348, Hardinge to Nicolson, June 9, 1911.
15. PRO, FO 535/14, No. 4, Buchanan to Grey, January 14, 1911.
16. National Library of Scotland, Edinburgh, Minto Papers, 4E 351, Morley to Minto, January 3, 1908.
17. Cambridge University Library, Hardinge Papers, vol. 70, no. 156, Chirol to Hardinge, June 14, 1912.
18. *Ibid*, Chirol to Hardinge June 28, 1912.
19. A.K. Wu, *China and the Soviet Union*, London: Methuen, 1950, pp. 39–40; Hosoya Chichiro, 'Japan's Policies Toward Russia' in *Japan's Foreign Policy, 1868-1941: A Research Guide* (ed. J.W. Morley), New York: Columbia University Press, 1974.
20. IOR, Curzon Papers, F112/213(b),; PRO, FO 371/382, no. 2244, Nicolson to Grey, January 6, 1907, Comment by Hardinge, Comment by Grey; nos. 41, 42, Comment by Hardinge. Morley to Curzon, September 10, 1919.
21. IOR, Bell Papers, F80, 5E 21/26, Bell to India, February 21, 1921.
22. IOR, Reading Papers, E238/3, Montagu to Reading, April 12, 1921.
23. IOR, Curzon Papers, F112/302, Curzon to Alston, August 26, 1921.
24. PRO, FO 371/6608, No. F3380/59/10, Minute by Curzon, September 12, 1921.
25. Clive Christie, 'Great Britain, China, and the Status of Tibet, 1914–21', *Modern Asian Studies* (Cambridge), vol. X, October 1976, pp. 507-8.
26. IOR, L/PS/10/148, No. 31724, Jordan to Grey, January 14, 1907.
27. C.P. Fitzgerald, *The Chinese View of their Place in the World*, London: Oxford University Press/RIIA, 1964, p. 71.
28. Stuart R. Schram, *The Political Thought of Mao Tse-tung*, New York: Praeger, 1965, p. 257.
29. S. Hay, *Asian Ideas of East and West*, Harvard University Press, 1970, p. 320.
30. Ibid., pp. 124–245.
31. W.F. van Eekelin, *Indian Foreign Policy and the Border Dispute with China*, The Hague: Martinus Nijhoff, 1964, p. 21.
32. Michael Brecher, *Nehru, A Political Biography*, Oxford University Press, 1969 p. 559.
33. K.P.S. Menon, *China Past and Present*, Bombay: Bharatiya Vidya Bhavan, 1972, pp. 48-9.
34. K.M. Panikkar, *In Two Chinas*, London: Allen and Unwin, 1955, pp. 26-7.
35. *China White Paper*, 1960–62, Delhi.
36. 'India and Anglo-American Imperialism', *World Culture*, Shanghai, 1949.

37. Patel to Nehru, December 7, 1950, quoted in J. Dalvi, Appendix 1: General Kulwant Singh, a distinguished field commander, was appointed to head a committee in 1952 to study the military threat to India's northern borders. His comprehensive report was shelved, as was General Thorat's on the defence of India's North East Frontier Agency in October 1959. See Brigadier J. Dalvi, *Himalayan Blunder*, Bombay: Thacker & Co., 1969, pp. 22, 23; and Lt. General S.P. Thorat, *From Reveille to Retreat*, Delhi: Allied Publishers, 1986, pp. 196–203.

38. L.F. Rushbrook Williams, *The State of Pakistan*, London: Oxford University Press, 1962, pp. 120–1, quoted in S. Gopal, *Jawaharlal Nehru*, vol 2, London: Macmillan, 1979, p. 243 (footnote).

39. Amaury de Riencourt in *Jawaharlal Nehru* (ed. S. Gopal), Delhi: Oxford University Press, 1989, p. 147. When asked by a *Times of India* correspondent why he and his party had chosen India as their sanctuary in 1959, the Dalai Lama referred to India as Buddha's land, the source of Tibet's spiritual inspiration. 'Geographically speaking', the Dalai Lama added, 'India is our next door neighbour. Therefore it was quite logical for us to seek refuge in India. Before we crossed the Indian border, we were wondering whether we should go to Bhutan or India. We were not sure of the attitude of the Indian Government. We sent some of our officials in advance to find out India's response and we were informed that India was ready to receive us. We also received a telegram from Pandit Jawaharlal Nehru expressing warm feelings. On April 23, 1959, I reached Mussoorie. When I met Nehru, we exchanged ideas. Although he showed a little temper on some occasions generally he was very warm. I felt relieved and relaxed after talking to him. He said we were not refugees but his guests. He said it was essential to keep the Tibetan question alive and felt the need to educate the new generation as also to get the cultural traditions going. Today we are enjoying the results of the seeds we planted together.' *Times of India*, June 23, 1991.

40. India, *White Paper* vol. xi, p. 12

41. Dalvi and Thorat (*op. cit.*); K.S. Shelvankar, 'China's Himalayan Frontiers, India's Attitude' in *International Affairs* (London), vol. 38, no. 4, October 1962.

42. Nehru discounted the possibility of a limited Chinese attack, believing wrongly that it would herald a wider international war and the possible use of nuclear weapons. Hardinge in 1911 told Nicolson that a Chinese attack along India's North-East Himalayan belt would invite a British response on China's coast. Given the global situation at the time this was unlikely.

    Having humiliated India in October–November 1962 on the battlefield, the Chinese withdrew behind the border into Tibet. The political gains for China from the whole exercise were in the short and medium term far in excess of its military success.

43. I.F. Stone, *New York Review of Books*, June 29, 1972. Two indispensable works of reference are: Tsepon W.D. Shakabpa, *Tibet, Political History*, New York: Potala Publications 1984; and Hugh Richardson, *Tibet and its History*, London: Shambala, 1984.

THE NATIONALITIES POLICY OF THE CHINESE COMMUNIST PARTY AND THE SOCIALIST TRANSFORMATION OF TIBET

Warren W. Smith

The Nationalities Policy of the Chinese Communist Party (CCP) had as its primary goal the integration of minority nationality areas into the administrative structure of the People's Republic of China in preparation for their 'socialist transformation'. The CCP's policy of regional autonomy for nationalities was presented as a solution to the nationalities question which had 'never before been seen in history'. The CCP is usually thought to have achieved the socialist transition – that is, collectivisation – without the resistance which accompanied that process in other countries. While this is essentially accurate for Han (ethnic Chinese) areas, there was violent and sustained resistance in nationality areas, especially in Tibet. This paper attempts to illustrate the contradictions within the CCP's nationalities policy and its failure to achieve either the unity of, or autonomy for, the nationalities.

Socialist Transition

The underlying issue in the socialist transition process is the role of the state. The socialist ideal requires that the choice for the socialist path be both popular and voluntary, and it requires a high level of development of 'proletarian socialist consciousness'. This consciousness could be taught, but not imposed without violating the principle of voluntarism and the ideal of socialist democracy:

The difficulty with the socialist ideal for revolutionary activists was to wait patiently for society to develop the conditions necessary for the 'natural' transition to socialism: at the heart of socialist development lies the tension between the vision of the socialist future projected by the leadership . . . and the principle that working people . . . must shape the future. Within the Marxist tradition, that tension has historically been embedded within the . . . concepts of the dictatorship of the proletariat as put forth by Marx and Engels and developed by Lenin, of democratic centralism and the vanguard party as developed by the Bolsheviks, and of mass line politics linking leadership and masses as refined in China . . .[1]

The essence of the socialist doctrine requires a transition not only in the forms of production but in the substance of actual control of production by the direct producers. To achieve the democratic promise of socialism, the transition process had to be both voluntary and productive of actual economic and social benefits. Lenin recognised that coercion was anathema to true socialist democracy:

> Cooperatives must be organised as to gain the confidence of the peasants . . . coercion would ruin the whole cause. Nothing is more stupid than the very idea of applying coercion in economic relations with the middle peasants.[2]

Marx postulated that socialism would evolve naturally out of capitalism; capitalism would produce capital, industry and the proletarian class – the 'forces of production' which were prerequisites for the transformation in the 'relations of production' to proletarian ownership. However, the impatience of revolutionary activists for revolution in pre-capitalist societies led them to formulate strategies for an accelerated revolutionary process which would skip the capitalist stage of economic and social development.

Lenin and Trotsky developed a strategy which called for the proletarian class to seize control of the 'bourgeois-democratic' revolution, which was imminent in Russia, and transform it into a socialist revolution by means of a 'dictatorship of the proletariat'. Because there was no true proletariat in Russia sufficiently enlightened to represent itself, the revolutionary activists, constituted as a Communist party, would represent the interests of the proletariat and assume its historic role of leading the socialist revolution. This strategy substituted revolutionary activism for Marx's historical determinism and depended upon the activists representing the interests of the proletarian class rather than themselves as a new class.

The concept of a 'dictatorship of the proletariat' in a society which had very little social and economic preparation for socialism necessitated more, not less, state power, and created more, not less, antagonism between the people and their leaders. At the same time, protection of the individual against the powers of the state was eliminated by the theoretical identity of the people and the state.

The dangers inherent in increased state control became manifest when Stalin attempted to employ 'socialist accumulation' to reverse stages of development, which required socialist relations of production, or collectivisation, to produce industrialisation, the forces of production. Socialist accumulation meant that the state acquired, by means of the collectivisation of agriculture, 'surplus' agricultural products which were then sold, often on the foreign market, to finance industrialisation. Stalin achieved industrialisation in the Soviet Union, but only at the expense of socialist democracy.

Nationalities Policy

Although Marxist nationalities policy was introduced only by Marx's successors, the fundamental contradiction in that policy was inherent in Marxist theory. Marx believed that economic class interest and identification would ultimately prevail over ethnic and national interest and identity. He misinterpreted nationalism as a transitory phenomenon at a particular stage of economic development. Marx considered that nationalism was a progressive force during the capitalist stage because the nationalist political format facilitated the accumulation of capital and the organisation of the proletarian class; however, he thought that it was only an invention of the bourgeois class which was employed to preserve economic monopolies and to create national divisions within the otherwise internationalist proletariat.

Lenin's policy for accelerated revolution sought to employ the progressive social and economic benefits of bourgeois nationalism while simultaneously preparing the stage for the elimination of nationalism in favour of proletarian internationalism. Therefore, the bourgeois-national revolution would be led not by the bourgeoisie, but by the proletariat or the revolutionary activists who theoretically represented the proletariat. This strategy contradicted Marx's doctrine that the socialist revolution would be the result of the objective conditions of mature capitalism, not the conspiracies of revolutionary activists.

This process in relation to minority nationalities would have to be initiated and led by revolutionary activists who represented neither the nationality nor its proletarian class. Lenin attempted to resolve this contradiction, and reintroduce the principle of voluntarism, by his doctrine on self-determination of nations.

Lenin's policy was based upon the premise that, given a completely voluntary choice free of oppression, any minority nationality would make the more economically advantageous choice of union with the larger and more advanced state rather than independence. Lenin adamantly insisted that the doctrine on self-determination must include the right to secession, which he thought was the essential issue and one which would gain the trust of the nationalities. Minority nationalism could thus be defused by elimination of the majority oppression upon which it thrived. Minority nationalities might in this way benefit from the assistance of the proletariat of an advanced socialist state, enabling the nationality to skip the capitalist and bourgeois-nationalist stages and advance rapidly to socialism.

The problem with Lenin's nationalities theory, and the ideology of accelerated revolution in general, was that revolutionary impatience and majority nationalist chauvinism were hard to resist. Knowing that any nationality's union with the advanced socialist state was theoretically advantageous to the nationality concerned and that the general advance to socialism was inevitable, it was hard for the revolutionary activists to avoid choosing on behalf of the nationality, both for union with the majority nation and for the socialist path.

The Soviet Union was organised in this manner; the Soviet nationalities were given the right to self-determination, but the Russian proletariat, or its representatives, knew what was best for the nationalities and therefore determined that the nationalities would join the Soviet Union. Soviet nationalities doctrine was characterised by the contradiction of theoretically supporting minority nationality autonomy while actually working to undermine it in favour of proletarian internationalism.

Chinese Nationalism and Chinese Nationalities Policies

The evolution of the Chinese state was characterised by the predominance of culture over ethnicity to the extent that cultural unity became the essential legitimising factor for Chinese political ideology. Cultural unity was maintained by the traditional ideology of universal harmony, or *datong*, the 'great togetherness', by which conflict between individuals and nations could be avoided by egalitarian communalism and uniformity of thought. In the political realm this ideal was expressed in the concept of the 'Mandate of Heaven' by which universal political harmony was maintained through centralised political control and universal dominance of Chinese culture.

The evolution of Chinese cultural identity and the process of state formation took place by absorption of the 'barbarians' within the Chinese ecological zone and by tributary relations with those without. China's consciousness of its political and cultural universe was therefore one in which the spread of Chinese civilisation into a universe of 'barbarian' darkness was a natural process. Illusions of universal Chinese cultural superiority are due to the lack of awareness of any culture of comparable sophistication within the Chinese geographical area.

China's encounter with European imperialism in the 19th century created a dilemma for Chinese political ideology. The European nations obviously enjoyed material superiority, and they refused to recognise the superiority of Chinese culture or the universal political authority of China. Foreign imperialism, especially that of Japan, another Asian state which China had traditionally considered inferior, was instrumental in the development of modern Chinese nationalism which was therefore of a defensive and anti-imperialist nature.

The lessons learned by Chinese nationalists about the effects of foreign imperialism on the development of national consciousness were not applied to China's own relations within what it considered to be its traditional sphere of influence. Chinese nationalists, though anti-imperialist, did not recognise the nationalist aspirations and rights of those on China's territorial frontiers, especially Turks, Mongols and Tibetans, whom it considered to be already within the sphere of Chinese cultural and political assimilation.

Sun Yat-sen maintained that China was basically one nationality and that in China state and nation were synonymous. He favoured the dying-out of the small minority of non-Han races in favour of the unity of the whole. Chiang Kai-shek went even further, claiming that all China's nationalities were of one common race, the only differences being due to geography and religion.[3]

The CCP's nationalities policy not only included all of the contradictions acquired from Marxist–Leninist doctrine, but those of traditional Chinese chauvinism as well. Mao Zedong compounded the Chinese misconception of nationalism by his extreme Marxist opinion that 'the national question is in essence a class question'. Mao thought that nationalism had no significance except as a means of class oppression; once class oppression is eliminated, nationalism would have no basis. Mao, who employed Chinese nationalism in the anti-Japanese resistance, recognised the power of nationalism but not any inherent rights of nationalities.

The fundamental purpose of the Chinese nationalities policy was to deny nationalities' separatism in favour of multinational unity, to diffuse nationalist sentiments and to prepare the way for the socialist transformation of nationalities areas in a process common with Han China. Chinese control of many nationalities' areas, or knowledge of their conditions, was very slight. Much emphasis was placed upon propaganda to convince members of minority nationalities that their true interests lay in union with the Chinese socialist masses in opposition to their own exploiting classes. At the same time, the upper classes were co-opted by means of the United Front policy, which maintained local leaders in authority (with new titles and large salaries) until CCP authority could be established.

The Leninist doctrine on self-determination was dropped after the founding of the People's Republic because, it was claimed, the Chinese nationalities had already determined their choice by 'common revolutionary struggle', along with the Han, in opposition to foreign imperialism:

> . . . the Chinese nation as a whole has long been a nation suffering external imperialist oppression; among our various nationalities they have shared weal and woe and cemented a militant friendship in the revolutionary wars, culminating in the liberation of this big family of nationalities. The relations among ourselves and our relations with the outside world do not require us to adopt the policy as was followed by Russia at the time of the October Revolution, which laid emphasis on national self-determination and at the same time allowed secession of nationalities.[4]

Elaborate evidence was evoked to demonstrate the voluntary nature of the nationalities' common revolutionary struggle with the Han and their voluntary choice both for inclusion within the Chinese state and for the Chinese path to socialism. The right to secession was said to be no longer an issue as minorities had expressed their irreversible decision for unity with the Han:

> . . . it was in accord with the noble wish of the people of all nationalities that the CCP advocated the principles of nationalities' equality and national regional autonomy within the unity of the great family of the motherland and discontinued the slogan of national self-determination and federalism. Consequently, the question of national division or national separation does not even arise in present-day circumstances: such schemes would inevitably meet with the violent opposition of the broad masses of all nationalities.[5]

The 'broad masses of all nationalities' included the Han, defined as one of the nationalities of 'multinational China'; therefore the noble wish of the people of all nationalities was in fact the will of the Han majority. Han determinism had been substituted for self-determination.

The CCP adopted the system of regional autonomy, rather than federalism, based upon the theory that China was a 'unitary multinational state'. The Chinese nationalities had supposedly opted for union with China's 'big family of nationalities' as part of a natural historical process, and furthermore had integrated to such an extent that none now occupied a distinct territory without inclusion of Han or other minority nationalities.

CCP ideologists explained the obvious exceptions of Xinjiang and Tibet by claiming that Xinjiang 'had few Han but was otherwise composed of 13 nationalities', and that Tibet was 'comparatively unmixed, but this was only in the area of the . . . Tibet Autonomous Region, whereas in other places the Tibetans live

among other nationalities'.[6] Zhou Enlai further elaborated the
theory in a speech on nationalities policy in 1957:

> Fairly large numbers of Tibetans live in compact communities in Tibet.
> However, if the Tibetans who live in Szechuan, Chinghai, Kansu and
> Yunnan Provinces are taken into account, it is true to say that the
> Tibetans, like the other minority people of China, are dispersed in dif-
> ferent areas of the country and do not live in compact communities in a
> single area.[7]

These rationalisations ignored the lack of any legitimacy of Chinese
rule in either Xinjiang or Tibet, or the arbitrary political divisions
of Tibet by the Chinese themselves. Zhou also failed to mention
that all of the Tibetan cultural areas, divided by the Chinese into
different provinces, were contiguous and formed a single cultural
territory virtually without inclusion of any other nationality. They
were only 'dispersed in different areas' by the artificial political
divisions created by the Chinese themselves.

Socialist Transformation

Integration of the nationalities into the PRC political system was
a pre-requisite for their socialist transformation. The socialist transition process itself was a method to increase central control over
minorities. The nationalities were to be politically mobilised for
socialist construction and transformed in social structure, economic relations and cultural ideology. Autonomy for nationalities
was to be confined to such superficial aspects of nationality culture
as song and dance which were in any case, according to Marxist
ideology, the only meaning of nationality.

The CCP was adamant in its assertion that the nationalities could
not develop, culturally or economically, without the assistance of
the 'advanced nationality', the Han:

> As the Han nationality is the bulwark of the revolution . . . and represents
> the pivot of solidarity among the various nationalities in our country, the
> strengthening of the solidarity centered on the Han nationality . . . [is] the
> basic task concerning the settlement of the question of nationalities . . .
> For the sake of development and progress of the various national minori-
> ties and for the sake of building socialism . . . the national minorities
> should strive to learn from the Han nationality and welcome the help given
> by the Han nationality . . . the question of whether or not to seek help
> from the Han nationality and learn from the Han nationality is . . . the
> question of having or not having socialism and seeking or not seeking to
> develop and prosper the nationalities. Any thinking against learning from
> the Han nationality and against welcoming the help given by the Han
> nationality is completely wrong. Any conduct against the Han nationality

is contradictory to the basic interests of the people of the national minorities and therefore must be resolutely opposed.[8]

The transition to socialism in Chinese practice was of three stages: 1. democratic reforms (land reform); 2. co-operativisation (mutual-aid teams (MATs) and agricultural producers' co-operatives (APCs)); and 3. collectivisation (advanced co-operatives, or collectives, and amalgamated collectives, or communes).

The Chinese Communists were initially intent upon avoiding the traumas and violence which had accompanied forced collectivisation in the Soviet Union. Collectivisation would have to proceed by careful stages initiated only when peasants themselves were convinced that collectives would outperform individual farming both in production and distribution. Democratic reforms and founding of the mutual-aid teams in the early 1950s had proceeded on the initiative of the peasants themselves; in some cases the Party even had to restrain the enthusiasm of the poorest peasants.

By 1955 Mao was convinced that the peasants were ready for, even demanding, higher stages of collectivisation. He believed in the efficacy of class struggle as a catharsis for social transformation; his dictum on the transition process was 'never forget class struggle'. In order to ensure support from poor and lower-middle peasants for the next stage, and to create the class struggle which he believed was necessary for socialist transformation, Mao created a further, entirely artificial, division between lower- and upper-middle peasants.

In 1955 Mao adopted the Stalinist theory on socialist accumulation and Stalinist methods of state coercion. With the mobilisation of the Chinese masses for socialist transformation, Chinese agriculture would provide the basis for industrialisation which would then make the mechanisation of agriculture possible.

In late 1955 and early 1956, during the 'high tide' of collectivisation, 88 per cent of China's peasants entered advanced APCs. The collectives were initially supported by poor peasants because they expected personal gains similar to those they had received during the previous land reforms. Many middle peasants, however, experienced the transition as a loss of personal property and freedoms to increased state control. Another source of peasant discontent was the very high rate of socialist accumulation; agricultural 'surplus' was very liberally defined in favour of state accumulation, and agricultural products were priced low in relation to manufactured products.

During the Great Leap Forward of 1958, collectives were amalgamated into communes. The communes were the first level of collectivisation which transcended traditional village organisation. The coincidence of communisation and the Anti-Rightist movement of 1958, which was against those who had criticised the Party during the 1957 Hundred Flowers liberalisation, led to an equation of any criticism of communisation with rightist anti-Party, anti-socialist opposition. This added a new level of ideological and physical coercion to communisation.

Mao's vision of the socialist transformation required mobilisation of the peasants on a scale transcending the traditional village and required essentially military methods of organisation. During the Great Leap, basic-level government administration was shifted from villages to the communes which were then placed under direct Party control. The collectivised peasants were organised into People's Militia, which facilitated their mobilisation for large-scale land reclamation and water-works projects. A slogan of the time reveals the militarist frenzy which characterised this period: 'Militarise Organisation, Turn Action into Struggle, Collectivise Life!'[9] Military mobilisation was also intended to 'repel imperialist aggression and their running dogs'.

In 1958, due to the euphoria of the impending transition to Communism in China and of the advantage in ballistic missiles which had been gained by the Soviet Union, Mao assumed very aggressive domestic and foreign political stances. His international adventurousness resulted in the Taiwan Strait crisis, while his domestic policies led to the break with the Soviet Union, and his precipitous attempts to pursue socialist transformation of the minority nationalities led to the revolt in Tibet. Disasters of the Great Leap eliminated even peasant support for collectives and communes, maintenance of which then relied upon increased state coercion. The promise of socialist democracy in China was rapidly being eliminated in favour of state control, collectivisation and industrialisation, as had happened in the Soviet Union.

Mao had counted on collectivisation to produce socialist consciousness, but the economic failure of the collectives forced him to seek other means to achieve this goal. Mao suffered a political decline in influence from the end of the Great Leap until he was able to regain control of the Party. This he did in 1966 when he began the Great Proletarian Cultural Revolution by calling on students to overthrow the Party apparatus. The Cultural Revolution was intended to instil socialist consciousness by means of mass action where other methods had failed; it was therefore an unplanned stage of the socialist transition process.

Socialist Transformation of Nationalities

The CCP's nationalities policy was characterised by a misinter-
pretation both of nationalism and of the legacy of Han relationships with the minority nationalities. The essential requirement of
nationalities policy was to avoid resistance to centralised control
and to maintain the illusion that the choice of union with the Han
and the socialist path had been made by the minorities themselves
as a part of their own self-determination. It was essential to maintain the principle of voluntarism in nationalities affairs in order to
preserve the substance of autonomy and to avoid resistance to Han
imposition of reforms.

The nationalities policy of the early 1950s concentrated on propaganda to create solidarity with the Chinese masses against both
foreign imperialism and the exploiting classes within each nationality itself. Nationality leaders were co-opted into the United Front
and sustained with large salaries paid by the central government
while actual control was exercised by the PLA and Han cadres.
Resisters were purged while collaborators were forced to accept
actual Han control.

In 1955 Mao proclaimed that minority nationalities were ready
for reforms, and that the opinion that they were not ready was an
attitude of 'looking down' on them.[10] Minority nationalities were
subsequently included in the Hundred Flowers and Anti-Rightist
movements. Criticism by minority nationalities of Party policies
during the Hundred Flowers led to an equation of 'local nationalism' with anti-Party, anti-socialist opposition:

The struggle against local nationalism constitutes a kind of revolution on
the political and ideological fronts and represents an important part of the
struggle between the two roads of capitalism and socialism in our country
during the transition period.[11]

Social education and anti-Rightist struggles among the minorities have the
same content as in the Chinese areas, but stress should also be laid on
opposition to tendencies of local nationalism. It should be clearly recognised that all those who make use of local nationalist sentiments and the
estrangement between nationalities left over from the past in order to
divide national unity and undermine the unification of the motherland act
contrary to China's Constitution and jeopardise the socialist cause of our
country. They are all anti-socialist Rightists.[12]

Many nationalities areas were precipitously communised in August
1958 without regard to the previous level of reforms or socialist
transformation. Tibetan areas, which had not even completed
'democratic reforms', were communised 'in a single stride'. By skip-
ping the stage of co-operatives, the possibility of a voluntary

evolution of organisation based upon traditional political units was eliminated. Party and state control were combined at the commune level, eliminating all vestiges of traditional leadership. Restrictions on private enterprise and mobility affected traditional means of livelihood. Reforms and communisation in Eastern Tibet, which had not been integrated politically with China, led to revolts which in turn increased the already extreme militarist hysteria of the Great Leap.

The failures of nationalities policy culminated in the Tibetan Revolt of 1956–9. The extreme embarrassment this caused the CCP was compensated, however, by its gaining complete political control in Tibet. The Party attempted to salvage as much as possible of its reputation with the 'Socialist Education' campaign of 1962–3. The minority nationalities were told to increase their class awareness and socialist consciousness by a ritual of 'remembering bitterness', the conditions of life before liberation.

The minority nationalities were singled out as targets in Cultural Revolution campaigns because they epitomised the failure to achieve socialist consciousness. Their customs and traditions, especially their religious beliefs, were the most obvious and blatant examples of the noxious 'four olds' (old ideas, old culture, old customs, old habits), against which Mao's Red Guards were unleashed. The minorities suffered accordingly.

The CCP declared itself judge of which parts of minority culture were innocuous and would be allowed to survive, and which were incompatible with socialism and would be eliminated:

We feel that the customs and practices of each nationality consist partly of factors favourable to socialism and helpful to the nationality concerned, and partly of factors unfavourable to socialism and prejudicious to the development of the nationality concerned.[13]

Since religion is harmful to the socialist construction of the mother country, it will inevitably prove harmful to the progress and development of the minority nationalities. Religion is not a condition for the formation of a nationality, still less is it a condition for the development and advance of a nationality. All national characteristics unfavourable to socialist construction and national progress can and should be changed.[14]

Paradoxically, the cultural oppression and destruction conducted by the Han during the Cultural Revolution increased rather than reduced the nationalism of minorities. The process of democratic reforms, which was effected with popular support in Han areas, meant for nationalities the elimination of indigenous political, cultural and religious leadership in favour of Chinese state control. 'Nationalities policy' and the 'socialist transition' were perceived by minorities as Han control and cultural destruction, or essentially a national decapitation effected in the guise of class struggle. The failure of CCP policies and increased minority resistance led to a gradual abandonment of the mythology of the voluntary nature of reforms and of Han–minority co-operation in favour of increased physical coercion.

Gaps in the perceptions of both sides were evident; many minorities assumed that autonomy meant an end to Han interference: 'In certain districts, some of the minority nationalities thought that after the realisation of regional autonomy, they could live separately from the Hans and get along without the Han people.'[15] The Han, on their part, imagined that, except for the machinations of class enemies and imperialists, minority nationalities would naturally seek multinational unity and the benefits of Han culture and socialist progress. As a Han spokesman wrote at the time: '. . . almost every rebellion in the minority nationalities region has been instigated by secret agents and counter-revolutionaries and has resulted from senior individuals of the minority nationality being first duped by the enemy plots.'[16]

The Socialist Transformation of Tibet

The nature of China's 'peaceful liberation' of Tibet reveals the fallacies of the CCP's nationalities policy and its misconceptions about China's traditional relationship with Tibet. The compulsion to invade Tibet and impose an 'agreement' which had many of the characteristics of a treaty between states belies the claims of a peaceful liberation and reveals that Tibet was far from being an integral part of China.

For the Chinese, the 'liberation' of Tibet merely restored Tibet's historical status as part of China, a status, it was believed, which was accepted by the Tibetans themselves, except perhaps for a few 'reactionaries and tools of foreign imperialism'. The CCP hoped that the Tibetan upper classes could be co-opted or suppressed, which would enable Tibetan 'local nationalism' to succumb to proletarian internationalism and socialist development. To the Tibetans, however, the issue was one of loss of independence, whether that had been exercised under the Lhasa Government or under autonomous political leaders. The greatest fallacy of Chinese nationalities policy was the hope that it could deny or suppress the reality of Tibetan cultural separateness and political independence.

The 'Seventeen Point Agreement for the Peaceful Liberation of Tibet' was an implicit admission of China's tenuous political status in Tibet. The Chinese had an almost non-existent physical presence in any Tibetan cultural area. When the PLA vanguard units moved into the Kanze (Tibetan *dKar-mdzes*; Chinese: *Ganzi*) region of Kham in 1949, Chinese logistics, even in this area which China had claimed to have administered since the early 1900s, were so tenuous that supplies had to be air-dropped to the troops. Money in the form of silver dollars was lavishly distributed to the Tibetans, local Tibetan officials were awarded new titles and paid large salaries, and the PLA troops were paid for all transportation and food requirements; 'not even a single needle and thread' was taken from the people.

The role of the PLA vanguard troops was to 'make friends and do good deeds' while propagandising unity of nationalities against class exploiters and foreign imperialists. The PLA employed mass meetings, film, drama and the ubiquitous loudspeakers to convey their message. Tibetans from all areas repeat the same version of the message the Chinese gave in justification for having entered Tibet: they had come to Tibet to help the Tibetans and they would leave when Tibet had been 'improved'.

The PLA entered Tibetan areas within Gansu and Qinghai (the Tibetan province of Amdo) in the summer of 1949. Tibetan resistance was immediately aroused against the Chinese presence and included armed revolts in Choni, Nangra and Trika. Chinese policies in Amdo seem to have been somewhat modified after the signing of the Seventeen Point Agreement, although the Chinese specified that the agreement applied only to the actual domains of the Dalai Lama's government. In Amdo, in response to revolts, the Chinese promised to delay reforms for three years. Local Tibetans report that this restriction was violated within three months.

After the signing of the Seventeen Point Agreement, PLA advance units marched from Chamdo to Lhasa, entering Lhasa in a famished condition which did little to impress Tibetans with the glory of the New China. The Tibetan economy was disrupted by the Chinese presence, and existing tensions were exacerbated. The first PLA troops who entered Lhasa were from the South-West Military Command which had its headquarters in Sichuan; later PLA units of the North-west Military Command, headquartered in Xinjiang, arrived from the north via Gansu and Qinghai. These two PLA commands were to form the basis of a factional rivalry among the military, and later civilian, administrators of Tibet. The Xinjiang faction also retained direct administration of western Tibet under the authority of the North-west Military District.

The Chinese treated as Tibet only that area under the actual authority of the Dalai Lama's government in 1950; this was to become the Tibet Autonomous Region (TAR). The former domains of the Muslim warlord of Qinghai, Ma Pufang, were made into the Qinghai Autonomous Region. Tibetan areas of eastern Amdo became 'autonomous districts' in Gansu, while those of southern Kham were included in Yunnan with the same status. The remaining area of Kham, which had been conquered by Zhao Erfeng between 1905 and 1910 and declared the 'province' of Sikang by the Nationalist Government in 1939, but which had never actually been administered by the Chinese, remained a separate province until it was incorporated into Sichuan in 1955.

More than half of the Tibetan territory and population was thus excluded from the TAR and either included in Chinese provinces or in the 'autonomous prefectures' within Qinghai Province. Not only did Tibet contradict Chinese assertions that no nationality occupied an exclusive territory, but the PRC found itself with three entirely or predominantly Tibetan provinces (TAR, Qinghai and Sikang), a situation only somewhat alleviated when Sikang was incorporated into Sichuan. The policy of treating significant areas of culturally Tibetan territory as parts of Chinese provinces, where the restrictions of the Seventeen Point Agreement would not apply, was to lead to revolt by Tibetans in those areas, especially in the early and mid-1950s, while the area of central Tibet, the TAR, remained relatively calm until 1958.

In 1954 Tibetan leaders of Amdo gathered at Kumbum monastery near Siling (Xining) to present a petition to the Dalai Lama, then returning from his meeting with Mao in Beijing. The Amdowas asked to have themselves put under the authority of Lhasa, and consequently under the restrictions of the Seventeen Point Agreement, in order to avoid the 'reforms' being propagated by the Chinese in Amdo. After the Dalai Lama departed for Lhasa, the petitioners were arrested and subjected to public criticism.

By 1956 the 'high tide' of collectivisation had begun to affect minority nationalities' areas. Mao declared that minorities also needed the benefits of collectivised production and should not be excluded on account of their backwardness:

. . . democratic reform is the process through which the people of various nationalities must pass in order to attain socialism. Without reform a clear class distinction cannot be drawn . . . broad masses of the labouring people cannot be mobilised and organised . . . it will be impossible to cultivate large numbers of activists . . . or establish a solid political power at the basic level . . . the reform must necessarily be a violent, sharp and most complicated class struggle.[17]

Reforms for agricultural areas were propagandised in the Kanze (Ganzi) Autonomous *Qu* (in Kham) in January 1956. By September, 95 percent of the population were reported to have been collectivised.[18] Reforms were implemented more rapidly in agricultural than in pastoral areas, but in 1956 the Party began to propagandise the advantages of fixed settlements to the nomads: 'Fixed abode and nomadic herd-raising has one important significance at present, namely, the promotion of the mutual-aid and co-operation movement.'[19] Zhu De instructed that 'all nomadic herdsmen should settle in order to facilitate socialist transformation and socialist construction'.[20]

By the spring of 1956 the pastoral areas had also been caught up in the frenzy of socialist collectivisation:

. . . patriotism has been continuously propagandised among the masses in all tribes. In the spring of this year [1956], the policy of mutual aid and co-operation was propagandised. In this way, the broad masses of the herdsmen began to understand the preparations that were being made for the socialist transformation in the pastoral areas.

. . . The broad masses of the herdsmen lived in abject poverty and misery. Some of them lived to be over 60 years old without ever seeing a fried noodle. Culturally they were even more backward.

Resistance to Chinese reforms began in Amdo and Kham in 1956 when 'democratic reforms' were first announced. The Chinese denied that the revolts had any nationalist content and claimed (in this case, about the Lithang revolt) that they were not even in Tibet at all, but 'in Western Sichuan, in the Ganzi Autonomous *Qu*, on the border of Tibet'.[21]

The Dalai Lama was allowed to travel to India at the end of 1956 for the 2,500th anniversary of the birth of Buddha. He was restricted in that all his public statements were written for him in advance by his Chinese advisers and he was accompanied everywhere by the Panchen Lama, who was accorded equal status. When the Dalai Lama indicated to Nehru that he intended to seek asylum in India, Zhou Enlai paid a hasty visit to New Delhi where he assured both Nehru and the Dalai Lama that reforms would not be carried out against the will of the Tibetan people.

In Beijing, Mao declared as part of his speech 'On Contradictions Among the People' in January 1957 that the TAR would be exempted from reforms for the period of the next five-year plan (1957–62) and for the subsequent plan as well if the Tibetans themselves were not ready to accept them.[22] Han cadres were to be reduced in number and the administration of the TAR was to be nationalised: 'Apart from a few whose service is indispensable, most of the Han people now working in Tibet will be dispatched to other parts of the country.'[23] With these promises the Chinese secured the return of the Dalai Lama from India.

It is uncertain to what areas the Tibetans understood this new policy to apply, but in the Chinese interpretation it was definitely restricted to the TAR. That reforms would continue in other areas of Tibet was made clear in the official proclamation of the policy in Lhasa:

The reason for the continuation until fulfilment of the democratic reform in Tibetan nationality areas in Sichuan and Yunnan provinces should be solemnly pointed out. The continuation of reforms in those areas is a good thing determined by the local people . . .; people in Tibet [TAR] should sympathise with the reforms undertaken by people in those areas, and should neither take conditions in Tibet as a basis nor take the case of Tibet as a precedent in interfering with the democratic reform of the Tibetan nationality areas of Sichuan.[24]

The reluctance of the Chinese cadres in Tibet to implement the retrenchment policy, even within the TAR, is evident in the official proclamation. The proclamation claimed that many Tibetans wanted 'democratic reforms' and, of course, Chinese assistance in achieving those reforms, but because the majority were not prepared for them, the Party would accede to their wishes. Whereas Tibetans may have hoped for a permanent relief from the Party's plans to transform Tibet, it was clear that the Chinese regarded this as a temporary measure until Tibetans could be convinced to accept the reforms. Much praise was heaped on the Han who had contributed to the socialist construction of Tibet, and the inevitability of ultimate reforms was made clear:

. . . without the Chinese Communist Party there would have been no New China – no prosperous and happy mother country; without a socialist mother country there would not be a prosperous and happy new Tibet.[25]

To be able to live happily, the Tibetan people must take the road of socialism; and to enforce democratic reform is the unavoidable path the Tibetan people have to follow . . .[26]

The Tibetan people have ultimately realised that the only road to happiness for the nation is to take the word of the Communist Party and follow the road to socialism.[27]

By June 1957 reforms were renewed in Eastern Tibet and extended to include the Chamdo region of the TAR which Mao and Zhou had earlier promised would be excluded from all reforms.[28] The Chamdo area seems to have been chosen because it was contiguous to the areas of Eastern Tibet where reforms had already been initiated. Reforms in the Chamdo area were resisted by the Tibetans who were well aware that they were definitely excluded by the policy proclaimed just six months previously. Chinese cadres tried to convince or coerce Tibetans to request that reforms be implemented, and in this way to circumvent the restrictions of the no-reform policy.[29] General organised resistance began in the Chamdo area and also in areas of Kham east of the Yangtse when these reforms were announced.

In the summer of 1958 agricultural and pastoral areas were communised regardless of the status of democratic reforms or the previous level of collectivisation:

On September 15, the entire Gannan *Qu* [Southern Gansu] was completely communalised . . . 93.58% of the herdsmen have joined the communes. The Tibetan herdsmen, on the basis of suppression of counter-revolutionaries and social reform, have flown over several ages and singing and dancing reached heaven in one stride, taking them into People's Communes in which are carried the seeds of communism.[30]

The revolution has been accomplished without going through a systematic democratic reform. With one stride instead of two the democratic revolution and the socialist revolution have been pushed through.[31]

The great socialist revolution in the pastoral areas has been a very violent class-struggle of life and death. At the debate meetings, the masses were so excited that they shouted continuously: Long Live Chairman Mao! Long Live the Communist Party! We Are Liberated![32]

Class struggle, which for Tibetans meant the purge of Tibetan leaders and coerced denunciations of Buddhist monks and lamas, was also initiated. The propaganda of the campaign singled out the religious class:

The masses indignantly exposed the counter-revolutionary elements and bad elements in the religious circles who had been working under a religious cloak. In this fiery anti-feudalistic accusation struggle, the vast labouring herdsmen masses further strengthened their class sentiment and promoted their thought for collectivism.[33]

In fact 'democratic reforms' and communisation in 1958 produced large-scale revolt, especially in Amdo and Kham. The Amdowas rose in general mass revolt which was suppressed with great loss of life. In Kham revolt was continuous from 1956 until the early 1960s.

The socialist frenzy of the Great Leap led the Chinese to pursue their reforms despite increasing revolt in Eastern Tibet and tensions within the TAR as well. As revolt in Tibet escalated, the Chinese gradually abandoned the strategy of the nationalities policy in favour of coercion. The situation in Tibet was a result, in part, of the policies of the Great Leap, but the revolt and the measures taken to suppress it also contributed to the militarisation and xenophobia of Chinese politics at the time. The Tibetan Revolt was a major international embarrassment for the Chinese and for Mao;

it must be considered one of the factors in Mao's eclipse and in the retrenchment policies of the early 1960s.

Tibetans suffered greatly from the famine of 1960-2 which had resulted from the Great Leap. None of the areas of Tibet had poor harvests, but food was taken from Tibetans for the Chinese in Tibet and for the provinces adjacent to Tibet. The Chinese explained that Tibetans were now part of the Chinese masses and therefore bore responsibility to share the fate of the Chinese; they must also support the PLA and Chinese cadres in Tibet in return for the help which they had provided to Tibet. Thousands of Tibetans who had been imprisoned after the revolt were confined in agricultural labour camps where they produced food for the Chinese while they themselves were starved.

'Democratic reforms' were implemented in the TAR immediately after the revolt, but collectivisation was pursued, at first, with caution. Temporary mutual-aid teams were organised in 1960; by 1964 90 per cent of the TAR's 'peasant households' were said to have been organised into permanent mutual-aid teams.[34] Communes were set up on an experimental basis in 1964, with some 130 established by 1966.[35]

Han Red Guards arrived in Tibet from Beijing and Shanghai in 1966. Tibetan Red Guards from the Institute of Minority Nationalities at Xi'an were sent to Lhasa in the same year. Red Guards initiated the destruction of Tibetan culture and religion by their vandalism of the Jokhang temple in Lhasa on August 26, 1966.[36] Chinese cadres in Tibet resisted the attempts of the Red Guards to 'topple the Party bureaucracy' by establishing their own Red Guards faction, known as Nyamdrel in Tibetan, which was composed of Hans and some Tibetan collaborators. The other faction that appeared, known as Gyenlok, was more militant and was composed of radical Han Red Guards and some Tibetan students. Because the Nyamdrel faction represented the Chinese administration, a gradual polarisation took place during which Nyamdrel became predominantly Chinese while Gyenlok became predominantly Tibetan.

Tibetans took advantage of Mao's call to overthrow the bureaucracy in order to attack Chinese, not only in Lhasa but in many areas of Tibet. By 1968 open revolt had spread to twenty of the fifty-one districts of the TAR as well as to parts of Kham and Amdo. The Chinese attempts to pursue communisation during the Cultural Revolution also contributed to the revolt. The revolt finally had to be put down by PLA troops from the North-west (Xinjiang) Military District (which included Western Tibet) because the PLA in Tibet was also split by the Red Guard factions. This situation increased the influence of the Xinjiang PLA faction in Tibetan politics. The significance of this revolt was such that the Chinese in Tibet referred to it as the 'Second Tibetan Revolt'.

Mao's attempt to democratise Chinese society (and recover his own position) by encouraging the youth to overthrow the Party bureaucracy had unforeseen consequences in Tibet. For many Tibetans the Cultural Revolution was an unprecedented opportunity to criticise and 'struggle' against Han cadres and their Tibetan collaborators. Factional strife within the Red Guards turned violent after the PLA in Tibet became involved.

The Cultural Revolution had for some Tibetans, especially students, a democratising effect in that they learned that they could oppose Han dominance by their own proficiency in Marxist dialogue. Some Tibetans then began to demand the rights of autonomy which they were legally guaranteed by the Chinese constitution and the minority nationalities policy. The political involvement of Tibetans in the Cultural Revolution, combined with their reaction to the destruction of Tibetan culture during that period, produced in some a revival of nationalist consciousness.

Factional strife in Tibet during the Cultural Revolution resulted in control by the hard-line faction, associated with the former PLA cadres of the Xinjiang command, until the early 1980s. Collectivisation was continued under the guidance of Ren Rong, who emerged as the TAR Party Secretary. Communes, which had been experimentally established in 1964, were set up in 34 per cent of the townships of the TAR by 1970 and in 90 per cent by 1974.[37] Tibet was said to have leap-frogged the stage of co-operatives.[38] Ren Rong was accused by many Tibetans of having consistently exaggerated reports of increased production and progress in Tibet in order to perpetuate his own rule. Informants said that the situation had become so bad by the end of the 1970s that, had there been no liberalisation, another revolt would have been likely.[39]

Liberalisation in the TAR was initiated by Party Secretary Hu Yaobang in the spring of 1980. Hu visited Tibet and was reportedly appalled by Chinese mismanagement there; he removed Ren Rong from his position and personally escorted him back to Beijing. Ren Rong's claims of progress in Tibet were belied by the necessity of increasing subsidies for the Tibetan economy during the 1970s; these continued into the 1980s. Economic subsidies became a major part of Chinese policy for defusing Tibetan discontent in the 1980s. Although the subsidies were greatly increased, they were of less benefit to Tibetans than to Han cadres who were able to enrich themselves and who resisted repatriation because of the opportunities available to them in Tibet. The subsidies also produced an

Nyemo rebellion, 1969. The major panel of text reads: 'The Nimu Counter-revolutionary Rebellion: at daybreak on June 13, 1969, bandits such as Rangqiong [Rangchung], who is the main backbone of the counter-revolutionary rebellion, with acute hatred of the Party and the masses, instructed by the nun [Thinley Choedron], slaughtered all of the 14 cadres and soldiers of the PLA Propaganda Entertainment Troupe at the head-quarters of the Ba-khor [rba-'khor] district authority, as well as nine state cadres, and many other revolutionary masses. The blood of the martyrs ran free, heads fell, the scene was too cruel to behold. On some of the martyrs' bodies there are several tens of knife cuts and impressions where stones have hit them. Stones have also become weapons for killing our martyrs.' The other captions give details of six Chinese soldiers who were killed by the 'class enemies'. The Army moved into the area and executed the rebels, including Thinley Choedron. (*TIN, 1992*)

Nyemo rebellion, 1969: photographs from an exhibition in a Tibetan
village in 1992 showing two Tibetans executed for taking part in the Nyemo
rebellion. The captions say 'Execute Rindron' and 'Execute Dorje'. The
crosses over the name indicate that the executions were carried out.
Rindron (*left*) has a placard around her neck which reads 'Backbone of
the Nimu (Nyemo) counter-revolutionary rebellion'. (TIN, 1992)

influx of destitute Han from Sichuan, and Hui (Chinese Muslims)
from Gansu, which negated attempts to reduce the number of Han
in Tibet.

Chinese policies of liberalisation in Tibet and of opening to the
outside world, although at first seemingly successful, had repercus-
sions which increased Tibetan nationalist sentiments. Liberalisation allowed the resurgence of autonomous social structures which
were inherently nationalistic. Tourism, which was intended to
increase revenue, and incidently to marginalise Tibetan culture,
had the opposite results when many foreigners, instead of being
impressed by Chinese 'improvements', were made aware of the
colonialist nature of the Chinese presence in Tibet. Many of these
foreigners became sympathetic to Tibetan culture and even supporters of the Tibetan political cause.

Chinese policy in the 1980s reverted to the policy first employed in the 1950s – the United Front – thus implicitly acknowledging the failures of the past and the still very embryonic stage of Sino-Tibetan integration. Current Chinese nationalities policy relies on slogans of the past, such as 'The United Front is still the magic weapon!'[40] In the late 1980s a campaign was announced to 'revive the spirit of the PLA's ·entry into Tibet'. This refers both to the optimism with which the PLA had entered Tibet with the task of liberating Tibet's people and also to the regained dominance of veterans from those PLA units belonging to the South-West Military Command (the 18th Army) who had fought at Chamdo and been the first to enter Lhasa.

Conclusion

The nationalities policy of the Chinese Communist Party, like Chinese Communism itself, derives from the line of succession of Marx–Engels–Lenin–Stalin–Mao, and has inherited the contradictions introduced by each of its patriarchs. Marx introduced the fundamental contradiction with his theory that economic interests would always prevail over nationalism, and that nationalism, like the state itself, would simply 'fade away'. Lenin eliminated socialist democracy in favour of the dictatorship of the proletariat by his attempt to accelerate the stages of socialist development. Lenin's nationalities policy required that nationalities should simultaneously flourish and assimilate to the majority.

Stalin reversed the stages of the socialist transition, requiring that socialist relations of production should produce the forces of socialist production rather than vice versa. Stalin eliminated voluntarism in the socialist transition process in favour of coercion. Finally, Mao eliminated self-determination of nationalities in favour of Han determinism.

The contradictions of Marxist–Leninist nationalities policy are inherent in its contradictory goals. Marxist–Leninist policy aims at minority nationalities autonomy while the ultimate goal is assimilation. The promise of nationalities autonomy in China was belied by the ultimate intention that all minorities be assimilated into the Chinese 'big family of nationalities'. The inclusion of the Han nationality as one of the 'big family' ensured Han dominance. The Chinese justified socialist assimilation as entirely different from capitalist assimilation. Zhou Enlai defined the former in a speech on nationalities policy in 1958:

Assimilation is a reactionary thing if it means one nation destroying another by force. It is a progressive act if it means natural merger of

A Chinese cadre teaching Tibetans during the Cultural Revolution. (*China Now*)

nations advancing toward prosperity. Assimilation as such has the significance of promoting progress.[11]

Socialist assimilation was, by definition, natural and voluntary, as it was in the best (economic) interest of the people and was in any case the 'inevitable course of history'.

The failure of Chinese policy in Tibet derives from the misconceptions and contradictions inherent in Chinese nationalities policy and the denial of the realities of Sino-Tibetan relations and of the history of Tibetan independence. Precipitous and coercive methods of 'socialist transformation' eliminated what little chance this policy might have had of success. The growth of Tibetan nationalism under the conditions of Chinese colonialism might have been predicted by Marxist theory had the Chinese not convinced themselves that their role was not colonialist at all, but emancipatory.

Liberalised policies since 1980 have further complicated the situation; with the abandonment of socialist economic policies the benefits of socialism no longer provide legitimation for the Chinese presence in Tibet. Economic development alone is insufficient legitimation, especially since the Chinese themselves are often the greatest beneficiaries. Tibetans' experiences in rebuilding the institutions of their own society, especially Buddhism, have increased social autonomy and national awareness. The rights of autonomy guaranteed to Tibetans in theory have been increasingly demanded in practice by Tibetans whose political consciousness of their own nationality has been raised by Chinese ideology. Ideological propaganda is now less effective among Tibetans due to reduced means of actual social control and an increased spirit of resistance. The Chinese administrators have had essentially to abandon ideological legitimation in favour of intimidation and outright use of force.

The essential issue in Tibet remains that of the legitimacy of Chinese rule. This issue is intentionally not addressed by Chinese nationalities policy because this policy assumes that the issue of legitimacy is already settled. China has no solution to Tibetan nationalism within either Marxist theory or traditional Chinese culturalism. Neither repression nor liberalisation now seems to reduce Tibetans' nationalist sentiments. Tibetan nationalism has reached a stage which assures its further increase rather than diminution. China's only solution is to recognise this fact or attempt a forcible assimilation of Tibet within the Chinese masses.

NOTES

1. Selden and Lippit, *The Transition to Socialism in China*, Armonk, NY: M.E. Sharpe, 1982, p. 12.
2. Lenin, quoted in Selden and Lippit, *op. cit.*, p. 78.
3. June T. Dreyer, *China's Forty Millions: Minority Nationalities and National Integration in the People's Republic of China*, Harvard University Press, 1976, p. 16.
4. Zhou Enlai, *Beijing Review*, March 3, 1980.
5. Chang Chih-i, quoted in George Moseley, *The Party and the National Question in China*, Cambridge, MA: MIT Press, 1966, p. 57.
6. Wang Ke, 'Regional Autonomy for National Minorities', *Peking Review*, May 6, 1958.
7. Zhou Enlai, *Beijing Review*, March 3, 1980.
8. 'Carry Through the Socialist Education Movement Opposing Local Nationalism', in Ling Nai-min (ed.), *Tibet 1950–1967*, Hong Kong: Union Research Institute, 1968, p. 271.
9. Franz Schurman, *Ideology and Organization in Communist China*, Berkeley: University of California Press, 1968, p. 479.
10. Dreyer, *op. cit.*, p. 148.
11. 'Carry Through the Socialist Education Movement Opposing Local Nationalism', *Tibet 1950–1967*, p. 276.
12. Deng Xiaoping, 'On Minorities', *Report on the Rectification Campaign*, Beijing: Foreign Languages Press, 1957, p. 41.
13. 'Carry Through the Socialist Education Movement Opposing Local Nationalism', *Tibet 1950–1967*, p. 281.
14. 'Communists Are Complete Atheists', *Tibet 1950–1967*, p. 246.
15. 'Summary of Basic Experiences in Promoting Regional Autonomy Among Minority Nationalities', *Tibet 1950–1967*, p. 29.
16. *Ibid.*, p. 31.
17. 'Plant Red Flags in Every Corner of the Tibetan and Yi Regions of Szechuan', *Tibet 1950–1967*, p. 323.

18. *Ibid.*, p. 321.
19. 'Positively Promote Fixed Abodes and Nomadic Herd-Raising', *Tibet 1950–1967*, p. 296.
20. *Ibid.*, p. 298.
21. 'Liu Ke-ping Denies Rumored Tibet Rebellion', NCNA, August 7, 1956.
22. Mao Tse-tung, *On the Correct Handling of Contradictions Among the People*, Beijing: Foreign Languages Press, 1958, p. 44.
23. 'Tibetan Preparatory Committee for Regional Autonomy to be Reorganised', NCNA, Lhasa, August 9, 1957.
24. 'Outline of Propaganda for CCP Tibetan Working Committee Concerning the Policy of Not Implementing Democratic Reform in Tibet Within Six Years', *Tibet Daily*, Lhasa, August 2, 1957.
25. 'Report of the Work Committee on Problems Relating to the Nationalities Policy', *Tibet Daily*, Lhasa, October 15, 1957.
26. 'Outline of Propaganda for CCP Tibetan Working Committee Concerning the Policy of Not Implementing Democratic Reforms in Tibet Within Six Years', *Tibet Daily*, August 2, 1957.
27. 'Communalisation in a Single Stride', *Tibet 1950–1967*, p. 30.
28. Abu Chonga, Abu Gongkar, Nyima Assam, Lobsang Tenzin, Kalsang Wangdu, in oral interviews, Dharamsala, January 1990.
29. *Ibid.*
30. 'Communalisation in a Single Stride', *Tibet 1950–1967*, p. 330.
31. 'The Socialist Revolution in the Tsinghai Pastoral Regions Must Be Carried to Its End', *Nationalities Unity*, March 1960.
32. 'Herdsmen on the Tsinghai Pastures Advancing Bravely with Flying Red Flags', *Nationalities Unity*, September 6, 1958.
33. 'Communalisation in a Single Stride', *Tibet 1950–1967*, p. 331.
34. 'Mutual-Aid Teams Develop in Tibet', NCNA, Lhasa, December 23, 1964.
35. *Peking Review*, July 31, 1970.
36. Dreyer, *op. cit.*, p. 217.
37. *Beijing Review*, July 19, 1974.
38. *Beijing Review*, July 18, 1975.
39. Tsering Wangchuk, interview, Dharamsala, January 1990.
40. National United Front Theoretical Work Conference, February 6, 1985, published in *Issues and Studies*, Institute of International Relations, Taipei, Taiwan, vol. 25, no. 7.
41. Zhou Enlai, *Beijing Review*, March 3, 1980.

CHANGE, CONFLICT AND CONTINUITY AMONG A COMMUNITY OF NOMADIC PASTORALISTS

A CASE STUDY FROM WESTERN TIBET, 1950–1990

Melvyn C. Goldstein

Introduction

Objective assessment of the situation in Tibet since 1950 has become entangled in the politics of the 'Tibet Question', that is, in the political status of Tibet *vis-à-vis* China. Strong feelings about whether Tibet was independent or part of China in the past, and whether it should now have the right of self-determination, have produced diametrically contradictory versions of modern history from Beijing and the Tibetan exiles in Dharamsala (and their supporters in the United States and Europe). Events have typically been portrayed as all black or all white, as horrendous oppression or magnificent progress. This, of course, is not unexpected, given the stakes involved. What is more surprising, however, is the dearth of objective and impartial *academic* accounts of social, political and economic changes in Tibet during the forty years since 1950. This dearth, I suggest, has enhanced the ability of politically motivated writers to portray the period in question according to their political agenda. One such issue that has been politicised in an unfortunate way is the meaning or referent of 'Tibet' itself. The problematic here is simple: what constituted the Tibetan polity at different times in its history, particularly in the modern era, and what that means *vis-à-vis* the 'Tibet Question'.

What is Tibet? – Fact and Fancy

Ethnic Tibetan populations are distributed over an area as vast as Western Europe. They are found not only in the Tibet Autonomous Region (of China), the traditional heartland of political Tibet, but also in parts of the neighbouring Chinese provinces of Qinghai, Sichuan, Gansu, Yunnan and Xinjiang, as well as in parts of other nations such as India (Ladakh, Sikkim, Northern Uttar Pradesh and Arunachal Pradesh), Northern Nepal and Bhutan. Although all of these regions were once united under the rule of the early kings of Tibet, during the eleven centuries following the breakup of that kingdom in the 9th century many of the regions on the periphery became independent or fell under the authority of neighbouring states.

The detailed history of all of these peripheral areas is not well documented in the literature on Tibet, and this introduction will not attempt to consider each of them. Rather, it will be limited to those most relevant to this discussion, namely, the easternmost extension of ethnic Tibetan populations – the two major sub-ethnic regions known in Tibetan as Kham and Amdo.

The 'modern' Sino-Tibetan border in these two regions was generally established during the mid-18th century when the Tibetan Government lost political control over most of these areas to Manchu (Qing) China. While the Tibetan Government has never accepted the loss of these regions as permanent or *de jure* – for example it claimed all of Kham and Amdo in the Simla Convention of 1913–14 – most of these areas in fact were not a part of its polity for the two centuries preceding the rise to power of the Communists in China in 1949. Consequently, the convention used in Tibetan historiography in the West has been to differentiate analytically between the political entity Tibet and other areas outside it where ethnic Tibetans lived.

For example, Hugh Richardson, the well-known British diplomat and historian, for practical purposes differentiated the Tibetan world into two categories. Following the work of Sir Charles Bell, he used the term 'political' Tibet for the polity ruled by the Dalai Lamas, and the term 'ethnographic' Tibet for other areas such as Amdo and Kham which were outside that state. He explained his rationale as follows:

In 'political' Tibet the Tibetan government have ruled *continuously* from the earliest times down to 1951. The region beyond that to the north and east [Amdo and Kham] . . . is its 'ethnographic' extension which people of Tibetan race once inhabited exclusively and where they are still in the majority. In that wider area, 'political' Tibet exercised jurisdiction *only in certain places and at irregular intervals*; for the most part, local lay or monastic chiefs were in control of districts of varying size. From the 18th century onwards the region was subject to sporadic Chinese infiltration. But in whatever hands actual authority might lie, the religious influence of Lhasa was a long-standing and all-pervasive force and large donations of money and valuable goods were annually sent to the Dalai Lama . . . In the text that follows Tibet means 'political' Tibet except where otherwise stated. . . . (Richardson, pp. 1–2; emphasis added.)

The convention used by Richardson, therefore, is simple and straightforward. The term 'Tibet' refers to the political state ruled by the Dalai Lamas; it does not refer to the ethnic border areas

Melvyn C. Goldstein

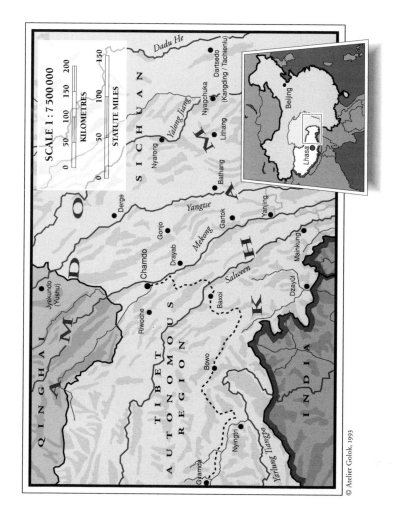

© Atelier Golok, 1993

Border region of Kham, Amdo and 'political' Tibet. The dotted line shows the road from Chamdo to Lhasa.

such as Amdo and Kham which were not part of that state in
modern times, let alone to Ladakh or Northern Nepal. Until
recently, this convention was, as far as I can discern, universally
accepted in the scholarly literature.[1]

Nowadays, however, this convention is increasingly being abandoned in favour of what seems to me to be a political definition
of Tibet that includes all of the ethnic Tibetan areas of the Chinese
provinces of Qinghai, Sichuan, Gansu and Yunnan under the
rubric 'Tibet'. In this perspective, an event said to have occurred
in 'Tibet' in the 1980s (or 1940s or 1840s) may well have occurred
in areas not part of the polity Tibet, i.e. in 'ethnographic' Tibetan
areas such as Amdo. The most striking example of this position is
the contention that Tibet was invaded by China in 1949. This was
the year, to be sure, when Amdo and the eastern part of Kham
became part of Communist China, but were these areas then part
of Tibet? And if they were not, is it valid to say that *Tibet* was
invaded at that time?

Proponents of the view that Tibet was invaded in 1949 appear
to believe that these areas were part of Tibet; they also appear to
believe that this assertion is not only good politics, but also good
history. Phintso Thonden, the former director of the Office of
Tibet in New York, for example, suggests that these areas were part
of the Tibetan state until the Chinese Communists conquered
China:

Since China's invasion of and occupation of Tibet, the Chinese have
incorporated the whole of Amdo and parts of Kham into the neighbouring
Chinese provinces of Qinghai, Szechuan, Kansu and Yunnan – *leaving
only* U-tsang and other parts of Kham as the so-called Tibet Autonomous
Region [TAR]. This was done with the view that should Beijing be forced
to give up its spoils in Tibet, it would give up only the TAR and hold
on to the more economically valuable regions of Kham and Amdo. . . .
(Thonden, p. 12; emphasis added.)

Thonden, therefore, appears to be asserting that these areas were
part and parcel of Tibet until the Chinese Communists invaded
Tibet in his terms in 1949. However, in another part of his article
he seems to contradict this by writing that the Central Tibetan
Government may have temporarily lost control of some areas of
Amdo and Kham in the 1930s and '40s (*ibid.*, p. 13). He implies
that this was due to the death of the 13th Dalai Lama in 1933 and
a subsequent weak interregnum government headed by regents.

My reading of modern Tibetan history suggests strongly that
both of these assertions are incorrect. Kham and Amdo were not
part of Tibet in 1949 and were not temporarily lost only in 1930–40.

Thonden's article may be good politics, but it is bad history. Let me, therefore, discuss briefly the historical situation in Kham and Amdo.

Observations on the History of Kham and Amdo

Although the history of the numerous Amdowa and Khamba areas has yet to be seriously addressed, there are enough available data to construct a general sketch of their situation over the past 250 years.

The Manchu Dynasty dealt with minority peoples in a number of ways including military conquest and absorption, the establishment of military colonies and the confirmation of native officials under the well-known *T'u-ssu* (pinyin: *Tusi*) system. In the latter system, the hereditary élite of ethnic areas was loosely integrated into the imperial system through the granting of court titles. In return for this 'confirmation' of its right to rule its own peoples according to its own cultural laws and traditions, this élite was responsible for various tasks such as the taking of censuses, the collection of taxes and the keeping of peace. In many cases this situation amounted to virtual independence for these native states since the Manchu tendency was to avoid interfering with local affairs unless developments directly threatened imperial control of the area.[2] By and large, the *T'u-ssu* system was the strategy utilised by the Manchu Empire in Amdo and Eastern Kham when it intervened in these regions in the early 18th century.

Joseph Kolmas, in a study of Tibet and Manchu China, commented on the Manchu ascendancy in this area:

The Tibetan policy of the next Manchu Emperor, Yung-cheng (1723–1735), though inconsistent, brought many important changes in Sino-Tibetan relations. The financial difficulty of maintaining numerous government troops in so remote an area as Tibet led the Emperor to order the withdrawal of the imperial troops from Tibet in the first year of his reign (in 1723). It also proved expensive and inefficient to attempt to control Eastern Tibet by maintaining Manchu-Chinese Civil Magistrates as had been done sporadically after 1720. For this reason in 1725 it was decided to replace the cumbersome and unwieldy direct control of the border zone by a sensible and flexible form of protectorate . . .

In this connection also a new boundary was drawn between Szu-ch'uan [Sichuan] and Tibet (in 1727), formed by the Ning-ching-shan range dividing the waters of the Chin-sha River (the headwaters of the Yangtze) from those of the Lan-ts'ang River (Mekong). According to this settlement, the territory east of Ning-ching-shan was to be incorporated in China proper, but the administration was to be carried on by the local chieftains (T'u szu) under the nominal supervision of the Szu-ch'uan provincial authorities, whereas all territory westwards was to be administered by the Lhasa government.

Thus the territory Tibet, handed down almost unaltered through the previous centuries, underwent for the first time a drastic reduction in area. If we add the territory of A-mdo (Ch'ing-hai), separated from Tibet in 1724, then the original size of Tibet as a politico-geographical unit has been reduced almost by half. (Kolmas, pp. 41–2)

Petech's classic study of China and Tibet in the 18th century presents a similar account. For example, regarding the time of the Dzungar conquest of Lhasa in 1717, he wrote:

Thus far the Dsungars held only Lhasa and the country to the north of it. The situation in the rest of the country can be summarized thus: Western Tibet and gTsan were for the moment politically a no man's land soon to be galvanized into active resistance . . . K'ams [Kham] was practically independent of Lhasa under its great lamas, and Chinese political influence was growing stronger and stronger; Amdo and Kukonor were under the sway of Mongol chieftains under Chinese suzerainty. (Petech, p. 42)

The revolt [in Kokonor-Amdo] was repressed in . . . 1724. The emperor [of China] seized the occasion for establishing solidly his sovereignty in Kukunor, which became from that time onwards an integrant part of the Chinese dominion. (*Ibid.*, p. 85)

This, as mentioned above, did not mean that China actually exercised day-to-day administrative control in Amdo and Kham, or even collected taxes, but it does indicate that from the early 18th century the Tibetan Government, with only a few exceptions mentioned below, did not rule these areas. Cultural, religious and economic ties continued, but these 'native states', as the British called them, were not part of the Tibetan polity.

The well-known Tibetan scholar-politician, the late Tsipon Shakabpa, discussed this issue in a parallel fashion:

In 1722 the K'anghsi Emperor died and was succeeded by his son, who became known as Yung-cheng Emperor. In 1723 the new Manchu ruler began a policy of retrenchment. He withdrew the garrison from Lhasa, leaving the administration of central Tibet entirely in the hands of Tibetan officials, without any military support from the Manchus.

In the first year of the Yung-cheng Emperor's reign, Mongols in the Kokonor region, led by Chingwang Lozang Tenzin, a grandson of the Qoshot Gushri Khan, revolted against the Manchus. The rebellion was suppressed, and in early 1724, the Kokonor [Amdo] region *was integrated into the Manchu Empire.* (Shakabpa, p. 141; emphasis added.)

For the more recent periods, we are fortunate to have available several straightforward firsthand accounts of a number of different border regions in Qinghai and Sichuan in the early 20th century. One such account concerns the ethnically Amdowa native state called Choni (now part of Gansu Province). The author of this account, Robert Ekvall, was an American Protestant missionary who was born in the Sino-Tibetan borderlands and lived in the Choni area from 1923 till 1935. His record of the history of the area parallels that presented above:

In the time of the Manchu dynasty, the entire region was administered by a viceroy of the Imperial Government. That portion of the country occupied by Chinese Muslims and some other, smaller, racial units was under traditional Chinese law. The Tibetans enjoyed almost complete independence and varying degrees of prestige. The Chone Prince ruled over the forty-eight 'banners' of one group of Tibetans; other Tibetan rulers or chiefs held grants or commissions – some of them hundreds of years old – from the Imperial [Manchu] government.

. . . Since the establishment of the Republic in 1912, changes have occurred. Although the region nominally owes allegiance to the Central Government of China, the administration has been split between Moslem and Chinese factions . . . the Chinese government has attempted to exercise considerably more power over the Tibetans than formerly. This has resulted in the establishment of a greater degree of control over the Tibetans along the border but has alienated those Tibetans who persistently maintained their independence, even enhancing that independence, which is combined with a half-wistful nostalgia for the days of the [Manchu] Empire. (Ekvall, pp. 6–7)

Ekvall's study focuses on what he saw as one of the most important issues of the day: the relationship between the ethnic Tibetans and the non-Tibetans living in the area (the Han [native Chinese] and the Hui [Chinese Muslims]). His study helps to clarify that issue but also leaves unanswered many questions regarding the precise nature of the political status of these areas *vis-à-vis* the Chinese Government. However, his work does demonstrate clearly that these areas were not then part of political Tibet.

Another Western first-hand observer, Hans Stubel, provides an account of the same region of Amdo. Like Ekvall, Stubel talks of an area which in 1936 was inhabited by Han, Hui and Tibetans. Referring to the political status of the ethnic Tibetans, he notes that they were organized into tribes which were nominally under China, not political Tibet, but in most ways were effectively independent: 'Although the Tibetans living here are under Chinese administration, they are not dependent on the Chinese and are not particularly influenced by Chinese culture'. (Stubel, pp. 6–7)

A third Western account was written by Eric Teichman, a scholarly British consular agent who was stationed in Western

China (and present in Kham) in the 1911–18 era. Steeped in the history of this area, his account echoes the observations of the above-cited authors, albeit for Kham not Amdo:

The boundary between China and Tibet was demarcated by a pillar, said to have been erected in the year 1727 . . . on the Bum La (in Chinese Ning-ching Shan), a small pass two and a half days south-west of Batang. The country to the west of this point was handed over to the rule of the Dalai Lama under the suzerainty of the Manchu Emperor, while the Tibetan Chiefs of the States and tribes to the east of it were given seals as semi-independent feudatories of China. This arrangement lasted for nearly two centuries, until the Chinese forward movement initiated in 1905 as a result of the British advance on Lhasa in the preceding year. (Teichman, p. 2)

At the beginning of the present century, before the British expedition to Lhasa in 1904 and the subsequent Chinese forward movement in Kam, that portion of High Asia inhabited by Tibetan-speaking peoples, and labeled *Tibet* on European maps, consisted of three separate entities, firstly, the Lama Kingdom of Tibet with its provinces and dependencies, secondly, the semi-independent Native States of Kham under Chinese protection, and thirdly, the Kokonor [Amdo] Territory under the control of the Chinese Amban residing at Sining in Kansu.
    The Kingdom of Tibet, ruled by the Dalai Lama from Lhasa . . . extended north to the Dang La range separating it from the Kokonor and east to the Bum La, the frontier pass near Batang. (*Ibid.*, pp. 7–8)

A firsthand account by Aten, a Tibetan exile from Nyarong, an Eastern Khamba area, supports this analysis. In his discussion of the rise of the famous Nyarong chieftain Gombo Namgye in 1860, Aten wrote as follows:

Then, in the early nineteenth century, there rose a man in Nyarong who, through sheer ability and ruthlessness, united the whole of Eastern Tibet, drove the Chinese back to the border of the ancient emperors, and made the Manchu Emperor of China quiver in his satin shoes . . . He failed only to conquer the province of Amdo, the extreme northern extent of Tibet. Otherwise he had taken back and united every inch of land within the frontiers established by the ancient Tibetan emperors . . . The Manchu Emperor of China became enraged. This barbarian upstart, this petty chief of some insignificant Tibetan tribes, had in a few strokes deprived the Celestial Empire of the fruits of centuries of painful conquests and brain-racking intrigues. (Norbu, pp. 25–6)

Like Teichman's account, Aten, therefore, indicates that at the time Gombo Namgye rose to power in 1860, Nyarong and the surrounding Khamba areas were under China (at least nominally), not the Lhasa-based Tibetan Government.
    Gombo Namgye's conquest of the neighbouring ethnic-Tibetan (Khamba) states, such as Derge and the Hor States, led them

to appeal to both the Chinese and Tibetan Governments for help against the Nyarong invaders. China was then deeply involved with the Taiping rebellion and the machinations of imperialist nations and, as Teichman puts it, was 'unable to take any action towards restoring order in the Tibetan States under their nominal protection' (Teichman, p. 5).

The Tibetan Government, however, sent an army to pacify Gombo Namgye in 1863 and, two years later in 1865, defeated him by trickery, burning his castle with him and his family inside. Tibet then took over the formal administration of Nyarong, and appointed a high commissioner (*nya-rong sbyi-khyab*) to govern the area. According to Teichman, Derge and the Hor States, which lie north of Nyarong, were 'freed from the Nyarong invaders and restored to independence under the rule of their own native Rajahs' (*Ibid.*).

Teichman further elaborated:

The Tibetan claim to Nyarong, and to a lesser extent to De-ge and the Hor States, dated from this time (1865). Nyarong appears to have been annexed by the Dalai Lama with the approval of the Manchu Throne. (*Ibid.*)

The trouble resurfaced in 1894 when the Tibetans of Nyarong invaded Chala (Tachienlu). Teichman describes this interesting incident as follows:

The Viceroy of Szechuan [Sichuan], Lu Ch'uan-lin, despatched a Chinese force which occupied Nyarong and suppressed the disorders. Viceroy Lu thereupon proposed, in a Memorial to the Throne, to take over the administration of Nyarong with Chinese officials. In this he was, however, opposed by the Manchu Amban at Lhasa and the Manchu Commander-in-Chief at Chengtu, while the Dalai Lama also sent representatives to Peking *via* India and the sea route protesting against any Chinese annexation of Tibetan territory. As a result of these representations Viceroy Lu's Memorial proposing the changes was rejected by the Throne, and the Tibetan Governor was reinstated in Nyarong. (*Ibid.*, p. 6)[3]

Aten, the Tibetan exile from Nyarong, discusses the fall of Gombo Namgye in a manner parallel to Teichman, concluding: 'However, Gompo Namgyal's efforts were not entirely in vain, for Eastern Tibet was *reunited* with the rest of Tibet. For about 40 years we were free.' (Norbu, p. 27; emphasis added) In other words, just before this incident he again indicates that this part of Kham was not included in the Tibetan polity.

Aten then continues his account of the history of Nyarong:

Nevertheless, the Tibetan Government could not retain Gonpo Namgyal's conquests . . . In 1903 . . . the Chinese Army under General Chao Er feng

[Zhao Erfeng] invaded Litang and Batang from the south . . . Little by little, the frontiers began to fall and gradually the whole of Eastern Tibet was occupied by the Chinese. (*Ibid.*, p. 28)

Zhao actually reset the border at Giamda (Gyamda) in Kongbo (Kongpo), less than 350 kilometres east of Lhasa, and started to subvert the 'native chief' system by deposing them and bringing their states under more direct Chinese rule via Chinese magistrates (*Tusi*) and so forth. After forty years under the Tibetan Government, these areas once again fell under the control of China, this time under more direct, day-to-day administration.

For this part of Kham, however, the frontier remained unstable, and border skirmishes between Tibetan and Chinese troops led to an outbreak of warfare in 1917–19 between Tibet and China. In this confrontation the Tibetan army soundly defeated the Chinese forces and, with the 1918 Treaty of Rongbatsa (brokered in large part by Eric Teichman), Tibet regained Chamdo, Traya (Drayab) and Markham – states located to the west of the Yangtse River – as well as Derge to the east of that river. However, Nyarong and many other Khamba areas east of the Yangtse River, such as Litang, Kanze (*Ganzi, dkar-mdzes*), Batang and Tachienlu, remained part of China and outside the territory of the Tibetan Government. This demarcation remained in place until 1931 when new fighting between troops of the Tibetan and Chinese Governments erupted in the Kanze area. Aten commented as follows:

But in the Spring of 1931 . . . the monastery of Dhargay in Tri Hor [part of the Hor States], north of Nyarong, revolted against its Chinese overlords . . . The Chinese rushed in soldiers to quell the rebellion, and fighting broke out in that area. The monastery was besieged, and in desperation the monks appealed to the Tibetan Government in Lhasa for help. (*Ibid.*, p. 22)

A Tibetan army was sent and at first the Chinese were badly defeated, with the Tibetan soldiers not only taking control of Nyarong, but also most of Eastern Kham. This victory was short-lived, however, and a Chinese counter-attack in 1932 drove the Tibetan army back to the Yangtse River. Aten describes this poignantly:

After about a year, the Tibetan Army suffered drastic setbacks in its advance east. The retreating Chinese, now strengthened with reinforcements, pushed back our small army and finally poured into Eastern Tibet. It was a bitter day for all of us when our ancient Lion Standard was hauled down, and the red and yellow flags of the Chinese Nationalists flown from the Castle of the Female Dragon [in Nyarong]. (*Ibid.*, p. 47)

This defeat of the Tibetan army set the *de facto* border in Kham at the Upper Yangtse River (the Drichu). From 1932, none of the ethnic Tibetan (Khamba) areas east of the Yangtse River was under the control of the Tibetan Government. Thus, while the Sino-Tibetan border in Kham fluctuated during the period 1865–1932, after 1932 it remained constant. And Amdo remained outside Tibetan Government control from the early 18th century until 1949. Consequently, when the People's Liberation Army (PLA) took control of Sichuan/Sikang, Qinghai and Gansu in 1949, these Tibetan areas were not part of Tibet. Aten's account, for example, explicitly states this: 'When the Communist army invaded Eastern Tibet, most of it was already under the rather desultory occupation of the Nationalist Chinese.' (*Ibid.*, p. 79) Thus, the recent practice of writing about the Tibetan areas of Amdo and Eastern Kham as if they were part and parcel of Tibet until 1949, when the Communists conquered and separated them, is clearly historically incorrect.

Consequently, the increasingly common claim that Tibet was invaded by the Chinese Communists in 1949 is also incorrect. This, to be sure, is the time when Amdo and Eastern Kham were conquered by the PLA; but as elaborated above, Amdo and Eastern Kham were not part of the Tibetan state at that time.

This, moreover, is not simply the view of a Western historian in the 1990s. It was also the view of the Tibetan Government in 1949, which did not consider the Chinese Communist conquest of China (including Amdo and much of Kham) as an invasion of its territory. As a result, in 1949 it neither sent its troops to defend these areas nor issued any protests, appeals or charges that its territory had been invaded. On the other hand, when the PLA crossed the Upper Yangtse River in October 1950, the armies under the command of Ngabö (Ngapo), the Tibetan Governor-General, at once engaged the Chinese forces in battle. On November 7, 1950, the Lhasa Government issued an emotional plea for help to the United Nations protesting against the invasion of its territory:

While these negotiations were proceeding in Delhi [that is, negotiations between representatives of the Tibetan Government and the Chinese Communists], Chinese troops, without warning or provocation, crossed the Dre Chu River [the Upper Yangtse River], *which has for long been the boundary into Tibetan territory*, at a number of places on 7th October, 1950. In quick succession places of strategic importance . . . fell to the Chinese . . . The armed invasion of Tibet for the incorporation of Tibet within the fold of Chinese communism through sheer physical force is a clear case of aggression [emphasis added].[4]

The Tibetan Government's understanding and use of the term 'Tibet' in 1949–50, therefore, was identical with that of Richardson in that it did not include the ethnic areas not under its control.[5] The Tibetan Government, to be sure, did not relinquish its claims to these areas, but there was no question of where the authority of its state ended.

Because the future re-integration of Kham and Amdo with what was political Tibet (now the TAR) appears to be a very emotional issue for many Tibetans in exile and Westerners who support them, let me add that the historical information I have outlined above does not in any way preclude Tibetan nationalists such as Thonden from today advocating and working to reunite these areas into a unified 'greater' Tibet in the future. Nor does it argue against the legitimacy of creating such a 'greater' Tibet since these areas share obvious cultural characteristics and were once part of a unified Tibetan state. On the other hand, scholars such as myself did not make Tibetan history – Tibetans did – and it might be useful if they and their Western supporters tried to understand it objectively.

What Difference does the Location of the Border Make Today?

Differentiating between what was political Tibet and the ethnic Tibetan borderlands in modern times is more than an arcane scholarly issue. It is an essential prerequisite for understanding clearly the issue under discussion, namely what has happened to Tibet since 1950 and what is happening now. The reason for this is obvious: the ethnic Tibetans in the borderlands, by and large, were outside the rule of Lhasa and experienced political, legal and economic histories different from those of their ethnic brothers in political Tibet. There is, therefore, every reason to assume that present conditions in 'ethnographic' Tibet (Kham and Amdo) do not necessarily parallel those in 'political' Tibet (today's TAR). Consequently, conditions in ethnographic Tibet cannot be extrapolated *a priori* to reflect those in today's TAR, and any convention which attempts to conceal such different conditions is methodologically and conceptually flawed.

Let me give a few examples of why it is methodologically important to avoid referring to events in ethnographic Tibet as if they occurred in political Tibet.[6]

First, China treated ethnographic Tibet very differently from political Tibet during the 1951–9 period because ethnographic Tibet was not formally covered by the terms laid down in the Seventeen

88 *Melvyn C. Goldstein*

Point Agreement, which applied only to political Tibet. As a result, while the traditional economic-religious system continued in Tibet *per se*, China attempted to impose reforms in ethnographic Tibet, which precipitated bloody rebellions in 1955–6 and considerable loss of life. To describe these uprisings in ethnographic Tibet as revolts 'in Tibet', as is common today, is deceptive since there were no revolts at this time in political Tibet, where the Chinese were very careful to adhere to the Seventeen Point Agreement. Similarly, to refer to the numerous ethnic Tibetans who died in this rebellion as Tibetans killed in Tibet is misleading, since any reader of such a statement would naturally assume that these deaths occurred in, and reflect Chinese policy and actions in, political Tibet. What happened in the area that was political Tibet (today's TAR) at that time, therefore, was very different from what happened in ethnographic Tibet and should be reflected and not obscured in our accounts.

In *The New York Times* of October 27, 1990, a letter to the Editor from Tseten Wangchuk, a Tibetan living in New York City, further illustrates this kind of confusion. After declaring that Tibet includes Kham and Amdo, Wangchuk wrote: 'In my father's home-town of Gyelthang in Kham, after four decades of political rule and cultural encroachment [1950–90], it is so hard to find Tibetan teachers that children no longer speak or study Tibetan.' While this may be the case in Gyelthang, one of the Eastern Kham areas that was not part of political Tibet for hundreds of years before 1950, it does not reflect the situation in political Tibet. By referring to this as Tibet, the author leaves the reader with the impression that Tibetans *in Tibet* do not speak their language, and by inference, that the Chinese policy in political Tibet is to not teach the Tibetan language to Tibetans. While there are certainly important language policy problems in the TAR, this is not one of them. In today's TAR one finds not only that Tibetans speak Tibetan, but that all teaching in Tibetan primary schools is conducted in Tibetan, Chinese language being started only in the third grade.[7] And in Lhasa there are two TV stations that broadcast daily in Tibetan. Consequently, the language issue in Gyalthang, if Wangchuk's account is correct, is likely to be the consequence of the very different historical experiences of this area *vis-à-vis* those of political Tibet, which illustrates precisely why it is so important methodologically to indicate clearly whether an event is occurring in political or ethnographic Tibet.

Another important area where this kind of politico-historical revisionism has serious consequences is the controversy over Chinese colonisation in Tibet. There are recurrent charges that

Tibet after 1949 has been, and is being, swamped with hundreds of thousands of Han colonists. An advertisement in *The New York Times* of January 31, 1992, for example, states: 'Over 7.5 million Chinese [have been] transferred to Tibet [and] outnumber the 6 million Tibetans.' This is obviously a critical issue since in-migration of Han populations, whether transferred by Beijing or moving voluntarily in search of economic gain, threatens the viability of Tibetan culture in Tibet. But again, to understand this in a meaningful way one must distinguish carefully between ethnographic and political Tibet.

There were no Han farmers or nomads in political Tibet at the time the Chinese Communists took control of Tibet in 1951 or in the past. My understanding of the current situation in the TAR is that there are still no rural Han farmers or nomads. The large numbers of Han who reside in the TAR are urban-based and are either government officials, construction workers or petty entrepreneurs. Moreover, all the Han in the TAR, including those with permanent-residence permits (*hukou*) and those with temporary-residence permits (*linshi-hukou*) but excluding military personnel, appear to amount to at most several hundred thousand, not millions.

On the other hand, the number of Han in Amdo–Kokonor and Eastern Kham (that is, in Qinghai, Gansu and Sichuan provinces) is more substantial and includes Han farmers. But how much of this Han presence is rural rather than urban, and when this Han in-migration occurred, is still empirically unclear. Certainly, only a portion of in-migration occurred after the establishment of the People's Republic of China: it is well documented that Han and Hui farmers were present in ethnographic Tibet in the 1920s and 1930s, and probably since the Manchu domination of the area in the 18th century. Robert Ekvall's above-mentioned firsthand account of Chinese–Tibetan interactions in the 1920s in Amdo–Kokonor illustrates this unambiguously. He wrote:

The second problem . . . is the infiltration of Chinese into the region occupied by the Tibetan farming population, many instances of which are found all along the border between the Chinese and Tibetan country. In the region of the Koko Nor an extensive colonization project is in the process of development, and the government is putting all possible pressure behind it. Land has been pre-empted from the Tibetan tribes, with scant regard for their desires, and is being granted to Chinese colonists. In still other districts turbulent Tibetan villages have been brought under strict rule by Chinese authorities . . . (Ekvall, p. 29)

Following the river up this steadily changing valley, we pass from one clearly defined culture pattern to another . . . Thus, a trip of seventy or

Melvyn C. Goldstein

eighty miles takes one through a veritable laboratory of culture change . . .
In the first village Chinese culture is dominant, and there are only vague
traces of Tibetan influence; as one moves on, Tibetan influence increases
to a point where the two cultures are evenly balanced; and from there on
Chinese influence decreases until in the farthest villages the Tibetan aspect
of life and manners is virtually unadulterated.

Such a trip likewise recalls . . . almost a journey into the past; for
leaving the first village . . . one leaves, in a sense, the present and travels
gradually backwards in time until he reaches the last village, which, with
its dominantly Tibetan character, represents what the now definitely
Chinese village once was. (*Ibid.*, p. 80)

Assertions, therefore, that many Chinese now live and farm in
'Tibet', while certainly true for ethnographic Tibet, are not true for
the TAR; nor do they mean that this is a recent phenomenon in
ethnographic Tibet. What portion of in-migration occurred since
1949 is an empirical issue. The problem regarding in-migration
into the TAR, however, is still a very serious matter, but its true
nature can not be understood if we obscure the very different
historical experiences of the TAR and ethnographic Tibet. Failure
methodologically to deconstruct 'Tibet' can only lead to gross dis-
tortions of the contemporary situation.[8]

This lengthy introduction may seem to labour an obvious point,
but I admit to surprise that some 'academics' follow the
'Greater Tibet' practice, and apparently consider their position
factually correct. Let me now turn to the main topic of this paper:
Tibet during the four decades from 1950 to 1990.

Methodology

In order to convey some of the salient aspects of social and economic change in Tibet from 1950 to 1990, the standard approach
would have been to examine Chinese Government statistics for this
area. However, because of the general, and to an extent well-
founded, scepticism most Western scholars have towards such
data, I decided that the most appropriate approach would be to
provide an account of Tibet from the perspective of one group of
nomadic pastoralists with whom I have conducted research. I
believe that their experiences are generally typical of those of other
nomads in Western Tibet, and that the trade-offs from this
approach – greater accuracy and insight – are worth the loss of
representativeness in sample. Thus, most of this paper will use what
in anthropology is called the 'case study' approach. My research in
Tibet consisted of five visits to the TAR (1985, 1986, 1987–8, 1990
and 1991) amounting to thirty months of fieldwork.[9]

Fourteen months of this time were spent in a community of

Nomads with their animals in Pala. (*Melvyn Goldstein*)

about 265 nomadic pastoralists who live in a relatively isolated, traditional nomad area called Pala. This area is located about 300 miles north-west of Lhasa and 115 miles north of the TAR's main east–west road on the western Changtang or 'Northern Plateau'.

Traditional anthropological methods such as participant observation and in-depth, open-ended interviewing provided the data for this paper. Interviews ranged from quasi-formal, where notes were taken and tape recorders often used, to informal, where data were collected as part of conversations. No restrictions were placed on meetings or interviews, and officials did not accompany us. All interviewing was conducted in Tibetan and virtually everyone in the community was repeatedly visited and interviewed. For most of the time with the nomads, my colleague, Professor Cynthia M. Beall, and I were alone with our private Tibetan research assistants, but for a portion of the study we were joined by a young Tibetan researcher from the Tibet Academy of Social Sciences who assisted us in data collection.

1951–9: Co-existence under the Terms of the Seventeen-Point Agreement

The establishment of the People's Republic of China (PRC) in 1949 set in motion events which two years later altered the 'Tibet Question' in favour of China. The new Chinese Government not only proclaimed the re-integration of Tibet into China as one of its prime goals, but in October 1950 forced it to the negotiating table by crossing the Upper Yangtse River and invading the eastern part of the Tibetan polity. Within a matter of weeks, it captured the bulk of the Tibetan army, together with Ngabö (Ngapo), the Governor-General who was one of Tibet's four council ministers. The Tibetan Government sent a delegation to Beijing to negotiate, and in 1951 reluctantly agreed to a 'Seventeen-Point Agreement for the Peaceful Liberation of Tibet' in which Tibet formally acknowledged Chinese sovereignty over Tibet in exchange for Chinese agreement to maintain the Dalai Lama and the traditional politico-economic system intact until Tibetans themselves wanted change.[10] Chinese troops moved into Lhasa in the autumn of 1951, and have not left.

Although 1951 marked the end of what then was a *de facto* independent Tibetan polity, the Dalai Lama and his government remained in place as did the traditional Tibetan political economy. Beijing left the quasi-feudal economic system intact.

The years 1951–9,[11] therefore, saw virtually no changes in Pala. The nomads continued to be *mi-ser* (serf-like subjects) of the Panchen Lama, belonging to his vast pastoral estate known as *Lagyab Lhojang*. This meant that they were, like Tibet's farmers, hereditarily tied to the land of their lord, and that they owed taxes to him in kind and in *corvée* labour. However, they owned their livestock, as farmers owned their crops, and had full rights over their disposal. The household was the basic unit of production and consumption. All of this continued in place until March 1959, when the Dalai Lama fled into exile and China assumed direct administrative control in Tibet after suppressing a large uprising. The period known as the era of 'democratic reforms' (*dmang-gtso'i bcus-sgyur*, mangtso jügyur) then began.

Direct Chinese Rule in Tibet: 1959 until the Cultural Revolution

The history of Tibet since 1959 is a complex story that will take years of detailed research in different sub-regions to elucidate adequately. The following account, therefore, can be thought of as an incipient examination of events during that period as experienced by Tibetans in one rather remote nomad area, rather than as a definitive exposition. On the other hand, during the course of my research in Pala I had the opportunity to hold a number of conversations about this period with farmers who had come to Pala to work for the nomads, and on the basis of this I think that the findings from Pala are basically congruent with the experiences of rural farmers, at least in this part of Tibet. I certainly would not, however, preclude future research revealing different patterns in other regions of Tibet.

In Pala the seventeen-year period from the time of the flight of the Dalai Lama into exile in 1959 to the end of the Cultural Revolution in 1976 can be divided into two phases: first, the early years from 1959 until the onset of the Cultural Revolution in 1966, and secondly, the era of the Cultural Revolution, from 1966 to 1976.

In Pala the events of 1959 began in a rather surprising way. Because the Lagyab Lhojang nomads refused to join a group of neighbouring Nagdzang nomads and rise up against the Chinese, they (including Pala) found themselves embroiled in warfare with the rebels when these nomads and their monk allies, who were mostly from Ganden Chugor monastery, began to launch punitive raids against them. This ended only towards the end of 1959 when a unit of the PLA came to the aid of Pala at the request of the nomads. Guided by local Lagyab Lhojang nomads, it engaged and defeated the rebel force.

After this, Pala underwent changes that seem to parallel those of other rural areas in Tibet. Beijing now had complete control in Tibet and started the process of land reforms, the uprising, the Chinese argued, having voided their agreement not to start reforms until at least 1962. However, Beijing decided that the Tibetan peasantry was not ready for a major transformation (communisation) of its economy along the lines of the one that had taken place in China proper. Instead, it adopted a policy of bringing Tibet into the 'socialist line' gradually. This meant some land reforms (expropriation and redistribution of land from those who were involved in the 1959 uprising), but no immediate establishment of communes. It also meant that, although the mass of monks were sent home from their monasteries, Tibetans were still permitted to practise individual Buddhism, including going to temples and monasteries.[12] And although new local officials were appointed by the government from among the poor nomads, and a new and formal 'class' structure was created, class struggle sessions were restricted to those who had supported the uprising and the Dalai Lama – the so called 'reactionaries' or *log-spyod-pa* (lokjüba) – or those who had administered estates particularly brutally. In Pala, this fate befell only one leader whose property was confiscated and redistributed. He committed suicide just before his scheduled appearance at a struggle session. The rest of Pala's better-off nomads, even the very wealthy leader of the entire Lagyab Lhojang area, kept the animals they held in 1959. Consequently, the poor nomads and the nomad beggar and servant classes in this area did not benefit much from the start of 'democratic reforms', because only the one herd was available for redistribution.

In early 1961, the relatively benign policy called 'mutual aid' (*rogs-ras*) was implemented in Pala. In this system, in nomad country, several households from the 'lower-middle' and 'poor' classes were formed into mutual-aid teams that co-operated in tasks such as herding; management and economic decisions, however, remained rooted at the household level, as did all income. This era also brought the first serious persecution of the members of the former nomad 'wealthy' class who, having already lost all their authority and status, were not permitted to 'join' the mutual-aid system and were forced to pay higher taxes and wages. But their animals were not confiscated and they were permitted to continue hiring other poor nomads as servants and shepherds, albeit at higher wages than those which the 'middle' and 'poor' class nomads paid. They could also still sell their products as they wished. The main thrust of the government's policy during this period was to establish infrastructure for later reforms and to reduce the tremendous income disparities of the 'old society' (*spyi-tshogs rnying-pa*, jitso nyingba) as the traditional era was now called. In villages this was easy to accomplish since the demesne land of the aristocratic and monastic lords was available for redistribution,[13] but with nomads it was more difficult because the former lords held only pastureland, so there were no animals to redistribute. The government ultimately imposed greater equality by heavily taxing the rich, that is, by reducing their income.

The 'Cultural Revolution' that began in China in 1966 dramatically changed all of this. In Pala, word of the impending creation of communes in 1969 precipitated a revolt among the nomads, who adopted the name Gyenlo, from one of the two Red Guard groups in Lhasa.[14] After killing some local district officials who had declared themselves supporters of the Communist regime – which in this area meant the Nyamdre or 'Alliance' Red Guard group – and imprisoning others, the nomads seized power in their area for three months, declaring religious and economic freedom. They had heard, and believed, that the PLA would remain neutral in the struggle between the two Red Guard groups, so they thought that they were safe even though their platform was not revolutionary reform but a return to what in essence was a modified pre-1959 state. This was a bizarre misunderstanding of events in China and Lhasa, and the PLA, guided by the 'Alliance'-member Tibetan cadres who had fled the district, came and reasserted their control.

At this point, the full weight of the Cultural Revolution fell on the nomads, transforming their lives.

The nomads were restructured into communes,[15] and, like farmers throughout Tibet and China, earned food, goods and cash on the basis of the 'work points' they received for their labour. The technology of pastoral management stayed the same, but now work was not organised on a household basis. The commune leaders decided who would do what work.

During the commune period (1969–81), no attempt was made to diminish the geographic scope of pastoralism by expropriating nomad pastureland or resettling nomads in agricultural areas. Nor was there any attempt to settle Tibetan or Chinese farmers in the nomad areas. However, several programmes to increase yields by irrigating and fencing pastures were tried in Pala, and an agricultural test plot was also set up in one small area. The nomads opposed this and the programmes all failed.

The Cultural Revolution also re-examined the class system that had been established in 1959–60. Using new and stricter criteria, a class of rich nomad exploiters of the poor was identified. Class conflict then became the dominant task, with severe struggle sessions occurring periodically. Those designated to have 'bad class origins' were at first prohibited from joining the commune and had difficulty even staying alive: a number died during this time. This restriction, however, eased after one or two years.

Although no attempt was made to resettle Han or to use Chinese language, Tibetan traditional cultural values, beliefs and norms now came under full-scale attack. One nomad described what happened to him when one day in 1970 Tibetan officials suddenly came to his tent and immediately took him into custody:

They called me a reactionary and a class enemy and told me: from today on, all your animals and goods are confiscated and you will live under the 'guidance' of the people just as the poorest of the poor lived in the old society. We had about 1,200 sheep and goats and 100 yak at this time. Right then and there they ripped off my earring, rings, necklace, my silver flint-striker and bullet holder. They also confiscated my new sheepskin robe saying that it was too good for the likes of a class enemy like me. In its place they gave me an old, worn one. But this was not all. They also took all of my family's household possessions and food stores, leaving us only one pot, one bag of 55 pounds of barley grain per person, and a little *tsampa*. And then they took away our fine yak-hair tent giving us in its place an old, tattered canvas tent. We were stunned – our whole life's wealth was eliminated in a matter of minutes. We didn't know how we would survive since they also said that we could not join the people's commune but had to fend for ourselves, alone and without help. Our sole means of support were the 40 goats they left us [eight goats per person], only ten of which were milk goats.

The campaign known as 'destroying the four olds' (old ideas, old culture, old customs and old habits) was energetically launched with the aim of eliminating the traditional culture and creating in its place a new atheistic Communist class system. Private religious activities were forbidden, religious buildings (including monasteries, temples and even prayer walls) were torn down and Tibetans were forced to abandon traditions that went to the core of their cultural identity. Everything was deliberately turned topsy-turvy. The class struggle sessions conducted by Tibetan cadres were frequent, going on until late at night, and there was a constant barrage of propaganda that contradicted and ridiculed everything the nomads understood and felt. Moreover, food was often inadequate since leaders claimed false production gains which, in turn, required higher taxes and left less to divide among the members.

Thus, during this phase of Chinese rule, all traditional social and economic institutions were destroyed – or at least banned – and a full-scale effort was launched to transform the values and belief systems of the nomads and of course everyone in Tibet and China. If there is a period where the term 'ethnocide' could be applied, it would clearly be the decade from 1966 to 1976.

Chinese policy in Tibet in the post-Mao Era: 1976 to the Present

The death of Mao Zedong in 1976 and the rise to power of Deng Xiaoping created a new cultural and economic policy in China that changed China and Tibet for the better. The full impact of these changes reached Tibet in 1980 when Hu Yaobang, General Secretary of the Party, visited Tibet with Wan Li, then Vice-Premier, and launched a new reform policy there.

The background to this intervention is not public, but informed sources suggest the following scenario. While China was discarding the ideological and economic baggage of Maoism and the Cultural Revolution in China proper, Ren Rong, the First Secretary of the Chinese Communist Party in the TAR, was reporting that conditions in Tibet were excellent and that the masses, shoulder to shoulder with their Han brothers, were dedicated to Communism and the revolution. Some Tibetans in Tibet now say that one or two Tibetan cadres may have made critical counter-reports to Beijing, but it appears clear that even if this is true, the full extent of the situation was not felt until the Chinese invited the exile Tibetan government to send a 'fact-finding' delegation to Tibet in 1979.

This delegation was the outcome of suggestions made in 1978 to both China and the exile government by John Dolfin, an interested middleman in Hong Kong, who believed that the time was ripe to open a new round of discussions on the 'Tibet Question'.[16] This quickly brought the Dalai Lama's elder brother, Gyalo Thondup, who lived in Hong Kong, into contact with representatives of the Chinese Government, and finally led to the Chinese issuing an invitation to the Dalai Lama to send a delegation which would have freedom to travel throughout Tibet and observe conditions there for themselves.

Beijing obviously accepted Ren Rong's reports that conditions were sanguine in Tibet, and consequently believed that once the delegation saw the progress that had been made in Tibet, *rapprochement* would be easier. Led by the late Lobsang Samten, another of the Dalai Lama's elder brothers, the Tibetan delegation visited a number of areas. Before going to Lhasa they went to Amdo (Qinghai Province), the birthplace of the current Dalai Lama, and there received a tumultuous welcome. Tibetans flocked to see the delegation, prostrated before them, gave them ceremonial scarves, and so forth. This reception was unexpected by the Chinese, and Beijing, embarrassed by such overwhelming expression of support for the Dalai Lama, contacted Ren Rong in Lhasa to ask him what would happen if the delegation continued according to plan and visited Lhasa. Ren is said to have told them that the Lhasa people were more developed then the simple herders of Qinghai and strongly supported the ideals of the Communist Party: there would be no such problems in Lhasa.

The magnitude of the local Han administration's ignorance of the sentiment of the masses in Tibet – namely the Tibetan people's intense dislike of the Chinese and Communism and their devotion to the Dalai Lama – is illustrated by their decision to organise a bizarre series of neighbourhood meetings in Lhasa just before the arrival of the delegation so as to exhort the local Tibetan masses not to let their hatred of the 'old society' induce them to throw stones or to spit at the Dalai Lama's delegates, since they were coming as guests of the government. The local Lhasa Tibetans[17] politely said 'yes' to the cadres' exhortations, chuckling inwardly, and then gave a welcome surpassing the one that the delegation had received in Qinghai. Thousands upon thousands of Lhasa people, tears often streaming from their eyes, mobbed the delegation, prostrated, shouted Tibetan independence slogans, offered ceremonial scarves and fought to touch the Dalai Lama's brother. Because Beijing officials were accompanying the Tibetan delegation, there was no way for Ren Rong and the other Tibet administrators to cover up this fiasco and the pro-Dalai Lama and anti-Chinese emotions it revealed.

When the delegation returned to Beijing it did not make a public statement on its observations, but privately informed the Chinese about its shock and dismay at the universal religious and cultural destruction it had witnessed, and at the overall poverty and backwardness of Tibet. The delegation said that, apart from criticising the massive cultural and religious destruction, it saw no evidence even of material progress in Tibet. Twenty years of Chinese Communist rule, the delegates chided, had not even brought Tibetan areas such basic things as good roads or buildings at a level parallel to those in Han areas. These private criticisms and the reality of the spontaneous affection and support demonstrated by the Tibetan masses shocked the highest reaches of the Party. It had expected to demonstrate to the refugee delegation and to the Dalai Lama the progress Tibet had made under Chinese rule and thereby to set the stage for serious negotiations to settle the 'Tibet Question' once and for all in a manner favourable to China. Now, faced with highly critical reports, the Party was forced to reassess the situation in Tibet and, if Tibet really had not progressed, to decide what should be done about the politically sensitive minority area.

After considerable preliminary investigation, the General Secretary of the Central Committee of the Chinese Communist Party, Hu Yaobang, made an unprecedented fact-finding visit to Tibet in May 1980, to see for himself the conditions there. He apparently was deeply dismayed by what he saw and heard, and not only insisted that Ren Rong return on the plane with him to Beijing, presumably so Ren could cause no more trouble – but publicly announced an extraordinary six-point report on Tibet which included among its salient points:

2. In view of the relatively difficult situation in Tibet, the policy of recuperation must be unswervingly carried out to lighten the burden of masses.

Compared with other provinces and autonomous regions of the country, it is conspicuous that in Tibet the people's living standards lag far behind. This situation means that the burden of the masses must be considerably lightened. The people in Tibet should be exempt from paying taxes and meeting purchase quotas for the next few years. They will definitely be exempt from paying taxes, and state purchase quotas should not be assigned to them. All kinds of exactions must be abolished. The people should not be assigned any additional work without pay. Peasants' and herdsmen's produce may be purchased at negotiated prices or bartered to

supply mutual needs, and they should be exempt from meeting state purchase quotas. It is believed that the broad masses of peasants and herdsmen will support the policy of purchasing goods at negotiated price, bartering and exchanging products of equal value. This policy will promote the development of agriculture and animal husbandry.
3. Specific and flexible policies suited to conditions in Tibet must be carried out on the whole economic front of the region, including the agricultural, animal husbandry, financial and trade, commercial, handicraft and communication fronts, with a view of promoting Tibet's economic development more rapidly . . .
5. So long as the socialist orientation is upheld, vigorous efforts must be made to revive and develop Tibetan culture, education and science. The Tibetan people have a long history and a rich culture. The world renowned ancient Tibetan culture included fine Buddhism, graceful music and dance as well as medicine and opera, all of which are worthy of serious study and development. All ideas that ignore and weaken Tibetan culture are wrong. It is necessary to do a good job in inheriting and developing Tibetan culture. Education has not progressed well in Tibet. Taking Tibet's special characteristics into consideration, efforts should be made to set up universities and middle and primary schools in the region. Some cultural relics and Buddhist scriptures in temples have been damaged, and conscientious effort should be made to protect, sort and study them. Cadres of Han nationality working in Tibet should learn the spoken and written Tibetan language. It should be a required subject; otherwise they will be divorced from the masses. Cherishing the people of minority nationalities is not empty talk. The Tibetan people's habits, customs, history and culture must be respected. (SWB, FE/6436/BII/4, June 4, 1980)

This public statement, moreover, was mild compared to the secret report (said to contain 39 points) and speeches of Hu Yaobang to the Party cadres. One point of the report is said to have gone so far as to equate the previous twenty years of Chinese rule in Tibet with colonial occupation. This decision on the part of Hu Yaobang and the Central Committee of the Party to support those who criticised conditions in Tibet formed the basis on which a series of reform measures was implemented in Tibet in the following years.

The major reform, known as the system of 'complete responsibility' (*'gan-tshang*, gen-dzang), dissolved the communes and restored the household as the basic unit of production. For the nomads in Pala, this resulted in all the commune's animals being divided equally among its 57 households with all infants and senior citizens receiving the same share.[18] The nomads owned these animals and were free to utilise them as they wished. Pastures were also divided at this time, but were allocated to small groups of several households (called *dzug*) rather than to individuals. These *dzug* then held exclusive usufruct rights over them: that is, the families in a *dzug* had exclusive right to use these pastures. However, in Pala they were not permitted to sell or even lease them.

This system in some ways was similar to the one prepared for farmers, and in others very different. As with the nomads' animals, all the commune's arable fields were divided among its members, normally on a *per capita* basis. However, farmers not only legally held long-term usufruct rights to their land, but most villages actually allowed the farmers to use the land as if they owned it. Households, therefore, could lease their fields for fees if they wished and could decide how much to give as an inheritance when their children married. In most villages, moreover, this land stayed with the household when a member died, although in some areas where land was scarce it reverted back to the village and was then re-allocated to landless (such as new-born) villagers.

At the time of decollectivisation, each nomad in Pala received 39 animals from the commune: 4.5 yak, 27 sheep and 7.5 goats.[19] In addition to this, households were allowed to retain the 'private' animals that they had held during the commune era.[20] This raised the *per capita* average to 42.4 animals: 4.7 yak, 27 sheep and 10.7 goats. Using the average household size in Pala of 4.7 individuals, this meant that each household had about 200 animals. In the pre-1959 era this would have situated them in the lower-middle rungs of the economic hierarchy.

Administratively the new reforms signified the end of the commune and brigade structure. In its place, the government returned to the pre-commune unit called the *xiang* in Chinese (and now also in Tibetan). *Xiang* is the traditional Chinese term for 'township', but it is usually equivalent today to a village or unit of several villages. In Pala, the *xiang* consisted of two sub-units identical to the two brigades during the commune era. The two brigades, in turn, were divided into ten *dzug*, each consisting of from two to nine households and associated pastures. Membership in a *dzug* was permanent, although households could, and did, shift so long as they secured permission from the members of the receiving *dzug* and the local *xiang* government, a task not very difficult in Pala.

The *xiang* administration functions primarily to collect local data, such as the number of animals, for the higher governmental levels. It also implements decisions passed down from above and serves as the primary legal-juridical body dealing with divorces, disputes and so forth. It is headed by two officials known as *shang-drang*, a phonetic rendering of the Chinese term *zhang* for the head of a *xiang*. These *shang-drang* are local nomads elected by secret ballot from a list of candidates compiled by the level of government immediately above the *xiang*, the 'district' or *qu*.[21] In 1988 there was talk of allowing nominations to be made by the local inhabitants for these positions, but this has still not been fully implemented. Nevertheless, local political leadership has undergone a marked change because district cadres in the mid-1980s began to give the nomads more choices in these elections. Not only did they select more candidates for the elections, but the lists included individuals who were formerly classified as class enemies. The nomads have responded by electing leaders with regard to their ability and their manifestation of basic nomad values, rather than to their political ideology. Thus, one of Pala's two *shang-drang* is an intelligent ex-monk who was a persecuted class enemy during the Cultural Revolution.

The district headquarters is located about three days' walk to the south of Pala. Its officials are all Tibetan, albeit mostly from non-nomad backgrounds. It functions as the intermediary between the *xiang* and the more distant 'county', known as *xian* or *dzong*, the headquarters of which is located about twenty days' walk to the south-east at Ngamring. Above the *xian* is the 'prefecture' of Shigatse and, above it, the government of the TAR.

The language used in administration at the district and *xiang* levels is Tibetan, and all letters and notices sent to Pala are written in Tibetan. At the county level, Chinese is often used by the higher officials, particularly in dealings with the prefecture and the autonomous region governments, and there are a number of Han officials.

Education is available in nomad country through a primary school located at the district headquarters. This school teaches completely in the Tibetan language, its main subjects being written Tibetan and arithmetic.[22] Nomad children who attend primary school live at the school and are provided free food and housing by the government. However, there were complaints about the poor quality of the food there throughout our stay in Pala and the nomads seemed generally uninterested in sending children to school despite repeated urgings by the district and county.

The 'responsibility system' mentioned above was implemented throughout China, so Tibet was not singled out especially in this regard. However, Beijing attempted to redress some of the wrongs that had been done to Tibetans in a number of ways.

Improving the standard of living of Tibetans, particularly the rural farmers and herders who comprise about 90 per cent of the population, was immediately addressed by exempting farmers and nomads in Tibet from both taxes and the quota system whereby farmers and herdsmen are required to sell fixed amounts of their produce to the government at prices slightly below free-market prices. This nation-wide system of quota sales provides the government with its main source of farm and animal products. The exemption meant that until the late 1980s Tibetan farmers were free to utilise their entire crop as they saw fit, and to sell or barter as much as they wanted or none at all. For the nomads in Pala, however, the government continued to utilise a system of compulsory quota sales of key products such as wool, cashmere and skins, euphemistically calling this a programme of voluntarily negotiated sale contracts. The nomads were free to sell their produce on the free market only after these 'quotas' were met. This element of compulsion was a source of irritation for many nomads, but because the prices the nomads received for their wool and cashmere were not much below market prices and rose markedly during the 1980s, the discontent over this was not great. For example, between 1985 and 1988 the prices of wool and cashmere rose by 50 and 150 per cent respectively.

These exemptions and the overall increase in prices for animal products have allowed Pala households to generate profits from what is still basically a traditional system of production. Although this is still a poor area even by Tibetan standards, by 1990 many of the households had purchased new manufactured commodities such as tape recorders, sewing machines and a few bicycles.

Another sign of the new disposable income was the re-emergence of the temporary summer in-migration of Tibetan farmers from villages 20 to 30 days' journey to the south. This traditional pattern had been forcibly terminated during the Cultural Revolution and spontaneously re-emerged only in about 1985 when scores of farmers again came to Pala and the surrounding nomad areas. As in the old days, these farmers tanned the nomads' skins, made *ma-ni* walls for nomad households, carved religious stones and even built houses. The nomads paid well for these services: for example, one sheep or goat for every nine to ten skins tanned. By 1990, roughly one quarter of Pala's households had hired such villagers to construct new storehouses or winter residences for them.

Tremendous cultural changes also occurred following the new reforms, which created a process of revitalisation. The nomads were informed that it was now permissible to practise religion and express other aspects of their culture. Depending on the interests and values of individual nomads, traditional religious and cultural practices gradually became active. In essence, the nomads began a dynamic process of re-creating their traditional cultural system, knowing there were probably still limits, but without being sure what these limits were.

Individual Tibetans, therefore, began to practise traditional Tibetan Buddhism openly, worshipping by circumambulating holy sites, turning prayer wheels and placing prayer flags on their tents. They also helped to fund the rebuilding of local monasteries and temples, and used them for religious purposes. Many began to make offerings to deities, monks and lamas, as had been the custom in the old society. Altars were again set up in tents, and by 1985-6 monks were being invited to perform prayers in people's tents. The monastery even set up a 'tent monastery' at the district horse-racing festival. The depth of these changes was pointedly illustrated one afternoon in December 1987 when a few nomads brought a newly purchased radio to our tent and sat listening to All India Radio's Tibetan-language short wave broadcast of news and religious prayers. Because they had the volume turned up and our tent was just a few feet from that of a Party leader, we asked if they weren't concerned that he would hear what they were listening to. The nomads laughed, saying 'Why should he care? He listens too.'

Institutional religion – monasteries and nunneries – also saw a renaissance, although it remained an area over which the government retained some control, particularly with regard to limitations on the number and selection of monks. In Lagyab Lhojang, work began in 1986 on rebuilding a small Drigung Kagyupa monastery in Tongling. The site for construction was beside the district centre that had been destroyed during the Cultural Revolution, and funds for the building were donated by the local nomads. It re-opened in 1988. The monks in this monastery were supported by their families during the year, and by the monastery when they gathered for prayers in winter and in the holy fourth Tibetan month. The costs of these 'prayer meetings' were met partly by yields from a herd of several hundred sheep and goats that had been donated to the monastery by individual nomads, and partly by direct gifts from nomad patrons.

These traditional practices did not reappear all at once or in an orderly fashion. At first the nomads feared that the new policy was a devious trick launched to expose pockets of 'rightist' thinking, and individuals were reluctant to take the lead and risk being singled out. Change occurred only gradually as individual nomads took specific actions that, in effect, tested the general policy. When no protest or punishment came from the district officials above them, all of whom are ethnic Tibetans, a desirable practice spread and continues to do so. The re-emergence of nomad 'mediums', individuals whom deities possess and speak through, exemplifies this. It is an aspect of the traditional Tibetan Buddhist religious system that is considered an 'unnecessary' superstition not only by the Communists but to an extent also by the Dalai Lama's exile government. Yet it reappeared in Pala in the winter of 1987 when an adult in one camp took ill and was in great pain for days before be died. A man from the same encampment went into trance spontaneously during the illness and was possessed by a deity who gave a prognosis and explanation of the disease. When no official criticism of this event occurred in the ensuing weeks and months, he and others fashioned the traditional costume worn by mediums, and he was sought after by others in Pala in cases of illness. By 1990, however, the district officials had passed down word that for lay people to become possessed was not acceptable, so the shaman was forced to continue practising in a surreptitious fashion.

What has been occurring, therefore, is a form of 'cultural revitalisation'. The term 'revitalisation' was used by Anthony Wallace in the 1950s to describe a number of movements of native peoples, such as cargo, nativistic and messianic cults that evolved in situations of socio-cultural stress and disorganisation, as 'conscious, organized efforts by members of a society to construct a more satisfying culture'. Wallace saw these revitalisation movements arising in response to an 'identity dilemma' that was common in contact situations where two cultures, one politically dominant, clashed. He wrote:

[Revitalisation movements] originate in situations of social and cultural stress and are, in fact, an effort on the part of the stress-laden to construct systems of dogma, myth, and ritual which are internally coherent as well as true descriptions of a world system and which thus will serve as guides to efficient action. (Wallace (1966), p. 30)

The Tibet situation conforms to Wallace's conditions for the emergence of revitalisation movements in a general way.[23] In their contact with the dominant and alien 'Communist' cultural system, the nomads were told that their traditional leaders were contemptible enemies of the people and that their old values and norms were immoral and exploitative. Compelled to abandon the traditional beliefs and symbols that gave meaning to the world around them and actively to embrace new 'Communist' norms and values that they considered repugnant, they experienced a crisis of morality and meaning. This was further exacerbated when they had to put the new morality into practice by persecuting and physically punishing the newly defined 'class enemies', many of whom were friends and kinsmen.

In another important sense, however, the Tibetan situation is inconsistent with the Wallace model since the response in Tibet has not involved a 'conscious' and 'organised' effort on the part of an individual or a group to rectify the *anomie* by innovating a new cultural system. Rather, what has occurred is a spontaneous, diffuse process wherein members of a society individually have resurrected and re-integrated components of their traditional cognitive and effective systems to relieve stress and dissonance and reconstruct for themselves a more satisfying culture. This process of diffuse revitalisation in Pala extends to all facets of the cultural system. Butchering livestock, for example, is again taking on the stigma it had in the traditional society. Since Buddhism teaches that taking life is sinful, the nomads traditionally relegated slaughtering activities, as well as castrating and cutting ear marks on livestock, to an hereditary 'unclean' social stratum: the very poor or the irreligious. This custom has again emerged in Pala and throughout Tibet, and most nomads no longer slaughter their own livestock.

An incident that occurred during our field-work in Pala illustrates the extent to which the traditional cognitive system has been re-integrated into the present system. A former *üpung* – 'poor class' – nomad, who had been an official during the commune period, sold a lactating sheep to a trader before milking it. By doing so he was breaking a traditional taboo, for nomads in Pala traditionally believed that such an act could affect negatively the milk production of the entire camp. A man in the same camp as the former poor class nomad, and someone who had been persecuted as a class enemy, became incensed. He berated the seller and words soon turned into pushing and fighting. They took the case before the local *xiang* government, the poor-class nomad arguing that the wealthy-class nomad looked down on him and was trying to impose reactionary superstitions on him. The local and district officials, however, were not impressed with what had become an anachronistic perspective and did not side with him. Instead they fined both men for fighting, in the process validating the acceptability of even this type of traditional taboo. On another occasion, when a goat of one of Pala's four Party members was accidentally strangled during milking by the rope that tied it, he threw the carcass into the adjacent lake. This is because it is traditionally taboo to eat the meat of an animal which had been killed, albeit inadvertently in this case, by female milkers.

Current marriage patterns also illustrate the re-emergence of traditional attitudes and values. A number of today's wealthy nomads, for example, favourably consider a potential spouse who has a high-status family background from the old society, and most nomads now refuse to marry those from the traditional 'unclean' stratum. Similarly, nomad practitioners of traditional Tibetan medicine are again active in the area, and traditional singing and dancing often spontaneously erupt when the young from several camps come together.[24]

One traditional pattern that has continued unrestrained through-out the period from 1959 to 1990 is that of having large families. Despite repeated claims in the West that the Chinese have imposed a strict policy of birth control in Tibet, where 'forced abortions, sterilisations and infanticide are everyday occurrences' (*New York Times*, 31 January 1992), there was no policy of restricting repro-duction in Pala, let alone evidence of forced abortions, sterilisa-tions or infanticide.

By 1988 some Pala nomads had heard that there was a way to stop getting pregnant, but there was no pressure to utilise family planning to restrict family size. In fact, one woman with many children actually came to us asking if we could help her obtain birth control 'medicine'. When we looked into this, we found that con-traceptive injections were available at the district health post, three days away by horseback, and that IUDs were provided and sterilisations done at the more distant county headquarters. Before 1989–90, however, no concerted propaganda programme extolling the value of small families was implemented. In that year, small numbers of contraceptives, of the injection and the pill types, were distributed to the local *xiang* officials who were instructed to ask each reproductive-age woman whether she wanted to use con-traception. There was still no pressure or coercion, however, to use them.

Not surprisingly, the nomads, including their officials, had large families. The fertility history of Pala's four Party members, all of whom were nomads who had joined the Party during the Cultural Revolution, reflects this. Of the three who are married, the Party Secretary's wife has had seven children, of whom six are alive; the two (successive) wives of a second official have eight living children; and the wife of the third has had seven births, of which six were living. These general observations of high fertility are sup-ported by demographic information for all the females in the nomad community.

Based on our own demographic surveys, the crude birth rate (CBR – the number of births per 1,000 population in a given year) was 35 per 1,000 over the four-year period 1986–90, and the crude death rate (CDR – the number of deaths per 1,000 population in a given year) was 30 per 1,000. Pala's fertility, therefore, is 67% higher than that of China as a whole. The crude rate of natural increase (CBR minus CDR), was 5 per 1,000 for 1986–90, which shows an annual growth rate of 0.5%. This represents a very modest population doubling time of 140 years.

BIRTHS TO PALA NOMAD WOMEN AGED 15-59, 1985

	All women		Parous* women	
Age	Average no. of births	No. of women	Average no. of births	No. of women
15-19	–	12	–	–
20-9	1.3	20	2.3	11
30-9	3.3	18	3.8	16
40-9	5.4	11	5.9	10
50-9	5.4	10	6.8	8

* I.e. women who have given birth to at least one child.

Our crude birth rate and crude death rate figures for Pala, however, are based on births and deaths over only a four-year period. To obtain a better understanding of population dynamics in this community, fertility histories were collected from a total of seventy-one females aged from 15 to 59. The Table above presents the actual number of births experienced by these women. It is clear that reproduction starts relatively late but that by the age 30-9, women have an average of 3.3 children. And by the age 40-9, women had experienced an average of 5.4 births, with 4.9 of these surviving in 1988. This relatively high fertility would be even higher if it were not for the late average age at first birth (22.4 years) and the large number of women who have never given birth (5 of 39 aged 30-59). Columns 4-5 present data only for 'parous' women, those who have actually borne children. This gives a better picture of fertility by eliminating infertile couples and unmarried females who have not yet conceived. The fertility of this sub-population of women averages 0.5 to 1.8 births more than that for all women, and is far in excess of any limit of two or even three births per couple.

Despite such strong evidence that fertility is very high in Pala, these data do not preclude the possibility that coercive birth control limitations have been implemented only recently. Our data, however, also indicate this has not happened. Between 1984 and 1988, seven Pala women gave birth to their third surviving child, four to their fourth, three to their fifth, five to their sixth and one to her ninth. The reproductive histories of Pala women at all ages, therefore, provide strong evidence in support of the conclusion that no population control policy restricting couples to two or even three births was or is operative. Furthermore, no Pala nomads have ever been fined for their third, fourth, fifth or subsequent children, and all such children and their families have full rights in the community.[25]

Taking all these changes together, this was a heady time. The nomads' devotion to Buddhism could be expressed by prayers and deeds, and their perception of the worth of their traditional culture had been vindicated. Told that their language and culture were primitive and 'feudal' during the Cultural Revolution, the new policies now proved, from their perspective, that they had always been right.[26]

Although Tibetan culture underwent a revitalisation, some traditional institutions such as polyandry remain illegal, and in others, such as '[spirit] possession', specialists have been forced to operate surreptitiously. There was also unhappiness with being forced to sell products to the government at non-market prices, and there is a controversy over the government decision to limit herd size in order to conserve the pastureland despite the nomads' claims that they were not overgrazing.[27]

One also must keep in mind that China's regard for human rights does not parallel our own, and although the new policies had a sanguine impact on life in Pala, there is obviously no democracy or freedom there as we know it in the West. Moreover, the nomads' knowledge and fear that the current government could intervene again at any time and impose its alien values is coupled with their knowledge that about 5% of the nomads seemed to prefer the more 'class'-oriented era of the Cultural Revolution. It will take a long time for the nomads to forget the first two decades of Chinese rule.

Let us now turn to comment briefly on the consequences of this reform policy for household wealth. Economically, the new policies were well accepted by the nomads. Nevertheless, although all started with the same number of livestock, a number of the nomads have amassed considerable livestock over the seven years from 1981 to 1988. Conversely, some have fared poorly enough to fall below the subsistence line, and one nomad has actually lost all his livestock. The number of animals per person now ranges from none to 154, and 10 households, or 18% of the total, were actually receiving welfare from the district. Consequently, a nomad economic hierarchy is re-emerging with poor families or individuals beginning to work for rich ones in a way somewhat analogous to that which existed in the old days, although the wages now being paid are quite reasonable: good food and one sheep per month. Thus, as in the rest of China, one of the consequences of the new reforms has been increasing differentiation of economic power, and all that it entails.[28]

Other consequences of the reforms are clearly under way. Roads have made it possible for nomads to get more directly involved in trade. While most have preferred to continue with straight animal husbandry, some have begun to explore the trade option. They were aided by a 1987–8 government programme for making loans for trade easily available to nomads with collateral. Some Pala nomads, therefore, have tried to sell sheep to Shigatse, which is a 2–3 day trip by truck away, and have converted the income from the sheep into manufactured commodities to resell in Pala. Others have simply used government loans to buy goods in Shigatse to resell among the herders. These innovations have had mixed results. The sheep scheme, for example, has not fared well because the Tibetan traders in Shigatse, knowing that the nomads have to leave when the truck that brought them departs, only buy at the last moment at a low price.

In general, these nomads have always been somewhat affected by world wool prices, and their entanglement is now closer and more direct. This will certainly have an increasingly strong effect on their lives. For example, following the recent collapse of the world wool price, the government stopped buying wool from the herders in 1990. The economic reforms discussed above, therefore, have started a process of change, the trajectory of which is not entirely clear. The economic situation is fluid.

In conclusion, the new reforms instituted in and after 1980 have provided a rich and nurturing matrix in which the nomads' strong convictions about the value of their way of life could express itself in the cultural and economic revitalisation here briefly described. There are problems, of course, and everything is far from perfect, but the transformation of their life has been remarkable. With no Han with whom to interact and with spoken and written Tibetan the language of administration, life in Pala, excluding of course the political system, is closer to traditional Tibet than at any time since 1959. While the same cannot be said for urban areas such as Lhasa, I think that the situation described above generally reflects the set of changes that have occurred throughout rural Tibet.

REFERENCES

Cincotta, R.P., Y. Zhang and X. Zhou, 'Transition in an Alpine Pastoral Production System: Relationships between China's Agrarian Reform, Livestock Development and Ecosystem Research' (ms.).

Clarke, G., *China's Reforms of Tibet and Their Effects on Pastoralism*, Institute of Development Studies, University of Sussex, 1987.

Dawa Norbu, 'China's Dialogue with the Dalai Lama 1978–90: Prenegotiation Stage or Dead End?', *Pacific Affairs*, 64(3), 1991, pp. 351–71.

Dreyer, J.T., *China's Forty Millions*, Harvard University Press, 1976.

Ekvall, Robert B., *Cultural Relations on the Kansu–Tibetan Border*, University of Chicago Press, 1977 (originally published 1939).

Goldstein, M.C., *A History of Modern Tibet, 1913–51: the Demise of the Lamaist State*, Berkeley: University of California Press, 1989.
——, and C.M. Beall, 'The Impact of China's Reform Policy on the Nomads of Western Tibet', *Asian Survey*, 28(6), 1989, pp. 619–41.
——, 'China's Birth Control Policy in the Tibet Autonomous Region: Myths and Realities', *Asian Survey*, 31(3), 1991, pp. 285–303.
Goldstein, M.C., C.M., Beall and R.P. Cincotta, 'Traditional Nomadic Pastoralism and Ecological Conservation on Tibet's Northern Plateau', *National Geographic Research*, 6(2), pp. 139–56, 1990.
Kolmas, J., *Tibet and Imperial China: A Survey of Sino-Tibetan Relations up to the End of the Manchu Dynasty in 1912*, Canberra: Australian National University Press, 1967.
Norbu, J., *Warriors of Tibet: the Story of Aten and the Khambas' Fight for the Freedom of their Country*, London: Wisdom Publications, 1986.
Petech, L., *China and Tibet in the Early 18th Century: History of the Establishment of Chinese Protectorate in Tibet*, Leiden: E.J. Brill, 1950.
Richardson, H.M., *Tibet and its History*, Boulder, CO: Shambhala, 1984.
Shakabpa, Tsepon W.D., *Tibet: A Political History*, Yale University Press, 1967.
Stubel, H., *The Mewu Fantzu: A Tibetan Tribe of Kansu*, New Haven: HRAF Press, 1958.
Summary of World Broadcasts, FE/6436/BII/4, June 4, 1980.
Teichman, E., *Travels of a Consular Officer in Eastern Tibet – Together with a History of the Relations between China, Tibet and India*, Cambridge University Press, 1922.
Thonden, P., 'On the Dragon's Side of the Tibet Question', *Tibetan Review*, 26(5), 1991, pp. 12–20.
Wallace, A.F.C., *Religion: An Anthropological View*, New York: Random House, 1966.
——, 'Revitalization Movements', *American Anthropologist*, 58, 1956.

NOTES

1. This general acceptance, of course, does not in any way mean that scholars using 'Tibet' in this way are conceding that Amdo or Kham should permanently be part of China. It says nothing at all about the political issue of which ethnic Tibetans areas should be part of a Tibetan state. It means only that the term 'Tibet' refers to a political entity – a polity – and should be used to refer only to people and events in that entity.
2. Dreyer, *op. cit.*, p. 10.
3. For a discussion of Sino-Tibetan interventions in Kham and Derge, see Teichman, pp. 6–7, and Shakabpa, pp. 260ff.
4. Cited in Goldstein (1989), p. 711.
5. When the PLA crossed the Yangtse River and invaded 'political' Tibet in 1950, the Khambas east of the Upper Yangtse River did not support the Tibetan Government's forces. In fact, rather than assisting the Tibetan Government by attacking the Chinese militarily from the rear and flanks, substantial numbers actually assisted the Chinese by providing transport and acting as guides and liaison-translators.
6. The same holds true for ethnic Tibetans in Ladakh, Sikkim, Nepal and India.
7. There is a Chinese-language track in TAR primary and middle schools in areas like Lhasa where there are thousands of resident Han. However, while some

Tibetans are allowed to matriculate in these, they represent only a small number of individuals.

8. Military camps in political Tibet, however, often engage in farming, and there is a new trend there wherein Han privately lease farmland from suburban Tibetans to grow vegetables.

9. These visits were sponsored by the US National Academy of Sciences' Committee for Scholarly Communication with the People's Republic of China (the US National Program for research in China), the National Geographic Society's Committee for Research and Exploration, the US National Endowment for the Humanities and the US National Science Foundation.

10. See Goldstein (1989) for a detailed account of this Agreement and the historical events leading up to it.

11. This period will be discussed in detail by the author in a monograph on Pala currently in preparation.

12. The three great monasteries around Lhasa remained open and some joint religious activities continued up to the onset of the Cultural Revolution. For example, there were several Monlam Chenmo (*smon-lam chen-mo*) festivals. This will be examined in a book about life in Drepung currently in preparation.

13. The new policy confiscated and redistributed all aristocratic and monastic demesne lands. However, aristocrats who were not involved in the 1959 uprising were compensated for the loss of their estates and were permitted to retain use of their homes in Lhasa.

14. This revolt appears, at least partially, to be related to others occurring at the same time in the areas of Nyemo and Biru.

15. The basic unit here was actually the *rukha* ('brigade'), which is technically a sub-unit of a commune (*gung-hre*).

16. Dawa Norbu.

17. I refer here to the *mangdzo* or 'common people'.

18. Losang Yexe (1988, p. 12), a nomad living in Damshung, an area north of Lhasa, also reports that animals were given to families on the basis of family size, but G. Clarke (p. 44) reports a variant system for Namtso, a pastoral area north of Lhasa. There, he says, 70% of the livestock went on a *per capita* basis among those aged 15 to 50 and the other 30% were 'allocated to the younger people and also to others who could work hard'.

19. There is actually some variation regarding these figures since one person sometimes received seven more goats, but then had this balanced by getting one less yak, etc. These data were copied from the original division list located in the *xiang*.

20. These 'private' animals were the equivalent of household garden plots on agricultural communes.

21. A new system was implemented in 1988–9 in which smaller *xiang* such as Pala were merged with contiguous larger ones. Thus, Pala no longer exists as a separate administrative unit.

22. No Chinese language is taught.

23. Wallace (1956).

24. Goldstein and Beall (1989).

25. Goldstein and Beall (1991).

26. There appears to be considerable variability depending on how local cadres interpreted the new policies, so anomalous situations probably exist. For example, in at least one nomad area north of Pala the commune was not dissolved and continues today (personal communication, George Schaller).

27. For a detailed discussion of this controversy, see Goldstein, Beall and Cincotta.

28. Goldstein and Beall (1989).

Part II
IDENTITY: LANGUAGE, RITUAL AND CULTURE

MOUNTAIN CULTS AND NATIONAL IDENTITY IN TIBET

Samten G. Karmay

> When secular customs break down, when traditional ways of life disappear, when the old solidarities crumble, it is, indeed, frequent that crises of identity arise.[1]

The early Tibetans, that is to say those of the Imperial Period which lasted from the 7th to the 9th centuries AD, were aware in many different ways of their own national identity. For example, they were very proud of the geographical location of the country. We find in ancient documents eulogies of the way in which the country is situated, its natural beauty, purity and wildness. One such hymn expresses this pride:

> Tibet is high and its land is pure.
> Its snowy mountains are at the head of everything,
> The sources of innumerable rivers and streams,
> It is the centre of the sphere of the gods.[2]

During this period, too, the country's geographical identity was expressed in terms of its centrality in relation to four other countries with which there was contact. India in the south was looked to as the source of religion; Iran in the west was envied for its great wealth; Turkestan in the north was feared for its military aggressiveness; and China in the east was admired for its knowledge of science.

One of the elements which play a significant role in Tibet's cultural identity, as much today as in the past, is the mountain cult. An example of this is the cult of Mount Lhari Gyangto in Kongpo, upon the summit of which, according to an ancient myth,[3] the first Tibetan king descended from heaven. The divinity of Mount Yarlha Shampo in Yarlung, which was considered to be the ancestral deity of the Yarlung Dynasty,[4] is also good evidence for this

112

cult. One of the early kings is even named Namri, 'Sky Mountain', which is one of the reasons why the Tibetan national flag has the image of a snow mountain and a snow lion, the emblem of Tibet, in its centre. This flag is now, of course, forbidden in its own land, even to the extent that a foreigner wearing a T-shirt or carrying a bag with this flag on it in Tibet runs the risk of being jailed. It is no wonder that these Tibetan national symbols should be considered so dangerous: they are not just recent means of identifying the country but go back to the Imperial Period.[5]

The concept of national identity in Tibet was, however, much more clearly expressed in ancient times than in, say, the Middle Ages. With the advent of Buddhism and particularly from the 11th century onwards, the national consciousness of the Tibetan people suffered greatly. This is, of course, not really surprising when we consider the manner in which Buddhism took hold on the minds of the people at large, especially with the prevailing monastic education. Nationalism requires will, self-assertion, self-identification and self-determination, and these notions have no place and receive no respect in Buddhist education as we know it. Tibetan monastic culture had a very strong tendency to discourage any contact with foreign religion and culture. If patriotism is the core of nationalism and if it were ever felt, it is often expressed in terms of protecting Buddhist doctrine and its institutions, and not the country as a nation or a state. In other words, there were periods when, immersed in the tranquillity of Buddhist compassion, the Tibetan people had almost forgotten who they were and where they were. When a Tibetan lama met a Mongol khan or a Manchu emperor, it was only on very rare occasions that the lama took the trouble to put his national interest first. This Buddhist equanimity exerted its effects not only in mentality but also in geography. A Japanese visitor in Lhasa in 1916 was shocked to note that when the Tibetan Government was asked for permission to climb Mount Everest from the Tibetan side by the British Mountain Climbers Association, it did not know that the northern side of the mountain lay within Tibetan territory.[6]

Since 1950 Tibetans have been merely reduced to a drop of ethnic essence in 'a vast sea of Chinese', as the Dalai Lama put it in a statement in 1985. Indeed, Tibet has not even the status of a stateless nation in international legal terms. Consequently, the integrity of its culture is in peril. But its national identity nevertheless remains alive and has even been reinforced and highlighted by Chinese repression since 1987.

During the last forty years, however, Tibetan Buddhism, which once worked to counter a strong sense of nationality, now works the other way. With the Dalai Lama as its spokesman and with his policy of non-violence, Tibetan Buddhism has come to symbolise Tibet's national identity. Moreover, it is proving an effective ideological counterbalance in the face of the advance of the Chinese brand of Marxism in Tibet.

In the process of awakening national identity there are two governing factors in Tibet's case: the experience of being under foreign occupation, and the close contact with Westerners in foreign countries and, in recent years, also in Tibet itself. The modern Tibetan nationalist often consciously wills his identification with the Buddhist culture. The greater the repression of his culture and identity, the more articulate he becomes.

In this regard it is important to note that during the Cultural Revolution a certain number of edifices regarded as national symbols were singled out to be razed. These monuments included, for example, the Yumbu-lagang, which is reputed to have been the palace of the first Tibetan king, Nyatri Tsenpo. This very concrete experience, which was and perhaps still is intended mainly to extirpate national sentiments and erase Tibet's national identity, has in fact taught the Tibetans to be more aware of their own culture than ever before.

The Tibetan nationalist's overt consciousness of his own identity is now expressed not only through his Buddhist culture – although Buddhism does largely dominate, since the idea of a Muslim Tibetan is almost unthinkable for Tibetans in general – but also through two secular traditions: epic literature and secular beliefs such as the mountain cult.

Unlike the mountain cult, the former is a written tradition, which has given us the world's longest epic. Epic literature was forbidden in monasteries and looked down on by the Buddhist clergy, but it has become the most popular reading in many parts of Tibet in recent years as a result of a period in which secular literature was encouraged in preference to religious material. The hero of the epic, King Gesar, the elected king, is in fact the personification of the ideal Tibetan man, that is to say a man who can perform supernatural feats when engaged in battle. When he is not so engaged, he simply goes into retreat in order to practise meditation as if he were a man of religion. It is evident that the stories of his conquest of different countries and his other heroic exploits, however fictitious they may be, have contributed to the awakening of the national consciousness, as have depictions of the characteristic boldness of the Khamba warriors and their patriotism. But it is particularly the literary and poetic language in which the epic is written, as well as the ideas it expresses, that illustrate Tibet's cultural identity.

During my research mission in Amdo in 1985 and in Lhasa in 1987, I noticed not only the abundance of printed copies of the epic literature, but also audio cassettes containing entire episodes of the epic, retold by famous bards. Posters showing different characters from the epic were also available in bookshops and markets, although some of this proliferation reflects to some extent the interest of the propaganda machine in this epic. The most glamorous printed poster was often not of King Gesar but of his elder half-brother, Gyatsha Zhalkar, whose mother is supposed to be Chinese, as is clear from his name. One of the characteristic elements which has contributed towards enhancing cultural unification among Tibetans is King Gesar's worship of Mount Gedzo, adjacent to Amye Machen. The early kings, who ruled the Tibetan empire at its height, regarded Mount Yarlha Shampo as their ancestral deity (*sku-bla, gtsug-gi-lha*). King Gesar, too, considers the deity of this mountain as his celestial father, in the same way as the Golok people in Amdo regard Amye Machen as their grandfather.

Here follows a short ethnographic description of the mountain cult, which belongs to what I call the 'unwritten tradition of the laity'. This is because neither Buddhist nor Bonpo clergy have any significant role in the cult, although it represents a supremely important element underlying Tibet's national identity. By the mountain cult I mean particularly the secular worship of the mountain divinity (*yul-lha, gzhi-bdag*), who is usually depicted in the style of a traditional warrior and is worshipped as an ancestor or an ancestral divinity for protection. This secular worship is in contrast to the cult of such mountains as Mount Tsari for Buddhists, Mount Kongpo Bonri for the Bonpo, or Mount Tise (Kailash) for both faiths. These mountains are designated as *gnas-ri*, 'holy or sacred mountains' and, being the object of Buddhist veneration, usually abound with small monasteries and hermitages on their peripheries. On important days, they often swarm with hermits and pilgrims performing circumambulations as a spiritual exercise. This type of mountain cult originates in Buddhism with its idea of devotional exercise, and so embodies no specific Tibetan ideas in its representations whereas the origin of the cult of *yul-lha*-type mountain divinities pre-dates the Buddhist era. The *yul-lha*-type mountains therefore do not attract devotees in a purely religious sense – for example, no circumambulations are performed around them. On the contrary, they are worshipped by the layman who may be a hunter or a trader concerned with purely mundane affairs, as we shall see.

The manner in which this type of mountain cult is practised varies from region to region, but the central idea remains the same everywhere. During my research mission in Amdo in 1985, I was able to make some observations of one such mountain-cult ritual in a region known by Amdowas as Sharkhog, or, in Central Tibet, as Zongchu. This region lies to the south-east of Amdo just to the north of the Chinese town of Songpan and is included in the present administrative unit of the Aba (Ngaba) Autonomous Prefecture under the Sichuan provincial government. Songpan is an important trade centre, situated as it is on the threshhold of the main and narrow route leading from the south-east of Amdo to Sichuan province proper. A Dunhuang document states that the Tibetan army first penetrated the area in AD 701.[7]

The people of this region are known locally as Sharwa, a term derived from the local name of the region, Sharkhog. Our historian (Gendun Chomphel) Gedun Choephel has suggested that most of these Amdo people are descendants of the royal army from Central Tibet who came to the area in the 7th century,[8] an idea which seems to fit the Dunhuang records. The population of the region, who are sedentary, number around 24,000, according to the local administrative authority.[9]

The predominant religion of the Sharwa is Bon, but small pockets of Gelugpa and Sakyapa followers are also found in the area. Villages used to be grouped according to a political federation system in which from four to seven villages, with a sacred mountain and a monastery for education and religious gathering, comprised a federation. Each federation had its own leaders as well as social and political institutions: elected council, militia for self-defence (each family needed to have a good horse and a gun ready whenever required) and a general assembly of adult men. Like most parts of Amdo, the region of Sharkhog was a semi-independent principality before 1950; it paid no kind of tax either to Central Tibet or to the local Chinese authorities. The historic relationship between this Tibetan region and the local Chinese town is one of conflict. The region was totally unknown to Westerners since no Christian missionaries penetrated there as they did in Tachienlu (*Dar-rtse-mdo*) or Bathang in Kham; and the few Western travellers who went there early in the 20th century either ventured no further than Songpan or just passed through the region without taking much interest.

The local social and political organisation of Sharkhog was, of course, completely shattered after the 1960s. Previously, there were annual religious and secular festivals which took place either at village, federal or regional levels. Each federation had a different date for its own festivals. During one of these festivals, which I witnessed in 1985, it was the mountain cult that reminded me of my own participation in such a ritual in my childhood. The ritual was forbidden from as early as 1960 and only re-instated in 1983; we know why it was so feared. The prohibition was so ferocious that in Sharkhog even the cairn on the mountain was scraped out.

The festival takes place on the 15th day of the sixth month and lasts two days. Only men take part, and in the ritual I observed in 1985 there were about 200. On the first day, the men gather together with their horses and tents on a plateau in front of the sacred mountain. Each man must bring an arrow (*mda'-rgod*) 5 or 6 metres long, which has been prepared in advance (fig. 1) and which is made from an entire young pine tree cut down in nearby forests (fig. 2). Early in the morning of the second day the men begin to climb the mountain with their arrows, at first on horseback and then on foot, until they reach the cairn high up on the mountain. At the cairn, a fumigation offering (*bsang*) takes place before the ritual of planting the arrows in the cairn; this is then followed by the scattering of what are known as 'wind-horses' (*rlung-rta*). These pictures of wind-horses, printed on small, white squares, are launched in their thousands by each participant into the wind, which carries them into the air like a multitude of tiny kites.

Whilst scattering the 'wind-horses' each person, at the top of his voice and in total disregard of others, beseeches the mountain divinity for his personal protection and for the realisation of other particular ambitions, or asks simply for help in subduing his enemy (fig. 3). Indeed, this cacophonic uproar on the summit of the mountain has a very strange ring. The ritual then concludes with oratorical speeches, songs and dances, horse-races and a shooting contest (this last is now no longer included).

The arrow is man's symbol and the ritual gesture of planting it in the cairn places each man who does so under the mountain divinity's protection; in the same way, by ritually scattering the 'wind-horse' – itself a symbol of fortune – into the air, each man calls upon the mountain divinity to increase his fortune, since it is the divinity who is regarded as the giver of glory, honour, fame, prosperity, power and progeny. Participation in such a ritual therefore implies total integration into the community: this in turn implies inherited social and political obligation, moral and individual responsibility, and an affirmation of communal and national solidarity in the face of external aggression. By the same token,

Above and opposite page: The mountain-cult ritual at Sharkhog in July 1985. (*Samten Karmay*)

internal conflict and disunity engender the withdrawal of the divinity's favour which will affect the power and prosperity of the community.

The mountain cult in Tibetan culture therefore plays a very significant role in the building up of national identity through each individual's identification of himself as an active member of the community and as a patriot of the nation. This notion is at work in the functioning of the social and political organisations in Tibetan society. It is in fact a survival of the ancient tradition which the spread of Buddhism never totally effaced. Indeed, it is deeply rooted and more marked among Tibetan communities in the border areas, where the Bon religion is often dominant and where encounters with people of different cultures who display their own national aggressivity are a daily experience.

According to theories of nationalism and identity, it is consensus, not ethnography, which is at the basis of the state.[10] In other words, the essential factors are will and determination rather than facts such as having a separate language and writing, literature and history, economy and geography, custom and belief. However, in Tibet's national identity, basic elements such as religious culture, secular literature and popular beliefs have not only helped to engender Tibetan identity but also exert a political force in its aspiration to regain independence.

NOTES

1. Claude Lévi-Strauss, *L'Identité*, Paris 1977, Preface. Translation by present author.
2. S.G. Karmay, 'King Tsa/Dza and Vajrayana' in *Tantric and Taoist Studies in Honour of R.A. Stein*, Brussels, 1981, vol. 1 (Mélanges chinois et bouddhiques, vol. XX), p. 207.
3. On this mountain, see S.G. Karmay, 'A Pilgrimage to Kongpo Bon-ri' in *Proceedings of the Vth International Seminar on Tibetan Studies*, Naritasan, Japan, 1989.
4. J. Bacot, F.W. Thomas and Ch. Toussaint, *Documents de Touen-houang relatifs au Tibet*, Paris, 1940, pp. 81, 86.
5. The *Blon-po bka'-thang*, which is said to have been rediscovered by O-rgyan gling-pa (1323–74), contains such indications that could be considered as of ancient origin (*bKa'-thang sde-lnga*, Mi-rigs dpe-skrun-khang, 1986, pp. 437–9).
6. Tokan Tada, *The Thirteenth Dalai Lama*, East Asian Cultural Studies Series, no. 9 (Tokyo, 1972), p. 72.
7. J. Bacot *et al., op. cit.*, p. 39.
8. *Bod chen-po'i srid lugs dang 'brel-ba'i rgyal-rabs deb-ther dkar-po*, mKhas-dbang dge-'dun chos-'phel-gyi gsung-rtsom phyogs-sgrig, Chengdu, 1988, p. 41.
9. A more detailed anthropological study of this population and of the country, in collaboration with my French colleague Philippe Sagant, is under way, and we hope to publish it in the near future.
10. E. Gellner, *Culture, Identity and Politics*, London, 1987, pp. 9 ff.; *Nations and Nationalism*, Oxford, 1983, pp. 53 ff.

TIBETAN PUBLICATIONS AND NATIONAL IDENTITY

Heather Stoddard

THE YEAR OF THE WATER PIG

In the year of the pig I went home
I thought to meet my parents
I saw but ruins everywhere
My country a nightmare from hell
My country
Full of soldiers, the city of Lhasa a wall of blood
Amdo full of Chinese
This land is a prison
The East divided above, divided below
My country
Chakpori is earth and stone, Ganden a tomb
Human rights the soles of boots
The heart of the religion of man is at the crossroads
The paradise of the red god is a pattern on water.
My parents' eyes are filled with tears
Their brief testament:
Trust not the red man – your heart will cleave in two.
The honey of today is tomorrow's poison –
Keep that in mind.
My country is a ruin
My parents innocent prisoners.[1]

Introduction

Given the question of Tibetan national identity during the period 1950-90, it may seem rather timidly Tibetological to have chosen to answer the question. 'What is national identity?' by examining literary output. It is not so much the question of literature as that of publications which is relevant here. The choices that a literate society makes, and the censorship it imposes on those who wish to express themselves in writing, reflect to a large degree the ideals and aspirations of that society.

The Tibetans in the diaspora are busily occupied with salvaging their cultural tradition and diffusing the *Dharma* in the West, while the constraints imposed on editors in the People's Republic of China, both Tibetan and Chinese, have been so great that we should expect almost no independent activity at all. Choosing to look at the literature they have produced, however, does offer great potential for exploring the nuances of development in Tibetan consciousness on both sides of the Himalayas. The sources for this study are in fact extensive and largely unexamined, and have the makings of a book rather than a short chapter. This paper treats essentially the situation inside the People's Republic, and of course specifically the high Tibetan Plateau, with only very short general observations on the diaspora.

First of all, if there be a national identity, then there must be a nation. When Ernest Renan (1823–92) asked, in his *Discours et Conferences*, 'What is a nation?', he gave the following definition:

A nation is a soul or spiritual principle. These are but two aspects of the same thing. One is in the past, the other in the present. One is the common possession of a rich legacy of memories; the other is the present consent, the desire to live together, the wish to continue to assert the undivided heritage that has been handed down. A nation is therefore a huge solidarity, constituted by the feeling of sacrifices that have been made, and which will continue to be made. It supposes a past, but it nevertheless comes down to the present in a tangible fact: the consent, the clearly expressed desire to continue living together.[2]

According to this definition, Tibet stands at the present time as a nation. The rich legacy of memories and the clearly expressed will to continue to live together are both undeniably present. It is a divided nation, but the last few years have clearly shown that the 'consent' is there.

One of the richest remaining expressions of the Tibetan past is its literature. There is a veritable ocean of Tibetan literary expression, linking countless individuals through thirteen centuries and across much of Inner Asia, within a cultural ethos whose fundamental view is that of Mahayana Buddhism. This inherently universal idea of existence goes beyond specific national and cultural boundaries, but in as much as the vehicle used in its transmission is the Tibetan language, mastery of which is a prerequisite for understanding that legacy, it remains an essential expression of Tibetan civilisation.

The territory of that civilisation is vast and the population small and scattered. According to one of the best-known Tibetan sayings: *Lung-pa re-re skad-lugs-re/bla-ma re-re chos-lugs-re* – 'To each valley its dialect, to each lama his religion'. A multitude of dialects, many mutually incomprehensible, has developed in Eastern Tibet – in Khams (Kham), A-mdo (Amdo) and rGyal-mo-rong (Gyemorong) – as well as in Central Tibet – in dBus (Ü),

gTsang (Tsang), Lho-kha, Kong-po, Dvags-po (Dagpo) – and in
Western Tibet – in sTod mNga-'ris (Tö Ngari) – and throughout
the nomad lands that spread from Mount Kailash in the extreme
west through the Byang-thang (Changthang) and far up into the
region of the Tshva'i-gdam (Tsaidam) and the great Blue Lake of
mTsho-sngon (Kokonor). Communication through travel, trade
and pilgrimage, and through the congregating within the larger
monasteries of monks from all over the high plateau and beyond
for the study of philosophy and dialectics, allowed for different
levels of standardisation in the spoken language. However, the
essential communication link lay, and still lies, in the written
language, through which a rich body of literature has been created
over the centuries, with the earliest texts dating from the 8th and
9th centuries. Much of this literature remains quite unknown to the
outside world.

The will or consent to continue to live together, stated in these
terms whether in writing or in speech, is a new phenomenon related
to historical events that have taken place over the years since 1950.
This must be the most critical period in the history of Tibet. Only
once before, during the expansion of the Mongol empire in the
13th century, has the distinct cultural entity that is Tibet been faced
with a situation so grave, involving its possible extinction. But
during this period the threat has been threefold: weighty ideological
opposition from the occupying power, massive population influx
from China and the pressures of the modern 20th-century world.
That is why this period has also seen the conscious desire for self-
determination come to the fore, and why this desire is expressed
with particular energy by those who are inside Tibet, where tensions reach their highest point.

The members of a traditional society express their identity and
particular role or place of origin clearly in the robes or adornments
they wear, in the type of dwellings in which they live and in the
functions they occupy. However, it is not until they go outside that
tradition or are forced to come to terms with it because of external
aggression that they realise its existence.

The civilisation that the outside world calls Tibet is a distinct
cultural entity, a high-altitude civilisation, which has functioned
uninterruptedly since the 7th century AD, and which is circum-
scribed and protected by a specific geographical environment. It
is also a civilisation defined by its relations with its northern
(Mongol) and eastern (Chinese and Manchu) neighbours. This relationship was directed, from the 13th to the early 20th centuries,
through a specific, privileged alliance, that of 'priest and patron',
which, in spite of contention concerning the relative status of each

party, functioned remarkably well over the centuries, over vast territories, and without the need for armed confrontation.

The whole basis of this relationship changed radically when the Younghusband invasion of 1904 provoked a violent reaction from the Manchu (Qing) Empire. The Sichuanese General Zhao Erfeng arrived in Eastern Tibet in 1905 to undertake, as an officially condoned project, the extermination of the Tibetan clergy and the Buddhist religion, the assimilation of Tibetan territory into regular provinces of the Manchu empire, and the repopulation of the Tibetan Plateau with the poor peasants of Sichuan. This was the first concrete attempt at assimilation in the history of Sino-Tibetan relations. When Zhao Erfeng entered Tibet through Khamba territory, the Khambas suffered most keenly, but during the following decades the Amdowas suffered as well, because it was the whole of Eastern Tibet that was most accessible to the Manchus – and later to the Republican Chinese. Central Tibet, being two to three months' caravan travel from the nearest point in China, was well protected: which is why the Tibetan Government remained in what might be called slothful rather than innocent bliss until 1950. That is also why there developed in Eastern Tibet both major resistance and the first stirrings of a national consciousness. This was first expressed in terms of Eastern Tibet alone, and subsequently in terms of a re-unification of the whole of the Tibetan Plateau as a *Bod Chen-po* (Great Tibet), as it was at the time of the Yarlung Dynasty. The Eastern Tibetan proposals, which also demanded the establishment of a new type of political regime, were rebuffed and rebuked time and again in the 1930s and 1940s by the Tibetan Government in Lhasa.

It is necessary to address this problem of profound regional separation in order to grasp the weakness of the Tibetans at the time of the invasion in 1950, and thus to evaluate the different developments both inside and outside Tibet following that date. It is a problem that the exile Tibetan Government has preferred to put aside, along with any serious debate on the historical questions that have laid the foundations for the present crisis of national identity and survival. It is the same basic problem that the government of the People's Republic of China turned to its own advantage right from the outset, using the precedent conceived in the Republican period, by which the three major traditional provinces of Central Tibet, Amdo and Kham were carved up and redistributed among the four Chinese provinces of Sichuan, Yunnan, Qinghai and Gansu, and the Tibet Autonomous Region. The new administrative divisions have underlined and exacerbated the internal regional divisions among the Tibetan people, and nascent national sentiment has been accordingly diluted and deflected.

After Zhao Erfeng failed in his attempt at the violent assimilation of Tibet, and was beheaded at the fall of the Manchu Empire, another Sichuanese – a warlord of the Republican period, Liu Wenhui, who was much more of a Confucian gentleman – decided that it would be better to assimilate Tibet through education. No doubt he was inspired also by Chiang Kai-shek, for he estimated that through education 'within 10 to 20 years the people will have forgotten even the names of the minority groups.'[3] Liu Wenhui, who operated in Kham in the 1930s and 1940s, revealed in this bald statement not only the continuing intentions of the Chinese for the complete assimilation of Tibet from the start of the 20th century, culminating in the total effacement of all specific cultural identity during the Cultural Revolution, but also the enormity of the misunderstanding among cultured Chinese of non-Chinese people.

In the period preceding 1950 several factors are present: the concept of Tibetan identity was already awake in the eastern part of the plateau, and although many well-to-do families had previously sent their children to China for a modern education, they took an ambiguous stand that included both sympathy for the new democratic and socialist ideologies and a certain awareness of the dangers presented by the assimilation that had motivated all the recently attempted Chinese interventions in Tibet. In Central Tibet, on the other hand, a number of progressive nobles had also been looking outwards, both to China and to India, where they had been sending their children for education in British schools. They were also in an ambiguous position with regard to both the British and the Chinese.

The Tibetan people at large were aware essentially of two types of identity: religious and regional affiliation. People belonged to a particular school or monastery, looked up to a particular religious leader, and owed allegiance, often of life and death, to their own regional group, be it a valley, a confederation or a region. At the outside they considered themselves as members of one of the three *chol-ka* or provinces, as *Khams-pa* (Khamba), or *A-mdo-ba* (Amdowa), or Central Tibetan, and within the latter region as *dBus-pa* (Ü-pa), *gTsang-pa* (Tsangpa) or *sDod-pa* (Dö-pa – those from the south-western regions). The general appellation of *Bod-pa* (Pö-pa) or Tibetan, as it is used today, indicated specifically the Central Tibetans, as against Eastern. All, however, spoke a dialect of Tibetan – *Bod-skad* (Pö-ke), as they would call it – and those who were literate wrote in the common language of literary Tibetan.

Thus, in the first half of the 20th century, encouraged by the example of the 13th Dalai Lama, or awakened to new things by their experience in the outside world, a small number of progressive Tibetans, often living on the periphery, began to express new ideas in writing. The first newspaper in Tibetan, written in *dbu-med* (ü-me) or cursive script, was published in 1904, not by a Tibetan but by the Moravian missionary, A.H. Francke, in Ladakh. It was called the *La-Dvags kyi ak-bar* (the *Ladakh News*), and had the aim of presenting a new type of non-religious secular writing which was in correct classical Tibetan but close to the colloquial language.[4] Then, in Kalimpong, in 1926 another missionary, this time a Bhotia from Kunawar called Tharchin, put out the first cyclostyled edition of his Tibetan newspaper, the *gSar-gyur me-long* (the *News Mirror*). Although Tharchin's long-term intentions, like Francke's, were those of awakening the flock to the truths of Christianity, thus largely restricting the real impact of his newspaper, he provided a unique forum in which other Tibetans could express their ideas on politics, science and history. It was in the *Me-long* that the first articles on early Tibetan history by dGe-'dun Chos-'phel (Gendun Choephel) appeared in the 1930s, as well as political declarations by Tibetans who were close to China and sympathetic to Republican ideas, such as Rab-dga' sPom-mda'-tshang (Ranga Pangdatsang).[5] The *Me-long* is a mine of information on events in Central Asia and the Himalayas in the mid-20th century.[6]

Another example of the early awakening of national identity is in the ancient name for Tibet: *Bod* (Pö). Its use can be observed in 1935 among the Khambas when Sangs-rgyas Ye-shes (Sangye Yeshe, later called Tian Bao, who was to become the Chairman of the TAR in 1979) formed, not as we might expect the first 'Khamba', but the first 'Pö-pa' Communist area in dKar-mdzes (Kanze) in Kham. Then, accompanied by his 'Independent Pö-pa division', he marched to join Mao Zedong at Yan'an.[7] It is very important to keep in mind here that in the *Soviet Constitution of China*, dated 1931, the political theory for the future People's Republic allowed, in imitation of the Soviet model, full rights of secession, self-government and self-determination for each ethnic group or nationality. All those who so desired were to be given full freedom to form their own state.

Here we can see the power of the written word. When the Eastern Tibetans sympathised with and joined the Communist movement in China, they must have been inspired and motivated by this Soviet vision of the future. Already, only one year later, there appear the first demands by the Khambas to form a separate state between Tibet and China. These demands were stifled, but they gave rise, or so it seems, to the fictitious province that was named by the Chinese 'Sikang' (literally 'West Kham', as opposed to 'West Tibet' or 'Xizang', as Central Tibet was called by the Republican Chinese and still is by the Communists). Was the creation of Sikang on the Republican maps a Chinese attempt to counteract what was designed by the Khambas to be a separate state? Had the Khamba aspirations to a Soviet model been scrapped on the way by the Republicans and turned into what they projected as a regular Chinese province? We have seen what Liu Wenhui thought about the assimilation of non-Chinese. Furthermore, throughout the 1930s and 1940s, the scheme was rubbished by both the Tibetan Government in Lhasa and by the British.

We may go on from this introduction to ask the following question: in what ways are the Tibetan people, under the present highly stressful circumstances, expressing that solidarity and that consent to live as a nation to which Renan referred? And what ways are open to us in the attempt to evaluate the evolution of that expression during the years since 1950?

Until 1959, many of the contemporary Tibetan scholars whom we know today were still inside Tibet, living in a society that functioned essentially along traditional lines. Except for a few outstanding individuals, such as Lu-khang-ba, there were few in the Tibetan Government who spoke up in public against the Chinese presence. Society continued, to all intents and purposes, to function as before. The Seventeen Point Agreement, signed on May 23, 1951, guaranteed, on paper at least, that this should be so.

From 1959 there followed twenty years during which Tibet became more hermetically sealed than ever before, and any information that was gleaned came through the opaque filter of Chinese Communist and Cultural Revolution propaganda. Along with the China watchers, a few Tibet watchers tried to grasp what might actually be going on by looking in the very small spaces between the lines of the endlessly repetitive and stereotyped clichés of the Chinese press.

From 1978 onwards the situation began to improve, beginning with the release of political prisoners, many of whom had been interned since 1959. A number of Western scholars were lucky enough to visit the high plateau during the 1980s, and even to carry out research there. I myself went six times between 1982 and 1992, for a total of twelve months, spanning the very beginning of the relaxation of tension, the short period of relative freedom that led up to the outbreak of anti-Chinese demonstrations in 1987, and the following rise in tension and violence. It is thus possible for me to draw some conclusions on that particular time partly from first-hand experience.

In Marxist societies in their most totalitarian phases, the efface-ment of external distinctions – whether of social or ritual roles, or of regional costume and adornment – is pursued to the limit. Indi-viduality is criticised as bourgeois and reactionary and traditional customs are considered backward, superstitious and feudalistic. Even traditional dwellings, considered unhygienic in the PRC, have been and still are bulldozed to make way for the construction of identical concrete blocks of flats. Under such circumstances what means are there for people to express their own identity? Language, literature and religion come to the fore as the focus of national expression. In traditional Tibet immense sacred value was placed on the written word. A piece of writing was never knowingly destroyed or placed on the ground; this very sacredness encouraged the Chinese during the Cultural Revolution to use holy texts as soles for shoes and *ma-ni* stones for paving toilets. It is remarkable that when the refugees escaped over the Himalayas to India many of them carried on their backs heavy loads of sacred books, and one of the first activities in the diaspora was the republication of these religious texts. Since the early 1960s, this activity has seen the reproduction of thousands of volumes from every school of Tibetan Buddhism, as well as of Bon. Buddhism has come to be the major expression of Tibetan identity in the outside world and Tibetan lamas are busily occupied with the enormous task of the transmission of Vajrayana to the West, as their legacy to the world. Translations into Western languages are increasing day by day.

In the PRC, however, all publications were directed towards a different end: that of changing radically the existing political system, of enforcing a new type of education, of educating the masses in Marxism–Leninism and of creating the conditions for mass indoctrination. All discussion and thinking that did not con-tribute to the creation of the ideal socialist paradise was banned as reactionary or counter-revolutionary.

As we have seen, Tibetan society on the eve of the Chinese inva-sion was not quite as homogeneously traditional as we sometimes might like to believe. The absence of any real occupying imperial power (compared to other countries of Asia) had retarded the formation of a new intelligentsia who might have been capable of formulating and imposing Tibetan national interests in the inter-national arena. Nevertheless, the processes of change and adapta-tion to the 20th century had already quietly begun under the 13th Dalai Lama. It is clear that when the Chinese arrived in Lhasa in 1951 a number of progressivist Tibetan intellectuals were already prepared to set up translation committees capable of putting into concise modern Tibetan the thoughts of Marx, Engels, Lenin and Mao Zedong. There is no doubt at all that these new Tibetans were inspired by the ideals of socialism and by the fundamental rights of nations as expressed in such publications as the *Constitution of the PRC* (Beijing, 1954) and the *Text of the Policy for the National Minorities* (Beijing, 1952).[8] By the early 1940s, Sun Yat-sen's *sanminzhiyi* – the 'Three Principles of the People' – had already been translated into Tibetan. The translation is claimed to have been made by two of the leading Eastern Tibetan intellectuals of the time, the layman and Kuomintang member Rab-dga' sPom-mda'-tshang (Ranga Pangdatsang) of Mar-khams (Markham) in Kham, founder of the Tibet Progressive Party, and the *dge-lugs-pa* teacher *dge-bshes* Shes-rab rGya-mtsho (Geshe Sherab Gyatso), of rDo-dbyis (Do-ji) in Amdo, who was to become, for many years, Chairman of the All China Buddhist Association of the PRC.[9]

The Khambas had been rebuffed by the *bde-ba-gzhung* (the Dewa Shung, or Cabinet) in Lhasa in their attempts to awaken Tibetans to the profound changes taking place in the world outside, and in their evolving demands which now called for the unification of the provinces of Eastern Tibet – Kham and Amdo – with Central Tibet; they had turned this way and that through the 1940s, only at the last moment siding with China and helping to set up what was to be the new socialist paradise on the Tibetan Plateau.

My doctoral thesis traces these events outside and inside Tibet during the first half of the 20th century.[10] dGe-'dun Chos-'phel (Gendun Choephel) is the main figure in this story, for he was the first to realise the vital necessity of history – the collective memory of an ancient and glorious past – for the construction of a modern nation, and the importance of critical scientific analysis as a fundamental tool in the acquisition of knowledge. Knowing only too well his own people and their profound religious faith, as well as their equally profound regional divisions, he advocated (jokingly) uniting them by first taking the most revered statue of Tibetan Buddhism, the *Jo-bo* (Jo-wo) of the *Jo-khang* in Lhasa, and placing it in a new temple at the junction of the three provinces of dBus-gTsang, Khams and A-mdo, which lies at sKye-sku-mdo (Jyekundo, now called Yushu by the Chinese). Having done that, he said, we shall then set about destroying religion. In dGe-'dun Chos-'phel's eyes, Buddhism had destroyed Tibetan national identity. Among those who joined the translation bureaux in the early 1950s were several of his close disciples.[11]

PUBLICATIONS INSIDE TIBET

1950–66: Establishing the Marxist society

When the PLA marched into Lhasa in 1950, led by 'Ba'-ba Phun-tshogs dBang-rgyal (Baba Phuntsog Wangyal), one of the first Tibetan Communists, many of the progressive Tibetans went straight over to the Chinese side and started working, as we have said, as translators for them. While the old Tibetan society con-tinued to print its own monastic publications, the translation com-mittees began to publish works on Marxism, socialist reform, economic policy, and so on. In Amdo, where the number of early publications on economics and politics is indicative of the presence of a group of progressive Eastern Tibetan intellectuals, their con-cern for Tibetan identity is clear from the publication of Tibetan grammars, and of the first set of modern textbooks for Amdowa children. Religion was eclipsed and science was introduced: Tibet had launched itself into the translation of an entirely new ideology. This was the second time in Tibetan history that such a feat had been attempted: the importation of Mahayana Buddhism had been admirably accomplished between the 7th and 12th centuries. Now Marxism–Leninism was to be introduced, but in a much shorter period of time.

In order to create the new idiom and the new terminology that were required, Tibetan scholars used three processes: they trans-cribed Chinese terms phonetically (these are relatively few); they translated directly from Chinese, using the same semantic elements; or, most often, they created new vocabulary directly from the rich fund of classical Tibetan. In the beginning, the translations of both Marxist and Chinese texts on science and economics were made by anonymous collectives and committees. The austere white book-covers were adorned only with red titles, and the text was printed in excellent quality Tibetan metal type, with various calligraphic styles. Even reproduction rights were mentioned.

An example of such a book is the *Mi-rigs srid-jus kyi yig-cha* (the *Text of the Policy for the National Minorities*) which was published in Tibetan in 1952 with a print run of 15,000 by the Nationalities Affairs Commission of the Central People's Govern-ment.[12] In this publication – produced only one year after the Seventeen Point Agreement – the earlier provision for the right of secession from the PRC that Mao had included in his draft consti-tutions has disappeared. The text, however, speaks in concise and clear modern Tibetan of equality among the different nationalities in the PRC, of the their right to autonomy and to the development of their specific regions, of friendship, solidarity, patriotism and internationalism, and of the need for liberation from foreign imperialism. Despite this clarity, one feels that the language is already somewhat weighed down with the repetitions and formulae that are to become clichés repeated *ad infinitum*, almost as if they were *mantra*s of the Marxist dogma.

1966–79: 'The Great Proletarian Cultural Revolution'

The Cultural Revolution and its aftermath brought the destruction of an estimated 95 per cent of the cultural heritage of Tibet. I have been to Tibet four times, travelling extensively through Amdo, Gyarong and Central Tibet, and sincerely believe that this figure is not an exaggerated one.

In terms of literary and artistic activity, this period is one of the leanest in the recent history of mankind, and certainly in the histories of both China and Tibet. For over a decade practically all publication came to a standstill. If we are to believe the propaganda organs, indoctrination was intensive and focussed to the extent that the intellectual effort of the entire population of the PRC was centred almost completely on the memorising, reproduction and endless discussion of the works of Chairman Mao, who had seen in the unlettered peasant masses of China an unwritten page on which to imprint his own revolutionary dogma. This policy was applied to the same degree all over the Tibetan Plateau. Images of nomads of the Changthang gathered in circles, studying the Word after a day's herding, became commonplace in the glossy propaganda magazines that were translated into a large number of languages, and which gave the world the desired image of the New China. The extent to which the propaganda was accepted in the West is astounding, underlining the power of repetition as both a religious and political device.

Newspapers and journals in Tibet were limited to a few official organs such as the *Bod-ljongs nyin-re'i tshags-par* (*Tibet Daily*), *Dar-dmar* (*Red Flag*), *Krung-go brnyan-par* (*China Pictorial*) and *Mi-rigs brnyan-par* (*Minorities Magazine*), the contents of which were simple translations of official centralised policy distributed from Beijing. Even economic, agricultural and pastoral questions were subordinated to the absolute necessity of strict adherence to whichever line was politically correct at each given moment.

Tibet became more closed and impenetrable than ever before. For the twenty years between 1959 and 1979, but especially between 1966 and 1978, it was not known whether people in Tibet were dead or alive.

At this time Tibetan studies in many Western universities were considered essentially to be the privilege of a chosen few, who treated the subject as the Latin of Central Asia. Tibetan was a dead language, interesting only as a branch of Buddhist studies, and Tibet was a civilisation eclipsed. At the first seminar I attended as a student at the School of Oriental and African Studies in London there were five lecturers and only one student. The only texts deemed acceptable were Buddhist translations. Two or three years later we were three students, and we made a little revolution when we asked to read the *Deb-ther sngon-po* (*The Blue Annals*), and the *Mi-la-ras-pa'i gur-'bum* (*The 100,000 Songs of Milarepa*, also known as the *gSung-gur*) as part of the curriculum. In 1968, in England as in China, indigenous Tibetan literature was considered to be of no value whatsoever.

The vast majority of Tibetan monastic libraries, manuscripts, woodblock prints and the woodblocks themselves were burnt, buried, made into the soles of shoes, used for toilet paper, for building and so forth. The last great library burning was reported as late as 1978, in Phenpo, north of Lhasa, where the fire from burning books and xylographic woodblocks lasted for three weeks.

1978–90: The New Nationalities Policy

The new nationalities policy officially began with the first release of political prisoners in 1978 and the opening of one or two major monasteries. With Hu Yaobang's visit to Tibet in May 1980 the liberalisation policy seemed to be genuinely under way.

For Tibetans all over the plateau it would appear that this important development had started some time earlier, an indication perhaps that the centralisation policy of the PRC was less effective at this time. On October 14, 1975, the 'First Co-operative Conference of the Five Provinces and Regions' was convened in Lhasa to discuss the collective translation and publication of Tibetan-language books. This appears quite remarkable given the political context, though it is not surprising to learn that its objective was 'to encourage the translation and publication of books in minority languages, under the guidance of Marxist, Leninist and Mao Zedong Thought, while taking the party's basic line as a key link'.[13] This was a year before the death of Mao, at a time when the Gang of Four was prominent and Jiang Qing, the 'dauntless warrior', was implementing her programme of activities in the field of Literature and Art. Under the benevolent wing of the Party's Democratic Centralism, publications were still minimal and art consisted of a handful of Jiang Qing's revolutionary ballets, such as *The White-Haired Girl, Taking Tiger Mountain by Strategy* and *The Red Detachment of Women*. This was towards the end of the Cultural Revolution but still two years before the human rights question came to the fore for the first time following the protests in Tiananmen Square, and three years before Chinese writers and artists took up activities after twelve years of interruption.[14] Yet in 1975 Tibetan scholars were quietly getting together to organise a publication programme for the whole of the Tibetan population in the PRC.

Both politically and from the standpoint of the development of national identity, this last period of reconstruction and re-affirmation of Tibetan culture may be broken down into two phases. The first phase, 1978–87, is characterised by the reconstruction of monasteries and temples all over the plateau, as well as the publication of classical Tibetan texts and new literary works. The second phase, 1987–90, saw outbreaks of demonstrations, demands for independence, and the recommencement of reprisals and repression. Lhasa was under martial law for the year before the summer of 1990, being lifted in May of that year apparently to allow for the partial resumption of the tourist trade. Publications continue to come out but the dearth of foreign scholars in Tibet made it much more difficult to obtain books, periodicals and information concerning them.

In 1990–2 the character of publications changed as a more aggressive economic climate developed in Tibet, with the implementation in early 1992 of 'fast-track' economic reforms and 'opening up'. In certain ways less attention was paid to the quality of publications: there seemed, for example, to be fewer notes, colophons or well-documented introductions. In Beijing the Tibetology Institute, which had produced, using computer technology, the first volume of a comparative text of the Kanjur, sought to establish a lead in the field of Tibetan studies in the PRC. In Tibet private funds had to be found in order to publish even the most scientific works, while teachers were encouraged to raise money by running food stalls, to the detriment of their academic work.

During this period there occurred a number of important events connected both with questions of national identity and with publications, namely the founding of the University of Tibet in Lhasa in 1985; the establishment of five schools of Buddhist study, one in Beijing and the others in places associated with important traditional monastic centres over the whole plateau – Nechung, Dzogchen, Dartsedo and Labrang; and the official announcement, in July 1986, that Tibetan would be the first official language of the TAR.

The implementation of this new law would not be easy: Tibetan culture has been presented as backward and second-rate for over thirty years, and habits, fear and incomprehension remain obstructions to the realisation of this ruling. But a new principle had thereby been established.

Presenting the official point of view, 1978–90. From 1978 publications outlining the new policy, in Chinese or in Tibetan translated from Chinese, give a glimpse of the official point of view. In 1980, a series of speeches on the 'Tibet Question' was published in *Construct New Tibetan Responsibility and Work Means* (Chinese: *Jianshe xin Xizang de renwu he fangzhen*) by the Nationalities Affairs Commission in Beijing. The second of these was the speech, *Six Necessary Tasks for the Construction of Tibet*, given by Hu Yaobang in Lhasa to the Assembly of Cadres on his 1980 visit to Tibet, when he discovered the appallingly backward conditions.

In his speech he underlines as the first task the necessity for real autonomous power of decision, 'without which', he notes, 'the unity of the nationalities is impossible.' In the fifth task he evokes the value of Tibetan civilisation. 'It is erroneous to denigrate it', he says, adding that 'it merits research and development.' He declares the education system to be bad, stresses the need to organise universities and schools and declares that 'it must be made obligatory for the Chinese cadres to learn both spoken and written Tibetan.' He also stated that they should respect Tibetan customs, history and culture.

All the while the government made sure that no-one would mistakenly think of Tibet as being anything but an inalienable part of China. Publications supporting the Chinese views of history, society and religion were regularly published. Among these were *On Some Principle Points of the Nationalities Theory and Certain Questions of the Nationalities Policy* (Chinese: *Guanyu minzu lilun he minzu zhengce de ruogan wenti*; Tibetan: *Mi-rigs kyi rigs-pa'i gzhung-lugs dang mi-rigs srid-jus skor gyi gnaddon kha-shas*) by Li Weihan, published in 1980, and in 1983 the *Selected Contributions on the Question of Intellectuals* (Chinese: *Zhishifenxi wenti wenxian xuanbian*; Tibetan: *Shes-yon-can gyi gnas-don skor gyi tshad-ldan yig-cha bdam-bsgrigs*) was translated into Tibetan. In *Who's Who in the History of the National Minorities of China* (*Zhongguo shaoshu minzu lishi renwuzhi*, Beijing, 1983), out of a total of 140 entries only ten Tibetans were named.

Also in 1983 *A History of the Relations between the Nationalities of China: Selected Essays* (Chinese: *Zhongguo minzu guanxi shi. Lunwen xuanji*) was published by the Gansu Minorities Research Department. In 1984, the Tibetan translation of *Feudalistic Super-*

stition and Gods and Demons (Chinese: *Guishen yu fengjian mixin*; Tibetan: *Lha-'dre dang bkas-bkod rgyud 'dzin gyi rmongs-dad*) was published in Qinghai. In 1986 *Collected Materials for the History of the Tibet Region of China* (Tibetan: *Krung-go'i Bod sa-gnas kyi lo-rgyus yig-tshang phyog-btus*) came out in Chengdu, and in the same year *Tibet is an Inalienable Part of China* was issued in Lhasa, in Chinese (*Xizang difang shi Zhongguo bu ke fenge de yibufen*). This last publication lists an impressive array of contributing institutions: the Tibet Academy of Social Sciences (TASS), the Nationalities Research Centre of the Chinese Academy of Social Sciences, the Central Institute of Nationalities and China's No. 2 Institute of History; but no authors are identified. This tradition has continued in the last few years in the area of applied anthropology, with pseudo-scientific statements being published to provide biological arguments for Tibet being part of China.

In 1989 a new series of scientific, historical and social monographs was launched from Lhasa called *The Knowledge of Tibet Series of Booklets* (Tibetan: *Bod-ljongs shes-bya'i deb-tshogs chung-ba*). The subjects have presumably been selected with a view to reinforcing the legitimacy of the present regime. The following volumes are known to have been issued in Chinese, each with the titles on the cover given in Tibetan as well as Chinese:

– *Changes in Tibetan Demography* (Chinese: *Xizang renkou de bianqian*; Tibetan: *Bod-ljongs kyi mi-grangs 'pho-gyur*)
– *The Mon-pa, Luo-ba and Muslims of Tibet* (Chinese: *Xizang jingnei de Bazu, Luobazu he Huizu*; Tibetan: *Bod-ljongs nang-khul gyi Mon-pa rigs dang Lho-pa rigs Hu'i rigs*)
– *Relations between the Centre and the Tibet Region in the Yuan and Ming Dynasties* (Chinese: *Yuan Ming liang dai zhongyang yu Xizang difang de guanxi*; Tibetan: *Yon Ming rgyal-rabs gnyis kyi krung-dbyang dang Bod sa-gnas bar gyi 'brel-ba*)
– *Foundations and Development of the Qing Dynasty Institution of the Amban in Tibet* (Chinese: *Qingchao zhu Zang dachen zhidu de jianli yu yange*; Tibetan: *Ching rgyal-rabs skabs Bod sdod am-ban lam-lugs kyi gsar-'dzugs dang 'phel-rim*).

Tibetan studies. During the 1980s Chinese Tibetologists were at the same time becoming aware of the interest that the outside world invests in Tibet and in Tibetan studies. Although they consider it to be their special field – and indeed they do have special access both to the land and to the resources – they have come to realise that they are far behind their Western colleagues. A serious programme of translation into Chinese of the major works of Western Tibetology was launched in the early 1980s. Sometimes foreign authors who happen to be on their way through Beijing might be astonished to find that their masterpiece has, unknown to them, already been translated into Chinese. Astonishingly, it is through these Chinese publications that the Tibetans in Tibet learn about Western interest in their civilisation. According to an oral communication, Neville Maxwell's *India's China War* (New York, 1970) was translated and the stocks rapidly sold out. Even John Avedon's frankly pro-Tibetan account, *In Exile from the Land of Snows* (New York, 1984), was translated into Chinese in 1988. Through a bureaucratic error, copies of the translation of Avedon's book were placed in a Lhasa bookshop: all copies were sold out in two days, later changing hands unofficially at vastly inflated prices.

Apart from the translations themselves at least three descriptive volumes and a regular bulletin are published which give biographical data of Western Tibetologists and short reviews of books on Tibet written in English, French, German and Italian. The bulletin, published by the Tibet Academy of Social Sciences, is called *Foreign Tibetology* (Chinese: *Guowai Zangxue*; Tibetan: *rGyal-phyi'i Bod-rig-pa'i skor*); the sixth fascicle was issued in 1986. This and *An Outline of Foreign Tibetological Research 1949–1978* (*Guowai xizang yanjiu gaikuang 1949–1978*, Beijing, 1979), plus two other volumes – *Selections from Foreign Tibetology* (*Guowai Zangxue yanjiu xuanyi*, Gansu, 1983) and *Selections from Translations from Foreign Tibetology* (*Guowai Zangxue yanjiu yiwenji*, Lhasa, 1987) – show how seriously Western and Japanese research is taken by Tibetologists in China.

Tibetan Publications, 1978–90.[15] Tibetan editors have also been busy producing books from the five main publishing houses for Tibetan publications in the PRC, which are in Lhasa for the TAR, Chengdu for Kham, and Xining and Lanzhou for Amdo. Beijing produces political texts and many of the major publications. The principal publisher in these five cities is the Minzu Chubanshe (Nationalities Publishing House), although several others, in particular the Chinese Academy of Social Sciences, handle books in Tibetan as well. The following selection also includes some books by Tibetan authors on Tibet but written in Chinese.

EDUCATIONAL MATERIAL

Between 1978 and 1983 over twenty books on grammar, calligraphy, language, poetics and regional dialects were published, as well as a few dictionaries. In 1983 a series of school language textbooks came out. Known as *sKad-yig* (ke-yik), they were published in seven small graded volumes and destined, for the first time, for Tibetan children all over the plateau in junior and middle schools. Published in Lhasa and Chengdu, the textbooks were written by a committee which met in Xining in 1982 under the auspices of the State Nationalities Affairs Commission, and which included 'the comrades responsible for the education [of Tibetan children] in the four provinces [Qinghai, Gansu, Sichuan and Yunnan] and in the Tibet Autonomous Region'. They instituted the series because 'it is very important to develop the education programme, and to encourage and increase the number of educated people, to put into practice the organisation of the five areas of Tibetan population'.[16] The contents of the books are a mixture of traditional Tibetan wisdom and stories, of Chinese morality (both classical and Marxist), of the modern world and of popular science. It would not be surprising to find that some of the participants had also been present at the first publications meeting of the 'Four Provinces and the Tibet Autonomous Region' in 1975.

Since 1983 several other language publications have become indispensable tools for students of Tibetan. The most significant of these is the three-volume *Bod-rGya tshig-mdzod chen-mo* (the *Great Tibetan-Chinese Dictionary*), published in Beijing in 1985. Other specialist dictionaries are on medicine, astrology and Buddhist terminology. Among several volumes of collected wise sayings one is devoted only to those found in the Gesar epic, and another contains nothing but comic proverbs.

From 1980, a variety of manuals of popular science have been published on such subjects as mathematics, physics, chemistry, biology, hygiene, astronautics and photography. From 1981 to 1986 a series of twenty-six or more booklets on modern knowledge was published in Beijing, perhaps mainly destined for middle-school students, under the title *Shes-bya'i zegs-ma* (*Drops of Knowledge*). No. 26 gives world records held by China between 1958 and 1983, ranging from the production of wool, rice and bicycles to sewing machines and books. In 1983, for example, a total of 350,000 titles, amounting altogether to over 5.8 billion copies, were printed in China, according to the booklet. Unfortunately no figures are given for Tibetan titles. In 1987 *Shes-bya'i kun-btus* (*General Knowledge*) was published in Lhasa as a series with more specifically Tibetan content: articles on news and current affairs, legal affairs, agricultural policy, nomads and peasants, culture, Tibetan children of the high plateau, natural resources, general living and knowledge. Control of the content, however, must have remained with the Chinese.

HISTORY

In 1985–6, bSod-nams dBang-'dus (Sonam Wangdu), head of the Archaeological and Art Department in the Norbulingka, published five books on Tibetan monasteries, ancient constructions and prehistoric sites. Much of the work, including accurate floor plans and description of contents, had been done in the early 1960s before the destruction of the majority of the sites during the Cultural Revolution. As a result the information given therein is particularly valuable, although criticisms have been made, including the fact that they were published only in Chinese and not in Tibetan. The main title was *Karuo* (Beijing, 1985), a detailed monograph of the neolithic village that the author excavated in mKhar-ro (Karo) in Kham, and identified as a specific Tibetan Plateau neolithic culture known as *mKhar-ro* after the site. It was accompanied by four separate regional studies published in Lhasa in 1985–6 and edited by bSod-nams dBang-'dus, giving details of historical sites and monuments in the areas of Lhasa, Ne'udong, Dranang and Phyong-rgyas (Chongye).

In this period Dunhuang studies have also been revived, which has allowed for new research to take place on the founding of the Tibetan state and the Yarlung Dynasty period, using as its source the Dunhuang manuscripts and the lithographic inscriptions on the *rdo-ring* stele and the bronze bells found in or near the early temples. Between 1983 and 1984 four publications came out under the editorship of Wang Yao, with the help of other scholars such as Dung-dkar Blo-bzang 'Phrin-las (Dungkar Lobsang Thrinley) and bSod-nams-skyid (Sonam Kyi, a Chinese scholar and wife of the Tibetan grammarian sKal-bzang 'Gyur-med (Kelsang Gyurmed).

In 1983 the *Tufan zhuan* (the annals of the Tang Dynasty) were published in complete Tibetan translation with a Tibetan/Chinese index, as *Thang-yig gsar-rnying las byung-ba'i Bod Chen-po'i srid-lugs (The Political System of Great Tibet according to the Old and New Tang Annals)*, in Qinghai.

Perhaps of greater significance for the study of Tibetan history are the re-publications of Tibetan historical texts. In the following list those which were previously unavailable or rare outside Tibet are marked with an asterisk (*). These extremely rich and valuable sources for Tibetan history will in the next few years allow for considerable advances to be made in research on the ancient and middle periods of Tibetan history:

– **sBa-bzhad (The Chronicles of Ba*, Beijing, 1980) by sBa gSal-snang, final composition *c*.14th century
– *sDe-dge dkar-chag (The Catalogue of the Derge Printing House*,

Chengdu, 1981, 395 pages) includes a list of all woodblocks available in the only surviving traditional printing house on the Tibetan Plateau
- *Deb-ther dmar-po* (*The Red Annals*, Beijing/Lhasa, 1981) by Tshal-pa Kund-dga' rDo-rje, written between 1346 and 1363
- *Deb-ther dmar-po gsar-ma* (*The New Red Annals*, Lhasa, 1982), written by Pan-chen bSod-nams Grags-pa in 1538
- *rGyal-rabs gsal-ba'i me-long* (*The Clear Mirror of the Royal Genealogy*, Beijing, 1982) by Sa-skya bSod-nams rGyal-mtshan, written in bSam-yas in the Earth Dragon year (1328?)
- *rGya-nag chos-byung* (*The History of China*, Chengdu, 1983)
- **Myang chos-byung* (*The History of Myang*, Lhasa, 1983) by Jo-nang Taranatha (1575–1634)
- *Deb-ther sngon-po* (*The Blue Annals*, Chengdu, 1984) by 'Gos lo-tswa-ba gZhon-nu-dpal (1392–1481)
- **rGya-Bod yig-tshang chen-mo* (*The Great History of China and Tibet*, Chengdu, 1985) written by sTag-tshang rDzong-pa dPal-'byor bZang-po in 1434
- *Legs-bshad mdzod* (*A Treasury of Good Sayings: A History of Bon*, Beijing, 1985) by Shar-rdza bKra-shis rGyal-mtshan, 20th century
- *rLangs po-ti bse-ru* (*The History of the Lang Clan*, Lhasa, 1986) written in three sections. Sections 1 and 2 are by rLangs Byang-chub 'Dre-bkol (963–1076), and section 3 is by Phag-mo-gru-pa Byang-chub rGyal-mtshan (1302–73)
- *bKa-'thang sde-lnga* (*The Five Testaments*, Beijing 1986), a *gter-ma* text found by U-rgyan gLing-pa (1329–67)
- **lDe'u chos-'byung* (*The History by the Scholar De'u*, TASS, Lhasa, 1987), in short and long versions, *c.*12th century
- **Rab-brtan Kun-bzang-'phags kyi rnam-thar* (*The Life of the Prince of Gyantse*, Lhasa, 1988), a biography of the builder of the rGyal-rtse *sku-'bum* written by Bo-dong Pan-chen 'Jigs-med Grags-pa in 1421
- **Mi-nyag mkhas-dbang lnga'i rnam-thar* (*The Lives of the Five Scholars of Minyag*, Chengdu, 1987), 13th-14th century
- **Chos-'byung me-tog snying-po sbrang-rtsi'i bcud* (*The History of Buddhism*, TASS, Lhasa, 1988) by Nyang-ral Nyi-ma 'Od-zer (1124–92)
- **Yar-lung Jo-bo'i chos-byung* (*The History of Buddhism by Yarlung Jowo*, Chengdu, 1988), *c.*14th century.

A number of studies by contemporary Tibetan historians have also been produced:

- *Bod kyi chos-srid zung-'brel skor bshad-pa* (Chinese: *Lun Xizang*

zheng jiao heyi zhidu, Beijing, 1981; also published in English as *On the Dual Politico-Religious System of Tibet*) by Dung-dkar Blo-bzang 'Phrin-las, one of the most learned contemporary Tibetan scholars
– *Bod kyi rig-gnas lo-rgyus dpyad gzhi'i rgyu-cha bdams-bsgrigs* (*Selected Research Materials for a Cultural History of Tibet*, Lhasa, 1982–9; eleven volumes to date), edited by the *Bod-ljongs chab-gros rig-gnas lo-rgyus dpyad gzhi'i rgyu-cha zhib-'jug u-yon lhan-khang*; essays by a number of contemporary leading figures in Tibet on different aspects of social and political life in Tibet in the first half of the 20th Century
– *Krung-go'i Bod sa-gnas kyi lo-rgyus yig-tshang phyog-btus* (*Collected Texts for a History of the Tibet Region of China*, TASS, Lhasa, 1986)
– *Deb-ther kun-gsal me-long* (*The Clear Mirror Annals*, Lhasa/ Qinghai, 1987) edited by Phun-tshogs Tshe-ring. It covers the period from the Yarlung Dynasty to the 14th Dalai Lama, and is written to prove that Tibet is a part of China.

Preliminary attention has been turned to the history of individual monasteries, leading to the publication of photographic albums with short texts on the most important religious seats: Jokhang, Potala, Sa-skya (Sakya), sKu-'bum (Kumbum), bSam-yas (Samye), and others. A number of slim editions of guides to specific monasteries, including Bya-khyung (Chakyung), sNar-thang (Narthang) and bSam-yas, have also been published.

ARTS AND SCIENCES

Several volumes exist with colour plates showing *thang-kas* or wall paintings from the surviving collections, of which *Bod kyi thang-ka* (*Tibetan Thangkas*, Lhasa, 1985), from the Potala collection, is the best so far produced, with bilingual text and descriptions. Individual volumes of the texts of *A-lce Lha-mo*, the traditional Tibetan opera, have been published, as well as one volume of collected texts of the eight main operas, *Bod kyi lha-mo'i khrab gzhung* (Lhasa, 1989).

In anthropology the best-known work in China by a Tibetan anthropologist is dGe-legs' *On the Origins of Tibetan Culture and the Links with Surrounding Peoples* (Chinese: *Lun Zangzu wenhua de qiyuan xingcheng yu zhouyuan minzu de guanxi*), published by Zhongshan University Press in 1988. dGe-legs (Gelek), born in Kanze in 1948, is the first Tibetan of the new generation to obtain a doctorate in anthropology and, apart from the above-mentioned book, has published many articles on social studies, prehistory and anthropology. Since 1978 he has been researching the history of minorities at the Central Institute of Nationalities. He studied in Zhongshan University (1983–6) and dedicated his book, which is based on his doctoral thesis, to his teacher, Professor Liang Jian-nao, who had just died. dGe-legs discusses relations with the Han Chinese, the Mongols, the Tanguts of Xixia, the Naxi on the eastern border of Khams, and India, and no doubt supports the political theory of the regime in the PRC. dGe-legs is now working under rDo-rje Tshe-brtan (Dorje Tseten), director of the newly founded Chinese Institute of Tibetology in Beijing.[17] Some twenty of dGe-legs' articles are also mentioned in the bibliography, including 'Tibet is also a place of the origin of mankind', 'The gods of the Tibetan religion of Bon', 'On the origins of the Qiang and Tibetan peoples', 'On links between the earliest Tibetan culture and the region of the Central Plain [of China]', 'Shamanism and the Bon tradition', 'On the origins and development of Bon', 'Studies on the aboriginal nomads of the Seta plain in Sichuan', 'Research and field studies on religion, law, kinship and marriage of a Tibetan aboriginal nomad tribe' and 'An historical discussion on the Tibetan Autonomous Prefecture of Kanze'.

Some publications have looked at traditional Tibetan sciences. In the 1983 volume, *Traditional Tibetan Astrology*, the introduction is in the form of a poem in traditional *kavya* style which opens with the obligatory mention of the motherland (meaning China) followed by a lyrical description of the Land of Snows, before beginning on the subject of Tibetan astrology. The author traces the tradition first in Tibet, then through China and India. He takes the Tibetan tradition back to the first king, and to the Bon religion, and gives ethnological detail about the Mon people and other Tibetan groups who make their own sundials by holding a straw upright. He then analyses the traditional astrological texts.

Medicine was the one domain of Tibetan traditional learning which was not completely interrupted by the Cultural Revolution. A considerable number of books of recipes, *materia medica* and treatises, as well as such works as the biography of the doctor gYu-thog, have been published. In 1986 a large volume of the *Tibetan Medical Atlas* was produced, based on a series of *thang-ka* paintings made in the former medical school of lCags-po-ri (Chakpori) in Lhasa. It follows exactly the text of the *rGyud-bzhi* (*The Quadruple Treatise*), which is the *summum* of Tibetan medical theory and practice composed by sDe-srid Sangs-rgyas rGya-mtsho (Desi Sangye Gyatso, 1653–1705). Chinese equivalents are given for each of the hundreds of vignettes taken from the whole collection of seventy-eight *thang-kas* now kept in the sMan-rtsis-khang (Mentsikhang) in Lhasa.[18]

In the mid-1980s a rectification of the transcription of geographic names in Tibet (and other parts of the PRC) gave rise to the publication of new maps and, to accompany them, a booklet published in Beijing in 1986 giving a list including the former sinicised place names and the new versions. These are considerably closer to actual Tibetan pronunciation, though still in many ways unnecessarily tributary to the Chinese *pinyin* system and phonology. A number of other small booklets on environment and wildlife are beginning to appear, containing interesting local maps and some photos.

LITERATURE

A number of literary periodicals are published in different areas: these include *Lho-kha'i rtsom-rig sgyu-rtsal* in Lhokha, *sBrang-char* and *Zla-gsal mTsho-sngon slob-gso* in Amdo, *Bod kyi rtsom-rig sgyu-rtsal* in Lhasa and *Jo-mo-glang-ma* in Shigatse. There are also a number of learned journals: TASS has published regularly, since the beginning of the 1980s, *Bod-ljongs zhib-'jug* (*Tibet Research*), which covers a broad range of subjects. The *Bod-rig-pa'i gros-dmol tshogs-'du'i ched-rtsom bkod-bsdus* (*The Collected Papers of the First China Tibetological Conference*, Qinghai, 1987) has appeared, as have a few collections of learned articles or monographs and scientific reports. In 1989 the first volume of *Krung-go'i Bod kyi shes-rig* (*China Tibetology*) was published, and a more popular English-language quarterly – *China's Tibet* – appeared in the spring of 1990. Both reflect, no doubt, the name of the new research institute established in Beijing: the Chinese Institute of Tibetology or Zhongguo Zangzu yanjiu zhongxin.

The *Zangzu wenxue shi* (*A History of Tibetan Literature*), first written in Chinese and published in Chengdu in 1985, is now being enlarged and translated into Tibetan. This is the first attempt at an overview of Tibetan literature, from the Dunhuang manuscripts right up to the 20th century. The only comparable work published to date in any language is the study by the Russian scholar A.I. Vostrikov, *Tibetan Historical Literature*, which was published in Calcutta in 1970.

At least three collections of classical literature have appeared or are being compiled. *The Bonpo Kanjur* (Chengdu, 1984–90) is a new edition of the first part of the Bonpo Canon (altogether 300 volumes) based on the unique copy from Gyarong. It is now available, though in limited numbers. The two other collections are the *Shes-bya kun-khyab* (*A Compendium of Knowledge*, Beijing 1985) by Kong-sprul Yon-tan rGya-mtsho (Kontrul Yonten Gyatso 1813–99); and the *bKa'a-'gyur bstan-'gyur* (*The Tibetan Canon*, Beijing, 1988). A team of about twenty Tibetan experts has started a major definitive project, in which all existing versions of the Tibetan Buddhist canon will be compared, collated and annotated.

A few books on *tshad-ma rig-pa*, traditional Tibetan logic, have been published, as have several studies of traditional Tibetan poetics, based on the Indian tradition taken from Dandin's *Kavya-darsa*. The Tibetan tradition of the life-story has also received some attention, and a number of important classical biographies have been republished, several of which, marked here with an asterisk (*), remain unobtainable or very rare outside Tibet:

– *Mi-la-ras-pa'i gsung-mgur* (*The 100,000 Songs of Milarepa*, Qinghai, 1981) (1042–1123) by gTsang-smyon Heruka rus-pa'i rGyan-can (1452–1507)

– **Tshang-dbyangs rGya-mtsho'i gsang-ba'i rnam-thar* (*The Secret Biography of the Sixth Dalai Lama*, Beijing/Lhasa, 1981)

– **Mid-dbang Pho-la-nas* (*Lord Phola-ne*, Chengdu, 1981) by mDo-mkhar Tshe-zhabs, 1733

– **Thang-strong rgyal-po'i rnam-thar* (*The Life of the King of the Empty Plain*, Chengdu, 1982), by Gyu-med bDe-chen, a 17th century biography of the Tibetan *yogi* Thangtong Gyalpo (1385–1464), who was famous for building iron bridges and for founding the Tibetan traditional theatre

– **rJe-bstun Shes-rab rGya-mtsho 'Jam-dpal dGyes-pa'i bLo-gros kyi gsung-rtsom* (*The Collected Writings of the Venerable Sherab Gyatso*, three volumes, Qinghai, 1982); Sherab Gyatso was a *dge-lugs-pa* scholar, and intimate of the 13th Dalai Lama, who became Chairman of the All-China Buddhist Association, 1955, and who was killed at the height of the Cultural Revolution

– *Mar-po lo-tswa-ba'i rnam-thar* (*The Life of Marpa the Translator*, Chengdu, 1983) by Khrag-thung rGyal-po, end of 15th century

– **Zhabs-dkar kyi rtogs-brjod* (*The Life of Zha-kar*, three volumes, Qinghai, 1985), the autobiography and mystic songs of the *rnying-ma-pa yogi* from Reb-kong in Northern Amdo, Zhabs-dkar Tshogs-drug Rang-grol, composed in 1781

– **rDo-ring Pandita'i rnam-thar* (*The Scholar of the Family Long Stone*, Chengdu, 1987), an autobiography written in 1810 by bsTan-'dzin dPal-'byor (b. 1760).

As for the oral tradition, a considerable number of volumes of collected songs, folk tales and sayings have been collected from all parts of the high plateau including, most notably, over forty volumes of the *Ge-sar*, which, with over a million lines, is the longest poem in the world. The living tradition of this poem is represented by its latest chapter, or rather volume, which is reported to be the *'Ja-gling g.yul 'gyad*, the story of the Jews and the Germans, and the Second World War. One imagines that somewhere in the grasslands a new chapter must be in the making on the battles of the Cultural Revolution.

NEW AUTHORS

The first modern novel of any length is *sKal-bzang Me-tog* (*The Flowers of the Good Age*),[19] which is by 'Jam-dbyangs rGya-mtsho (Jamyang Gyatso), now a research fellow at the Chinese Academy of Social Sciences in Beijing and head of their Gesar Research Institute. In a short preface he indicates the political aim of the book: to demonstrate the great benefits of the new socialist era. This is not achieved without a little realistic criticism of both regimes, giving the book its saving grace. The theme is that of a young man from a poor family in Kham who is chosen one day, unbeknown to his family, to become the scapegoat (*klu-dgong rgyal-po*) for the New Year festivities, and thus to carry away with him all the misfortune of his people. He flees eastward and meets the 'golden divine army' – the PLA – coming to liberate Tibetans from their old, superstitious and outdated society. In spite of the over-riding political input the novel possesses a certain literary quality.

Another well-known modern writer, perhaps almost a cult figure, is Don-grup rGyal (Dondrup Gyal). He was born in Amdo, and committed suicide by putting his head in a gas oven in 1985, aged approximately forty. Somewhat Bohemian and fond of wine and women according to reputation, he was perhaps one of the most original and gifted Tibetan writers of the new generation. The articles he published used to be avidly devoured by young, literate Tibetans. A series of his writings appeared either in *sBrang-char* (*Honey Rain*) or *Zla-gsal* (*Clear Moon*), the main literary journals in Amdo,[20] and one poem, *mTsho sngon-po* (*The Blue Lake*), was particularly famous. Other publications of his include:

– *'Bol-rtsom zhogs-pa'i skya-rengs* (*Dawn Pillow Writing*, Qinghai, 1981), a series of short stories, one of which gives an account of how a Gesar bard managed to survive the Cultural Revolution.
– *bTsan-po Khri-lde-srong-btsan gyi lo-rgyus mdo-tsam brjod-pa*

(*A Brief Account of Dhri-de Srongtsen*, Beijing, 1984). A traditional *kavya* poem prefaces a historical study of this particularly murderous time in Tibetan history: thus 'the gorgeous day of the [new] policy of the [Chinese Communist] Party dawns . . .' The author does not forget to excuse his limited knowledge and capacity while calling for precious criticism from his colleagues.

– *mGur-glu'i lo-rgyus dang khyed-chos* (*History and Specificity of the Tibetan Tradition of Narrative Song*, Beijing, 1985). This, his doctoral thesis, is a major study of the ancient indigenous poetic tradition of the Tibetans at the time of the creation of the military empire in the 8th and 9th centuries, according to the contemporary manuscripts found in the walled-up cave temples of Dunhuang. After a thoughtful introduction, the songs are presented, each with an analysis of the legend to which it is related, and with a translation into modern Tibetan. The study also includes a commentary on the earliest poetic tradition of Tibet.

A third writer is dPal-'byor (Paljor), who was born in Lhasa of a noble family. His only published writing to date is a full-length novel entitled *gTsug-gyu* (*The Turquoise of the Crown*).[21] This is the first modern novel in Tibetan in which there is none of the obligatory mention of the socialist regime. However, through the complicated fortunes of a turquoise and of a young man of very humble origin, the author relates the intrigues and dramas of the old society, and the relations between the different social strata in Lhasa before 1959; his class consciousness and Marxist education can be read between the lines. The style, a complicated flowing unbroken prose typical of Central Tibet, is very different from the other two authors.

bKra-shis Zla-ba (Tashi Dawa; Chinese: Zaxidawa) is another well-known writer among the new generation of Tibetans educated by the Chinese. Although he apparently writes only in Chinese – his father was Tibetan, and his mother Chinese – the subject matter is that of contemporary Tibet. *Horse of the Winds*[22] is almost surrealistic in its use of Buddhist notions of *karma* and rebirth, and in the ellipses of time. Of course there is much Chinese influence in his writing, but the whole effect is of a new kind of Tibetan writing. This may be compared with the writing in English by young Tibetan intellectuals in the diaspora such as Jamyang Norbu.

Recent reports in *Bod-ljongs nyin-re'i tshags-par* (*Tibet Daily*) and *Lasa Wanbao* (*Lhasa Evening News*) have given details of publishing activities and writers. For example, on August 16, 1990, the *Lasa Wanbao* (it is published four times a week, and only in

Chinese) reported on the Fourth National Minorities' Social Science Periodical Editorial Meeting in Lhasa, and on their resolutions: 'how further to combine dialectically the two basic points of sticking to the four basic principles . . . with close reference to the realities in the minority area'. Later articles in the *Lasa Wanbao* on September 18, 1990, and in the *Bod-ljongs nyin-re'i tshags-par* (published six times a week in separate Tibetan and Chinese editions) on October 6, 1990, gave a little more concrete information. Of the 1,800 members of the 'Association for Minority Writers' in the PRC, drawn from forty nationalities, thirty were Tibetan. A few of their names were given in Chinese: Cidanpingcuo (Tshebrtan Phun-tshogs/Tseten Phuntsog), Yixidanzeng (Ye-shes bsTan-'dzin/Yeshe Tenzin), Labapingcuo (Lhag-pa Phun-tshogs/Lhakpa Phuntsog, Director of TASS and a Vice-Governor of the TAR), Zaxidawa (Tashi Dawa, author of *Horse of the Winds*), Sebuo (Tsephul), Banjue (dPal-'byor/Paljor), and Yangzen (Yangzom). Since 1980, the newspapers reported, a total of 957 pieces of writing, including short stories, reports, prose collections and thirty-one long novels, had been published by members of the Association, of which 600 were by Tibetan writers. There was no indication as to whether these works were published in the TAR or were written in Chinese or Tibetan. And since 1970, the articles say, 1,500 titles in 20 million copies have been published by the Tibetan People's Publishing House, although again no indication is given of how many are in Tibetan.

The *Tibet Daily* article of October 6, 1990, presented the official view of the sources which had inspired this new Tibetan literary activity, and indicated the policy change which had allowed it to come to the surface. 'The comrades from the propaganda department of the Autonomous Region's Party Committee said that *before Liberation literary creation in Tibet was zero*, and after Liberation a branch of army writers and Chinese writers came along to write a large amount of works on the life of the Tibetan people. However, the Autonomous Region's Party Committee believes that it is necessary to educate a class of Tibetan writers to reflect Tibetan history and its changes completely. Since the establishment of the Autonomous Region, the education of Tibetan writers has been considered a big thing . . . [author's emphasis]'.

Another article in the *Tibet Daily*, which appeared on the same day under the title 'The Prosperous Tibetan Publishing Industry', talked of Tibetan participation for the first time in the (third) Beijing International Book Fair, held in September 1990, as well as in the First National Periodicals Exhibition, held in the same month, at which sixteen (of a total of nineteen) Tibetan periodicals were presented, in both Tibetan and Chinese, and some in English versions. According to this article, the first Tibetan publishing house was established only in 1971. After the Cultural Revolution a specific demand was made by the TAR Party Committee and by the People's Government for the press to publish mainly in Tibetan, and mainly popular writings; such Tibetan school textbooks as existed at the beginning of the reform were described by the newspaper as 'blank'.

In the *Tibet Daily* of October 13, 1990, a report was printed on the Publishing Meeting of the Tibet Autonomous Region which was held in Lhasa and concerned particularly with the circulation of seven newspapers and one periodical. By the end of 1990 an expected total of 226,000 copies of newspapers would have been published. Xiangbaqudeng (Byams-pa mChod-rten/Chamba Choeden), the Vice-Director of the TAR Postal Management Bureau, suggested that for the future they should first strengthen the 'organisation and leadership' of the system of newspaper subscriptions and propaganda, secondly 'adopt many methods to make propaganda' for the newspapers, and thirdly 'strengthen the professional qualities of the leadership and guarantee the qualification of the personnel.'

TRANSLATIONS

A number of literary works have appeared in translation. One republication, originally translated from Sanskrit into Tibetan, was re-issued in Chengdu in 1981. It is the translation of and commentary on the *Ramayana*, by Zhang-zhung-ba Chos-dbang Grags-pa (1404–69), a disciple of Tsongkhapa. Among several new translations from Chinese into Tibetan are two of the great novels of Chinese literature: *Thang-sin bla-ma'i rnam-thar* (Chinese: *Xiyouji* [*The Journey to the West*], abridged version, Beijing, 1981); and *Khang-chen dmar-po'i rmi-lam*, (Chinese: *Hongloumen* [*The Dream of the Red Chamber*], Beijing, 1983). Another translation is of the great early Chinese classic on warfare, *Sun-tsi'i g.yul bkod* (Chinese; *Sunzi bingfa xinzhu* [*Sunzi's Art of War*], Qinghai, 1986), translated into concise literary Tibetan by Tshe-ring Don-grub and the Scientific Committee of the PLA in Qinghai. The preface quotes heavily from Mao's writing to justify the translation, and the text has a lengthy Tibetan commentary.

Translations from Tibetan into Chinese include several chapters of the *Ge-sar* epic, several volumes of folk tales, biographies of the Dalai Lamas and Panchen Lamas,[23] and *The Tibetan Medical Atlas*.

China's Tibet, in its spring and winter editions of 1990, announced the publication of a number of new books, although it did not specify whether the books would be published in Tibetan or Chinese. These included: *Wedding Congratulations* from Amdo; *Tibetan Ironware* by Zhaxi (Bkra-shi); 132 stories about *A-khu sTon-pa*; a *Ge-sar Dictionary* edited by Tubdan Nima (Thub-gten Nyi-ma); volumes 1–3 of the *Catalogue of the Nationalities Library*; volumes 12–14 of *Literary Selections of Tibetan Language* – on the rise and development of the *rnying-ma-pa, bka'-brgyud* and *sa-skya* schools – by Campus Cenam and Bewar Qime Doje; *Research on the History of Tibetan Religion* by Li Anzhai; two parts of *Tibetan Literary Selections throughout the Ages*, by Qi Shunlai, the first consisting of 170 excerpts from original texts from the 7th-20th centuries; a *History of Tibetan Religion* by Yang Huaqun and Song Xiaoji (December 1990); *In Memory of the 10th Panchen Lama*; a collection of photographs by Zhang Ying and Zhang Ziyang on *Tibetan Mythical Dance, Opera and Mask Arts*, with text by Qu Liuyi; *Selected Works on Ancient Tibetan Qigong*, eight articles by Tibetan authors, edited by Duoshi (December 1990); *New Proverbs of Tibet* by Joba Donzhub [*sic*] (July 1990); and *Records of Natural Disasters*, a series edited by the Chinese Tibetology Publishing House, including *Snowstorms* (1985), *Floods* (1990) and *Historical Records on Earthquakes in Tibet*.

More titles were listed in the *Tibet Daily* of October 6, 1990: an *Index of the Manuscripts in the Potala Palace* (Chinese: *Budalagong dianji mulu*); *Biography of the 7th Dalai Lama* (Chinese: *Diqishi dalai lama zhuan*); *Biography of the 5th Dalai Lama* (Chinese: *Diwushi dalai lama zhuan*); *Biography of the 4th Panchen Lama* (Chinese: *Disishi banchan lama zhuan*); and *Grand and Unique Index of the Nanzan Tribe* (Chinese: *Nanzanbu weiyi lhuangyan mulu*).

Thus, from 1978, we observe the beginnings of a new modern Tibetan literature, the diversification of subject matter and the appearance of the first few glossy books on Tibetan society, art and the 'minorities'. The appearance of a number of new Chinese authors publishing on different aspects of Tibetan culture is also to be noted. The publication of ubiquitous Chinese political tracts does not in any way impede what is no doubt the most important activity on the part of the Tibetan editors, namely – in spite of the declaration that literary creation was 'zero' before 1950 – the reprinting and re-editing in good quality printed book form of many of the major works of Tibetan classical literature.

An evolution in the presentation of the re-editions may be noted through the 1980s: at the beginning of this period first each volume was rigorously presented, with tables of contents, sometimes even indexes, and introductions giving details on the author and perhaps a commentary on the contents. This attention to good editing does not preclude a little censoring of undesirable details in the text, although often the introduction provides a suitable apology for the credulity and superstition of the modern Marxist Tibetan's forebears. However, all this rigour faded somewhat as the 1980s progressed, and publications fell back into being simply reproductions of traditional Tibetan texts. Maybe this reflected a relaxing of vigilance by the authorities, and perhaps, before October 1987, a vague anticipation of a return to 'good old times'?

It would be interesting to compare the quantity and quality of these re-editions in the PRC with the considerable number of re-editions of classical Tibetan texts produced in India from the early 1960s, and those which were produced under the protection of the American Library of Congress from the 1960s onwards.

PUBLICATIONS BY TIBETANS IN THE DIASPORA, 1959-90

The major contribution of the Tibetan refugee community has been the reprinting of thousands of religious texts brought with them over the Himalayas when they escaped in 1959. Already in 1960 two young Bonpo monks had set up reprinting facilities in Delhi, and were redistributing texts to their community who had donated the funds for their work. Others soon joined in and from the mid-1960s up to the beginning of the 1980s the American Library of Congress provided for the vast majority of these reprints, encouraging all schools and lineages to produce a maximum quantity of texts; even manuscripts from Ladakh and Nepal were procured and copied in the crowded workshops of Old Delhi. It was during the winter months when the printers came down from their mountain refugee camps to spend the days and nights in assuring the survival of the vast body of Tibetan literature that activity was most intense. The work took place on a huge scale. The Library of Congress gave to each printer sufficient funds to reproduce a minimum of twenty-four copies of each volume. These were sent to twenty-four university libraries in the United States, and any copies that were extra could be donated or sold by the printer for his profit. The system had some undesirable effects: for example the printers were encouraged to put 600 pages in each volume, neither more nor less. This meant of course that often several books went into a single volume, and that the last text would be truncated, with part of it in another volume. Also the price was fixed at 300 rupees, a sum out of proportion with the economic realities of India. Professor Lokesh Chandra, who was producing very similar editions of Tibetan texts from his father's collection, sold the *Satapitaka* series on the market in the late 1960s for only 60 rupees. In spite of this, the Library of Congress's programme, and the dedicated work done by Gene E. Smith, must be counted as one of the major factors in the salvaging of traditional Tibetan learning during those vital years when the monastic libraries in Tibet were being ransacked and burnt to the ground.

As the tide of reprints eventually slowed down to a trickle, another activity took over: the transmission of Buddhist teachings to the West. With the teachings there came the immediate necessity of translation, both simultaneous oral translation and the slower textual translations. Over the last ten years the flood of books of religious teaching published in Western languages by a number of specialist publishers reflects the energy of the lamas travelling and teaching in different parts of the Western world, and now practically the whole world over. Western disciples are becoming more and more proficient in the technical language of the *Dharma*, and already translators are gathering together to try and work out standardised terminology.

We should consider the danger to national identity and survival that lies in the spread of Mahayana Buddhism. In the busy transmission of the teachings of Tibetan Buddhism to the West, will not its very success cause the Tibetan part to be in the long run forgotten? This may be considered irrelevant by those involved in spreading the teachings of the Buddha around the world, but for the survival of Tibetan identity and language it may prove to play a somewhat dangerous role. While the Tibetans outside Tibet may voice their dismay at the poor education system on the Tibetan Plateau, and the almost compulsory use of Chinese for all higher education, we may also wonder at the lamas who teach more and more directly in English, as well as the young Tibetan intellectuals graduating from Indian universities who feel more at ease in the language bequeathed by the British to India. If the Tibetan language, as a vehicle for communication in the world of the 21st century, is not made viable by systematic use in all contexts relevant to the modern world, if Tibetan – both spoken and written – is threatened from without and within, is not the very core of Tibetan national identity threatened? Is not the language and literature of a people a key to its survival as a separate entity?

It is, on the other hand, fair to say that the exile Tibetan government has; since the arrival of the refugees in India, paid great attention to the establishment of schools and to the education of its children. In the 1960s a series of textbooks was compiled by a group of scholars with the aim of passing on to Tibetan children traditional knowledge and values. The realisation of the importance of education has been widespread among the refugee population, and many children, orphans or those with parents in difficult material situations have been given over to the care of the children's villages, where they can at least receive basic instruction in Tibetan, English and mathematics. In recent years, considerable numbers of Tibetans from Tibet, both children and adults, have gone to India in search of the education they could not obtain in the PRC.

In the 1960s, immediately after arrival in India, a series of manuals on language and traditional Tibetan science and knowledge was compiled for the schools. At the same time, a programme of translation into Tibetan of Western works of general knowledge was launched by a group of young Tibetan scholars who knew English. But this was unfortunately cut short when it was found that H.G. Wells's *History of the World*, which was then being translated, contained no mention of Tibet, and moreover interpreted the evolution of mankind in a way that was alien to the Buddhist world-view.[24] Since that time little progress has been made in school textbooks either, and it is now quite clear that the Tibetans inside Tibet have better resources (albeit still limited) than those in the diaspora for giving their children a modern education in Tibetan. On the one hand, the liberty of expression and the importance of the traditional educational system in India attract many families in Tibet who make considerable efforts to get their children over the Himalayas and so to school in India. On the other hand, the development of language tools, manuals, dictionaries, textbooks and popular science inside Tibet will, without any doubt, contribute in an important way to the future education of all Tibetan children, on both sides of the Himalayas.

A certain amount of attention has also been paid to political and historical writing. It is clear here that some of the important texts indicate both a desire to adapt to the 20th century and the need for an official political history of Tibet. These are some of the principal examples:

- *Bod kyi rtsa-khrims* (*The Constitution of Tibet* [bilingual text in Tibetan and English], New Delhi, 1963)
- *'Gro-ba-mi'i thob-thang gi yig-cha* (*The Universal Declaration of Human Rights* [Tibetan translation], Dharamsala, 1970)
- *Bod kyi srid-don rgyal-rabs* (*A Political History of Tibet*), first published in English [New Haven, 1967], and then in an enlarged

version in Tibetan in two volumes (Kalimpong, 1976), by Tsepon Shakabpa
– *Bod kyi lo-rgyus phyogs-bsdus Bod dang Bod-mi* (*Tibetan History, Tibet and Tibetans*, New Delhi, 1980) by Khang-kar Tshul-khrims sKal-bzang (Tsultrim Kelsang).

Other significant contributions in Tibetan are: *Bod dmag gi lo-rgyu* (*A History of the Tibetan Army*) by rGyal-rtse rNam-rgyal dBang-'dud (sic) (Gyantse Namgyal Wangdu, Dharamsala, 1976); and *rGas-po'i lo-rgyus 'bel-gtam* (*The Long-winded Story of an Old Man*, Dharamsala, 1982) by Khe-smad bSod-nams dBang-dus (Khe-me Sonam Wangdu).

A considerable number of new books written in Tibetan, however, sometimes at the behest of Dharamsala, have been censored or banned from publication because they do not conform to the desired image of traditional Tibetan society. Any serious discussion of history and of possible shortcomings in the society before 1959 is taboo, thus maintaining the historical consciousness of the Tibetans outside Tibet within an ideological framework that is of course radically different from the Marxist one, but equally rigid. The positive role of critical historiography in the forging of national consciousness is not yet tolerated. While censorship is being carried out with very different aims on both sides of the Himalayas, a small amount of pirating also occurs. For example, a number of volumes of the *Ge-sar* epic, the scabrous tales of *A-khu ṣTon-pa* (Aku Tonpa), published in the PRC and unavailable in India, are being reproduced by the refugee community. On the other hand, the newly written Tibetan historical work *gLang Dar-ma* by the Tibetan scholar S.G. Karmay was originally sponsored by Dharamsala but later refused publication by the *bka'-shag* (Kashag) because of its historical non-conformity. It has since been published in Beijing at the demand of the Tibetologists there. It relates the period of the notorious King Lang Darma according to contemporary sources in the Dunhuang manuscripts, and therefore gives a very different image of the fall of the Yarlung Dynasty from the later Buddhist version. The pressure of tradition in India is strong, while the desire to sweep away all tradition in the PRC makes it possible to look with different eyes upon the evolution of Tibetan history.

An interesting development in the diaspora is that in the 1960s, for the very first time, ordinary lay men and women, as opposed to teachers and incarnate lamas, began to write their life stories, often at the behest of sympathetic Western friends. These writers give detailed personal descriptions of Tibet before and during the

Chinese takeover with the aim of letting the world know the plight of the Tibetans. Thus the traditional function of the *rnam-thar* or life-story has been altered radically from describing the journey of a holy being towards enlightenment, where it serves as a model for others. The modern biographies represent one of the earliest and fullest expressions of a new kind of awareness concerning Tibetan identity. Unfortunately, being destined for a Western audience, these are most often written only in English, and we see again that the concern for survival and communication with the outside world, the lack of which did much to bring about the present situation in Tibet, leads Tibetans to neglect their own language. So at the same time as new forms of expression of national identity emerge, so the very essence of national identity is truncated.

As for folk tales and popular tradition, a small number of publications have appeared which concern popular traditions in Tibet before 1959. These publications are highly interesting, but their very paucity indicates how little store is set by non-ecclesiastical life. Those who have felt the urge to record oral traditions, it would seem, have received little encouragement; thus another possibility for developing and diversifying Tibetan literature has been blocked.

Over the last thirty years attempts have been made at launching new writing among young educated Tibetans. A group in St Joseph's College, Darjeeling, brought out a series of cyclostyled literary magazines called *North Pointer*; another series was called *Fresh Winds*. Writers of high quality exist, such as Jamyang Norbu and the late Trungpa Rinpoche. But again much is done in English and little seems to appear in Tibetan. Of the four long-established periodicals and newspapers published by the Tibetan community in India, two are in Tibetan – *Shes-bya* (*Knowledge*) and *Rang-dbang gsar-shog* (*New Freedom Press*) – and two are in English – *Tibetan Review* and the *Tibet Journal*. Apart from the last, which is a learned quarterly, the others are essentially politically oriented, and each has its own distinct style. More journals have appeared more recently in other countries, including *Tibet Forum*, an occasional Tibetan newspaper edited in New York by political dissidents from the PRC, which is unique in that it appears in both Tibetan and Chinese editions (Tibetan: *Bod don gleng-stegs*; Chinese: *Xizang luntan*).[25]

It might be thought that some forms of resistance literature must exist, written or sung by those who have lived and died inside Tibet since 1959. Up till now very little has appeared before the general public, though such works must surely exist, scattered among the thousands of letters that have come out of Tibet since 1978, as well as in the oral tradition inside Tibet itself. The song at the beginning of this article, though written by someone who returned to Tibet from India, bears witness to it.

Conclusion

In spite of the considerable output of publications on both sides of the Himalayas, there is a remarkable absence of translation work into Tibetan. Of course, inside Tibet great efforts have been made to adapt to the modern Marxist society: political and economic translations abound. That is part of the new system. The entire body of Marxist-Leninist and Maoist doctrine has been put into Tibetan, and quite competently, thus for the second time in history importing an entire doctrinal corpus into Tibetan. The Tibetan language is rich and pliable, and perfectly capable of creating and expressing all that is necessary in the modern technological world. But what else is there? In the last few years we have seen in Tibetan *The Dream of the Red Chamber, The Journey to the West* and *Sunzi's Art of War*; these are but three classics among the vast and beautiful body of Chinese literature. Shakespeare's *Coriolanus* and one of Agatha Christie's novels make up the very short list of European works known by the author to have been published in Tibetan in the PRC; these were no doubt translated through Chinese versions. No other models of foreign literature are available on the high plateau, except of course Chinese translations of Japanese, Russian and Western literature permitted in the PRC.

In the diaspora the situation is similar. In the 1970s, L. Lhalungpa published his Tibetan translation of *The Life of Mahatma Gandhi*, and Dr Samten Norbu in Darjeeling is currently translating a work by Tagore. Apart from these, and the *Universal Declaration of Human Rights*, what other work has been done? Where are the translations of world literature, poetry, philosophy, art, science and social studies? Where are the attempts to understand and describe, in modern Tibetan, the modern world? They are almost nil. All energy is going into the survival of a people, the survival of their traditional civilisation and their national identity. The problem remains almost the same as in 1959. Without enrichment and interaction with the outside world, is it possible to survive? But with interaction traditional life is diluted and altered. The major effort is directed, as we have noted above, towards the translation of the *Dharma* into Western languages: this is seen as the legacy of the Tibetan Buddhist masters to the West, and indeed they have a great treasure to hand on to all of mankind, in which they transpose as well as translate their tradition, in the same way that

Indian Buddhism was transformed in its assimilation into Tibetan society. After the older teachers are gone, the West will possess their knowledge. But what of Tibetan identity itself? Will there be such a thing as a new Tibetan identity in the 21st century?

NOTES

1. *Songs of Tibet*, vol. 2, composed and recorded by Potala Band, produced by the Tibetan Association in Germany, and recorded in Hilden, Switzerland, June 1988.
2. E. Renan, *Discours et Conférences*.
3. J.T. Dreyer, *China's Forty Millions*, Harvard University Press, 1976, p. 36.
4. John Bray, 'A.H. Francke's *'La Dvags Kyi Akbar*. The First Tibetan Newspaper', *Tibet Journal*, vol. XIII, no. 3 (1988), pp. 58–63.
5. *Me-long*, December 24, 1936.
6. A complete set of copies of *Me-long* should be collected together for public use before it is too late.
7. *Issues and Studies*, Institute of International Relations Taipei, December 1979.
8. Chinese: *Minzu zhengce wenjian*; Tibetan: *Mi-rigs srid-jus kyi yig-cha*, State Nationalities Affairs Commission, Beijing, 1952.
9. See H. Stoddard, *Le mendiant de l'Amdo*, Société d'Ethnographie, Université de Paris X, 1985, pp. 87–8, 103, and H. Stoddard, 'The Long Life of rDo-sbyis dGe-bshes Shes-rab rGya-mtsho (1884–1968)', *Studia Tibetica* (Munich), vol. II, 1988, pp. 465–72.
10. See note 9.
11. For example, Zla-ba bZang-po (Dawa Zangpo) and Hor-khang *dge-bshes* Chos-grag (Horkhang Geshe Choedrak).
12. See note 8. The first print run for the Tibetan translation was 1,000 in September 1952; in December 1952 there was a second print run of 14,000 copies.
13. *Issues and Studies*, Taipei, December 1975, p. 109. 'Five' refers to the provincial level areas in the PRC that include Tibetan inhabitants within 'Tibetan autonomous' administrative areas of one size or another, i.e. the four provinces of Qinghai, Gansu, Sichuan and Yunnan, plus the TAR.
14. *Bulletins Internationaux*, 14 August 1978.
15. The following information on publications does not pretend in any way to be exhaustive. It is limited mainly to material available and known to the author in 1990. (See notes 24 and 25.)
16. *'zhing-chen dang rang-skyong-ljongs lnga'i slob-gso'i sde-tshan gyi 'gan-'khur blo-mthun . . .'* (vol. 7, p. 76). See note 14.
17. Both were invited to the SOAS Conference 'Forty Years On: Tibet, 1950–1990', but were unable to attend.
18. *Bod-lugs gso-rig rgyud bzhi'i nang don bris-cha ngo-mtshar mthong-ba don-ldan*, edited by Wang Le, Wang Lei and Byams-pa 'Phrin-las, published in a Tibetan/Chinese edition by the Bod ljongs mi-dmangs dpe-sprun-khang (Tibetan People's Publishing House), Lhasa, 1986. See also the edition of the Medical Atlas covering the same materials but prepared from the only other known set, which is kept in the former Soviet Republic of Buryatia: *Tibetan Medical Paintings: Illustrations to the Blue Beryl Treatise of Sangye Gyamtso (1653–1705)*, ed. Yuri Parfionovitch, Gyurme Dorje and Fernand Meyer, 2 vols, London: Serindia Publications, 1992.

19. Beijing: Nationalities Publishing House, 1982, 547 pp.
20. I have not had access to these.
21. People's Publishing House, Lhasa, 1985, 303 pp.
22. Translated into French by Bernadette Rouis as *Les chevaux du vent* (Paris, 1990).
23. Some of these were in process of being translated in 1988 by a team of young Chinese-educated Tibetans.
24. A major translation project was initiated in July 1992, after this chapter was written, by the Amnyemachen Institute, a new non-governmental academic organisation based in Dharamsala. Works being translated into Tibetan include Brown's *Bury my Heart at Wounded Knee*, Thomas Paine's *Common Sense*, Orwell's *Animal Farm*, Solzhenitsyn's *One Day in the Life of Ivan Denisovitch*, and Harrer's *Seven Years in Tibet*. The Institute, dedicated to advanced Tibetan studies and particularly its non-religious dimensions, and independent of the exile Government, was founded in 1992 by its directors Tashi Tsering, Pema Bum, Lhasang Tsering and Jamyang Norbu. [Editor's note]
25. At least three new literary and political journals of note have started regular production in India since this chapter was researched, in large part as a result of the flight to India of Tibetan writers and intellectuals educated in Amdo: *dMang-gtso* (Mangtso, *Democracy*), *lJang-gzhon* (Jangzhon, *Young Saplings*), and *Zla-gsar* (Dasar, *New Moon*). [Editor's note]

POLITICISATION AND THE TIBETAN LANGUAGE

Tsering W. Shakya

When the Chinese established control over Tibet in the 1950s, it was not only an attempt to assert political control over the territory. The new Communist state also viewed its task there as one which would promote fundamental social change and transform Tibet into a 'socialist society'.

From the start this task was fraught with difficulties. It was clear that there was little or no basis for a socialist revolution in Tibet.[1] Moreover, there was no indigenous Communist or political movement within the country which could be relied on for support. Tibet had for centuries remained culturally and socially isolated from the major social movements in the world, and 20th-century political phenomena such as socialism and nationalism had had no major impact on Tibetan society or on the development of Tibetan culture. Neither had any Western literature been translated into Tibetan that might have provided a potential source of change by introducing minor variants into Tibetan culture.[2]

When the Communists entered Tibet they were immediately confronted with problems of how to promote and develop socialism in a society where there was a very low material base. One of the major problems was how to communicate socialist ideas and propaganda to the masses. To the vast majority of the Tibetans, Communism was a totally alien ideology. If it were to be successfully transplanted in Tibet it was necessary to develop mass propaganda and socialist consciousness among the people. The major resistance to the development of Communism was not the resistance of guerrilla fighters or of the Tibetan army: it was the objective socio-cultural conditions in Tibet.

The problem was not only that Communist ideology was alien to Tibetans, but that there were no linguistic means of communicating the Communist ideals and concepts to them. So the Communists in Tibet had to develop a new Tibetan lexicon to promote unfamiliar political and social ideology. Thus, since the 1950s the Tibetan language has undergone fundamental changes in order to adapt to the prevailing political ideology. Of course there is nothing new in language adapting to political realities, but in the case of Tibet it became necessary to invent new linguistic categories to propagate the new ideology.

On a more practical level, the question of the nature and style of Tibetan itself and also of the medium of communication further complicated the problem. Traditionally, Tibetans have viewed written language as sacred, and Tibetan literature has been dominated by religious discourse, and no popular literary genre has developed.

As a result, the Communists in the 1950s were confronted with two major socio-linguistic problems. First, no adequate lexicon existed in Tibetan to discuss modern political ideologies, and literacy was primarily associated with Buddhism. Furthermore, the spoken language was hierarchically structured, with complex honorific rules of verbal discourse which reflected the traditional stratification of Tibetan society. This hierarchical structure in Tibetan was seen as incompatible with the egalitarian ideology of the Chinese.

Secondly, there was no infrastructure to deal with the total shift in the nature of Tibetan political participation. For the first time mass meetings were held in villages and localities to discuss such varied subjects as American imperialism and Soviet revisionism. The Tibetan peasantry was being mobilised into political action. It was not important whether the people understood the complexity of these political debates; but it was important that, for the first time, a new language should be available to articulate these issues.

If socialism was to succeed in Tibet, it was apparent to the Chinese that, above all, there needed to be an appropriate language to reflect the egalitarian ideology and philosophical bases of Marxism, and an infrastructure, such as printing presses and a modern media system, for language production.

In the 1950s, after the Communists had established effective control over Tibetan-speaking areas, they set out to publish Communist propaganda literature in Tibetan. The first Tibetan-language newspaper was started in 1950 in Amdo, from where it was issued every ten days.[3] Monks from Labrang monastery were recruited to the work of translation from Chinese and the paper also carried speeches given in Tibetan by the Panchen Lama and Geshe Sherab Gyatso. The first Communist literature to be translated was the Eight Point Proclamation of the PLA, which embodied the basic policies of the CCP. Whenever the PLA entered Tibetan-speaking areas it was this document that was distributed.

The Chinese also realised early on that the effectiveness of the printed media was limited by the extent of illiteracy in Tibet. Therefore, from the very beginning, the Chinese used radio broadcasts as a method of disseminating information and propaganda.[4]

Although it was only during the Cultural Revolution that radio became an important medium of propaganda, these radio broadcasts were to lead to the development of a particular style of language.

The primary need for language change in Tibet was to spread mass information and propaganda among the people, but the secondary need, to further the transformation of Tibet into a socialist society, could only be achieved if the Tibetans developed socialist consciousness. I have already mentioned that a new lexicon was introduced to accommodate socialist terminology, but this was not in itself enough: a new literary style had also to be developed to establish a popular literary genre which could be understood by the masses. This genre was mainly used for the Party's propaganda purposes and became the standard form for newspapers like the *Tibet Daily*.[5]

The new literary style was closer to colloquial Tibetan, or *phal-skad*, literally 'common speech', since it was envisaged that the masses would be able to understand it more easily. In conformity with Communist ideology the principal objective of this language change was to develop a simplified system of orthography and grammar which would be closer to the spoken language. As a result 'spoken language' became the standard measure for correct usage.

In the 1960s some minor grammatical changes were made so that written Tibetan would be closer to colloquial Tibetan. For example, in written Tibetan there are five genitive particles (*'brel-sgra*): *gi, gyi, kyi, yi* and *'i*. The use of a particle is governed by the preceding suffix or consonant. But in spoken Tibetan no differentiation is made and the particle *gi* is used. Accordingly, in the 1960s the particles *gyi* and *kyi* were eliminated from general use. As in spoken Tibetan, only the particle *gi* was used in publications. After the period of liberalisation began in the 1980s, however, all publications reverted back to the traditional use of the complete range of genitive particles.

It is difficult to ascertain, in retrospect, whether such choices were made according to purely linguistic principles or whether political considerations were paramount in reaching these decisions. It is, however, apparent that abrupt shifts in language use must have been sanctioned or patronised by those in power, and so must have reflected their political aspirations.

Similar difficulties surround the question of the success of the changes. Today, illiteracy is still widespread in Tibet, and the main means of propaganda besides public meetings remains radio broadcasts and, now, television. However, all publications still tend to adopt the new style.

During the Cultural Revolution (*rigs-nas gsar-brje*) the idea of 'egalitarian language' was taken to its extreme. The pamphlets published by the Red Guards (*srung-dmag dmar-po*) demanded the abolition of the honorific in Tibetan, the elaborate system of which was regarded as a remnant of feudal tradition (*bkas-bkod rgyud 'rjan lam lugs*) and as the language of the aristocracy (*sku-drag skad-bcad*). One pamphlet demanded 'that the *Tibet Daily*, Radio Lhasa and other broadcasting offices must use and propagate the language of the working class [*ngal-rtsal dmangs skad-bcad*] and seek to eradicate the language of the aristocracy and the upper class.'[6]

The abolition of the honorific caused considerable debate among the Red Guards and staff in publishing houses. I was told by one informant that at times the debate became farcical. As an example he described the argument over what sort of language was appropriate when referring to Chairman Mao: the honorific or colloquial (*phal-skad*) forms. If you used the honorific, you were likely to incur the wrath of a particular faction of the Red Guards and be accused of harbouring feudal sentiments. If, on the other hand, you chose to use common speech, you would be condemned by another faction of the Red Guards for not respecting Chairman Mao.

Change took place in other areas of language use as well. One of these was the translation of Marxist and contemporary political terminologies into Tibetan. The 1960s saw the development of a complex and innovative new Tibetan lexicon which was solely concerned with Marxist ideology and with the shifting nature of political culture. Just as the motivation for the change was political, so the greater part of the new terminology was related to the new ideology and politics, particularly key Marxist concepts, while the new lexicon was totally related to politics and economics.

One can illustrate this by examining how the term 'class' is translated into Tibetan. The central idea in Communist ideology is the concept of 'class' and 'class struggle'. The Marxist concept of 'class' was alien to Tibet and, moreover, there were no linguistic categories in Tibetan to describe this. Thus, the most innovative linguistic terminology is to be found in the field of class labelling.

The term 'class' itself was translated as *gral-rim* by using existing morphemes. The syllable *gral*, meaning 'row' or 'rank', was combined with the syllable *rim*, meaning 'order'. Thus the term 'class' was literally translated as 'row/rank order'. The term 'class struggle' was translated as *gral-rim thab-rtsod*. Here the word for 'struggle' has been created from a compound of the syllable *thab*, meaning to 'combat' or 'fight', and *rtsod*, meaning 'to argue', 'dispute' or 'debate'. These terms were translated from Chinese and in some cases directly reflected the composition of the Chinese word-phrase, which in the case of the word 'class' is made up of the characters *jie*, meaning 'row' or 'step', and *ji*, meaning 'rank' or 'order'. The Tibetan translators thus used the same conceptual framework that the Chinese had used in translating Western terms.

The method of forming or translating a new word by combining existing morphemes represents nothing new in Tibetan; indeed, numerous combinations can be made to coin new words or translate new concepts. This system provides flexibility and has been used by Tibetans in the past to translate new terms and concepts.

It was not only the key Marxist concepts, but new class categories that had to be translated and established by the Chinese. During the Cultural Revolution, class differentiation and labelling became major preoccupations. Every aspect of Tibetan society was classified and labelled. New social categories were invented to conform to the Marxist understanding of social class, so that terms like 'working class', 'upper class' and 'bourgeois' were translated into the Tibetan language and Tibetans were classified accordingly. The term 'working class' was translated as *'byor-med gral-rim*, which is made up of *'byor*, meaning 'wealth', and *med*, meaning 'without'. Thus, in Tibetan it literally means 'wealthless class'. The term 'upper class' was translated as *'byor-ldan gral-rim*, which literally means 'class with wealth'. The term 'middle class' was translated as *'byor-'bring gral-rim* – 'middle wealth class'. People are further sub-classified into categories such as *zhing-pa phyug-po*, meaning 'rich peasant', or *'brog-pa phyug-po*, meaning 'rich nomad'. These sub-classifications differed from place to place depending on the economy of the area.

The labelling and differentiation of class became major tasks for the *las-don ru-khag*, as the 'work teams' were called in Tibetan, and for the Red Guards during the Cultural Revolution. Everyone was classified into a particular class, thus giving Tibetan language a set of totally new categories and new concepts of social hierarchy.

People were given both class and political labels. For example, all those who took part in the 1959 uprising were classified as *log-spyod-pa*, meaning 'reactionary'. The word was coined from the elements *log*, meaning 'to turn', and *spyod*, meaning 'manner'. The worst political offence was being a 'counter-revolutionary', and this term was translated as *gsar-brje'i ngo-log-pa*,[7] literally meaning 'turning against modernity'. These new words became the standard rhetorical phrases of the Cultural Revolution and thence passed into everyday usage.

Another innovative and interesting example of new terminology is the translation of the concept of '-ism' as in socialism, capitalism or imperialism. This suffix was translated as *ring-lugs*, which is made up of *ring*, meaning 'long', and *lugs*, meaning 'tradition'. Thus the Western concept of '-ism' is rendered as 'long tradition' or 'established tradition'. Like '-ism' in English, the term *ring-lugs* is used as a suffix. Thus the term 'socialism' is translated as *spyi-tshogs ring-lugs*, a compound made up of four syllables. The first syllable *spyi* means 'common' or 'public' and the second syllable *tshogs* means 'to meet' or 'assemble'.

The term 'capitalism' is translated as *ma-rtsa'i ring-lugs*. Although *ma-rtsa* is a direct translation of the word 'capital', it only has Marxist connotations in this combination. The term 'imperialism' is translated as *btsan-rgyal ring-lugs*. The syllable *btsan* means 'to coerce', and *rgyal* means 'victory' or 'power'.

As stated earlier, the main impetus for linguistic changes arose from the need to translate Marxist concepts and ideology into Tibetan. The works and speeches of Mao were regularly translated into Tibetan and published in the *Tibet Daily*. The Party's theoretical journal *Red Flag* (*dar dmar*), now replaced by the magazine *Seeking Truth* (*Qiushi*), was translated into Tibetan in its entirety and the Tibetan edition was circulated to Tibetan Party members.

It was primarily the direct translation of Marxist and Party propaganda that established the standard requirements for translation. The major part of the translation and the standardisation of concepts and phrases were directly monitored by the Party. The institution responsible for translation, as well as for all Party and government documents, was the Beijing *yig-sgyur khang* (Chinese: *fanyi ju*), which is directly supervised by the Party through the United Front Department (*'thab pyogs gcig sgyur sgyor*).

Most of the new lexicon was directly related to social, economic and political issues. This was especially the case during the Cultural Revolution, when it was essential that everyone should be aware of the correct terminology and slogans. Although the majority of Tibetans were illiterate, they became aware of these words through public meetings and lectures organised by Party officials. New political concepts and ideas were explained to the people through the activities of the 'work teams'. Almost everyone was aware of terms like *log-spyod-pa* for 'reactionary', and *gsar-brje'i ngo-log-pa* for 'counter-revolutionary'. This vocabulary has since passed into everyday language, where they have become terms of abuse.

The new lexicon and terminology were not only centred around political phrases and slogans. They were also concerned with translating abstract concepts such as 'subjectivity' and 'objectivity'. The term 'subjectivity' is translated as *rang-shed* (*ring-lugs*). The word is made up of *rang*, meaning 'self', and *shed*, meaning 'to speak'. Here, words like *rang* and *shed* come from colloquial Tibetan, rather than from traditional Buddhist philosophical usage. (The Buddhist term for 'subject' is *yul-can*.) The term 'objectivity' was translated as *pyi-rol yul* (*ring-lugs*). The word is made up of *pyi* meaning 'external' or 'out', *rol* meaning 'side', and *yul* which, interestingly, is the term in Buddhist philosophy for 'object'. Thus the term 'objectivity' is literally translated as 'outside object', and 'subjectivity' as 'self speak'. (It is questionable whether equivalent terms exist in Buddhist philosophy. Although the terms 'subject' and 'object' exist in Buddhist philosophy, the Western notions of subjectivism or objectivism do not.)

The new terms and concepts were translated from Chinese into Tibetan and it is most probable that Tibetan translators did not have a direct knowledge of the European languages from which many of these new terms and concepts originated. However, they were aware at least of their historical origins, since they would have studied the history of socialism. On the whole, in rendering new terms into Tibetan, translators have drawn their inspiration from both colloquial and classical sources. They have not opted for the simpler route of transliterating and using loan words. Nevertheless, there are a number of terms that have not been translated into Tibetan. For example, it is interesting that the term 'party', as in political party, is not translated into Tibetan. The Chinese term for the 'Communist Party', *gongchandang*, becomes *gung-khran tang* (or a similar phonetic approximation such as *gung-bran tang*) in Tibetan, with the hybrid *tang-mi* (or the phoneticisation *tang-yon*) being used for the Chinese term *tangyuan*, a 'Party member'. So in fact the term 'Communism' has not been translated but transliterated.

The translation and emergence of new terminologies are related to the concurrent political and economic campaigns being initiated at a particular time by the Party. In recent years the opening of Tibet to tourists has necessitated more lexicographical invention, such as the coining of a new word for 'tourist': *yul-skor spro-cham-pa*. Similarly, the recent demonstrators were labelled as *kha-bral ring-lugs-pa*, meaning 'splittist' or 'separatist'.

Linguistic changes and innovation also occurred among the Tibetans in exile and it is interesting to note that the pattern of change was similar in both the exile and indigenous communities.

In both situations the primary structural reasons for the change were the shifting nature of political discourse between the political élite and the masses. For the first time in Tibetan history the masses were being mobilised and new political ideology was being inculcated. While socialism was fostered inside Tibet, the exile community was developing notions about nationalism and patriotism. For example, one of the most frequently used words among the exile community today is *sems shug*, made up of the two morphemes *sems*, meaning 'mind', and *shug*, meaning 'strength'. It can be translated as 'love of one's country' or 'having conviction in the cause'. The cause in question here is that of Tibetan independence. This term and *rang-btsen*, independence, form the core of the political vocabulary of the exile community, appealing to the sentiments of Tibetans and mobilising them to fight the Chinese occupation. Inside Tibet, on the other hand, the masses are rallied in the name of modernity and socialism. In both situations linguistic innovation reflects the prevailing political objectives.

The shift in Tibetan language over the past forty years has been a response to the changing political climates of Tibet and of China as a whole. To some extent this has been a technical response, in so far as the translation and innovation of the new lexicon are the product of political needs rather than of a genuine intellectual and creative exchange of ideas. People inside Tibet were not free to translate works as they wanted. The translation of and the need for new words were dictated by the needs of the Communist Party. However, this does not mean that translators lacked creativity. In fact the translators showed creativity and many of them may later be seen as successors in the long Tibetan tradition of the great *lo-tswa-ba* (translators) of the past.

NOTES

1. On April 6, 1952, Mao told generals leading the PLA forces that the situation in Tibet was 'completely different'. He said, 'We have no material base in Tibet. In terms of social power they are stronger than us, [a situation] which for the moment will not change.'
2. Western missionaries had translated the Bible. However, as Christianity did not have any impact upon Tibetan society, the Tibetan Bible still remains an atypical and idiosyncratic form of Tibetan literature.
3. Before 1950 the only Tibetan newspaper produced outside Tibet was the *Tibet Mirror* (literally, the *News Mirror*), published in Kalimpong, India, by Rev. Tharchin.
4. Immediately after coming to power the Communists used radio broadcasts as a means of establishing dialogue with the Tibetan Government. The Communists had no means of making representations to Lhasa and it was through a

radio broadcast that they invited the Tibetan Government to send a negotiating team to Beijing.

5. Despite the high rate of illiteracy, newspapers became one of the main media of communication. Communes and work units were encouraged to institute group reading and discussions.

6. This pamphlet was produced by the Red Guards from the TAR Teacher's College in 1966.

7. The word 'counter-revolutionary' is also used as a legal term. Anyone seeking 'to overthrow the rule of the Chinese Communist Party' is charged under laws against counter-revolution.

THE IDEOLOGICAL IMPACT ON TIBETAN ART

Per Kvaerne

It is surely no exaggeration to say that Tibet is passing through a period which is the most critical in its long history as a distinct and major culture in Asia, and since the first demonstrations in Lhasa in the autumn of 1987, has been the scene of a spiral of protest and repression. It is inevitable that the dramatic aspects of the conflict between China and Tibet should command our attention. The systematic repression of political protest and national sentiment, which has been put into operation in Tibet by the Chinese Government, has had the unintended effect of placing Tibet where it belongs: on the agenda of the international community. In fact, not only individuals and governments but also a growing sector of the academic community, whose interest in Tibet was till recently largely private or professional (and whose fear of being denied access to Tibet by the Chinese authorities was frequently less than lightly veiled), has in recent years refused any longer to turn a blind eye to the violations of basic human rights, the massive population transfer and the wanton destruction of the natural environment of Tibet. The comfortable illusion – so widespread in the 1980s – that a scholar need not (indeed, should not) get involved with 'politics' is untenable, for the simple reason that even the most virginal aloofness inevitably affects the course of events as much as fervent activism. Whatever part we choose to play, we cannot escape from the common stage in our 'global village'.

While the larger issues of human rights and national self-determination have an indisputable claim to our attention, it is my contention that Tibet is also being subjected to another, less dramatic but nevertheless profound impact. Ideological pressure, which is designed to influence people's values and perceptions of reality, does not in itself cause blood to flow or forests to disappear (though this, of course, may be the ultimate effect), but it may play an important part in determining the fate of any nation. I shall discuss two specific aspects of Tibetan culture – contemporary art and folk-dance – and I argue that they are consciously and systematically put to ideological use.

In *Mythologies*, Roland Barthes has shown that any object, provided it carries a meaning or message, may be regarded as a form of speech or discourse. While a particular *Weltanschauung* is, to be sure, also conveyed by means of writing and oral discourse, we shall focus our attention on art, for 'pictures . . . are more imperative than writing, they impose meaning at one stroke' (Barthes, p. 110). In other words, art constitutes a highly effective example of 'myth' (using the word in the sense that Barthes does, i.e., as synonymous with speech or discourse, which, as we have just noted, is not necessarily verbal). In the following, I attempt to view a particular type of contemporary Tibetan art as 'myth', more precisely as a group of more or less related myths that are designed to disseminate a particular ideology or world-view. Myth is more effective in this respect than analytical discourse, for 'myth essentially aims at causing an immediate impression . . . its action is assumed to be stronger than the rational explanations which may later belie it' (*ibid.*, p. 130).

Thus art, as a form of myth, can be an effective agent for ideological, political and social change. A precondition for this effectiveness, however, is that myth, if we regard it as discourse, employs a grammar and a vocabulary that are familiar. Therefore, while new times generate new artistic expressions, at the same time a minimum of traditional structural and semantic elements must be retained in order to render new messages acceptable. This is precisely what is happening in Tibet today.

Needless to say, outside influences continually made themselves felt on Tibetan art before the Chinese occupation in 1950. One need only think of the successive stylistic influences from Kashmir, Nepal, Central Asia and China which have at various times penetrated Tibet. It could also be argued that this art, most of which expresses Buddhist ideas and is intended to be used in connection with Buddhist rituals, meditation or lay devotion, was, particularly in its early phases, part of a conscious campaign of indoctrination. No doubt Tibetans who had not yet converted to Buddhism viewed this art with fear, disdain and, it may be assumed, incomprehension. No art, therefore, is immutable, and in the first half of the 20th century the greater world surrounding Tibet was, after a period in which Tibetan art had been characterised by stagnation and reproduction of traditional forms, once again slowly making itself felt, at least in the work of a few gifted individuals. One immediately thinks of Gendun Choephel (1905-51), 'one of the most brilliant and controversial figures of Tibet in the twentieth century' (Karmay, p. 145). A small number of his sketches have been preserved, which reveal a fluid, sensuous hand unfettered by traditional religious art.[1] He also made at least one painting copying the style of Russian icons,[2] no doubt a result of his association with the Roerich family. Another innovative artist was Gendun Choephel's pupil, Amdo Champa. In the Norbulingka he painted a fresco that portrays the members of the Tibetan Government in the 1940s in a very naturalistic style.[3]

In this paper, however, our concern is with a style of painting known as 'the Kanze [school of] New Tibetan Painting' (*dKarmdzes Bod-kyi ri-mo gsaŕ-pa*). This movement was started by two artists: a Tibetan, Rinzin Namgyal, and a Chinese, Mis Tingkha'e,[4] who founded the Association of Young Tibetan and Chinese Artists in 1980 in the Eastern Tibetan town of Kanze (Garze or Ganze in *pinyin*). From the start, they had the support of the Sichuan branch of the Artists' Association of China. Thus encouraged, and having 'understood the art of the masses, they decided to find a new path for Tibetan painting.' They jointly painted in the same year three paintings in the new style: 'King Gesar of Ling', 'Tashi Delek' and 'The Meeting in 1936 between Zhu De and dGe-stag Tulku'. These were shown the following year in Beijing at an exhibition of the art of 'national minorities'; the first two, especially, were highly praised and later transferred to the Cultural Palace of Minorities in Beijing.[5]

'King Gesar of Ling' has remained the classic piece in this tradition of New Tibetan Painting (fig. 1). The central figure, that of King Gesar mounted on a fiery, rearing steed, is traditional in content but not in style, which is that of contemporary Chinese (ultimately to a large extent Russian) fairy-tale illustrations. The structure of the painting as a whole is, however, that of a traditional *thang-ka*, with a central figure surrounded by an entourage (in this case, the thirty warrior-companions of Gesar), a lower sector full of lay-people and offerings, and an upper sector with three deities, painted in traditional style.

This combination of elements of traditional painting and modern Chinese art is typical of the New Tibetan painting. We shall take a closer look at a few examples of this art and attempt to elucidate their message and their 'myths'. In this we shall have recourse to a distinction made by the art historian Erwin Panofsky in 1932[6] between *Bedeutungssinn* ('intentional meaning') and *Wesenssinn* ('essential meaning').[7] The 'intentional meaning' is the meaning or the 'message' conveyed by the posture, character, colours, disposition of the figures, the background and the details. We can grasp this meaning provided that we are familiar with the literary sources which constitute the world of images, anecdotes and allegories of the painting; these sources provide an objective *Typengeschichte* ('history of forms'), against which our subjective interpretation must be tested. The 'essential meaning' is the implicit message, which is not directly expressed by the painting, but which is made

Fig. 1. 'King Gesar of Ling', according to the Kanze school of New Tibetan painting, 1980. (All the illustrations in this chapter were photographed by *Per Kvaerne*)

accessible by means of a deeper analysis. This analysis must, however, be continually tested against the objective norm of *allgemeine Geistesgeschichte* (the general 'history of ideas'), which tells us which ideas were in actual fact operative in a particular historical period, and which symbolic forms these ideas assume.

If, to return for a moment to Barthes, we regard a painting in itself as the 'form' of a myth,[8] we may say that the 'intentional meaning' of Panofsky is the myth conveyed by the painting when it is regarded 'without ambiguity', when 'the signification becomes literal . . . This type of focusing is, for instance, that of the producer of myths, of the journalist who starts with a concept and seeks a form for it'; whereas the 'essential meaning' emerges when 'I undo the signification of the myth, and I receive the latter as an imposture . . . This type of focusing is that of the mythologist: he deciphers the myth, he understands a distortion.'[9]

Let us now turn to one of the seminal works of the New Tibetan Painting: 'The Meeting in 1936 between Zhu De and dGe-stag Tulku' (fig. 2). Like the painting 'King Gesar of Ling' (and in this respect conforming to a common pattern in traditional religious art), the surface of the painting is divided into three horizontal sectors: a central sector in which are seated a Chinese officer and a Tibetan lama, framed by lavishly decorated Tibetan-style pillars and cross-beams; a lower sector that shows a Tibetan monastery in front of which a large number of blue-clad soldiers are parading; and an upper sector in which masses of red flags are to be seen in front of an inscribed pillar, flanked by angelic beings floating in the air. This, to use Barthes' terminology, is the 'form' of the myth. Proceeding to the level of 'intentional meaning', the myth itself is found to be entirely explicit. From a publication in which this painting is reproduced, we learn that the two central figures are Zhu De (Chu Teh), one of the leaders of the Communist forces on the Long March, and Getag (dGe-stag) Tulku (1903–50), 'a patriotic Tulku from Be-ri Monastery in the district of Kanze'. Getag Tulku 'mobilised the Tibetan masses and aided the Red Army' when the Communists passed through Eastern Tibet in 1936. 'Later, after the liberation of Sichuan, he became a member of the North-west Military Government Committee and Vice-Chairman of the People's Government of Sikang (Xikang) Province. In 1950 he died in Chamdo while going in person to Lhasa to seek a way of achieving the peaceful liberation of Tibet.'[10]

In other words, the painting depicts an exemplary religious figure who actively served Chinese interests (hence he is called 'patriotic') during the Long March in 1936 as well as during the 'liberation' of Tibet in 1950. As an aside it may be mentioned that Robert Ford

Fig. 2. 'The Meeting in 1936 between Zhu De and dGe-stag Tulku', Kanze school, 1980.

met Getag Tulku in Chamdo in 1950 when the latter was on his way to Lhasa and described him as (Ford, p. 76) 'a typical Khamba in appearance, with a noticeably angular nose; but in manner he was mild and quiet and reserved'. Getag Tulku travelled in the company of three Khamba girls, of whom it was said to Ford that 'they go to his room in the evenings to sing to him' (*ibid.*). According to Ford (whose radio transmitter was operated from the room directly above Getag Tulku's room), the girls 'were young and rosy-cheeked, and far too pretty for me to have allowed in my establishment . . . I did not hear them singing to him in his room' (*ibid.*, p. 77). Soon after, Getag Tulku died; Ford states that he was poisoned, and that he believes he knows who the murderer was, although he declines to reveal the secret (*ibid.*, p. 83).

Returning to the painting, we note that the two figures are surrounded by doves, a symbol of peace which, although of Western (and ultimately Christian) origin, has been fully appropriated by the Chinese Communists and frequently appears in examples of New Tibetan Painting (whereas doves had no such function in traditional Tibetan art). The doves underline the friendliness of the encounter and the peaceful intentions of the People's Liberation Army. Chrysanthemums and peacocks add to the impression of peace, goodwill and harmony.

Below, we see Getag Tulku's monastery. A large detachment of blue-clad Chinese troops are parading in front of it, while a smaller group, presumably officers, have dismounted and are greeted by a lama (identified by the ceremonial parasol) and an orchestra of monks. To the right, one can also see a motley crowd of Tibetan lay people, as well as a group of men and women who are clearly ready to perform for the guests. This scene carries the following explicit message: there is natural harmony and goodwill between Chinese (especially the armed forces) and Tibetans; for the latter, the presence of the army is an occasion for rejoicing, for it heralds liberation; as for the army, it acts in a disciplined way, scrupulous in its display of respect for local etiquette and religious sensibilities. The scene in fact aptly illustrates Point 7 of the Seventeen Point Agreement which was signed between the Chinese and Tibetan governments in 1951 – 'The religious beliefs, customs, and habits of the Tibetan People shall be respected, and lama monasteries shall be protected'[11] – and Point 13, where it is specifically said of the People's Liberation Army that it 'shall not arbitrarily take a single needle or thread from the people'.[12]

Such, then, is the political myth conveyed by the painting. However, underlying this intentional meaning is a deeper significance. The position of the two figures, facing each other but at the same time half turned towards the onlooker is a conventional one in many traditional *thang-kas*.[13] Thus the painting utilises a traditional composition which is likely to hold the attention of a Tibetan. A closer observation of the two figures reveals an utterly untraditional message: as is indicated by the gesture of his hand, it is the layman (a Communist leader, hence not even a Buddhist), who speaks, and not, as the entire weight of Tibetan culture would require, the lama who instructs the layman. The deeper significance, therefore, is that it is the religious man who is in need of instruction, not the representative of secular power, and that the former is not the equal of the latter. This, of course, is precisely the fundamental premise of the 'freedom of religious practice' granted by the Chinese in Tibet. Further, the officer is Chinese and the lama is Tibetan; the subtly dominating posture of the former serves to convey the paternalistic attitude of the Chinese towards the 'national minorities', the recipients of guidance which is benevolent but firm (indeed, the soldiers shown in the lower sector of the painting far outnumber the Tibetans). It is, after all, the Chinese who, whether their mandate has been given by Heaven or by the Party, have something to teach the 'minorities', and not the other way around.

So far we have been able to identify two myths conveyed by the New Tibetan Painting. 'King Gesar of Ling' represents what I would call a kind of 'historical triumphalism', in which the myth of a dashing, colourful heroic past is glorified. The ancient kings, especially Srongtsen Gampo and, not surprisingly, his Chinese spouse, are favorite subjects (figs 3, 4).[14] Princess Wencheng, as contemporary Chinese scholars point out (Wang and Suo, p. 20), 'worked untiringly in the interest of unity and friendship between her people and the Tufans [that is, the Tibetans]. She did a good job in strengthening the political ties between Tang and Tufan, enhancing the economic and cultural exchanges between them and spurring the progress of Tufan society.' This world of Tibetan kings and heroes is, however, a gaudy, one-dimensional, fairy-tale distortion of history, from which the great saints and ecclesiastical figures who have dominated Tibetan civilisation and played a decisive role in Tibet's history are conspicuously absent. We shall look in vain for a Milarepa, a Butön, or a 5th Dalai Lama.

The second myth is the one we have just seen exemplified by 'The Meeting in 1936 between Zhu De and dGe-stag Tulku': friendship and harmony between the army and the people, benevolent guidance of the Tibetans by the Chinese.

We now turn to a third myth which we shall identify on the basis of a painting bearing the title 'The Market' (fig. 5). The central

Figs. 3 and 4. Srongtsen Gampo and his Chinese wife Princess Wencheng.

Fig. 5. 'The Market'.

sector shows a young Tibetan couple, perhaps on their way home from the People's Department Store. The man is wheeling a motor-bike, while the young woman, whose head is turned backwards (giving the impression of gazing wistfully at the market-place they are leaving), holds a pinkish nylon umbrella. Above this couple stand five young Tibetan ladies, four of them with their backs to the onlooker (allowing the artist to display the elaborate head-ornament which one of them is wearing). Two of them are holding a piece of red cloth (perhaps a table-cloth), and seem to examine it with admiration. Framing the central sector are four rectangular panels containing market scenes in which large quantities of goods are offered for sale.

The 'form' of the myth is thus a collection of apparently trivial scenes from contemporary daily life in Tibet. The explicit myth – the intentional meaning – is perfectly clear. In the new Tibet there is an abundance of goods, both traditional handicraft and indus-trial products. Moreover, there is affluence, for the goods all find ready buyers. In particular, the young couple of the central scene display the supreme symbol of affluence and progress: a motor-bike. In fact, the painting eulogises the myth of 'consumerism', the materialistic paradise of consumer goods to which 'development' of 'backward' nationalities will, so the painting assures us, inevitably lead. While the myth of consumerism is the central theme of the painting, it is closely associated with a second myth which we have already encountered in various modes, *viz.* the 'unity and friend-ship' between the 'nationalities'. This is indirectly but clearly brought out by the young couple and the group of lady customers. All are ostentatiously wearing Tibetan dress – signifying the Cen-tral Government's benign policy of promoting 'minority' culture. At the same time, they also have discreetly non-Tibetan items of dress, such as the pullover worn by the man or the nylon umbrella of the woman. Such items eloquently illustrate the myth of the integration of minority culture into the mainstream culture of modern China, characterised by gaudy, mass-produced consumer goods. The small scenes in the panels along the borders of the pain-ting illustrate the same interweaving of traditional dress and minority culture with consumer goods imported from China: an old lady tries on Chinese canvas shoes, children gaze longingly at toy giraffes and balloons produced in Shanghai, and in the bottom panel two Tibetans have settled down with three bottles of beer – or, more likely, cheap fire-water from Sichuan.

All this constitutes the explicit 'intentional meaning' of the pain-ting, the unambiguous myth. There is, however, a deeper signifi-cance to it, which we, as 'mythologists' (in Barthes' sense), can 'decipher'. First of all, we once again note that the structure of the painting copies that of a particular type of traditional *thang-ka*, *viz.* that of a biographical *thang-ka* in which the subject of the biography occupies the centre, while square or rectangular panels on all four sides show scenes from his life to constitute a more-or-less continuous pictorial narrative.[15] The traditional structure of the painting prediposes the viewer to accord particular importance to the central part, which in 'The Market' is not, as would conventionally be expected, a saint, but a young couple. The presence of the young man and woman leads to a whole series of associations: sexuality, matrimony, lay life. In short, the painting glorifies the 'myth' of the primacy of secular life. The side-panels do the same, but with particular emphasis on 'consumerism'. It is, however, a consumerism which has a deeper, more sinister aspect, for it is based on an unequal relationship, or, more precisely, a colonial economy. Tibetans – as is shown in the painting – are the recipients of cheap, mass-produced industrial goods from China, whereas the Chinese – this is *not* shown in the painting – extract raw materials, especially timber, from Tibet to supply China's industry, with disastrous consequences for the natural environment of Tibet.

I would like to comment, albeit more briefly, on a few more paintings in which traditional structure, colours and proportions are made use of to express new myths. A good example is a mural, entitled 'Harvest Festival', in the 'Tibet Hall' in the Great Hall of the People in Beijing (fig. 6). The central figure is that of a young Tibetan woman striking a pose, *viz.* the graceful *tribhanga* which in traditional Buddhist art is characteristic of Bodhisattvas; the upper part of her body is surrounded by an aureole, her attribute is a sheaf of barley which symbolises the harvest, and although she is dressed in festive clothes (but then practically all Tibetans in Chinese art are), her head-scarf shows her working-class background. She is flanked by two acolytes, both elderly bearded men who represent folk-opera and folk-music. The remainder of the painting is filled with a hectic whirl of figures who are engaged in horse-racing, drinking and dancing, and who form the entourage of the central 'goddess of the harvest'. Once again a basically traditional method of structuring the elements of the surface of the painting, together with traditional 'icongraphical' elements, is employed to communicate a new set of myths: the primacy of youth, fecundity, labour, and the colourful and carefree quaintness and barbaric vital force of 'national minorities'. Characteristically, the painting is said to have been executed by artists of three different 'nationalities': Ye Xingsheng (presumably, since nothing else is stated, Chinese), Yixi Xirao (i.e. 'Yeshe Sherab, Tibetan), Zhu Yaotao (again presumably Chinese) and Abuyi (Hui), which thus sets an admirable example of friendly co-operation between the many 'nationalities' of the People's Republic of China. The example is all the more appropriate as the painting (together with a number of other similar pieces) was 'a gift of the Tibetan people for the 20th anniversary of the founding of the Tibetan Autonomous Region' (*Jubilant Tibet*, p. 122).

Another similar painting, likewise found in the 'Tibet Hall', is described as follows in the official publication in which it is reproduced: 'The work is done in rich golden colour in the style of the lamasery murals. But the way it gives expression to the personality of the images and the feeling of motion it creates shows a breakthrough of the traditional art. It is a painting of powerful spirit, dazzling colours, compact composition, combination of motion and stillness, and strong yet cheerful rhythm: a painting that eulogises the new life of the Tibetan people' (*ibid.*).

Another piece, emanating from the Kanze school of New Tibetan Painting, is entitled 'Jubilant Khambas' (fig. 7). In the centre are to be seen two yak-dancers, each with an acolyte, in a whirl of movement that suggests the barbaric vitality of a carefree 'minority'. This group is surrounded by a circle (a *parivāra*, if the term may be used) of spectators. The 'jubilant Khambas', who have clearly long ago forgotten the many years of fierce resistance to the Chinese invaders and the horrors of the Cultural Revolution, are seated comfortably under colourful umbrellas and are holding the inevitable balloons; they are all dressed in traditional costume, but the careful observer will notice Chinese mass-produced items such as tape recorders, a thermos flask and a musical instrument of impeccable ideological respectability, the accordion. The painting gives a highly suggestive glimpse of a make-believe Tibet in which suffering is no more, only blissful celebration of minority quaintness: umbrellas, balloons and butterflies. The formal structure is the traditional one of a central deity surrounded by its entourage (in fact, the upper yak mask forcefully suggests a likeness to a fierce tantric deity).

It is not necessary at this stage to enter into a detailed analysis of each painting, because their structural patterns and the myths they express – overtly as well as indirectly – will have become familiar. Thus it need hardly be said that this Brave New Tibet has its own *mandalas*, which are perfectly traditional in structure, but radically new in content. Instead of revealing the most profound spiritual insights of Tibetan Buddhism, a *mandalas* may now show a heroic scene, presumably inspired by the Gesar epic.

Fig. 6. 'Harvest Festival', a mural in the Tibet Hall of the Great Hall of the People, Beijing, by Ye Xingsheng, Yixi Xirao, Zhu Yaotao and Abuyi, 1985.

Fig. 7. 'Jubilant Khambas', Kanze School.

In the case of our final example of New Tibetan Painting, executed in 1986 and entitled 'The Land of Song and Dance' (fig. 8), one has to look twice in order to realise that the painting is *not* a traditional one. It is, in fact, from every formal point of view a traditional *thang-ka*, with a multi-armed figure, exactly like a tantric deity, which is surrounded by an aureole of flames, with a secondary, smaller figure immediately below within its own falling aureole, and an inner entourage that consists of two male and two female dancing figures, and an outer entourage of six rows of alternating male and female dancers. The central figure is, however, not a goddess but a young woman who strikes a dance posture while holding a drum and drumstick (her additional twelve arms, which are naked so as to suggest the arms of a deity, emphasise the movement of dance, but the *mudras* of the hands are without meaning). The message of the painting is totally secular and in complete conformity with the officially promoted myth of 'minorities' as exotic, colourful and, above all, given to song and dance.

It is not my task to act the part of the devil's advocate. But should we not reflect for a moment on this inordinate emphasis which is placed on exuberant folk-dance in the Chinese view of minorities? For it is a fact that in Chinese civilisation actors and dancing-girls have occupied the bottom rung of the social hierarchy. They have often been prostitutes, and generally the object of profound contempt. Social myths die hard, and we are probably not much mistaken if we sense the same thinly veiled contempt towards minorities, and towards actors and dancers, beneath the shiny, hectic veneer of this politicised art.

Bearing this in mind, we pass from art to real life (the distinction is a superficial one) – more specifically, to a local festival of folk culture, which was celebrated in a district of Amdo in the late 1980s. At this official festival of Tibetan folk-culture, Chinese pop, disco and break-dance dominated the programme in the local Palace of Culture for two consecutive nights. The ethnic touch was essentially a parody, whether it was in the form of an imitation of Tibetan, Qiang (Ch'iang) or Kazakh folk-dance. What was the message of this parody of Tibetan culture? Like New Tibetan Painting (with which the culture festival shared the same aesthetic universe), the myth, as I understand it, was twofold: on the one hand, there was affirmation of diversity and equality between the 'nationalities', great or small; on the other, a show of happiness under the leadership of the political establishment (whether local or central). This was the intentional meaning, the open political thrust of this festival of Tibetan folk culture. There was, however,

Fig. 8. 'The Land of Song and Dance', 1986.

a more subtle message, an essential meaning, which was conveyed by the dress of the dancers, and which was just as gaudy and unrealistic as any to be found in the examples of contemporary art considered above. Official minority folk culture in China is entertainment, circus, show – nothing more. Further, the personal appearance of the dancers – their heavy make-up and expressionless facial features – conforms to Chinese, not Tibetan aesthetic ideals. What we see there is not Tibetan folk-culture at all, but a modern Chinese cultural idiom masquerading as Tibetan.

Finally, let us look at the expression of the same messages in the parade on the concluding day of the festival of Tibetan folk culture. In that parade, groups of young men and women marched past in ethnic dress (or rather, since all are exactly alike, ethnic uniform), followed by monks whose participation in the parade with religious banners and musical instruments represented proof of the government's policy of religious freedom. The parade moved towards a plain outside the town where Tibetan horsemen assembled, brandishing the flag of the People's Republic of China. Some were dressed to impersonate ancient heroes – the theme is familiar. Others proudly rode that supreme symbol of progress, the motor-bike. As row upon row of young women and men, who were dressed up in imitations of the Tibetan *chuba*, filed before the local *nomenklatura*, one was struck not only by the incongruity of Chinese pink straw hats as part of Tibetan dress, but on a deeper level one realises that one is witnessing a call to blind political obedience, collective existence and cultural uniformity (fig. 9).

Among the many questions raised by the New Tibetan Painting, some must remain unanswered. One such question is whether this artistic idiom is *effective* as the expression of a particular group of myths. Is its intentional meaning in fact accepted? The skillful use of traditional structural and iconographic elements would suggest an answer in the affirmative. The fact that the myths concerning material progress and cultural characteristics of 'minorities' are continually propagated by the authorities in countless other ways could argue for the same conclusion. On the other hand, the stark contrast between the carefree universe of joy and plenty of the paintings and the conditions of poverty, cultural discrimination and political oppression under which most Tibetans live would suggest that this art is, in all likelihood, less than convincing. Reproductions of several of these paintings in the form of posters abound in Tibet and, although they are not infrequently found in private homes, there is no indication that they are treated as anything more than pieces of gaudy paper that are pasted on walls for lack of something better. Furthermore, the persuasiveness of the

Fig. 9. Official parade, with Tibetans in national costume, Amdo, late 1980s.

symbolism expressing the myths may have its own inherent limits. In the New Tibetan Painting we are dealing, obviously, with what Barthes styles 'myth on the Left'. This mythology is characterised by its poverty, for it expresses only a limited number of political notions. Not only does it not touch upon the spiritual world of religion, but 'Left-wing myth never reaches the immense field of human relationships, the very vast surface of "insignificant" ideology . . . it is a myth suited to a convenience, not to a necessity.' Barthes has something very pertinent to say concerning the type of myth which we have encountered in the New Tibetan Painting and in officially promoted folk-dance: 'It does not know how to proliferate; being produced on order and for a temporally limited prospect, it is invented with difficulty. It lacks a major faculty, that of fabulising. Whatever it does, there remains about it something stiff and literal, a suggestion of something done to order.'[16] This stiffness is perhaps due to the fact that the myths we encounter are myths of the *established* Left, of a regime,

184   *Per Kvaerne*

and not a genuine revolutionary or popular art. May we not assume that the mythological poverty of the New Tibetan Painting is perceptible to most Tibetans who encounter it?

A final question must also remain unanswered: is it not possible, indeed likely, that the 'consumerism' which constitutes one of the myths we have discussed corresponds in reality to a genuine aspiration of most Tibetans? Perhaps; but here we must make a careful distinction between an almost universal human desire for material comfort and status-conferring goods, and a colonial situation, characteristic of present-day Tibet, in which second-class citizens provide a market for imported goods, their territory a 'Western Treasure-house' (to use the Chinese term designating Tibet) for the world's last remaining colonial power. As a style or a school, the New Tibetan Painting has not been without a certain power of innovation; but it has surely already explored to the full its limited possibilities of expression. As for Tibetan folk-dance, its survival will entirely depend on whether it can still appeal to Tibetans outside the officially sponsored displays of 'minority' culture.

REFERENCES

Barthes, Roland, *Mythologies*, London: Paladin, 1973 (Paris, 1957).
dKar-mdzes Bod-ris, Chengdu, 1987.
Ford, Robert, *Captured in Tibet*, London: Harrap, 1957.
Goldstein, Melvyn C., *A History of Modern Tibet*, Berkeley: University of California Press, 1989.
Jubilant Tibet, Lhasa: Tibet People's Publishing House, 1986.
Karmay, Heather, 'dGe 'dun chos 'phel, the Artist' in Michael Aris and Aung San Suu Kyi (eds), *Tibetan Studies in Honour of Hugh Richardson*, Warminster: Aris and Phillips, 1980, pp. 145–9.
Lehmann, Peter-Hannes, and Jay Ullal, *Tibet. Das stille Drama auf dem Dach der Erde*, Hamburg: Geo, 1981
Pal, Pratapaditya, *Art of Tibet*, Los Angeles County Museum of Art, 1983.
Panofsky, Erwin, 'Zum Problem der Beschreibung und Inhaltsdeutung von Werken der bildenden Kunst' in Ekkehard Kaemmerling (ed.), *Ikonographie und Ikonologie. Theorien – Entwicklung – Probleme*, Köln: Dumont, 1979 (1932), pp. 185–206.
Stoddard, Heather, *Le mendiant de l'Amdo*, Paris: Société d'ethnographie, 1985.
Wang Furen and Suo Wenqing, *Highlights of Tibetan History*, Beijing: New World Press, 1984.

NOTES

1. Karmay, p. 147; Stoddard, ill. nos 27–35.
2. Stoddard, ill. no. 204.

3. Stoddard, ill. no. 377; Lehmann and Ullal, p. 119, has a reproduction of a mural from the Norbulingka, presumably the one in question, which is said to depict the Dalai Lama in 1956, surrounded by his family and ministers.
4. The Tibetan spelling is retained.
5. This is based on the Introduction (in Tibetan) to *Bod-ris*.
6. Panofsky, pp. 185ff.
7. The formulation of these two 'meanings' is preceded, according to Panofsky, by a primary *Phänomensinn*, a 'meaning of the phenomena', which is the ascertaining·of physical movement or position.
8. This 'form' (the mere interplay of mass and colour which conveys a myth only when it has been infused with meaning) could be seen as corresponding to the *Phänomensinn* of Panofsky.
9. Barthes, p. 128.
10. *Bod-ris*, p. 12.
11. Cited in Goldstein, p. 766.
12. *Ibid.*, p. 768.
13. For examples of this convention, see Pal, pp. 82, 89.
14. Another example of Srongtsen Gampo together with Wencheng, is a modern *thang-ka* displayed in the Great Hall in Beijing (reproduced in *Jubilant Tibet*, p. 120). The *thang-ka* is basically in traditional style, except for the inevitable stereotyped male and female dancers along the lower edge of the *thang-ka*. The royal couple (Tibetan king and Chinese queen) have supplanted the traditional triad of 'religious kings' as an 'iconographic' motif.
15. Pal, p. 15.
16. Barthes, pp. 145ff. I do not entirely follow the analytical scheme of Barthes, for he sees 'myth on the Left' as the myths of the oppressed, while the myths of the oppressors, the 'myth on the Right', are considered by him as far more rich, all-encompassing and diversified. Barthes is not entirely consistent, however, for he counts the Stalin myth as a myth on the Left; surely Stalin represents an oppressor if ever there was one.

Part III
EXILE: RESISTANCE AND DIPLOMACY

THE TIBETAN RESISTANCE MOVEMENT AND THE ROLE OF THE C.I.A.

Jamyang Norbu

In marked contrast to developments in other areas of Tibetan studies, very little attention has been paid to modern Tibetan history, and within that even less to the violent and cataclysmic period in the 1950s and 1960s when the Tibetan people, especially the tribesmen from Eastern and North-eastern Tibet, rose in revolt against Chinese domination. What few published accounts of the Tibetan resistance movement exist are on the whole vague about figures, place-names and details of the people involved. Books like *Tibet in Revolt* by George Patterson, *From the Land of Lost Content* by Noel Barber, *The Cavaliers of Kham* by Michel Peissel and *The Secret War in Tibet* by Lowell Thomas Jr. were good reads, very supportive of the Tibetan cause and probably the best that could be done at the time with the limited information available, but they were on the whole rather nebulous. In one of them the author even managed to make little or no mention of the real leaders and participants in the revolt, while glorifying as resistance heroes and leaders people who were clearly not.

There has also been a singular lack of inquiry into the resistance movement on the part of the exile Tibetan government. This government has always had an uneasy relationship with the resistance. The wide extent and popularity of the resistance highlighted the failure of the government's policy of co-operation with the Chinese occupation forces. Traditional prejudices between Khamba and the Lhasa government also played their part. Early in the 1960s the exile Tibetan government did attempt to gather statements from as many refugees as it could and collected a number of accounts from people involved in the resistance. These accounts were never very extensive or detailed, and only a few of them were ever published.

186

A number of these records seem to have been lost or misplaced, but an attempt is being made to put them back together as far as possible.

The resistance itself did not go in for documenting its activities in any systematic or extensive way, and was suspicious of other people's attempts to do so. With the establishment of connections with the CIA there was an almost obsessive insistence on secrecy that was carried to a degree where it did more harm than good. No real attempt was made to publicise the activities of the resistance to the world. Even within Tibetan society little attempt was made to inform people of its activities. Secrecy was also maintained so as not to embarrass the governments of India or Nepal where the resistance maintained bases and agencies.

After the closure of the last guerrilla bases in Mustang in 1974, the Four Rivers, Six Ranges organisation in India, which was mostly composed of former resistance members, made attempts to gather and record detailed histories of every guerrilla group or *dmag-sgar* that had belonged to the resistance movement. This project has apparently had considerable setbacks and it does not seem that it will be possible for these records to be published in the near future. A posthumous biography of the leader of the resistance, Gompo Tashi Andrugtsang, was published in India in 1973, but it was sketchy and badly translated.[1]

Lhamo Tsering, a leader of the Mustang guerrilla force and assistant to Gyalo Thondup, one of the Dalai Lama's elder brothers (who was a kind of overall leader of the resistance for some years), has also written his memoirs. The book is not published at the time of writing, but it promises to shed light on some aspects of resistance history, probably focusing on resistance activities in the 1960s and '70s when he was involved in a position of responsibility. Another person closely linked to the Tibetan rebellion, especially in the mid- and late 1950s, is the controversial Alo Chonze. He was one of the leaders of an underground Lhasa-based nationalist organisation, the *Mimang* (the People), which was the main source of anti-Chinese activities in the city. He is publishing, in instalments, a semi-historical, semi-autobiographical, account of the Tibetan uprising and of the politics of exile. Two volumes have been released of which the first provides interesting information on the uprising in Lithang and the formation of the Mimang organisation in Lhasa.[2]

Although many resistance leaders and fighters have died, a number are still alive in Nepal, India and Switzerland. Many of them these days seem willing to be interviewed, and to talk freely about their past. In a recent French television documentary on the

Tibetan resistance,[3] Khambas spoke openly about their activities, their old CIA connections and even their connections with the Indian intelligence and army.

Washington still regards American support for the Tibetan resistance as a sensitive issue, and the appropriate records remain security-classified. A few obscure newspaper articles[4] and some references in certain books on the CIA[5] are all that is available to the public on one of the few long-term and successful operations conducted by the American secret service. According to Fletcher Prouty, a colonel in the US Air Force who managed secret air missions for General Erskine's Office of Special Operations, Tibet is 'buried in the lore of the CIA as one of those successes that are not talked about'.[6]

Such lack of information on the Tibetan Revolt has enabled the Tibetan leadership successfully to rewrite history, playing down the role of the armed revolt and fostering the fiction that the popular resistance was non-violent. Though unhesitatingly subscribed to by many friends of Tibet, this story is patently untrue. There was never a non-violent campaign against the Chinese. Even the few public demonstrations before the uprising of March 10, 1959 were not a display of the public's commitment to non-violence: quite the reverse. They were a signal to the Chinese that the Tibetans were prepared to act violently to protect their leader and their religion.

The promotion of the non-violent interpretation of modern Tibetan history has accorded only a minor role to the resistance movement. It has even given rise to two very misleading assumptions, both of which we shall examine: first, that the overall scale of the uprisings had not been significant; and secondly, that the resistance movement had been supported and even possibly fomented by the CIA.

Magnitude of the Tibetan Uprising

From anecdotal evidence provided by surviving resistance fighters, refugees and recent escapees from Tibet, it would seem that during the uprising the scale of the fighting and the consequent death and dislocation in Eastern Tibet were enormous, and comparable in magnitude to the events in Afghanistan following the Soviet invasion. Though the effect of the uprising on China has not been as great as that of the Afghan conflict on the Russian people, especially since propaganda ensured that the Chinese people would be properly ignorant of it, the uprising has remained the one persistent running sore that has constantly spoiled China's otherwise successful efforts at keeping up appearances before the eyes of the world. Roderick MacFarquhar considered that the Tibetan resistance produced 'the gravest episode of internal disorder [in the People's Republic of China] prior to the Cultural Revolution . . .'[7]

Even if we were to discount the anecdotal evidence, the scale of demographic dislocation in Eastern and North-eastern Tibet, where most of the fighting took place, provides sufficient evidence to substantiate the claim of many refugees as to the massive extent of the fighting and casualties in these areas. One of the standard corroborations of this provided by refugees is that, subsequent to the crushing of the uprisings, all or most of the ploughing in their villages or districts was being done by women (unthinkable in the past) as there were no men left in the area. Chinese figures taken from their 1982 census,[8] fifteen to twenty years after the revolt had been crushed, indicate a much larger ratio of women to men in Eastern and North-eastern Tibet, even though a lengthy period of time had passed since then. Such disparate sex-ratio figures do not appear at all in other parts of Tibet or even China, although vast numbers of people died in these places too, for other reasons such as the 1960–3 famine (probably the greatest famine in human history), which affected both sexes equally. We must also bear in mind that the majority of the Tibetan people lived in Eastern and North-eastern Tibet where most of the fighting had taken place.

No substantive effort has been made by any person or organisation, not even the exile Tibetan government, to find out the number of people killed in the uprisings in Eastern Tibet, or in the rest of Tibet and Lhasa. In fact the only published figure we have for Tibetans killed in the Lhasa uprising and its aftermath is from official Chinese sources. A booklet marked 'secret' and published in Lhasa on October 1, 1960 by the political department of the Tibetan Military District, says of the aftermath of the Lhasa uprising: 'From last March up to now we have already wiped out [*xiaomie*] over 87,000 of the enemy.'[9]

Earliest Resistance to the Chinese

Prevalent at one time among journalists and academics sympathetic to China was the idea that the Tibetan revolt was essentially a conspiracy of the Tibetan church, the aristocracy and the CIA, and that even the Dalai Lama's flight to India was engineered by the CIA.[10] Vestiges of such notions still prevail today. Popular resistance in Eastern and North-eastern Tibet began long before any American involvement. In fact there is evidence to prove that sporadic resistance to Communist Chinese advances occurred in these areas even as early as 1949. We need not go into accounts here of earlier clashes between Tibetans and Communist forces, especially in 1934-5 during the Long March,[11] as these clashes were not connected to the actual invasion and occupation of Tibet in later years.

In a number of interviews I was repeatedly informed by tribesmen from Gyalthang in South-eastern Tibet, now part of Yunnan Province, that they had resisted the Red Army when it first advanced into their territory in 1949. Their claims are to some extent confirmed by the accounts of Peter Goullart,[12] a White Russian employee of the Kuomintang Government, who served in the late 1940s as an agricultural expert of sorts in the Nakhi (Naxi) town of Lijiang in Yunnan Province. Goullart states that in 1949, after the fall of Kunming, the provincial capital, and the Red Army push towards the west, Khambas from Gyalthang, which bordered Nakhi territory, came to Lijiang and, helped by local Nakhis, managed to inflict an initial defeat on an advance guard of the Red Army. Later the Communists used more subtle tactics and infiltrated agents among the younger Nakhis which led to their demoralisation and the fall of Lijiang to the Communists. Goullart also mentions that the Gyalthangwas were a more warlike and formidable people than the Nakhis.

Gyalthang's resistance probably explains why it was one of the first places in Eastern Tibet where 'democratic reforms' were carried out from as early as 1953. Gompo Tashi Andrugtsang mentions the event in his autobiography: 'In the area of Gyalthang Anthena Kham, the following year [1953] the local population was divided into five strata and a terror campaign of selective arrests launched by the Chinese. People belonging to the first three strata were either publicly humiliated or condemned to the firing squad.'[13]

Another area of early resistance to the Red Army came from somewhere geographically distant to Gyalthang, namely Hormukha and Nangra in Amdo, or North-eastern Tibet. Here, the fight against the Communists had been going on for a considerable time with Ma Pufang, the Kuomintang Governor (in reality a semi-independent Muslim warlord) of Qinghai Province, who led his Hui cavalry, and was allied with Amdowa and Mongol tribesmen.[14] But when Communist victory seemed imminent in 1949, Ma Pufang fled with his wives and treasure on two DC-10s. The Red Army reached Nangra and Hormukha in September 1949, according to an eyewitness, Rinzin,[15] who later also participated in the fighting.

In December of the same year the two chiefs of Nangra, Pon

Wangchen and Pon Choje, led their men in battle against the Chinese. There were a number of encounters, in one of which the son of Pon Wangchen was killed. Rinzin claims that the initial contingent of Chinese troops with whom they fought consisted of around 6,000 men, who were later reinforced by an additional 10,000 men from Rikong after the outbreak of fighting. The people of Hormukha joined in the fighting in February 1950, but by then it was too late to affect the outcome of the conflict as the Chinese had many more troops in the area. All the major Amdowa forces were destroyed. In one disastrous encounter Pon Choje was nearly captured but managed to escape attention by faking death. Nearly all the tribesmen were forced to leave their homes and take to the mountains from where they began hit-and run guerrilla operations against Chinese supply lines and patrols. These operations proved more successful than the pitched battles they had been conducting until then on more conventional lines. The Amdowas of Nangra claimed that, because of their determined resistance, the Chinese referred to Nangra as 'Little Taiwan'.

In 1952 a truce was arranged by some lamas of Dechen monastery. Pon Wangchen was taken to Xining and then to Beijing where he is said to have met Mao Zedong. There was a brief period of peace between 1952 and 1953, but once again the Chinese began denunciations, struggles, arrests and executions, and renewed fighting broke out all over the territory. The Chinese had by now built up an overwhelming superiority in numbers and in quality of arms, and there was no doubt as to the final outcome of the conflict. Many thousands of Amdowas were killed in the fighting, executed or sent to labour camps. Many also committed suicide. Some escaped to Lhasa. In the words of Rinzin, 'only a few blind men, cripples, fools and some children were left.'[16]

Such resistance against invading Chinese forces in the late 1940s and early 1950s was not a common phenomenon in Eastern and North-eastern Tibet at the time. Nor did the Tibetan Government forces receive much help from local Khambas when Communist troops attacked in October 1959. A considerable degree of the Tibetan Government's prestige and authority had waned in Eastern Tibet since 1917 when, under Kalon Lama Champa Tendar, Governor of Eastern Tibet and Commander of the Tibetan forces there, Tibetan power and influence in that entire area had been at its pinnacle.[17] Before the Chinese invasion of 1950 the Tibetan Government had attempted to arouse the people of the frontier regions to resist the Red Army, but without much success. Taktser Rinpoche, one of the Dalai Lama's elder brothers and abbot of Kumbum monastery in Amdo, told me that his monastery had received a letter from the Lhalu *zhabs-pad* (minister), the Governor of Eastern Tibet and Commander of the Tibetan army there a year before the invasion, instructing the monks of Taktser to resist Chinese forces. But Lhalu's efforts to rouse Amdowa and Khamba loyalty were not very successful, except in a few cases, as at the monastery at Chamdo.[18]

Isolated though they were, the outbreaks of fighting in Gyalthang, Nangra and Hormukha and certain other areas were of sufficient scale and ferocity to be indicative of the course that events in Eastern Tibet would run. Soon Chinese policies in Eastern Tibet began to create a new wave of hostility against the occupation forces that became particularly violent around the winter of 1955–6, one of the most immediate causes being the implementation by the Chinese of a set of programmes labelled 'Democratic Reforms'. The Chinese called this uprising the 'Kangding Rebellion',[19] after the Chinese name for the town of Dartsedo, which was the Chinese headquarters for the whole of Eastern Tibet. The revolt spread like wildfire all over Eastern Tibet, and soon tribal chiefs from diverse areas tried to organise a joint effort to defeat the Chinese. Yuru Pon, the paramount chieftain of the Lithang nomads, sent messengers all over Eastern Tibet calling for attacks on Chinese positions on the eighteenth day of the first Tibetan month of 1956. Monasteries and tribes in Nyarong, Kanze, Batang, Drango, Linkashiba and many other places responded to this call to action. Yuru Pon later died in the bombed ruins of the Great Monastery of Lithang after having killed two senior Chinese officers with a concealed pistol in a fake surrender.[20]

Dorje Yudon (Dorgee Eudon), the younger wife of the chieftain of Nyarong, Gyari Nima, stated in an interview[21] that the Gyaritsang family received a letter from the Lithang chieftain asking them to revolt on the eighteenth day of the first moon of 1956. He also wrote that he would send them another message confirming the date of the revolt as soon as he received answers form all the chiefs in Eastern Tibet. Since Gyari Nima had been summoned by the Chinese authorities to Dartsedo for a meeting, Dorje Yudon took up the leadership of the Gyaritsang clan and other tribes of Nyarong. When she organised meetings in various parts of Nyarong to persuade people to join her revolt, the Chinese authorities realised what she was up to and attempted to have her assassinated at her home by two Nyarongwa collaborators aided by two Chinese soldiers.

The attempt failed, as did other attempts to arrest Dorje's uncle and other leaders of the revolt in Nyarong. She was therefore forced to call the revolt four days earlier than the date agreed upon with Yuru Pon. The Nyarongwas were initially successful in destroying various small Chinese garrisons in the region and also in killing and capturing many collaborators. Surviving Chinese troops fell back on the Chinese administrative centre for Nyarong which was located in Drugmo Dzong, the Fortress of the Female Dragon. The surviving Chinese soldiers barricaded themselves behind the massive walls of the ancient fort and prepared to hold out. The Nyarongwas tried to storm the place a number of times but were unsuccessful.

The Chinese sent relief forces from Kanze which the rebels tried to intercept and ambush. Initially Dorje Yudon's forces were successful but after a month larger Chinese forces from Drango and Thawu (Dawu) managed to break the rebels' siege of the Fortress of the Female Dragon. Dorje Yudon recalls that twenty-three tribal chieftains in Kham first responded to Yuru Pon's call to revolt, and that they called their loose-knit alliance 'Tensung Dhanglang Magar', or 'The Volunteer Army to Defend Buddhism'.

The Character of the Revolt

Though there were obvious limits to which military action could be co-ordinated among all the various tribes of Eastern Tibet, the general uprising in 1956 did manage to succeed in clearing the Chinese out of nearly the whole province for a few months. The Red Army soon returned in greater strength and numbers, but that part of the story need not concern us here. Yet it is worth noting that, despite long-standing tribal animosities and differences, a fairly successful attempt was made to unite the efforts of Eastern Tibetans in rebellion against the Chinese. When one considers that this attempt at co-ordination had to cover many hundreds of miles of mountain wilderness, without even basic communication equipment, roads or motorised transport, it is remarkable that such a widespread rebellion should have successfully taken place, more or less around the date agreed upon.

The name that the Khambas gave to their resistance movement, 'the Volunteer Army to Defend Buddhism', reflects what may be called the ideological nature of the uprising, and thus the support it gained all over Eastern Tibet and later in Central Tibet. Dawa Norbu, in an article on the Tibetan Revolt, considered that the Khamba uprising was in defence of Tibetan Buddhist values, and of the political and sacred institutions founded upon such values. 'As long as the Chinese did not tamper with the objectively functioning social system and the value systems still considered sacred by members of that society, as happened in Outer Tibet, there was no revolt, although the unprecedented Chinese presence in the country caused great resentment and anxiety. But the moment the Chinese tried to alter the functioning and sacred social system in Inner Tibet which they considered *de jure* China proper, the revolt began.'[22]

This traditional ideology on which the revolt was based gave it sufficient popular appeal to transcend the borders of Eastern Tibet and to ignite passions and violence even in the Tibet Autonomous Region, where the Chinese had caused no disruption in the social system, and where the aristocracy and clergy were being actively courted by the Chinese authorities. Hence many Tibetans have considered the revolt a national one,[23] in the sense that the sentiment of the majority of the Tibetan people was involved. Yet the leaders and members of the resistance movement, mainly composed of Khambas and Amdowas, were too often unable to transcend narrow tribal loyalties for the movement to take on a fully national and dynamic character. The traditional Lhasa–Khamba divide, though bridged on a number of occasions during the revolt, was also never reconciled satisfactorily. The other name of the resistance movement, 'Chushi Gangdrug' – 'Four Rivers, Six Ranges' – an ancient name of Eastern Tibet, underlines the narrower and divided character of the movement.

With the savage suppression of the uprisings in Eastern Tibet and the large-scale movement of refugees to Lhasa, the focus of the resistance shifted to Central Tibet, where, under the leadership of the Lithangwa merchant Gompo Tashi Andrugtsang, the earlier very loose-knit confederacy of guerrilla bands was re-organized, and a single resistance army formally created on 16 June, 1958, in the district of Lhokha just south of Lhasa. Weapons were purchased secretly from India. Dawa Norbu points out that 'the vast majority of the 23 Khamba leaders of the Tibet Revolt were merchants who had made their fortune since the "liberation," as China kept pouring silver coins called *dao-yuan* into Tibet to pay the Tibetan ruling class and road workers. But instead of making more money or running away to India safely with their silver fortunes, Khambas spent the Chinese money for the purchase of arms and ammunition for the revolt.'[24]

The resistance also received information from sympathetic ministers and officials of the Tibetan Government on the location and content of secret government arsenals. From these they removed substantial quantities of arms and ammunition,[25] which enabled the guerrillas to cut off the three strategic highways south of Lhasa and nearly paralyse Chinese army operations in that area.

Limits of American Involvement

It is from these tumultuous and far-ranging events that the Tibetan resistance movement takes its origins. It was only after these events and other successes, reports of which reached the ears of the American Government in due course,[26] that the United States actually sent assistance to the resistance forces in Tibet, although this aid only began to reach the hands of the fighters in 1958. By all accounts, during the crucial period of the resistance in Eastern Tibet and during its greatest successes, no American arms or assistance of any kind were received by any resistance group.

Accounts of the CIA engineering the Dalai Lama's escape and escorting him[27] seem to be mostly the result of creative journalistic imagination. The only agents the CIA had in Lhasa who attempted to make some kind of connection with the Dalai Lama and the Tibetan Government were two Lithangwas, Atha and Lhotse, who had been parachuted near Samye some time before the outbreak of the revolt in Lhasa. Lhotse died a few years ago but Atha is still alive, in New Delhi. He told me that he and his partner secretly managed to see Phala, the Dalai Lama's Lord Chamberlain (*mgron-gnyer chen-mo*), who with Surkhang *zhabs-pad* was the leader of the nationalist faction in the Tibetan Government, and sympathetic to the resistance. Atha gave Phala a message from the American government asking for an official request from the Tibetan Government for American military aid. Phala told Atha that it was too late and that it would be impossible to trust the entire Cabinet or the Assembly with such a sensitive and potentially compromising message. Phala confirmed this story of his meeting with Atha in a conversation I had with him some years ago before his death. Phala planned and organised the Dalai Lama's escape using Atha and Lhotse with their radio transmitter to keep the Americans informed of developments in the escape plan, and later during the actual escape itself.

The true extent and implications of the Tibetan resistance have never been studied systematically. From the little understanding I have managed to gain through conversations and interviews with people who were involved, I have come to realise that the amount and quality of information on these events are frustratingly inadequate; the far greater mass of historical knowledge and memory floats undiscovered beneath the surface of our indifference and neglect. It is my hope that the present attitude of Tibetan officials, Buddhist followers, Western supporters and intellectuals, who regard the resistance movement as an embarrassment – either because it somehow detracts from the preferred peace-loving image of Tibet as a Shangri-la, or because the resistance committed the sin of taking weapons from the CIA – will change and a more realistic and inquiring attitude take its place.

NOTES

1. Gompo Tashi Andrugtsang. *Four Rivers, Six Ranges: A True Account of Khampa Resistance to Chinese in Tibet*, Dharamsala: Information Office of His Holiness the Dalai Lama, 1973.
2. Alo Chonze (Alo Chos-mdzed), *Bod kyi gnas-lugs bden-'dzin sgo-phye ba'i ldenmig zhes bya-ba (The key that opens the door of truth to the Tibetan situation)*.
3. Marie de Louville and Michel de Castelverd, 'Tibet. L'armee des ombres', broadcast in the series *Résistances* by the TV channel Antenne 2, Paris, September 2, 1991.
4. Jeff Long, 'Going After Wangdu: The Search for a Tibetan Guerilla Leads to Colorado's Secret CIA Camp', *Rocky Mountain Magazine*, July/Aug. 1981.
5. Victor Marchetti and John D. Marks, *The CIA and the Cult of Intelligence*, New York: Dell, 1980.
6. Fletcher L. Prouty, 'Colorado to Koko Nor: The Amazing True Story of the CIA's Secret War Against Red China', *Denver Post*, February 6, 1972.
7. Roderick MacFarquhar, *The Origins of the Cultural Revolution*, New York: Columbia University Press, 1983.
8. *The Population Atlas of China*, Oxford University Press, 1987.
9. *Xizang xingshi wenwu jiaoyu di jiben jiaocai*, Lhasa: Political Department of the Tibetan Military District, 1960.
10. Chris Mullin, 'The CIA: Tibetan Conspiracy', *Far Eastern Economic Review*, September 5, 1975.
11. Edgar Snow, *Red Star Over China*, New York, 1938; Jamyang Norbu, *Horseman in the Snow*, Dharamsala: Information Office of H.H. the Dalai Lama, 1979 (later published by Wisdom Publications as *Warriors of Tibet*).
12. Peter Goullart, *Forgotten Kingdom*, London: Readers Union, 1957.
13. Andrugtsang, *op. cit.*
14. Leonard Clark, *The Marching Wind*, London: Hutchinson, 1957.
15. *Tibet Under Chinese Communist Rule*, Dharamsala: Information Office of H.H. the Dalai Lama, 1976.
16. *Ibid.*
17. Eric Teichman, *Travels of a Consular Officer in Eastern Tibet*, Cambridge, 1922.
18. Robert Ford, *Wind between the Worlds*, New York: David McKay, 1957.
19. Anna Louise Strong, *When Serfs Stood Up In Tibet*, Beijing, 1960.
20. Alo Chonze, *op. cit.*
21. Holly Elwood, 'Dorgee Yudon: The Leader of the Rebels', unpubl. interview, May 21, 1989.
22. Dawa Norbu, 'The 1959 Tibetan Rebellion: An Interpretation', *China Quarterly*, no. 77, March 1979, pp. 74–93.
23. Phuntsok Wangyal, 'The Revolt of 1959', *Tibetan Review*, July–August, 1974.
24. Dawa Norbu, *op. cit.*
25. Andrugtsang, *op. cit.*
26. US Department of State, Office of Intelligence Research, Division of Research for Far East, Intelligence Report no. 7341, 'Unrest in Tibet', November 1, 1956.
27. Mullin, *op. cit.*

SINO-TIBETAN NEGOTIATIONS SINCE 1959

Tsering Wangyal

It is generally assumed that negotiations between the exile Tibetan Government and the Government of the People's Republic of China started in the late 1970s. Supporting this assumption is what has come to be known as 'delegation diplomacy', which describes the three official delegations sent from Dharamsala in rapid succession between 1979 and 1980 on fact-finding missions to Tibet.

There were indications, however, that the two sides had been in contact – maybe not directly but through intermediaries like Gyalo Thondup, the Dalai Lama's elder brother – since as far back as the early 1970s. In 1972 there were rumours in Lhasa that the Dalai Lama would soon be returning from his exile. Many refugees escaping to India at that time reported that the Chinese authorities in Lhasa were telling people to behave casually and not get excited in the event of the Dalai Lama's return. In June of that year the authorities ordered renovation of the Tsuglakhang (Jokhang) temple and proclaimed the 'Four Great Freedoms'.[1] Earlier, in May, a high-powered Chinese delegation was reported to have travelled through Western Tibet, village by village, instructing people how to behave when the Dalai Lama returned, which they said 'may be soon'.

Although Dharamsala never made any announcements at that time about any kind of negotiation with Beijing, it is impossible to believe that the Chinese would have been going through the whole exercise without receiving some sort of signal from the exile Tibetan Government. Judging from similar events in subsequent years, what probably happened is that Gyalo Thondup, either on his own initiative or with Dharamsala's knowledge, made tentative approaches to the Chinese, which Beijing interpreted as the Dalai Lama's desire to end his exile. In any case the visit never took place.

The Start of 'Delegation Diplomacy'

Dharamsala continued to deny that it was holding any negotiations with Beijing. However, there is no doubt that by the end of the 1970s both sides were planning to break the deadlock. The Dalai Lama started talking about the importance of Tibetan exiles being allowed to visit their relatives in Tibet and to assess the conditions

there for themselves. He also said that it should be made possible
for Tibetans in Tibet to visit their relatives outside and to find out
how the exiles were living.[2] At that time there were no Chinese
announcements on this move. It was not until 1988 that Lodi
Gyari, then Foreign Minister of the exile Tibetan government,
revealed in an interview with some French reporters that the
Chinese had made such proposals through Gyalo Thondup in
1978.[3]

So in October 1978 a group of fifteen Tibetan refugees, including
three government officials, applied for Tibet visas at the Chinese
Embassy in Delhi. On December 4, the Chinese replied saying that
they would grant the visas. The group then started making preparations for the visit, but at the last moment, on May 19, 1979, the
Chinese said that the visitors should carry Chinese travel documents describing themselves as 'overseas Chinese', and that they
should pay all their expenses in American dollars or pounds
sterling, the Indian rupee being unacceptable.

The Tibetans refused to accept these conditions, as the Chinese
must have known that they would; this suggests that the Chinese
did not want the visit to take place. One reason for their reluctance
may have been the Dalai Lama's acceptance at that time of an
invitation to visit the Soviet Union.[4] By imposing unacceptable
conditions for the visit of the fifteen, the Chinese may have been
showing their displeasure to the Dalai Lama, because they *did* give
a Tibet visa that same month to Tsultim Tersey, a Tibetan living
in Switzerland.

Around that time the Dalai Lama told an interviewer on BBC
television that Deng Xiaoping, then Vice-Premier, had invited
him to visit Tibet and that he had declined, saying that he would
not undertake such a visit until he was certain that the 6 million
Tibetans were happy and contented under Chinese rule.

It was probably with a view to assuring the Dalai Lama that all
was well in Tibet that the Chinese asked him to send fact-finding
missions. In August 1979 the first Dharamsala delegation left
for Tibet. It travelled via Hong Kong and Beijing, and did not
carry any visas. The Chinese were apparently certain that the
delegation would be favourably impressed by the conditions in
Tibet, so they invited, at the same time, forty-four foreign journalists based in Beijing to visit Lhasa. However, the exile Tibetan
Government sought to keep the visit secret from its own people
for as long as possible. The delegation left Delhi on August 2 but
the Tibetan National Working Committee, which was supposed to
be the highest decision-making body, was informed of it only on
August 1.

Among the journalists allowed into Lhasa were Audrey and Seymour Topping of the *New York Times*. Seymour Topping wrote a long report supporting Chinese claims of happiness in Tibet,[5] to which Dharamsala did not send a rejoinder. Even after the delegation returned and told some people of its experience, which supported previous refugee reports, the exile Tibetan Government still did not publicise the full report. Instead, in a small item in the *Tibetan Bulletin*, the official organ, the Chinese Government was thanked for allowing the visit and for making proper arrangements for the delegation, once inside Tibet, to move from place to place.

A Hitch in Delegation Diplomacy

Dharamsala sent the second fact-finding mission to Tibet in June 1980. The third was sent, albeit to a different part of Tibet, while the second was still there. The Chinese were apparently still confident that nothing would go wrong from their point of view and invited more journalists to the city. However, they received a rude shock when the people of Lhasa gave an enthusiastic reception to the delegation outside the Jokhang temple, some raising pro-independence slogans and wishing long life to the Dalai Lama. The Chinese were so indignant that the delegation's visit was cut short by six days.

Since the third delegation was already in the country it was allowed to continue. However, the fourth delegation, which was scheduled to visit in the summer of 1981, was cancelled. The reason given by the Chinese for its cancellation was that there had been little change in Tibet since the visit of the last delegation. However, Tibetans believed that the real reason was the experience with the second delegation.

Talks in Beijing

By this time Dharamsala seems to have decided that it had learned everything it needed to know through fact-finding missions and that it was time to start exploratory talks with the Chinese authorities. This became clear to me purely by coincidence. When in Dharamsala in March 1982, I happened to notice that the Cabinet staff were checking various books to find out the significance of the abbreviations 'SSR' and 'FSSR'. At that time I wrote an editorial in the *Tibetan Review* speculating that the Chinese might have offered Tibet a Soviet type of federation. I realise now that it may have been the Tibetan side which was toying with such an idea, since the concept of 'federation' or 'association' appeared six years later in the controversial Strasbourg Proposal.

A month after this event, a delegation composed of senior ministers in the exile Tibetan Government left for Beijing 'to continue the contact with Beijing established since 1979'.[6] Dharamsala said that the delegation was only going to hold 'exploratory talks' and not conduct any negotiations. However, on April 29 the Chinese told the *Economic Times* of Japan that they had allowed the Dalai Lama to set up an office in Beijing. Dharamsala promptly denied having made such a request.

When the delegation returned to Dharamsala in June there was once again no public statement, except to say that the visit had been useful. However, typically, this agreement to maintain secrecy did not seem to be binding on the Chinese side. Beijing told reporters that the delegation had visited Beijing with a message from the Dalai Lama asking for Tibet to be granted a status similar to that being offered to Taiwan. They further added that they had refused this request.[7] The Tibetan side then felt compelled to give their own version. According to them, what they had said to Beijing was this: 'If you are prepared to give so much to Taiwan, you should be prepared to give much more to Tibet.'

Subsequently Beijing–Dharamsala relations seem to have cooled down and there was no overture from either side for the next two years.[8] The dispatch of the delegation had also given rise to persistent rumours in the press and in the Tibetan community that the Dalai Lama would be visiting Tibet in 1985. Even the Chinese issued a five-point statement of conditions for his return, the important points being that he would be allowed to visit Tibet but not to stay or hold a 'local post' there and that he would instead be given a 'national post' in Beijing. The rumours came to a halt only when Dharamsala announced clearly on December 16, 1983 that the Dalai Lama would not be visiting Tibet in 1985.

Second Delegation to Beijing

Secret dialogue seems to have continued during this period, leading to the dispatch of another delegation to Beijing in 1984. The delegation was in China from September to November. On its return, Dharamsala for the first time issued a public statement on the negotiations. It said that both the delegations to Beijing had asked China to accept the historical status of Tibet and its right to self-determination, the right to reunification of the three traditional provinces of Tibet, the need for a relationship or alliance with China on an equal footing and the transformation of Tibet into a zone of peace.[9] The Chinese, of course, did not accept these proposals. The contact, however, was maintained and a fourth fact-finding mission was sent to Tibet. This delegation only visited the Tibetan areas of Gansu and Qinghai provinces. The Chinese said that they should not visit what they call the Tibet Autonomous Region because it was busy preparing for celebrations of the twenty-fifth anniversary of its founding. The delegation was in Tibet from July to September 1985. Upon their return the delegates said that the Chinese authorities had confiscated thousands of photographs of the Dalai Lama from their possession and that the people in the areas they had visited had not been informed beforehand of the arrival of a delegation.

Deterioration of the Relationship

In the mean time, apparently in response to the statement issued by the exile Tibetan Government, the Chinese Premier Zhao Ziyang said in London on June 9, 1985 that there was no question of considering the future of Tibet 'except within the framework of China'.[10] Since then there has been no indication that the stance taken by the two sides has been bridged to any extent. Incidents suggesting the deterioration of relations continued to occur.

In May 1986 Professor Thubten Norbu, the Dalai Lama's eldest brother and an American citizen, was denied a visa to visit his relatives in Taktser. No reason was given although Norbu had been allowed to visit the country on an earlier occasion.

Since 1986 there have been a number of arrests and executions in Tibet. As the Dalai Lama observed in his March 10 statement in 1987: 'It seems there is no desire on the part of China to resolve the issue on the basis of mutual respect and for mutual benefit.' He further angered the Chinese by adding: 'The issue of Tibet is fundamentally political, with international ramifications, and as such only a political solution can provide a meaningful answer.' The Dalai Lama also commented on the mass arrests, on the influx of Chinese immigrants and their taking of control over the economy, and the policy of deliberately encouraging bad habits like alcoholism and gambling among the youth of Tibet.

The fifth delegation to Tibet, which was scheduled to leave in June 1987, did not materialise because the Chinese once again introduced the unacceptable condition that they should travel as 'overseas Chinese'. The Chinese said that only Gyalo Thondup and others related to the Dalai Lama could travel without the Chinese document. From this the obvious inference to be drawn was that the Chinese wanted to deal only with delegations composed of members of the Dalai Lama's family. This would be quite in keeping with the impression that the Chinese wanted to give to the outside world: that there is no such thing as the issue of Tibet, only that of the return of the Dalai Lama. The exile Tibetan Government did not comply.

In September 1987 the Dalai Lama unveiled his Five Point Peace Plan, the Chinese denigration of which sparked off the September 27 demonstration in Lhasa which in turn led to further demonstrations, riots and their violent suppression over the next two years.

Then came the Strasbourg Proposal in June 1988. Although the Dalai Lama relinquished the right of Tibet to conduct its own foreign policy in exchange for total and real autonomy within the whole of traditional Tibet, Beijing described it as a demand for 'semi-independence or a disguised form of independence' and refused to have anything to do with it. The Chinese continued to say that they were willing to hold talks with the Dalai Lama, and added that these could be held 'anywhere in the world'.[11] Previously they had insisted that all talks should be held in Beijing or in Hong Kong. Dharamsala took this offer at its face value and hastily suggested that the talks might be held in Geneva in January 1989. The names of the Tibetan team for negotiations were also announced.[12] The Chinese again backed out, saying that they objected to officials of the exile Tibetan Government and a foreign legal adviser being included in the team.[13]

In Lhasa there were more demonstrations and more killings, local authorities having been instructed to 'use merciless repression in handling anti-Chinese activities', according to reports from Hong Kong newspapers.

The Chinese also told a Hong Kong newspaper that now they would only hold talks with the Dalai Lama and with no one else.[14] They are also reported to have said that they would only consider Beijing – and no other place – as the venue.[15]

With the imposition of martial law in Tibet in March 1989, even Dharamsala appeared to have stopped trying to maintain further contact with Beijing.

Conclusion

The Dalai Lama offered the Strasbourg Proposal as the ultimate compromise to China. He told his people repeatedly, including in a speech on March 10, 1990, that this was the lowest level to which he was prepared to come down. In other words, as far as the Tibetan side is concerned, any future negotiation with China could only take place with Strasbourg as the basis. However, the Chinese side have totally rejected Strasbourg and have said there can be negotiations on any subject except the independence of Tibet 'in any form'.

The Dalai Lama has made it clear that the main reason for putting forward the Strasbourg Proposal was to check the killings in Tibet and to make China reverse its population-transfer policy. Judging from the 'negotiating tactics' adopted by the Chinese, it seems that they are also thinking along the same lines, but in the opposite direction. They want to continue their present policies in Tibet while at the same time giving the impression that they are also ready to negotiate. In other words, to them negotiation is a strategy to buy more time so that they can complete their demographic invasion of Tibet. Secondly, it appears that whatever negotiations they are willing to hold will be solely concerned with the return of the Dalai Lama. They have no intention of discussing the future status of Tibet which, as far as they are concerned, will not change under any circumstances.

The inevitable conclusion we arrive at is that there will not be any further Sino-Tibetan negotiations, at least as long as the present regime in Beijing remains in power. There is a possibility of its resumption if Communism is toppled in China and if dissident leaders assume control. However, so far the Chinese dissident leaders have not sided with the Tibetans in political terms. They have professed respect for the Dalai Lama and have recognised the absence of human rights in Tibet, but they have not yet accepted that Tibet was historically independent, is still legally independent and is deserving of *de facto* independence as well. They have yet to accept that Tibetans are a separate people and not one of the so-called national minorities of China. In this way their current stand on Tibet is not dissimilar to that on Taiwan. They are willing to joint forces with the Tibetans in an effort to overthrow the Communist regime in Beijing, but they are not yet ready to see the independence of Tibet restored.

The Tibetans' only hope is if Chinese dissident leaders are willing to learn more about the subject of Tibet. If both these qualifications are fulfilled – that is, if the dissidents fully understand and appreciate the Tibetan point of view and if they come to power in Beijing – then the Tibetan government should be able to meet them on an equal footing, which was not the case with past negotiations. It was always the Chinese who dictated the terms, and Beijing was the venue for the talks, rather than Dharamsala, Delhi or Geneva. In addition, the Tibetan teams were headed by a minister, whereas Beijing deputed an official of lower rank from the Nationalities Affairs Commission.[16] Such issues of protocol reflect the central question underlying the negotiation process between the Tibetans and the Chinese: whether that process is being pursued in order to settle a minor dispute between the Motherland and one of its constituent minorities, or whether these negotiations are being held to settle a dispute between two nations, one of which is under occupation by the other.

The only benefit of the Dharamsala–Beijing contact that Tibetans both inside and outside Tibet have enjoyed so far has been the opportunity of visiting each other. Hundreds went back and forth, some many times. Although most of these trips were made to visit long-separated relatives, the more resourceful among them also successfully mixed business with pleasure.

It is not certain whether the Five Point Peace Plan and the Strasbourg Proposal can be described as part of the negotiations. They were not made in response to any Chinese call. They were, rather, the Dalai Lama's response to the failure of the contacts with Beijing. Until 1987 the Tibetan side is never known to have presented any proposal to Beijing. It contented itself with trying to find out what China was willing to concede. It seems unlikely that it had any proposal that it seriously intended to sell to the Chinese. For the Tibetan side negotiation with China meant devising a formula to have Tibet's independence restored. From the Chinese point of view, there is no such thing as a 'Tibet problem'. They were only interested in getting the Dalai Lama back and, as a reward, were willing to give small concessions in Tibet, such as increased freedom of religion. 'Independence' of the country in any form remained unthinkable to them.

The Dalai Lama decided to break the deadlock by announcing his two proposals. He was prompted no doubt by the decay of Communism in Europe and other unforeseen changes around the world. He might have thought that the Chinese themselves could see the inevitability of the collapse of their system as well, and that they would genuinely welcome these proposals as a face-saving device. As for the Strasbourg Proposal, it was certainly a genuine effort on the part of the Dalai Lama to seek a happier future for the Tibetans, and no evidence has appeared to support suggestions that it was influenced by the British Foreign Office, the US State Department or the various Indian intelligence agencies. It tends to be forgotten that the Strasbourg Proposal was never binding on the exile Tibetan Government or the people. The Dalai Lama described the proposal as his personal view on how a solution to the Tibetan problem might be found which would be acceptable to all. He remained personally in favour of the Strasbourg

Proposal, but announced in 1991 that he no longer felt himself obliged to adhere to it. This was not because he found the opposition to it too strong, he said, but because it had not elicited any favourable response from the Chinese side.

NOTES

1. The Four Great Freedoms were: freedom of worship, freedom to buy and sell (privately), freedom to lend and borrow (with interest) and freedom to employ servants (and labourers, etc).
2. For instance, the Dalai Lama said in his March 10, 1978, statement: 'If the Tibetans are really happy . . . the Chinese should allow the Tibetans in Tibet to visit their parents and relatives in exile. These Tibetans can then study the conditions of those of us in exile living in free countries. Similar opportunities should be given to the Tibetans in exile . . .'
3. This interview was held in Dharamsala on October 3, 1988. It is not known whether the interview was ever published. Purely by chance I obtained a copy of the transcript in 1990.
4. Agence France Presse reported from Beijing on May 28, 1979, that 'China has been irritated by the recent invitation from Moscow to the Dalai Lama to visit the Soviet Union and attend an Asian Buddhist Conference for Peace.'
5. 'Tibet's struggle for higher living standards' by Seymour Topping, *New York Times*, October 28, 1979.
6. The delegation members were: Phuntsog Tashi Takla, Minister of Security; Juchen Thubten Namgyal, Minister of Education and Religious Affairs; and Lodi G. Gyari, Chairman of the Assembly of Tibetan People's Deputies.
7. The Beijing–datelined Associated Press report on June 18, 1982, said: 'There simply does not exist the question of applying the nine-point policy to Tibet as in the case of Taiwan, a Foreign Ministry spokesman said in response to a reporter's question. Under the nine-point policy expounded last fall, China would give Taiwan almost total autonomy and virtual independence allowing it to maintain its social and economic system, foreign relations and even its armed forces.'
8. In October 1982 the Office of Tibet, New York, submitted a fourteen-page document entitled 'Chinese Human Rights Abuses in Tibet, 1959–1982' to the Subcommittee on Human Rights and International Organizations of the Committee on Foreign Affairs, US House of Representatives.
9. See full text in *Tibetan Review*, January 1985.
10. *Indian Express*, New Delhi, June 10, 1985.
11. The *Times of India* reported on September 23, 1988, that the Chinese Embassy in New Delhi had informed the Bureau of the Dalai Lama that talks could be held in Beijing, Hong Kong or any of the Chinese embassies and consulates abroad. 'If the Dalai Lama finds it inconvenient to conduct talks at these places, he may choose any place he wishes,' the Chinese statement added.
12. The names in the Tibetan negotiating team were, in fact, announced soon after the Strasbourg Proposal was made. The team consisted of three ministers of the exile Tibetan Government, one former minister and two general secretaries. Two aides and one legal adviser were also named. All were ranking officials of the exile Tibetan Government except for the legal adviser, Dr Michael van Walt, a Dutch citizen.

13. The rejection of the talks was made by Chen Xin, Vice-Minister of the Nationalities Affairs Commission, in an interview with the pro-Beijing Hong Kong newspaper *Wen Wei Po*, published on November 25, 1988.
14. *Ibid.*
15. This was told to *Tibetan Review* by a reliable source in Dharamsala who asked to remain anonymous. The Tibetan Cabinet, however, refused to confirm or deny this report.
16. The leader of the Chinese side in 1982 was Ulanfu, who at that time was the Vice-Chairman of the National People's Congress and had just retired as Minister for National Minorities. He was assisted by Xi Zhongxuan, who led the Chinese side during the 1984 talks.

Part IV

RESISTANCE IN TIBET 1987–1990

THE ANTI-SPLITTIST CAMPAIGN AND TIBETAN POLITICAL CONSCIOUSNESS

Ronald D. Schwartz

In the space of ten days in the autumn of 1987 three demonstrations took place in the centre of Lhasa. The first one, on September 27, was led by monks from Drepung monastery, who marched through the streets shouting for Tibetan independence and displaying the Tibetan flag. They were attacked and beaten by police, arrested and imprisoned. On October 1 a similar demonstration was staged by monks from Sera monastery. They too were attacked and beaten by police, then taken to a nearby police station. An angry crowd burned down the police station in an attempt to free the monks, and for several hours police shot into the crowd, killing at least eight people and wounding many more. In the third demonstration on October 6 monks from Drepung staged another protest.

In the following two years there were at least two dozen further demonstrations by monks and nuns in Lhasa, and dissident activity broadened to include the distribution of political literature, the mounting of wall posters and the creation of a loosely knit network of underground organisations. This paper examines the campaign launched by the Chinese Government in Tibet to suppress dissent and contain the demonstrations. First, it outlines the mobilisation of the apparatus of Party control as a response to nationalist unrest and analyses the role of ideology in the political meetings initiated to correct Tibetan thinking. Secondly, it documents the Tibetan response, and suggests reasons for the failure of the campaign to control unrest. The 'anti-splittist' campaign ('splittist' is the term used by the Chinese authorities to refer to Tibetan separatists) has in fact increased the social and symbolic opposition between Tibetans and Chinese. It has sharpened Tibetan political consciousness and enlarged Tibetan demands for independence to encompass a range of modern political ideas.

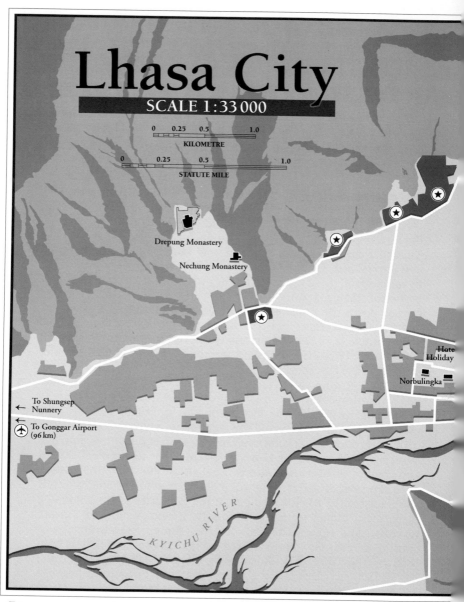

Lhasa City

SCALE 1:33 000

0	0.25	0.5	1.0

KILOMETRE

0	0.25	0.5	1.0

STATUTE MILE

Drepung Monastery

Nechung Monastery

Hote
Holiday

Norbulingka

To Shungsep
← Nunnery

← To Gonggar Airport
✈ (96 km)

KYICHU RIVER

 TIBETAN QUARTER   CHINESE QUARTER   ⭐ MILITARY OR PARAMILITARY CAMP

To Garu Nunnery ↑   Chubsang Nunnery

Sera Monastery

Sangyip Prison Nr.1

Sangyip Prison Nr.4

Sangyip Prison Nr.5

Drapchi Prison

Michungri Nunnery

Public
Security Bureau   People's Hospital

Potala Palace   Ramoche Monastery

To Gutsa Prison →

Jokhang Temple   Barkhor

TAR
Government Offices   Police station

Headquarters   Police station   Public Security Bureau

Tsangkhung
Nunnery   University
of Tibet

To Ganden Monastery
(40 km) →

Drib
Military Camp

© Atelier Golok, 1993

The front page of the *Tibet Daily* on October 2, 1987, the day following the violence at the police station, displayed two lead articles that between them bracketed the official Chinese response to the outbreak of nationalist unrest in Tibet. The first article reported a huge picnic, sponsored by the government on September 29 for 350 monks from Sera monastery and some 3,000 of the 'religiously faithful masses', which marked the end of the traditional summer retreat. The article bears the caption: 'Flying high the flag of patriotism and unity, protecting the unification of the motherland and opposing splittism'. The speeches delivered by leading Tibetan political figures representing the regional Chinese People's Political Consultative Conference (CPPCC), the United Front Work Department of the Party, the local Nationalities and Religious Affairs Commission, and the Buddhist Association, set out the Party's policy on religion and are in fact a clear warning to the monks of Sera not to repeat the mistake of the Drepung monks who had demonstrated on September 27. No doubt the article was prepared before the Sera monks themselves demonstrated on October 1, China's National Day.

In the article the leaders promise that the Party's policies on nationalities and religion, as well as the reforms and the 'open door' policy, will continue. In return, those with 'religious vocations' must display patriotism and support national unity and thus contribute towards the establishment of a 'new socialist Tibet based on unity, wealth and education'. This last slogan came into its present usage following Hu Yaobang's visit to Tibet in 1980. It signifies the current strategy of the United Front in Tibet, which aims to maintain political control through economic liberalisation, on the one hand, and carefully manage accommodation to national and religious sentiments, on the other.[1]

The second article is an 'announcement' from the People's Government of the City of Lhasa. It offers the official version of the events of October 1, which had Tibetan 'trouble-makers' seizing guns from the police and shooting each other. It goes on to lay out a series of 'directives' for combatting splittism through a political campaign. First, the 'broad cadres, workers, city residents and monks and nuns of the entire city' are required to comprehend the seriousness of the incident and 'adhere to a correct ideological view and a correct standpoint'. Party members, members of the Communist Youth League and cadres are expected to set an example in this regard; their readiness to do so 'without wavering in the slightest' is a test of their loyalty. Secondly, government units and departments are required to do 'good ideological work' in educating workers and cadres under their jurisdiction, who are in turn responsible for educating their families, children and relatives. Likewise the neighbourhood committees are required to carry out ideological education among the residents of the city so that 'the broad masses of the people reject the actions of a few' and understand 'that it is impossible for the disturbance caused by a few people to change the Party's policy'. Finally, it is necessary for the departments and neighbourhood committees to 'report any special information they come to know' to the authorities.

The announcement marked the beginning of a political campaign that has occupied the Government and the security apparatus in Tibet since 1987. The tone of the document is consistent with other political campaigns in China, with its emphasis on a 'correct view and standpoint' and the necessity for 'good ideological work' among the masses.

As the demonstrations continued and the scope of unrest broadened throughout 1988 and into 1989, the campaign went through several phases. The first phase spans the period from the first demonstrations in the autumn of 1987 to the riot following the close of the Monlam festival on March 5, 1988. During this phase existing local administrative structures were regarded by the authorities as adequate to deal with the problem. Following March 5, in the wake of widespread arrests and imprisonment, the burden of dealing with the unrest shifted to the security and prison apparatus, whose treatment of prisoners was intended both to frighten the masses and to isolate potential dissidents and organisers. At the same time the message broadcast to Tibetans indicated that any demonstrations would be violently and brutally suppressed. The third and final phase is marked by the declaration of martial law on March 8, 1989. Martial law was in a real sense an admission of the failure of the anti-splittist campaign. Demonstrations could be prevented, but only through a massive display of military force in the streets of Lhasa. Tibetans nevertheless continued to demonstrate. This has led to administrative measures implemented to search out splittists, measures originally seen as a temporary expedient, but which have become permanent and institutionalised. Each phase of the campaign has thus added an additional layer of organised repression.

Defending the Reforms in Tibet

In the initial phase, following the first wave of demonstrations in the autumn of 1987, the themes that would dominate the campaign were introduced. The demonstrations were blamed on the influence of foreigners and the work of saboteurs sent by the 'Dalai clique' who were confusing and tricking the masses. The policies instituted in Tibet during the reforms of the 1980s were regarded as essentially correct. In the autumn of 1987 wrongdoers were not yet described as 'counter-revolutionaries', a term that would justify the harshest treatment and the severest sentences, but only as common criminals. The overall thrust of the campaign at this point was to emphasise the positive aspects of the reforms in Tibet and the continuing need for 'unity and stability' if further progress and development were to be achieved.

Local Tibetan officials certainly had an interest in down-playing the significance of unrest in Lhasa in their reports to the central authorities in Beijing. They may have believed that the trouble-makers could be easily isolated, the population convinced of the need to support current reform policies in Tibet and the demonstrations suppressed without difficulty. In a speech to the regional People's Congress on January 19, 1988, the Panchen Lama went to some length to justify the policy of reform and the relaxation of controls in Tibet and attributed the demonstrations to persisting problems remaining after '20 years under the guidance of erroneous leftist ideology':

This state of affairs provided an opportunity which the splittists could take advantage of to create trouble. Various errors and loopholes in our work provided the conditions, like dry firewood, for the splittists to feed the flames and stir up trouble and disturbance.[2]

The Panchen Lama acknowledged that he had personally intervened to gain the release of most of those Tibetans who had been arrested following the demonstrations in the autumn, and insisted that the current policies must not be reversed. He warned, however, that those like himself who had been identified with the reforms were already under some pressure from others who would roll back the reforms, particularly on nationality and religious questions:

After the riots occurred in Lhasa some people thought it was because we had gone too far in setting aright the work guideline, redressing wrongs, implementing policies, and correcting errors in our previous work. Because we went too far in implementing the religious policy, the lamas became too arrogant; and because we went too far in implementing the nationality policy, narrow-minded nationality sentiments were abetted. So they held that after the riots occurred we should backtrack to the old practices, stop pursuing the current relaxed policies that we adopted after setting right the guideline[s], and adopt some high-handed measures; otherwise there would be no way to deal with the problems. Although not many people held such a viewpoint, they did account for a very small proportion of our cadres. We should adopt a prudent attitude toward such a viewpoint and idea and approach them seriously. Such a viewpoint and idea may cause great trouble if they continue to spread.[3]

Immediately following the demonstrations in October a whole series of 'forums' were announced within government departments responsible for the policy of relaxation and the implementation of the reforms in Tibet: the regional CPPCC, the local Nationalities and Religious Affairs Commission, the Buddhist Association and the United Front Work Department of the Party. One after another, Tibetan representatives were required to come forward and condemn the splittists who had incited the demonstrations, praise the Party's policy on religion and testify to the unity of the motherland and the unity of nationalities.

Attestations of loyalty from these groups of rehabilitated non-Party leadership ('the patriotic upper strata') seem to have served two purposes. First, by saying that things had never been so good – monasteries rebuilt, the economy improved, religious freedom reinstated – these rehabilitated Tibetan leaders lent legitimacy to the current regime. As the principal resource of the United Front in Tibet, they were expected to provide a counterweight to the exile leadership around the Dalai Lama and thus defuse nationalist discontent. Secondly, they were themselves targeted in the campaign against splittism. Whatever tacit support they had provided to separatist sentiments must be stopped. They needed to understand and attest to the fact that their own rehabilitation and positions of influence, as well as whatever progress had been made in religion and education, were also at risk. The campaign was thus a warning to them. For many of these Tibetan figures, denunciation of the Dalai Lama and the Tibetan national cause did not come easily. This was the first real test of their loyalty to the Chinese regime since their rehabilitation during the 1980s.

The Apparatus of Social Control

On October 13 the Propaganda Department of the Regional Party issued a notice defining the 'focal point' for the ongoing ideological studies initiated by units throughout the region. The points to be stressed were: first, that the disturbances were 'plotted and instigated by the Dalai clique'; secondly, that national unity is vital to the 'policies of reform, opening up to the outside world and invigorating the domestic economy'; and thirdly, the 'two inseparables': that Han and Tibetan peoples cannot live without each other.[4]

These ideological studies were to be carried out within the existing administrative structure of work units, government departments and neighbourhood committees, which has been in place in
one form or another since the inception of Communist rule in
Tibet. An important feature of this structure is the provision for
incorporating every individual into supervised study and discussion
sessions.[5] The very same structure also provides monitoring and
surveillance of the behaviour of individuals and has direct links to
the Public Security Bureau (PSB). During the reforms of the 1980s
the structure had fallen into disuse. After 1984 the number of
required political meetings was reduced from three times to once
a week. The subjects discussed at meetings could be both practical
and political: health, cleanliness and education were all regular
subjects. Before the demonstrations began the political content of
the meetings was largely laudatory, and would announce improvements made under the 'new Tibet policy' in economics and education. Questions of political loyalty and Tibetan independence never
came up.

Political education went on in both work units and residential
compounds, and individuals would have to participate in one or
the other depending on where they were 'registered' (*them-mtho*).
Within the Tibetan part of the city each residential compound
(*sgo-ra*) is placed under the administration of a neighbourhood
committee (*sa-gnas u-yon lhan-khang*). The latter has a headquarters and a permanent administrative staff. Normally its
meetings consist of the staff plus the leaders (*go-'khrid*) of each of
the compounds. Leaders go back to their compounds with topics
for meetings. During the early period of the campaign, workers
in government departments were told that they would be safer
if they shifted to their units from their residential compounds
to live. For the workers this was a way of avoiding the atmosphere
of intimidation and fear in the Tibetan areas. It probably was safer
for Tibetans in their work units than in the neighbourhoods,
because the presence of Chinese peers insulated them from the
campaign. Also, displaying 'wrong ideas' in the work unit sessions
might result in a warning and reprimand from the unit leader,
but would normally not lead to an investigation by the PSB and
possible arrest. However, as one worker in a government enterprise
explained:

The Government made this request because it was frightened. It was trying
to separate people from the movement. Many Tibetans are very angry, but
they are afraid to speak for fear of losing their jobs.

The neighbourhood committee meetings were organised in the first place to identify those who had been involved in demonstrations or were potential dissidents. According to one interviewee who had attended a meeting, leaders instructed those under their jurisdiction:

Whoever indulges in these anti-government demonstrations will be dealt with seriously. Persons who inform us about who is indulging in these demonstrations, who inform us about people putting up wall posters, will be rewarded. If you cannot inform in person, then write it on a slip of paper and push it under the door of the neighbourhood committee. We will check on the people you name.

Leaders were also asked to investigate links between families in their compound and the refugee community in India. One question asked was whether families had sent children to India for schooling, which would mark the family as politically suspect. The PSB also maintains a network of paid informers, Tibetans with ordinary livelihoods who receive extra cash for providing information about their neighbours. Particularly in Tibetan neighbourhoods, where many people are merchants or small traders and do not belong to work units, the system of informers has many of the characteristics of a 'protection racket'. Licences can be revoked and trade halted if individuals do not co-operate with the PSB, while special privileges such as freedom to travel are the reward for co-operation. These informers would also be present at meetings and report directly to the PSB on what was said.

Residents were regularly provided with subjects to think about or questions to discuss: for example, whether monks should be thrown out of the monasteries for demonstrating and what should be done with them afterwards. Individuals who spoke up in meetings in support of the Chinese found their statements used by the Chinese media for propaganda. An important function of the meetings was to identify potential dissidents by forcing attestations of loyalty. The names of those who refused to co-operate were noted. Though they were not usually arrested on the spot, following subsequent demonstrations they were among the first to be arrested. People would often make excuses for not participating in the discussions – they had not seen the demonstrations or they did not know enough to speak, for example. They might be coerced into declaring their support for the Chinese, but would do so unwillingly and without enthusiasm.

The real test of loyalty was whether Tibetans were prepared to criticise the Dalai Lama. Virtually no Tibetans would comply with this demand. Attempts at organising pro-Chinese/anti-Dalai Lama counter-demonstrations foundered on this point as well. Tibetans might be coerced into making perfunctory declarations of loyalty in political meetings, but they could not be coerced into attacking the Dalai Lama. The Chinese generally did not attack the Dalai Lama directly, and preferred to refer to the 'Dalai clique'. But Tibetans recognised the ambiguity in this and were quick to seize the opportunity. Thus, in one meeting in a government department, a young Tibetan responded: 'Whatever was done may have been very bad, but we should not curse the Dalai Lama and blame what has happened on the Dalai "clique" [*ru-tshogs*] because he is our religious leader.' The worker was later called into the office of the manager and told that his 'thinking' had to change, but nothing else was done to him.

Tibetans became adept at managing the ambiguity of the Dalai Lama's combined religious and political roles. Thus, in political meetings they would insist on their right to 'religious freedom' as defined by the Chinese and would refuse to criticise the Dalai Lama, while in the streets they would bring forth the Dalai Lama as the symbol of Tibetan independence.

Following the first demonstrations in the autumn of 1987 a special unit for political education and investigation at the monasteries and nunneries was organised. Notices were sent out to government departments, work units and enterprises to send selected cadres for training and assignment to political education squads referred to collectively as the 'work team' (*las-don ru-khag*).[6] During the course of the campaign, salaries for these cadres would continue to be paid by their units while they were on temporary leave. In addition they received a bonus for their political work. A similar work team was formed from the staff of the neighbourhood committees, given political training and then sent around to conduct political education with city residents. During the 1987–9 period the units assigned to monasteries and nunneries would stay for varying lengths of time, from several weeks to several months, in order to carry on their investigations, identify potential dissidents and hold meetings.

Initially, the work team was not responsible for political education in government departments and enterprises. Managers assumed this responsibility for themselves. As the campaign has progressed and as the unrest has continued, however, the effectiveness of control in these organisations has also come into question. The work team has become a permanent fixture of life in Tibet. Its function has become increasingly one for the identification of splittists within the Tibetan community. By November 1989, 300 cadres were reported to be assigned to the work team for Lhasa, and 1,000 for Tibet as a whole. They remain stationed at the monasteries and nunneries, but have extended their work to include institutions previously exempt. Meetings of four and five hours' duration are held in offices two or more times a week, during which workers are forced to discuss their views on the demonstrations. Neighbourhood committees have been instructed to separate those who are involved with the splittists from others who are suitable for re-education, and participants in earlier demonstrations have been re-investigated to see what their current views are. Under the guise of an 'opinion survey', suspect Tibetans have been interviewed in detail.

During training sessions in November 1989, cadres were assigned the task of screening out dissidents in every monastery, office and neighbourhood. The directives issued for monasteries and nunneries, for instance, were: first, to continue to resist the splittists and the 'Dalai clique'; secondly, to condemn and campaign against the award of the Nobel Peace Prize to the Dalai Lama; thirdly, to continue to identify participants in the successive demonstrations since 1987 at the monasteries and their supporters, particularly those who did not actively participate, and to expel unregistered monks; and fourthly, to go even to small monasteries and nunneries looking for splittists.

The last directive suggests a kind of quota, because it presumes that every organisation must in principle contain splittists. It was emphasised that this time the screening had to be 'complete'. The same procedures were to be applied in neighbourhoods and units, which were to be searched section by section for splittists.

The Tibetan who provided this current information suggested that the situation was reminiscent of the 1960s. However, it is significant that throughout the campaign no attempt has been made to return to the practice of 'class labelling', in which economic groups were singled out for persecution. The issue remains loyalty, not economic status. Nevertheless, many of those who have undergone intensive investigation have been Tibetans from families formerly labelled 'counter-revolutionary'. Recent directives also have indicated that families will be held accountable for the activities of their members. The campaign has extended into the schools with the appointment of cadres to oversee the participation of students in political education and to report on uncooperative students and parents. Families are thus subject to monitoring both through their own units and neighbourhood committees and through the schools that their children attend.

But there has been no return to the 'struggle sessions' of the Cultural Revolution, where neighbours and families were expected to attack targeted individuals in public meetings. Meetings during the anti-splittist campaign have consisted largely of lectures and threats from political workers. Discussion has been used mainly to identify potential dissidents. The activity of the work team has become institutionalised, with cadres identifying candidates for arrest and the PSB carrying out the task of interrogation and imprisonment. In this, the anti-splittist campaign represents the bureaucratic consolidation of the security apparatus rather than the orchestration of a popular movement.

Interrogation as Education

On March 5, 1988, just as the Monlam festival was drawing to a close, another major demonstration occurred. It began as monks from Ganden monastery encircled a group of assembled government officials and demanded the release of Yulu Dawa Tsering, a prominent scholar and member of the CPPCC who had been arrested in December 1987 for talking about Tibetan independence with a foreigner. In the course of the demonstration, a unit of the People's Armed Police entered the Jokhang and proceeded to savagely beat monks who had fled there for safety, killing a number of them and arresting the others. The demonstration erupted into a riot, and in the days that followed, a large number of Tibetans were arrested and taken to prisons around Lhasa (primarily Gutsa and Sangyip). Included were many who had not participated in the demonstration and riot, but who had been identified as political dissidents during meetings or had been named by others undergoing interrogation. The overwhelming impression gained from the reports of prisoners held following the Monlam demonstration is that the brutality in prison was intended to intimidate and create an atmosphere of fear.

Unlike the earlier demonstrations, the March 5 events were a direct confrontation between Tibetans and uniformed Chinese soldiers or security forces. The brutality within the prisons was systematic and widespread, and only incidently related to the need to obtain information and confessions. Those arrested following March 5 were subjected from the outset to beatings by police, soldiers and prison guards. The harsh treatment of prisoners – which included repeated beatings, shocks from electrified batons, suspension from ropes, shackling and attacks by dogs – continued throughout the period of imprisonment up to the time of their release. Most of the approximately 800 people arrested were released in July, several months later, with no charges laid.

The pattern that emerges from the accounts of released prisoners is that the meetings and interrogations inside the prisons were an extension of the political campaign on the outside, with the same goals and stressing the same themes, but with the responsibility now shifted to the administrative structure of the prisons. Systematic torture was always a feature of interrogation. Interrogation took place in a separate interrogation room in the presence of one or more guards, an interrogator and sometimes a translator. This account of interrogation at Gutsa prison was given by a shop assistant who was arrested for throwing stones on March 5 and released around July 25:

I was interrogated eight times during the first half of the month. They asked me, 'Why did you take part in the demonstration? What are your views? What does your family do?' . . . They punched my stomach quite frequently during the interrogation. One night they made me stand outside without sleep. It was very cold. The interrogator would say that Tibet could never be independent and what did I think we could achieve? Some of the interrogators were Tibetans . . . There were two or three police in the cell and one interrogator. At first it was a different interrogator each time. Later on, the same interrogator would come. Sometimes the questions were similar – 'How many times did you throw a stone?' Afterwards, they ask you about other people. This was really very difficult, I know how much I have suffered. I don't want to be the cause of this kind of suffering for anyone. If I had named someone, how could I face him or his relatives? When you don't give names of other people they really start to beat you. If you don't say anything they beat you. Later on they ask you, 'Who was the leader? Who incited you to revolt?'

In general, lay prisoners were under less suspicion than the monks. All of the prisoners were made to attend large meetings in which the 'correct' view of Tibetan history was explained. Three such meetings occurred between March and July in Gutsa, where most of the lay prisoners were held. Prisoners were reminded that if they gave names and confessed their crimes they would be treated leniently. The main political theme according to prisoners was the futility of revolt: 'They always began with stating how powerful China is and how could we ever think of overthrowing them. In 1959 the rebellion was crushed, despite the fact that we were well-armed and supplied from abroad. They say, "You have nothing now, what can you achieve?" '

The meetings were aimed at the politically unsophisticated: Tibetans who, in the view of their interrogators, had been incited by the ringleaders to demonstrate, but whose thinking might still be corrected. Thus, the political cadres who led the meetings in the prisons were careful not to attack the Dalai Lama directly, since ordinary Tibetans would be expected to retain religious devotion for him: 'They said the Dalai Lama is like a faithful dog who has been deceived by foreigners and is following them . . . You are all doing these things under the influence of a few bad foreigners and have been taken in by their deception. You should not do this. Tibet and China can never be separated. In terms of past history or in terms of the future, it is impossible for you to gain Tibetan independence.'

A major goal of the interrogations was to identify leaders and organisers of the demonstrations. In turn, the most significant evidence that a prisoner was a ringleader was the coherence of his or her political views. The more thoughtful and intelligent their answers to political questions, the less likely they were to be released. Prisoners were sometimes presented with political ideas about which they may not have been well informed, for example, the Five Point Peace Plan of the Dalai Lama. This may have been to gauge the depth of their political understanding or the extent of their contact with Tibetans in India. Prisoners were also asked whether they had relatives in India or whether they had been to India. A nun accused of being the organiser of a small demonstration by nuns in April 1988 described in detail the attempts of her interrogator to discover the depth and source of her ideas about Tibetan independence:

I was taken to a room and asked whether I knew, first, how many other nuns in the prison were from my nunnery, secondly, what I thought when they had been arrested, and thirdly, if I knew they had left the nunnery to take part in the demonstration. I said I didn't know anything about that. He claimed I knew about everything and it was I who had organised it all. Since he kept on insisting that I was the leader behind the demonstration, I had no choice but to say that I did organise it. Then he asked what my aims had been. I said, 'To have Tibet free.' He asked if I would get something to eat if Tibet becomes free. I told him we do not fight for a free Tibet in order to get something to eat, but for the same reason as you. You cry out to the outside world for your rights and fight to get them. We too strive for the rights we are entitled to. Secondly, we strive so that one day all Tibetans will get the opportunity to see the Dalai Lama in a free Tibet . . .

He asked if I had gone to India to attend the Kalachakra initiation last year. I replied that I did not know the way to get there. Then he asked if any monk had come to our nunnery after the Kalachakra. He said someone had incited us and asked who it was. I answered that we had received no incitement and that whatever we had done had been of our own accord . . . He then asked whether there really had been no one inciting us. I said we had done everything on our own initiative and that moreover we do not need anyone to incite us . . .

Then he said, 'This means you are a supporter of Kusho Yulu?' I said,

'Yes, I am a supporter of Kusho Yulu.' He said, 'Then are all these people in the prison supporters of Kusho Yulu?' I replied, 'Yes we are.' He asked if I knew what crimes Kusho Yulu had committed and I said, 'Our crimes are the same – to fight for a free Tibet. Other than this I do not know.' . . . The officer said that a free Tibet is impossible no matter how much we fight for it. Then he began telling a history about which I have no knowledge, so I kept quiet. He asked if I would be happy if Tibet became free, and I said, 'Yes, when Tibet is free there will be much happiness.' . . . Then he said that the policy of the present Chinese government is good, so I asked him, 'In that case, why are there so many beggars around the Barkor?' He said this was nothing special, there were more beggars under the old government. I replied that we were not talking about the old government but about the present one. He said I should also know that there were many beggars in India, and I told him that I had no idea since I had not been there. I said that he had started talking about the present government and therefore I had to say what I thought. He then said that would be all for now, but that I should think hard for three days.

The interrogator must have decided that this nun was not after all one of the organisers. She was released in July with most of the other nuns arrested from her nunnery. In fact, nuns received some of the most brutal treatment as prisoners. The nuns, for their part, refused to give ground. They certainly frustrated the efforts of the interrogators to get useful information and win confessions. They had no names to give, because they had acted alone and had all been arrested, and had nothing to confess, since they were unshakeable in their commitment to Tibetan independence, which they made no effort to hide.

By the autumn of 1988 most of the prisoners arrested following the March 5 demonstration had been released. Those that remained were Tibetans who for one reason or another had been identified as leaders and organisers. These included fourteen monks from Ganden, the monastery that had precipitated the demonstration on March 5, along with fourteen other nuns and monks from monasteries and nunneries around Lhasa. A few of these had demonstrated and been arrested more than once. Some had spoken out in meetings and displayed extensive knowledge of Tibetan history, an indication that they had studied banned literature. Some were accused of writing wall posters and pamphlets, or had been found with incriminating letters and documents in their possession. A few were older monks who had advocated boycotting the Monlam festival in 1988 and were held responsible for the actions of the younger monks in their charge. Between fifty and seventy-five lay Tibetans, both men and women, also remained in prison. They too were not necessarily held because of their participation in the demonstrations, but because of what they had said in meetings or under interrogation, or because they had been caught putting up wall posters or with Tibetan independence literature in their possession.

Tibetans nevertheless continued to prepare for demonstrations, and wall posters continued to appear around Lhasa. The political meetings were becoming increasingly ineffective, with more and more Tibetans speaking out in meetings against the Chinese. In the neighbourhood committee meetings the principal message communicated was that Tibetans would be 'gunned down in the streets' if there were any further demonstrations. To back this up, ever larger military patrols began to appear in the streets of Lhasa, especially when demonstrations were expected. The work teams returned to the monasteries in September 1988 to try to prevent further demonstrations. It was announced at the monasteries that large numbers of monks, particularly those who had demonstrated and been arrested, would be expelled. The monks seized the opportunity to resist and frustrate the political workers. A monk from Ganden described a meeting held there in September 1988 with monks recently released from prison. The meeting was called to discuss the expulsion of monks and the conditions for remaining at the monastery:

We were told to put forward our case and discuss. No discussion followed. Then they started questioning [us] one after the other. On that day three youths spoke from our side. They stated that the Communist Party had expelled them from the monastery and that they would have to leave, and they asked to be expelled from that day. It was obvious that there was nothing to be done, since the Communist Party had all the power. When they said this they were accused of reacting in a bad way. They were asked, 'Why do you say you are leaving? There are two paths. If one adheres to both patriotism [*rgyal gces*] and love of religion [*chos gces*], then one can remain in the monastery. If one rejects these, then one would have to leave.' So because the monks said they were leaving they were accused of being unpatriotic.

This was on the second day of the meetings. Our youths insisted that a decision should be reached that same night. They had to study from the next day onwards, they said. It was decided to reach a conclusion and a heated discussion took place. The Chinese threatened to adjourn the meeting to the next day if we wanted to get into such detailed discussion. One really could not get into a detailed discussion because there was no neutral person present. If one wanted to make a point it was useless because there was no mediator. If there were an impartial mediator, then we could state our case and the Chinese could state their case in an honest manner. But in the absence of such a mediator the situation was that the Chinese put the questions and then answered them as well. They carried on exactly as they liked, so the meeting ended this way.

The monks were in fact attempting to turn the argument with the political cadres into the kind of debate they are trained for as part of their religious education, and which they practise every day in the monastery courtyard. Logical reasoning is a major component of the curriculum in the monasteries, and much of the current thinking of the young monks about Tibetan independence has been developed in this form, that is, by examining the consequences of stated premises. Clearly, the cadres of the work teams sent to the monasteries were not prepared for this kind of argument. The Ganden monk explains what happened the next day:

The next morning they started by saying we had behaved in a disgraceful manner on the previous night and that we were still reactionaries poisoned to the root. They went on saying, 'Yesterday you demanded that the meeting should come to a decision. Do you want to go to prison again? If you want to be imprisoned we can oblige. If you want to drink the water of this land you have to observe the laws.' The chairman of the sub-committee [*las-don tshogs-chung*] spoke a lot. The young monks did not say anything more. Then I spoke, 'This is not the right way to speak to us. You are cadres [*las byed-pa*], we are just members of the public. Speaking for myself, I have just been released from prison. As regards the general state of affairs, I was not happy there, but I had no worries. I just had to think of myself. After coming here, there has been so much talk with the Chinese about this and that. You set me free from prison, but the feeling that I have is that I have been re-imprisoned. I did not ask to be released from prison and if it does not suit you, and you want to imprison me again, then send me back.' When I said this they accused me of having the wrong attitude. I added, 'When you start questioning us, why don't you hear us out?' They kept telling us to speak out, then they kept interrupting us.

Instead of convincing Tibetans of the correctness of the Chinese position, the political meetings had the opposite effect and provoked resistance. They functioned as solidarity-building exercises for the Tibetans. Individuals might be identified as trouble-makers by the political cadres and arrested, but there were always others to take their places as spokesmen when the occasion arose. By providing a public forum for Tibetan grievances through the meetings, however biased and intimidating the setting, Tibetans were able to confront Chinese authority collectively, even as they watched their 'heroes' taken away for punishment.

Perhaps the best illustration of this is the village uprising which was precipitated by the visit of eight cadres of the work team from the local county headquarters in Chushul to Ratö monastery, 30 kilometres south-west of Lhasa. During a meeting on September 29, 1988, one of the monks, Tsering Dondrup, stood up and began arguing with the political cadres who had been lecturing on the 'zombie' (*ro-langs*) of feudalism. He said, 'I didn't say anything about feudalism. Tibet has been independent for thousands of years. I said that Tibet has been under Chinese imperialism.' At that point forty or fifty monks all stood up and shouted out that Tibet is independent.

Tsering Dondrup was arrested that night, and a meeting was called on October 4 to announce that he would be taken away for trial. As he was led away, the monks began throwing stones at the cadres and the police. That night farmers from the nearby village joined the monks in attacking police and stoning cars – most of the young monks at Ratö are children of local families. The police and cadres left, but on October 6 about 200 People's Armed Police arrived from Lhasa and surrounded the monastery and the village. Skirmishes broke out again, but were quelled by the troops using tear-gas and firing guns into the air. People were beaten and four more monks were arrested.

There is some significance perhaps in the fact that the confrontation with the cadres took place in the monastery courtyard, the same place in which the monks practise debate. The cadres had set foot on Tibetan ground reserved for argument and discussion. The political meetings were enough like traditional debate for the monks to draw the comparison, yet sufficiently unlike free and fair discussion for the monks to find them intellectually deficient and absurd:

All these troubles had started in the courtyard of our monastery because we had chosen not to listen to what the Chinese were saying. The Chinese told us we were not behaving like monks, and therefore we were not monks. We asked them to give their reasons for making this statement. It was on that night also that Tsering Dondrup stood up and asked them if there was anything more they would like to tell us. They replied that if we monks thought we were so great, we should go to Lhasa to shout. It was after this that Tsering Dondrup, who could not take any more of this Chinese talk, shouted for an independent Tibet.

For their part, the arguments of the cadres lacked even ideological substance. They were little more than boasts of Chinese power and threats that only served to provoke the monks:

What did they say at the meeting? They said that Tibet had no army and that we were in a hopeless situation. The Tibetan Government once had army barracks all over the place, but they, the Chinese, had destroyed them in three months and we could not do anything about it. There was no one as powerful as them left in Tibet now, and even if they were to give each monk a rifle and a machine-gun we would still be helpless against them . . . They said, 'Tibet is not an independent country, you cannot lift the sky with fingertips nor put it in your mouths.' They asked us if we thought that *tsampa* and barley would fall from the sky if we got independence. 'You think if you became independent that life would be easier for you and that you won't have to work so hard? That is not the case: your present life is much better than before. You were all slaves and serfs then, and you had no food to eat although it was an independent country. There is no better policy than what you have now.'

The Symbolism of Protest

The anti-splittist campaign in monasteries, work units and neighbourhood committees was unsuccessful in altering the attitudes of Tibetans toward Chinese rule.[7] It also failed as a means of suppressing nationalist discontent or preventing demonstrations; instead it degenerated into threats and bullying. The growing reliance on the security apparatus, and finally on military force, is evidence of this. The anti-splittist campaign had the effect of sharpening Tibetan political consciousness and hardening Tibetan resistance. If the underlying rationale behind political education in China is to mobilise group pressure to effect changes in thinking, then the anti-splittist campaign clearly failed to do this. Instead it pitted Tibetans as a group against Chinese authority and to that extent enhanced Tibetan solidarity. Though the political cadres were for the most part Tibetan, their role within the meetings served only to emphasise the division. As the work team became a permanent feature of life in the monasteries, neighbourhood committees and work units, its cadres became increasingly isolated as opportunists and collaborators. The cadres must also have felt their growing isolation as they became identified, willingly or unwillingly, with a bureaucratic apparatus whose purpose was to select individuals for torture and imprisonment. If work of this kind was a necessary part of the job for political cadres, as well as an opportunity for career advancement, then enthusiastic compliance offered few advantages to ordinary Tibetans.

The structural changes in Tibetan society that followed decollectivisation and the reforms of the 1980s are largely responsible for the current situation. Without the total apparatus of collectivisation, it is difficult to see how political meetings and re-education can effectively change political ideas or even offer much in the way of social control. Tibetan social life has once again started to form around relationships beyond the reach of the state and frequently in opposition to it. This is self-evident in the case of the monasteries, which provide a natural basis for solidarity among a younger generation of Tibetans with a common experience of Chinese rule. Religion in general provides an obvious focus for Tibetan consciousness and opposition to the Chinese. In the absence of all-pervasive collective organisation, the political meetings reminded Tibetans of other bases for solidarity. Whether they defined themselves as benefactors or oppressors (and they did both in the course of the meetings), the Chinese always lay on the other side of a deepening divide. People can be bought or intimidated, but the Chinese system in Tibet no longer offers an organisational basis for groups that will root out and attack its 'enemies', as it did during the Cultural Revolution.

The continuing demonstrations throughout 1988 and 1989 can be properly understood in the context of the ongoing political campaign. For Tibetans the one was a reflection of the other, and both served to confirm and sharpen the social and symbolic opposition between Tibetans and Chinese. The demonstrations themselves were very much nation-building exercises. They were a novel response to the current situation in Tibet, they highlighted the separation of the Tibetan and Chinese world, and staked out and defended Tibetan territory in a manner that repelled Chinese efforts at incorporation. The form that the demonstrations took illustrates this point. In almost all of the more than two dozen demonstrations, small groups of monks or nuns assembled near the Barkor in the old Tibetan part of Lhasa, then proceeded to circumambulate the Jokhang temple, shouting 'Tibet is Independent' and 'Long live the Dalai Lama' (literally, 'May the Dalai Lama live ten thousand years') while displaying the banned Tibetan national flag. The demonstrations by monks and nuns were joined by ordinary people from the Barkor. The demonstrations would continue until they were violently broken up by the security forces and people were beaten, arrested and sometimes shot.

Circumambulation, or '*korwa*' (*skor-ba*), has a central place in Tibetan Buddhism. It is practised universally around temples and other holy sites, and is for lay Tibetans the most common means of accumulating merit. *Korwa* performed around the Jokhang temple in Lhasa, the holiest site for Tibetans, has special significance. At the same time, the Barkor circuit in Lhasa is the centre of the Tibetan city and the busiest market area for Tibetans. Circling the Barkor as a form of protest was an invention of the first group of Drepung monks who demonstrated on September 27, 1987. Their demonstration was prompted by attacks in the

Chinese media on the Dalai Lama's visit to the United States. But when the monks assembled in a teahouse early on the morning of September 27, they literally had no idea what to do next. Circling the Barkor was only one of several possibilities; marching down the main street and assembling in front of the government buildings were two others. The third demonstration on October 6, by monks from Drepung who were trying to win the release of those arrested on September 27, took place in front of the government compound.

There was also a demonstration on December 30, 1988, by students and teachers from the University, prompted by the shootings that had occurred on December 10, International Human Rights Day. The demonstration proceeded down the main street, but did not show the Tibetan flag; its demands were for disarming the police, allowing Tibetans more cultural and religious freedom, and greater use of the Tibetan language in education and government. This demonstration was not broken up by the police.

With the demonstrations around the Barkor, Tibetans were symbolically marking out their own territory. The government offices are Chinese territory, in the Chinese part of the city, and to protest there would be to acknowledge Chinese authority. This might have been the kind of demonstration the Chinese expected and would have understood, but it would have meant acquiescing in the Chinese understanding of the issues: for example, how much and what kinds of religious freedom are to be tolerated, what are the rights of nationalities, and so on. But *korwa* takes place on the home ground of Tibetans, in the vicinity of the Jokhang, and is an act that every Tibetan understands. Chinese, on the other hand, feel uncomfortable when they venture into this part of Lhasa. Following the first demonstrations, armed Chinese security forces began to patrol the Barkor in the anti-clockwise – thus anti-religious – direction. Whether the Chinese were aware of the symbolism of this or not, every Tibetan immediately understood. The Chinese were thus drawn into the Tibetan symbolism in a way that graphically illustrated their oppositional role.

In the second demonstration on October 1, an old monk who rushed into the burning police station to free those arrested was carried around the Barkor on the shoulders of the crowd. His act was immediately assimilated to the symbolism of *korwa* as protest, and thus simultaneously bravery, compassion and rebellion. The bodies of the dead were also paraded, during this and later demonstrations, around the Barkor by the crowd. Again, the religious significance was apparent to every Tibetan.

Religious Freedom

The invention of *korwa* as a form of protest draws attention to another dimension of the Tibetan response to the anti-splittist campaign: the contradiction between Tibetan and Chinese conceptions of religion and religious freedom. *Korwa* is for ordinary Tibetans one of the simplest and most visible forms of religious expression. At the same time – along with prostrations, turning prayer-wheels and burning incense – it conforms to the understanding of religion which is incorporated into the Party's policy for allowing the expression of 'voluntary religious faith' (*chos-dad rang-mos kyi srid-jus*). Religion is thus conceived as harmless superstition, at best a decorative feature of minority nationalities. Forcing it into this mould neutralises the explosive potential of religion to unite Tibetans as a nation. In the long run, modernisation and economic development are expected to make religious practices vestigial and irrelevant. It is on this assumption that religion is tolerated. What the monks are illustrating through their use of *korwa* as political protest is precisely the limits to Chinese-defined religious freedom. In effect, they are forcing the Chinese to strike out at religion by striking out at nationalism. At the same time, they are showing ordinary Tibetans how to transform their personal practice of religion, which Chinese policy allows, into a practice which, through recovering the symbols of nationhood, becomes an act of rebellion.

Tibetans developed a number of tactics for nationalist protest in the form of religious practice. After September 27, 1988, when the massive presence of security forces patrolling the Barkor made any demonstration to commemorate the previous year impossible, a crowd of several hundred Tibetans sat in the teaching area next to the Jokhang and recited prayers for several hours on behalf of those who had died the year before. No attempt was made to break up the crowd. On December 3, 1988, during the evening of the Butter Lamp festival, over 1,000 Tibetans gathered in front of the Jokhang and chanted the 'Prayer of Truth' (*bden-tshig smon-lam*) composed by the Dalai Lama, which calls on the 'protectors of Tibet to drive the barbarians from the land of snows'. In the days following October 5, 1989, as news that the Dalai Lama had been awarded the Nobel Peace Prize spread among the Tibetan population, Tibetans began to celebrate by burning incense and tossing handfuls of *tsampa* over each other (and at Chinese troops). When officials became aware of the significance of the celebrations, meetings were called to denounce the award to the Dalai Lama, and on October 13 troops were instructed to arrest and shoot Tibetans who were throwing *tsampa* and burning incense. A search was launched for the organisers of the celebrations, which were now branded splittist activities, and up to 200 people are said by one source to have been detained and interrogated.

The key religious symbol for Tibetans is, of course, the Dalai Lama. The dual nature of his role for Tibetans – both political and religious leader – has been an important political resource for Tibetans, who used the ambiguity of his status to counter attacks in political meetings. The Dalai Lama also embodies the central formula of Tibetan politics: 'religion and politics combined' (*chos-srid zung-'brel*).[8] But for Tibetans this formula has acquired a new significance that contrasts with its meaning in traditional Tibetan society, because the political side of the equation is identified with democracy, and the Dalai Lama as a world leader is understood by young Tibetans as a symbol of democracy and human rights.

The Chinese, on the other hand, are obliged to attack both. Religious faith must be subordinated to 'patriotism' – love of the nation – and thus religious tolerance requires submission to Chinese rule. Tibetan demands for democracy and human rights are in turn dismissed as attempts to restore the 'old society' (*spyi-tshogs rnying-pa*). Yet Tibetans understand the Chinese system to be deficient by world standards precisely because it cannot deliver democracy and human rights. One of the monks from Ganden recounts this line of argument in a political meeting at the monastery:

The Chinese say that our past government, which was temporal as well as spiritual, is totally unsuitable for the present situation . . . They said the Chinese government is much more advanced. They have a very high regard for their socialism and communism. They said their government is more suitable for the present-day situation of the world. They said our past government was unsuitable because religion and politics are incompatible.

We demand that the Chinese should leave Tibet. If they don't, it will be intolerable for us. We need freedom and independence. The Chinese don't know what we are suffering under their rule. They blame us for wanting to revive the old government. They claim that in our minds we have the goal to become the leaders. In fact we didn't shout to become leaders, but to bring happiness to the majority of the Tibetan people. We appealed to human rights organisations of the world and to the supporters of Tibet. For that reason we peacefully marched.

Tibetans will cite a whole series of restrictions on religion: on the reconstruction of monasteries, on the admission of new monks and nuns, on donations by lay people, on the performance of ritual services and so on. Religion is administered by a collection of official organisations responsible for implementing Party policies. From the Chinese side, the restrictions make perfect sense, because they impose conditions which in one way or another limit the autonomy of religious institutions and the growth of the individual elements of religion, which for Tibetans are intimately bound up with national consciousness. For their part, Tibetans try to ignore or work around the restrictions; sometimes they get away with it, but they are always aware that policies can be quickly reversed. The Ganden monk adds:

Under the Chinese there will be no freedom of religion. If Tibet is independent and has freedom, then there will be freedom of religion as well. Until then there will be no freedom of religion. It will be only in name, not in reality. They declared freedom of religion. They also declared a policy of relaxation (*srid-jus gu-yangs*). So they actually left us without any restrictions for a little while. Slowly, there came to be more and more restrictions on religion. So there's no way we'll get freedom of religion.

Human Rights

Tibetans to a large extent have taken Chinese declarations of policy and turned them around in an effort to clarify their own opposition. At the same time, the continuing flow of information and ideas from the outside world on democracy, human rights and national struggles has provided them with an alternative vocabulary (and alternative meanings) to the Chinese. Equally important has been the effort made by the Tibetans to align modern political terminology with conceptions of the world and man's place in it drawn from Buddhism. This is illustrated in a discussion of the meaning of terms like freedom and human rights from an interview with a young Drepung monk who took part in the first demonstrations in the autumn of 1987. First he states what Tibetan independence means for him:

If we get independence, from a narrow point of view all Tibetan desires will be satisfied. From a bigger point of view, if Tibet is independent, then the *Buddha Dharma* can prevail, can be spread. So if *Buddha Dharma* is strong enough and good, then it can bring peace and happiness in the world, not only for Tibetans. Here we are in our own country but our own body is not owned by ourselves. The Chinese say they have improved a lot in Tibet, that they take care of poor Tibetan families, giving them everything and so on. This is not true for me. Everyone is seeking freedom. Without freedom the human body is meaningless.

The monk goes on to state what human rights mean to him:

For us the Chinese are saying that you have freedom of everything, such as freedom of religious faith and so on. Human rights include freedom. But we need real freedom. Through freedom we can make preparations not only for this life, but work more for the future lives to come. As the Chinese reject the existence of future lives, that is one difficult point. If freedom is only to eat and drink, it doesn't have much significance. That can be done by any animal such as a dog or a cat who only worry about food or drink. So human beings are not the same. To be human has deeper meaning.

This young monk is in his early twenties. His education in Tibetan before entering the monastery did not go beyond the six years of elementary school. He was not allowed to continue his education because his family received a bad 'class label' (*gral-rim-pa*) during the Cultural Revolution. He had studied another four years in the monastery. The political words in his vocabulary have all entered the Tibetan language in the 20th century. Some of these words – such as 'democracy' and 'imperialism' – have acquired their modern political denotation largely through Chinese political material translated into Tibetan. It is not simply that as a monk he is inclined to gloss their meaning in religious terms. To give them meaning in terms of a wider and coherent view of the Tibetan situation under Chinese rule requires an appeal to a Buddhist framework, where a human rebirth is precious, where there is a need to do good for future lives and where *Dharma* has importance for the world.

Thus, independence implies freedom to practise the *Dharma*, but freedom in turn is senseless without acknowledging the human condition. 'Human rights' in Tibetan is literally the 'rights of human transmigrators/beings' (*'gro-ba'i mi'i thob-thang*), and 'transmigrator' (*'gro-ba*) remains a basic term in the language of Tibetan Buddhism. The three terms – independence, freedom and human rights – lead in order of ascending generality back to the issue of making human life meaningful. Religious freedom implies the right to prepare for future lives, which implies unselfish actions for the benefit of others – which includes political life in general as well as working for independence. Opposite to this are actions motivated by the selfish interests of this life, which here refer to Chinese promises merely to 'make life better'. Human rights, as the concept is understood by Tibetans, thus divide altruism from selfishness, the sacred (which includes both religion and politics) from the profane. What in a modern Western political context are essentially secular political values, are for Tibetans identified with the sacred side of the equation and are symbolically opposed to the Chinese system in Tibet, which belongs to the profane side. The monk adds:

'Reciting *Om mani padme hum*, visiting temples and making donations are not considered the real freedom of religion.'

Tibetans have long been aware of the existence of the United Nations, and regard it (perhaps naively) as a legitimate forum for their grievances; handwritten letters addressed to the United Nations are frequently slipped to foreign tourists to be smuggled out of Tibet. From 1987 onwards Tibetans described their protests not just as a struggle for national independence, but as a fight for human rights. The term appeared more and more frequently in these letters and on wall posters put up around Lhasa. For instance, in the days preceding the demonstration on December 10, 1988, International Human Rights Day, a political leaflet circulated informing people: 'Today is a day commemorating the struggle for human rights. Therefore, along with appealing to the United Nations and friendly countries in order to restore our just rights, we Tibetans would like to commemorate this day.'

The wall poster that appeared around Lhasa on the morning of December 10, added to the familiar slogans 'Long live the Dalai Lama' and 'Long live the restoration of Tibetan independence' new slogans such as 'Long live the new democratic constitution' and 'Let us remember the human rights of the United Nations'. These leaflets, letters and posters were crudely reproduced by woodblock or handprinted mimeographs, and were sometimes signed by groups giving themselves names like 'The Revolutionary Committee for Tibetan Independence' or 'Victorious Greater Tibet'. The names would change frequently, which reflects a loosely knit network of dissidents cutting across Tibetan society from shopkeepers in the Barkor to monks and nuns, office workers, students and Chinese-educated cadres. Posters were often put up by women making their rounds in the early morning. The penalty for being caught producing or distributing this literature is always imprisonment.

Closely associated with human rights in Tibetan thinking is the idea of 'truth' (*bden-pa*), which in Tibetan also carries both a religious and a political meaning (that is, justice). Tibetans speak of the 'truth' (or 'justice') of their cause, of their 'true rights' (*bden-pa'i thob-thang*) and of their 'true history', all of which the Chinese have denied them and which they are entitled to. Truth is also presented as a weapon in the fight against Chinese rule. This is in fact the standard answer to Chinese assertions that Tibetans have no army and can never defeat the Chinese militarily. In the words of a Drepung monk: 'The best way and the only way is to talk using the truth, otherwise we can't fight them. Even if we have the power to fight them, we won't do that. Instead we will fight with the truth.'

The appeal to truth, in both the religious and the political sense, counters Chinese 'lies', the only basis of which is power. The December 10 leaflet says: 'Recounting even a brief history will make the Chinese invaders feel ashamed.' Tibetans imagine an opportunity to argue their case before a hypothetical impartial forum, confident that 'truth will prevail'. One 'Letter to the United Nations' written in August 1989 (five months after the declaration of martial law) and later smuggled from Tibet, requests that 'you assemble all the people of Lhasa, monks and lay people, including the Chinese authorities, and without discriminating between Chinese and Tibetans give us the opportunity to talk about the true history'.

It is easy to discount these appeals to 'truth' as the only recourse of the powerless, as the Chinese have done. But the Chinese themselves have laid the foundation for Tibetan political consciousness through the campaign against splittism. Tibetans are, after all, invited to listen to Chinese arguments and discuss them. The exercise is largely a sham, but in the absence of other collective mechanisms to enforce ideological conformity and restrict discussion, Tibetans are capable of finding their own answers to Chinese arguments. No real attempt has been made to dismantle the reforms and re-institute collectivisation.

On the other hand, modernisation and economic development cannot function as effective ideological substitutes for socialism (which was hardly mentioned during the campaign). The Chinese would have Tibetans see them as modernisers rather than oppressors. But Tibetans have simply identified their own aspirations with 'modernity' in the global sense, a point of view that further highlights the deficiencies of the Chinese system in Tibet. The influx of foreign goods, foreign ideas and foreign visitors only helps this along: foreigners are almost always sympathetic to the Tibetan cause and critical of the Chinese system and are expelled from Tibet whenever trouble breaks out. The Chinese have wrongly assumed that they can 'modernise' Tibetan thinking along Chinese lines. Instead, the anti-splittist campaign has undermined Chinese claims to represent progress and modernity, while sharpening the Tibetan sense of nationhood.

The most remarkable document to come out of the current phase of nationalist unrest in Tibet was prepared by a group of young monks from Drepung monastery in 1988 using woodblocks. Entitled *The Meaning of the Precious Democratic Constitution of Tibet*, it was intended to be taken by monks back to their villages to provide an example of what an independent Tibet might look like. The authors had earlier been arrested during the first demonstration, on September 27, 1987, and released the following January. Some of the group were arrested again and sentenced to long prison terms on November 30, 1989; the leader, Ngawang Phulchung, received a sentence of nineteen years.

The constitution referred to is the 1963 plan for a democratic constitution drawn up by the Dalai Lama in exile. The Drepung text restates the principles of the 1963 constitution. It calls for 'equality' without discrimination based on sex, social origin, language, religion, race, wealth or regions, and declares the equal right to free speech, freedom of thought, freedom of assembly and association, and freedom of movement.

The Drepung text, however, is very much a reflection of the current situation and a Tibetan response to the campaign against splittism. It opens by calling on Tibetans to continue the struggle against the 'foreign Chinese invaders' with a determination based on 'a force whose nature is established truth' (*bsgrub-bya bden-pa yin-pa'i rang-bzhin gyi nus-shugs*). This formulation, which echoes the language of monastic debate, indicates the extent to which the monks are able to draw on the rational elements within religious tradition to counter Chinese arguments. The heart of the text is a discussion of the meaning of 'democracy combining political and religious principles' (*chos srid gnyis-ldan gyi dmangs-gtso*). This is, of course, the traditional formula for Tibetan politics, but here it is Buddhism which is described as compatible with democracy, while the Chinese system remains incompatible.

The text answers the claims made in political meetings that only the Chinese system is suitable to modern conditions. The language is simple and straightforward, but the style of argument again comes from the tradition of monastic debate. An explanation of the Tibetan term for 'democracy' (*dmangs-gtso*) is provided by breaking the term into its two syllables. The first syllable (*dmangs*) is defined to mean 'the broad masses' (*rgya-che'i mi-dmangs*) by excluding exceptions based on power, social class and kinship. Here the monks are borrowing a standard term from the Chinese Communist political lexicon and using it in the context of Tibetan independence to convey a very different meaning. The meaning of 'the broad masses' is then illustrated using the case of Tibet. Applying the same procedure with the second syllable (*gtso*), a short form of the word *gtso-ba*, meaning excellence or superiority, democracy becomes 'a practice for expressing the will of society that accords with making paramount the demands and wishes of the broad masses' (*rgya-che'i mi-mang gi dgos 'don 'dod-babs gtso bor bstun dgos-pa'i spyi mos kyi lugs srol*).

The Drepung text goes on to outline a simplified procedure for representative government. Its real significance lies, however, not in what it says about the provisions of the 1963 constitution for an independent Tibet, but in what it indicates about the level of political reflection going on in Tibet today. In taking up the question of the 'old society' in detail – rejecting the restoration of 'serf-dom' (*shing-bran gyi lam-lugs*) and the 'old system' administered by a succession of feudal masters (*bkas-bkod brgyud-'dzin-pa*) – the monks are responding to the principal line of argument taken by the cadres in the political meetings.

Without the meetings the monks might never have been forced to think about democracy in universal terms. Ironically, the meetings did succeed in their expressed aim, that is, raising political consciousness among Tibetans, but they did not succeed in such a manner as the Chinese might have wished for. The result has been to take long-simmering Tibetan hostility to Chinese rule and sharpen it by identifying Tibetan demands for independence with modern political ideas like democracy and human rights. This is perhaps all the more surprising because it has occurred during the course of a brutal campaign to suppress dissent. The level of real understanding may vary considerably throughout the population, but the majority of Tibetans probably at least know the words and associate them with the Dalai Lama and Tibetan independence. Democracy and human rights are now common and widespread ideas among Tibetans and it is taken for granted that this is what the fight for Tibetan independence is about.

Under Martial Law

After the declaration of martial law in Lhasa on the night of March 7–8, 1989, increasingly harsh measures became necessary to suppress dissent. The responsibility for maintaining order in Lhasa was assumed directly by the PLA. The events of the days before March 8 in fact suggest a plan to provoke Tibetans to riot, which would have justified the imposition of martial law and the stationing of PLA troops in the city, although the initial demonstration on March 5 had been small and peaceful and no different from several others in the previous months. After police opened fire on the demonstrators, security forces withdrew from the Tibetan part of Lhasa, leaving Tibetans free to riot. On the occasional forays the

> ## The No.3 Announcement by the People's Government of the City of Lhasa
>
> October 3rd 1987
>
> In order to ensure the smooth Implementation of the opening police, to promote the development of tourism industry in our region, to increase our economic and technical exchange and cooperation with different countries in the World, to avoid apprearance of displeasure in foreign affair's work, the city announces as follows:
>
> 1. We extende welcome to friends from the different countries in the World who come to our region for sightseeing, tour, visit, work, trade discussion and economic cooperation.
> 2. Who ever comes to our region must respects our State sovereignty, abide by the lows of our country. They are not allowed to interfere in internal affairs of our country and engage in activities that are incompatible with their status.
> 3. Foreigners are not allowed to crowd around watching and photographing the disturbances manipulated by a few splittists, and they should not do any distorted propaganda cocerning disturbances, which is not in agreement with the facts.
> 4. In accordance with our lows, we shall mete out punishment to the trouble-makers who stir up, support and participate in the disturbance manipulated by a few splittists.

Order issued by the Lhasa Government on October 3, 1987, prohibiting tourists from watching or filming demonstrations. (*Anders Anderson/ Tibet Image Bank, 1987*)

security forces continued to make into Tibetan areas, they fired at random and thus further enraged the crowd.

Martial law enabled the authorities to prohibit visits by all but a few selected foreigners and to restrict the movement of Tibetans. Displays of force – troops, armoured personnel carriers and military checkpoints – became a regular feature of life in Lhasa, and on March 4, 1990, tanks were stationed in the Jokhang square to prevent unrest on the anniversary of the declaration of martial law.

The main result of the anti-splittist campaign that followed the declaration of martial law was a steady stream of arrests and prison sentences for a variety of 'counter-revolutionary offences'. Most of these had nothing to do with the riots and demonstrations although the sentencing of large numbers of prisoners only began in earnest after March 8, 1989. The sentences became more and more severe in 1989 and 1990, with prisoners often receiving sentences of ten years or more for such crimes as 'teaching reactionary Tibet independence songs', singing songs praising the Dalai Lama, putting up wall posters, displaying the Tibetan flag, and writing or distributing independence literature. On January 23, 1990, a sentencing rally was held in which twenty-two Tibetans charged with counter-revolutionary offences, including a juvenile, were paraded in public.

Meanwhile, as the search for splittists continues, 'screening and investigation' have become routine features of life in Tibet. The work team, originally a temporary measure instituted for ideological re-education, has assumed under martial law an increasingly large role in monitoring and surveillance, and a permanent 'Office for Stabilising the Situation' has been created to investigate those reported to be uncooperative.

NOTES

1. See my article 'Reform and Repression in Tibet', *Telos 80*, Summer 1989.
2. Lhasa Xizang Regional Service in Mandarin, 1130 hrs GMT, February 9, 1988, in FBIS, February 10, 1988, pp. 36–7.
3. *Ibid.*, p. 37.
4. Lhasa Xizang Regional Service in Mandarin, 1130 hrs GMT, October 13, 1987, in FBIS, October 14, 1987, p. 30.
5. See Martin King Whyte, *Small Groups and Political Rituals in China*, Berkeley: University of California Press, 1974, for a discussion of comparable forms of political education throughout China.
6. The Tibetan term means simply 'work team'. The name of the teams in Chinese is *gongzuo dui* and has the same meaning as in Tibetan.
7. Whyte, *op. cit.*, also found that political meetings generally were not an effective means of changing attitudes. But he adds that other properties of group organisation nevertheless contributed to social control. These are precisely the organisational features on which the Chinese can no longer depend in Tibet. Compare the Tibetan situation with Whyte's conclusion that 'orders, threats and physical coercion have by no means been eliminated from Chinese life, but the new organisational model does seem to make it possible to keep these techniques of control in the background' (p. 233).
8. Margaret Nowak has an insightful discussion of the role this formula plays in the political thinking of young exile Tibetans in India. As she explains, along with the symbol of the Dalai Lama, it enables young Tibetans in a refugee environment to 'interpret the lessons of contemporary, alien, social experience in the familiar light of the traditionally ambiguous and therefore flexible ideology of *chos-srid zung-'brel*, "religion and politics combined" '. See her *Tibetan Refugees: Youth and the New Generation of Meaning*, New Brunswick, NJ: Rutgers University Press, 1984, p. 157.

SYMBOLS AND PROTEST
THE ICONOGRAPHY OF DEMONSTRATIONS IN TIBET, 1987–1990

Robert Barnett

In terms of Tibetan history the second week of March 1990 was a time of special significance. It was a key anniversary in the story of Sino-Tibetan struggle, and stood not just at the turn of a calendar decade, but at the turn of a ten-year period in Tibetan history. That significance can be summed up in a single iconographic statement: on Sunday, March 4, news reached the outside world that four tanks had been stationed outside the Jokhang temple, in the central square of the Tibetan quarter of Lhasa.[1]

The event was not itself of major news value, in the Western understanding of that term – there were no reports of serious protests or disturbances at that time – but the event was laden with symbolic implications. The redeployment of tanks on the streets of the Tibetan capital for the first time, as far as we know, in at least ten years brought an end to what should have been, and almost was, a decade of reform and liberalisation in Tibet.

The dates involved in this cycle of events covered exactly a decade. The process of liberalisation in Tibet had begun when the First Symposium on Work in Tibet was held by the Central Government in March 1980.[2] This conference decided that the priorities in Tibet were to correct the excesses of ultra-leftism and to use 'practice as the only yardstick for truth'. In other words, it recognised both that the depredations of the Cultural Revolution had to be rolled back, as they had already begun to be in China, and that conditions in Tibet were different from those in China and required special, more conciliatory policies.

With these key ideological concessions in place, the stage was set for Hu Yaobang, then Party Secretary, to make his May 1980 visit to Tibet – the first by a Party Secretary while in office. Hu was apparently horrified by what he saw, and some reports claim that he admitted that Tibet was poorer than when the Chinese took it over in 1959.[3] He pushed the pace of reform even further, and called for respect for Tibetan culture and a tax amnesty for Tibetan farmers and nomads.[4] Thus began a time of relative liberalisation for Tibet, after a twenty-year period of policies which had amounted to an officially endorsed attempt at ethnocide and which had in addition led to widespread impoverishment.

The policy of reform was not unsuccessful. The disbanding of the communes immediately allowed nomads to resume a way of life that was economically appropriate to their own conditions; their standard of living improved markedly as a result.[5] In the towns and villages too there was some increase in prosperity. Outward religious practice returned to a degree which must have been unexpected by the Chinese, perhaps by any observer, after twenty years of repression. Travel was allowed for Tibetans to visit relatives and pilgrimage sites in India, and tourism was encouraged as the key to urban development: these were the hallmarks of the policy of liberalisation.

The tanks that were stationed in the central square of Lhasa in March 1990 can be seen as the visible sign of the failure of that policy. Foreign tourists had been heavily restricted since late 1987, although 43,000 had visited earlier that year; by mid-March 1990 there were, I believe, just eleven in Tibet, and eight of those were only there because they had been turned back from the Nepal border by a snowdrift. The Lhasa valley had been under martial law since the previous March and travel abroad by Tibetans had been almost entirely prohibited. By that time the number of suspected dissidents arrested since 1987 had probably come close to 3,000.

What is more relevant, because it has always been the flagship of the Chinese claim to liberalisation, is what now appears to have been the erosion of religious tolerance. There were always those who argued that the new liberalisations were more cosmetic than actual, and it had been pointed out that, in some areas at least, religious practice was allowed while religious teaching was restricted. But it was only in the last weeks of 1989 that definitive signs emerged that the authorities had started to re-impose explicit restrictions on religious practice.

In this context the tanks take on a further significance. It was not only that they had been positioned on the streets of Lhasa that suggested a collapse in the policy of reform, but also that they had been stationed at the gates of the Jokhang temple, the heart of the spiritual world of Tibetan Buddhism, that also indicated the character of the divide in Sino-Tibetan politics at the time.

The Reclaiming of Anniversaries

Before analysing the decline of the policy of liberalisation, it is important to emphasise the resonance of the religious issue in Sino-Tibetan politics: although the struggle between the two sides is over sovereignty and national identity, the battleground on which that struggle is fought is religion. More specifically, it is the great festivals and anniversaries of the Tibetan religious calendar that provide the context and landmarks for the central dispute between the Tibetans and the Chinese. Furthermore, the key issue in that religious battle is not the apparent question, which is whether the great festivals will take place, but the underlying question, which is whether, when they do take place, they will signify the sustaining of a Chinese or a Tibetan state.

That is why the second week of March has a special significance in Tibet, for it is a week of anniversaries, and it is over anniversaries that political battles in Tibet are fought.

March 5: Raid on the Jokhang. Four different anniversaries fell within the second week of March, all of them of major political significance. Of those four events, it was the last – the religious anniversary – which was of the greatest importance. The first, which took place on March 5, 1990, marked the second anniversary of a major demonstration in 1988 when at least five people were shot dead by police,[6] and when, more particularly, the Jokhang temple was raided by the People's Armed Police.[7]

In 1989 the first anniversary of that incident was marked initially by a small demonstration of less than forty people. The incident escalated into three days of widespread protest and unrest when police opened fire on the group, thirty minutes after they had begun to chant pro-independence slogans; one Hong Kong paper later quoted an unnamed Chinese official as saying that 250 Tibetans had been killed by police in the days that followed.[8] It was at the end of those three days that martial law was declared. Some observers have suggested that the decision to bring in the army was premeditated, because Tibetans were expected to try to mark the March 5 anniversary in some way.[9]

March 8: the Imposition of Martial Law. The second anniversary remembered that week was on Thursday, March 8, 1990: one year after the imposition of martial law in Lhasa. This was another occasion which the Tibetans were expected to mark with protests. In fact the Chinese authorities themselves marked it in a distinctive way by staging the largest display of military hardware seen in the city for several years.

The parade included 1,800 armed troops, fifty lorries, twelve field guns, five armoured personnel carriers, and five multiple rocket launchers.[10] The Chinese authorities seem to have thought that the start of the second year of martial law was the most likely

Tanks passing the Potala palace, March 1990. (*DIIR, Dharamsala/Les Amis du Tibet*)

Soldier on sentry duty overlooking the Barkor square during martial law, Lhasa, 1989–90. (*DIIR, Dharamsala*)

occasion for a Tibetan protest, and they made sure that it was marked in the way they wanted rather than as the Tibetans might have preferred.

Paradoxically, they fell into something of a trap in doing so. The Tibetans may have failed to express their protest on that day, but the Chinese authorities themselves demonstrated in a highly visible way exactly what it was that Tibetans protest about: the Chinese presence in Tibet. This presence is at the core of nationalist discontent, and has been the subject of the demands of almost all the protests that have taken place in Tibet.[11] The Chinese army is the most obvious embodiment of that presence.

The authorities were not to know that, despite the ban on tourists in Lhasa that week, the outside world would find out about the display, including even the number of military vehicles which broke down during the course of the parade (one troop truck and one motorbike). The Chinese display of military force must have looked crude to foreign observers, but this was not its only drawback. The display may have been intended to have a symbolic purpose, presumably to act as a deterrent, but in fact it implied that those who needed to be deterred represented a powerful threat. The 1,800 troops and the multiple rocket launchers paraded on the streets of Lhasa effectively vitiated China's claim that the dissident element in Tibet consisted of only 'a handful of splittists' who, in addition, it had never seriously claimed were armed.[12] But the significance of the display goes further than that: by showing massive firepower the Chinese reinforced the persistent critique of those Tibetans who say that China's presence, besides being illegal, is essentially a military operation involving the disproportionate use of force.

In other words, in terms of ideology and credibility, the Chinese may have lost more than they gained by marking the March 8 anniversary in such an unambiguous way. Of the reactions of the spectators we know from eyewitnesses in Lhasa only that Tibetans watched the parade in silence, and that one old man, standing at the back of the crowd, made a thumbs-down sign as the troops passed. But it is not hard to imagine that the parade signified to Tibetans the bankruptcy of Chinese rhetoric. That view was anyway axiomatic among Tibetans. I recall in 1987 a Tibetan saying to me in Lhasa: 'If the Chinese say something, then it's a lie.' The Chinese commitment to liberalisation, even to anything other than power, was seen as progressively more suspect as they responded with growing incoherence to the protests of the previous thirty months. The March 8 parade may have been the least ambiguous choice for the authorities to make, but to a people whose entire culture is informed by symbolism it may not have meant what the government intended.

March 10: Uprising versus Reform. The third anniversary remembered that week fell on March 10. This marked the day in 1959 when thousands of Tibetans took to the streets of Lhasa to protect the Dalai Lama from alleged abduction by Chinese forces. The protest turned into an armed uprising, and led a week later to the flight of the Dalai Lama to India. On that occasion, the army defeated the rebels, and the death toll from casualties and later reprisals was immense: 87,000 killed in that year alone, according to a Radio Lhasa broadcast at the time.[13]

March 10 has a special significance as an anniversary in that both sides claim it as a highpoint in their histories. In what must have been an intentional effort to displace the Tibetan recollection of the day as a commemoration of rebellion, the Chinese authorities have claimed the same day as the anniversary of the implementation of democratic reforms in Tibet. This cannot actually have begun on March 10, 1959, since Lhasa at least was paralysed by protest at that time.[14] Nevertheless, each year there is still a conscious attempt by the authorities in Tibet to redefine the historical importance of March 10, and the occasion is now marked by official speeches on the success of the reforms.

In 1989 the March 10 speeches marking thirty years of democratic reform were given by the leading cadres at the western end of Lhasa while, at the other end of the city, just forty-eight hours after the imposition of martial law and twenty-four hours after the expulsion of all foreign tourists, there was a display of military force in the Tibetan quarter of the capital.[15] A platoon of military lorries had been positioned in the Jokhang square, each with Katyusha-type multiple rocket launchers targeted on the temple.[16] Again the authorities ensured that they controlled the visible symbolic content of the day; but again, with their heavy-handed symbolism they may have lost more than they gained. For a start, their deployment of heavy armour confirmed the Jokhang as the focus of Tibetan dissent.

The Jokhang versus the Norbulingka

Although the March 10 uprising in 1959 focussed on the Norbulingka, the summer palace of the Dalai Lama 3 kilometres outside the city, the centre of the 1990 anniversaries had become the Jokhang temple. The Tibetan pro-independence activists had made the Jokhang, and thus the old Tibetan quarter of Lhasa, the political focus of Tibet by staging all the nationalist demonstrations of the previous two and a half years outside or around the temple. In contrast, the Chinese vision of anniversaries in the reform era has always been centred on the Norbulingka, which, in comparison with the Potala, can be seen as the secular seat of the Dalai Lama: it is not revered by devotees to the same degree as an object of pilgrimage or circumambulation. It is at the Norbulingka that Chinese cadres have since the early 1980s staged official celebrations, and where they have marked official events such as Teachers' Day and folkloric events like Shoton (the 'Yoghurt Festival') by hosting picnics, giving long speeches on reforms and organising performances by local folk-dance troupes in the park. The events at the Norbulingka have thus represented the Chinese attempt to reconstruct on the site of the 1959 uprising an officially acceptable and specifically secular tradition of Tibetan anniversaries.[17]

It is perhaps significant, therefore, that the first major demonstration of the current wave of unrest broke out in front of the Jokhang on the same day and at the same time as a secular, official anniversary was being staged in the Norbulingka. This was October 1, 1987, China's National Day and the anniversary of the founding of the People's Republic in 1949. At the same time that the leading Chinese officials in Tibet were giving speeches at the Norbulingka about the thirty-eight years since the founding of the People's Republic, 3,000 Tibetans were burning down a small police station overlooking the Jokhang 3 kilometres away.

The Chinese press, in its accounts afterwards, was scathing about the insult offered by the demonstrators to the state celebrations in the Norbulingka that day. Symbolically, the rejection of the Norbulingka celebrations was an affront to Chinese sensibilities, and a rejection of the secular edifice that China had created in its reconstruction of tradition and its rebuilding of the city.[18] A year later the authorities took steps to strengthen the interpretation of October 1 as a secular, specifically Chinese anniversary, even trying to revalidate it by ascribing Tibetan folk superstitions to the day, rather than by allowing the pro-independence movement to claim it as a nationalist anniversary.[19]

These attempts made little headway against the interpretation of the day that had been created by the Tibetan demonstrators in October 1987. By their rejection of the Norbulingka event, they had reinforced the symbolic status of the Jokhang in Tibetan culture, and the role it had had for over a thousand years before the Chinese arrived in Tibet. In the late 1980s the repeated demonstrations there made it a symbol of Tibetan nationalist aspirations. Furthermore, although the majority of demonstrators in 1987 were lay people, they reinforced the religious element within the nationalist movement. The temple remains by its nature a symbol of specifically religious aspirations but came to represent the fusion of religious and secular aspirations that constitutes contemporary Tibetan nationalism, which in turn reflects the traditional Tibetan theory of the state as *chos-srid zung-'brel* ('religion and politics combined').

The Commitment to Religious Tolerance

Again, perhaps unaware of the power of symbolism, the Chinese themselves nourished the union of religion and politics in Tibet by staking the success of their reforms on the visible display of religious tolerance. In 1986, in a major ceremony at the Jokhang temple, the Chinese staged their most ambitious exhibition of reform by allowing the monks to hold for the first time in twenty years the Monlam (the 'Great Prayer Festival'). [20]

As a religious event, this celebration had to be held at the Jokhang, not at the Norbulingka; it was in any case essential for the authorities to show that their liberalisations included the religious establishment. It is not clear if they were aware that the traditional purpose of the Monlam was to allow the monks to convey some sort of spiritual or ecclesiastical endorsement on the Tibetan Government, in return for a commitment to the religious establishment. [21] Whether the authorities knew or not, their choice of symbolism led them to share the same fate that had befallen traditional Tibetan governments in earlier years: the religious establishment re-assumed control through the ritual of the festival over the secular polity.

In 1988 it became imperative for the Chinese Government to let the Monlam festival take place, as it had in the previous two years, to show to the world at large that its liberalisation policy in Tibet remained intact despite the 1987 demonstrations. Unlike the secular festivals at the Norbulingka, the authorities could not run the Monlam on their own: they had to have the co-operation – in effect, the traditional blessing and consensus – of the monks. Hundreds of monks announced that they would not go to the Jokhang for the Monlam in March 1988 in protest against the arrest of political dissidents after the October demonstrations. The Panchen Lama interceded and fifty-nine protestors who had been imprisoned the previous year were released. [22] But others remained in custody and many monks refused to take part in the Monlam;

more were arrested in the arguments that followed as officials tried to persuade them to give up their boycott.[23]

The authorities succeeded, with the help of the Panchen Lama, in persuading about half the monks to hold the festival, but on the last day, March 5, 1988, the major demonstrations mentioned above broke out. The protests led to the police breaking into the Jokhang and seizing the 400 or so monks barricaded inside. This was not a good move for a government bent on showing its commitment to religious tolerance.

The Fourth Anniversary: the Monlam Festival

The last of the four anniversaries that fall as a cluster in the second week of March is the Monlam festival itself, the most important of the four since it underlies and includes the others. All the other anniversaries commemorate incidents that arose because the Monlam was taking place, or was meant to be taking place, at the time. But the significance of the Monlam is not just circumstantial. As part of an old and pre-Chinese history, it embodies in itself the theory of state–church relations in Tibet and it retains an intrinsic power which makes it difficult for the Chinese to reshape it to their own needs.[24]

As an anniversary the Monlam festival differs from the others which Tibetan nationalists tend to mark with demonstrations. Tibetans have instead preferred to mark the Monlam by refusing to attend it;[25] this has given them greater leverage, and has forced the Chinese state on to the defensive. But it has another force in the rhetoric of Chinese political claims. As mentioned above, the series of illegal demonstrations – at least thirty of them from 1987 to March 1990 – had moved the focus of political protest in Tibet to the square outside the Jokhang. The Tibetan refusal to attend the ceremony in 1988 moved the debate actually into the temple itself.

When those who did attend the 1988 Monlam staged their demonstration, they deliberately waited until the conclusion of the religious festival, when the great statue of the Maitreya Buddha was taken back inside the temple. At that point the secular postscript to the festivities – a traditional weight-lifting competition in front of the highest state officials – began. It was at precisely this moment – 9.47 in the morning – that the monks began to demand political concessions from the cadres present on the podium, in this case the release of other monks from prison. The officials left the podium and the monks' demands became calls for Tibetan independence. They then marched three times round the temple, in the same way that other demonstrators since 1987 had aimed to do.

They then did what no other demonstrators had done before: they went back inside the temple and closed its massive wooden doors behind them. In a way they had reclaimed the precedence of the spiritual over the physical body, by refusing to allow the secular state activities that usually followed the religious part of the festival to take place without responding first to their own agenda: this is a claim that appears to have always been at the political heart of the Monlam festival in Tibetan history.

But, probably more by accident than by design, in closing those doors the monks achieved a more potent symbolism than the mere shutting out of the Chinese state from the centre of the Tibetan religious world. The high officials who had been on the podium, visibly ruffled and disturbed by the disruption of the weight-lifting contest earlier that morning, had for some reason retreated not to their vehicles and thence to their offices a kilometre or so away, but to the sanctuary of the Jokhang itself. When the monks had finished their three circumambulations of the Jokhang and closed the doors of the temple behind them, they locked several of the highest state officials in Tibet inside the temple.

By a further irony, the officials had actually gone to shelter in the rooms which a year earlier had been appropriated from the temple by the state: the rooms had been commandeered for use by a 'work team' (*las-don ru-khag*), a 'garrison' of political re-education cadres within the temple whose duty was to monitor the political thinking of the monks. It may have been to consolidate their claim to this little patch of territory within the temple that the officials had gone there, when the protests started, rather than to their own offices.

In any case, by 10.30 on the morning of March 5, 1988, the Chinese state found that some of its highest local officials were locked into a tiny suite of rooms within a temple from which they could not escape and which it certainly could not control. It was a potent piece of political symbolism. The precedence of the religious body over the secular was on this occasion as concrete as it can ever have been since the Chinese had invaded Tibet nearly forty years before.

Two hours later the People's Armed Police had to force open the doors of the Jokhang in order to gain entrance. Before doing this they were obliged to by-pass the temple doors by climbing up firemen's ladders to the first-floor windows of the work team's rooms: the whole scene looked like a medieval siege. But one thing about that raid was clear: by the time the PAP arrived, it was an exercise not in self-defence but in reclaiming from the Tibetan clergy the physical control of the place that had become for that moment, as it had always been during earlier Monlam festivals, the focus of political life in Tibet. In a way, one could say the Chinese were forced on that day to play out again in miniature, on a small but highly visible stage, their original invasion of Tibet. What made the exercise even more poignant was that this time they had to do this not to enforce a claim to neighbouring territory, but to rescue their own leaders who had been trapped and rendered powerless by the Tibetans.[26]

Monlam 1990: the Collapse of Religious Tolerance

The Monlam festival in 1990 was an anniversary of a different sort, unmarked by any Tibetan demonstrations. But it lay like a shadow behind the other – Chinese – demonstrations which that year marked the anniversaries of March 5, 8 and 10. Except for a report of a protest at the Jokhang temple by a small group of nuns on March 11, about which we have few details and no confirmation, the only demonstrations in March 1990 were those staged as displays of force by the Chinese army. These, as we have seen, in any case showed the Chinese responding to a Tibetan agenda, since they had to parade their troops and tanks around or close to the Jokhang, thus re-affirming its centrality in Tibetan political life. The most obvious evidence of concession to this agenda was that the Chinese sent their tanks to guard or threaten the Tibetan temple rather than to defend the government buildings, where one would expect the seat of power to reside. Even the Norbulingka, the would-be focus of the Chinese version of symbolic politics, had not taken the focus away from the Jokhang.[27]

The Chinese operation in Tibet is riddled with such anomalies. One of the most ironic is the fact that PLA and PAP soldiers on patrol around the Jokhang temple are obliged to march round it in an anti-clockwise direction. They have little choice because if they walked round the temple clockwise, as all Tibetans do, it might be taken to symbolise devotion and respect to the Buddhas within.

But the more potent symbolic agenda that the authorities had to answer in dealing with the Monlam festival in 1990 was whether to hold it at all. In the event, they cancelled it: monasteries were allowed to hold ceremonies within their own confines, but the great public celebration was cancelled for the second year running. Either way, the authorities lost the debate. By cancelling the festival they renounced the symbolic centre of their claim to tolerate religious practice in Tibet. It had been cancelled in 1989 too,[28] but since the Tibetans had nevertheless managed to stage three days of demonstrations, the symbolism in cancelling it was overshadowed by the stronger image of the Tibetan protests, and by the imposition of martial law that followed. The cancellation in 1990 indicated that, even with the full force of military rule behind them, the Chinese could not put into practice the rhetoric of religious tolerance.

Prohibitions on Religious Practice: Tsampa and Juniper

In the weeks before March 1990 it seems that there had been a practical change in religious policy. The authorities had already been manipulated into avoiding religious symbols, like the Monlam, that might lead to protest, but now they actually began to impose restrictions on religious practice and to forbid by law certain acts of religious devotion. This was a major setback for the authorities, who even in the August 1989 campaign against the 'six evils' – which included a prohibition on certain kinds of 'superstitious acts' – had not sought, so far as we know, to curtail religious practice (rather than teaching) in Tibet. Since March 1989 there had been, it seems, an informal ban on the admission of new monks to monasteries, and the re-building of monasteries destroyed by the Chinese before 1979 appears to have stopped in some regions. These delaying measures seem to have been augmented in late 1989 by specific prohibitions on religious practice.

The religious issue was and still is regarded by China's leaders as central to the 'Tibet Question'.[29] It was the view of Zhao Ziyang, then General Secretary of the CCP, perhaps under the influence of the Panchen Lama, that the key to the problem in Tibet was religion, and that religious repression would antagonise the Tibetan people irreconcilably. With the re-introduction of specific restrictions on Tibetan religion, the Chinese put at risk their entire claim to reform. The repressive policies with which they responded to the 1987 demonstrations have been viewed by China as a response purely on the level of security; in Chinese rhetoric, they did not indicate the collapse of a commitment to liberalisation, although they clearly do by Western standards. In terms of legitimacy, the apparently minor restrictions on popular religion that arose at the end of 1989 represented a more critical threat to the viability of China's political rhetoric than did the campaigns of arrest, torture and sometimes summary execution of Tibetan dissidents over the previous two years.

Tibetans in a field near Lhasa again perform the *lha-rgyal* ceremony, throwing *tsampa* in the air to celebrate the Dalai Lama's birthday, July 1991, one year after the lifting of martial law. (*TIN, 1991*)

The religious restrictions that materialised in those weeks involved a ban on the collective burning of juniper incense (the *bsangs-gsol*), and on the practice of *lha-rgyal*: the tradition of throwing in the air on special anniversaries handfuls of *tsampa* (*rtsam-pa*) or roasted barley flour. In banning these practices the authorities were again trapped into an agenda set by the Tibetans. As the onset of military rule had made it almost impossible to stage political demonstrations in the obvious way, Tibetan religious traditions, which had always tended to express nationalist feelings as well as spiritual ones, became more laden with political symbolism. This is a direct reflection of the whole problem of the Dalai Lama as faced by the Chinese Government: it is the problem of the Tibetan synthesis of church and state. 'Believing in the Dalai Lama and supporting Tibet's independence are two problems of diametrically different natures', asserted one official in 1988, perhaps more in hope than conviction.[30] The two issues are so closely intertwined that the Chinese authorities find it difficult or impossible to express relative tolerance for Tibetan religion without in some way tolerating or acknowledging the concept of the Tibetan State.

The authorities found themselves obliged to ban the *lha-rgyal* ritual on October 11, 1989, after Chinese troops and police had spent ten hours watching some 1,000 Tibetans walking round the Jokhang throwing *tsampa* over each other. Video film of the occasion shows soldiers and officials on patrol around the Jokhang as confused but tolerant observers of the unusual but good-natured celebrations going on around them.

It was only at about 7 that evening, when Lhasa must have run out of surplus *tsampa* anyway, and voluminous quantities of juniper had been burnt, that the authorities realised the significance of what they had been watching. As they must have surmised, it was a kind of religious festival, such as they were at the time committed to tolerating. But what the Tibetans were celebrating was an entirely new anniversary. They were celebrating, openly, but without words, the award of the Nobel Peace Prize to the Dalai Lama six days earlier.

It was presumably something of a humiliation to the authorities that their knowledge of Tibetan religious ritual was so superficial that they were unaware of the special relation of *lha-rgyal* to the person of the Dalai Lama. Officials were sent the next day to all offices and work units in Lhasa to hold emergency political meetings initiating a mini-campaign against *tsampa*-throwers and mass juniper branch-burners. The involvement of the police and officials was greeted with derision by Tibetans at the time. 'We threw *tsampa* at each other and at the soldiers and the police for hours before they realised why we were doing it', one young woman told a Westerner later. 'Then the PLA went searching for Tibetans with bags of *tsampa* and flour-covered fingers.'[31]

Lectures were given by the officials, and everyone present was asked to confess if they or anyone else they knew had thrown *tsampa* the previous day. There are some reports that a number of people were later arrested.[32] By December the government had issued statements that declared both *tsampa*-throwing and mass juniper branch-burning to be illegal. They became political crimes, and *tsampa*-throwers at least were declared in neighbourhood meetings that month to be liable to three years' imprisonment.[33]

This state of affairs had more serious connotations than at first appeared. Incense offering is central to Buddhist practice in Tibet, and is not a trivial ornament to ritual. The practice of *lha-rgyal* is less central, and probably stems from pre-Buddhist traditions, but is still a religious practice: its name means offering to the gods, and it is designed to ensure the future welfare of the person being celebrated, in this case the Dalai Lama.

The Tibetans themselves, in the messages that have reached the outside world, concentrate on the ban on *lha-rgyal* rather than on the incense restrictions. This may be because *tsampa* is the Tibetan national foodstuff, and so has a symbolic importance because it is something the Chinese never eat. But it may be more than just that: *tsampa* seems to have become a key symbol of Tibetan identity, in the sense that it indicates a specifically nationalist Tibetan identity. A schoolgirl who escaped to India in late 1989 said that when she was interrogated by police while in prison after demonstrating on March 5, 1988, the interrogators continually asked her who had forced her to join the demonstrators. She told them that she had merely heard the shout go up in the streets for all *tsampa*-eating Tibetans to come out, and therefore, as a *tsampa*-eating Tibetan, she had joined them. This account appears to use *tsampa*-eating to distinguish Tibetans who adhere to Tibetan traditions from those who have become sinicised; in other accounts the term '*tsampa*-eaters' is used by Tibetans to refer generically to themselves as a people. In banning the practice of *lha-rgyal* the Chinese may have been enhancing the identity of the Tibetan opposition rather than subduing it.

Conclusion

In the light of these events the Chinese authorities appeared to have become involved in a struggle over symbols in which they were constantly caught on the defensive. Although Party strategy has always laid a premium on the exhaustive re-writing of history, Chinese officials seemed unable to contain the historical resonances which the Tibetan nationalists evoked by their use of religious and nationalist anniversaries.

The Chinese position on religious tolerance was progressively invalidated as they found it harder to separate the attack on nationalism from that on the politico-religious symbols used by the pro-independence movement. The claim of tolerance was further weakened in March and April 1990 when monks and nuns suspected of supporting the pro-independence movement were expelled from their monasteries and nunneries; at the same time there were reports that all major religious ceremonies were forbidden except where official approval had been granted.

These reports did not represent a reversal of the policy of relative religious tolerance; they involved a tightening of bureaucratic controls over religion which the state had always retained but not always chosen to exercise.[34] Nevertheless, the drift of these developments was clear: the Chinese state was finding itself forced to make incursions into the thin but crucial fabric of religious tolerance in Tibet. What had been till then an ideologically manageable issue about security and the control of political dissidence became by late 1989 a challenge to China's self-proclaimed ability to accommodate a measure of religious and national or ethnic identity. The Tibetans had led the Chinese state into an arena rich in symbolism where, step by step, the ideology of Chinese liberalisation was stripped of value and exposed as rhetoric.

As mentioned earlier, the positioning of the tanks outside the Jokhang temple in March 1990 symbolised an end to the commitment to liberalisation that had begun exactly one decade before. By chance the Chinese authorities, in the timing of this deployment, provided an apt illustration of the richness of the symbolic battlefield in which this conflict is waged. They moved their tanks into the capital just as the festivities marking the Tibetan New Year, which culminates with the Monlam festival, reached their conclusion; in a sense it was the Chinese way of marking that anniversary. It is strange, therefore, to discover that the new year which began that week was, according to the Tibetan cycle, the Year of the Iron Horse, and there must have been more than one person who saw the Chinese tank as an expression of the iron horse predicted by the Tibetan calendar. Even in this action the Chinese authorities had revealed themselves more as servants than as masters of the powerful logic that underlies the political conflict in Tibet.

NOTES

1. 'Soldiers stand by for Tibet protests', *Guardian* (London), March 5, 1990; 'Tibet: Chinese Tanks take over Lhasa City Centre', Tibet Information Network (TIN), London, *News Update*, March 4, 1990. Officials in Beijing ridiculed the reports but did not explicitly deny them. Nong Deyi, a spokesman for the Beijing office of the People's Government of the Tibet Autonomous Region, told Hong Kong reporters that 'the Chinese Government had deployed sufficient martial law troops in Lhasa last March and there was no need to send tanks to the city.' Ren Yinong, spokesman for the Nationalities Affairs Commission, added that 'the situation in Lhasa has been restored to normal and the city has been very calm under martial law. What's the need to send tanks and armoured carriers to patrol in Lhasa?' However, he went on to say that 'overseas separatists are still instigating anti-Chinese activities in various parts of Tibet and they have not stopped their activities'. *Hong Kong Standard*, March 6, 1990.
2. See for example *100 Questions about Tibet*, Beijing Review Publications,

Beijing, 1989, p. 34. Yang Zhongmei translates the group's title as the 'Tibet Work Seminar', and notes that its report was approved by the Party Central Committee on April 7, 1990. Yang Zhongmei, *Hu Yaobang*, Armonk, NY: M.E. Sharpe, 1988, p. 142.

3. One classified Chinese press source quoted Hu as saying that he had 'seen very clearly that the scars a long history of feudal serfdom had left on society were very deep and could not be erased overnight. Many things that are the product of history will take time.' *Baokan Wenzhai* (Excerpts from the Press), Beijing, May 8, 1984, quoted in Yang, *op. cit.*, p. 196.

4. Yang, *op. cit.*, p. 143.

5. See for example G.E. Clarke, *China's Reforms of Tibet and their Effects on Pastoralism*, discussion paper 237, Institute of Development Studies, University of Sussex, November 1987.

6. The Panchen Lama said in a television interview in April 1988 that, apart from casualties among members of the security forces, five people had been killed in the unrest. 'NPC Deputies Ngapoi, Banqen Meet Press', Foreign Broadcast Information Service (FBIS) CHI-88-064, April 4, 1988, quoted in Asia Watch, *Evading Scrutiny*, July 1988, p. 20. Some Western journalists put the number much higher; see for example Jonathan Mirsky, 'Revealed: Temple Massacre of Tibetan Monks', *The Observer* (London), May 8, 1988.

7. Video footage that documents the protest of March 5, 1988, and which was filmed by Chinese officials or police for internal distribution, was obtained by TIN, London, in January 1989. The film shows the raid of the temple but does not show any shooting, presumably because those episodes had been edited out.

8. This figure was cited in an article in *Cheng Ming*, Hong Kong, May 1, 1989. Western journalists who were in Lhasa during part of the protest placed the death toll at between 75 and 150.

9. See for example *Martial Law in Lhasa – A Premeditated Plan?*, TIN, London, August 7, 1989.

10. 'Chinese Show of Force Chills Tibet', eyewitness report, *Guardian*, London, March 9, 1990, p. 24. The parade took place on Dekyi Shar Lam, known in Chinese as Beijing Donglu, the main street in Lhasa.

11. Demonstrations in Lhasa on May 19, 1989, were in sympathy with the pro-democracy movement and the hunger strikers in Tiananmen Square at that time. The students' demonstration of December 30, 1988 called for human rights and for the implementation of the promise to make Tibetan the official language in Tibet; some observers interpreted the green cloth they used for their banners as a veiled gesture of support for the Dalai Lama, with whom that colour is sometimes associated. There were no arrests at either of these protests. All other protests have called explicitly for Tibetan independence.

12. There were reports by Chinese news agencies in March 1989 (see for example 'Account of 5, 6 March Riots', NCNA, March 7, 1989, in FBIS, March 8, 1989) that guns had been found on and used by Tibetan demonstrators that month, but evidence was never produced to substantiate these allegations and they have not been repeated. For other examples see Asia Watch, *Merciless Repression – Human Rights in Tibet*, New York, 1990, pp. 16–20. Earlier, the Chinese Government had said on January 13, 1988, in a letter to the United Nations Commission on Human Rights (summarised in UN Document E/CN.4/1988/22, January 19, 1988, para. 81) that Tibetans had used firearms during the demonstration on October 1, 1987. But the allegations were later quietly withdrawn and are completely absent from the statement given to the Commission by the Chinese Government after a Western eyewitness testified to the contrary at the Commission (see UN Press Release HR/2159, March 4, 1988, p. 7).

The Panchen Lama's statement on the incident did not mention any Tibetan use of firearms either, and contradicted official statements that police had not used their guns. Radio Lhasa, February 8–9, 1988, in SWB, FE/0072 i, February 11, 1988.

13. Asia Watch cites not Radio Lhasa but *Xizang xingshi he wenwu jiaoyu di jiben jiaocai*, a booklet published by the Tibet Military District on October 1, 1960, as the source for this figure. See Asia Watch, *Human Rights in Tibet*, New York, 1988, p. 10.

14. Ngapo Ngawang Jigme unambiguously describes the 1959 rebellion as 'the March 10th incident' in his officially accepted accounts of the affair. He refers to the democratic reforms as the main target of attack by the rebel leaders, but does not say that they started on March 10. He is in any case ambiguous about the value of the reforms and notes that in 1956 'the central authorities decided that democratic reforms would not be introduced for at least six years' (*China Tibetan Studies*, no. 2, 1988, cited in *100 Questions on Tibet*, *op. cit.*, p. 116). Ngapo also gives details of Premier Zhou Enlai's personal promise to him and to the Dalai Lama in 1956 that there would be no reforms before 1962 at the earliest. He later criticises the extent of the reforms and notes that Mao told him once 'that it was wrong to form co-operatives then in Tibet'. The actual decision to implement the reforms was made 'soon after the insurrection was put down . . . at a plenary meeting' of the Preparatory Committee for the Tibet Autonomous Region, according to Ngapo ('On the 1959 Armed Rebellion', in *Tibetans on Tibet*, China Reconstructs Press, Beijing, 1988, p. 164). Mackerras notes that the resolution calling for reforms to take place in Tibet was passed by the National People's Congress in Beijing on April 28, 1959, and formally adopted by the Preparatory Committee on July 17. Colin Mackerras, *Modern China, A Chronology*, London: Thames and Hudson, 1982, pp. 489–90.

15. Meetings to celebrate the 30th anniversary of the implementation of democratic reforms in Tibet had continued throughout March and April despite the imposition of martial law. As a result, cadres' speeches dwelt on the successful suppression of the recent unrest, and so tended to imply a close parallel between the 1959 rebellion and the 1989 protests. In one speech celebrating the reforms, Hu Jintao, the Tibet Party Secretary, listed the 1987-9 protests as one of the four major incidents since 1959: 'In the major events [during the past thirty years] which include putting down the rebellion, democratic reform, counter-attack in self-defence [the 1962 Indo-China war], [and] suppressing the Lhasa Riots, the people of all nationalities in Tibet, in co-operation with the PLA units and armed police, used their practical deeds to safeguard unification of the motherland.' 'Secretary Addresses Tibet Meeting . . . to mark the 30th Anniversary of Democratic Reform in Tibet', Radio Lhasa, April 20, 1989. See also 'Anniversary of Tibet's Democratic Reforms Marked', SWB, April 4, 1989.

16. 'Forty truckloads each carrying at least twenty soldiers with sub-machine-guns were positioned in the Barkor . . . witnesses counted twelve trucks carrying hand-held rocket launchers . . . about five of these trucks carried Katyusha-type mounted rocket launchers with rockets arrayed in clusters of four or five for rapid succession firing . . . The trucks were positioned with the rockets pointing towards the Jokhang temple in what the source described as a clear attempt at intimidation. Similar vehicle-mounted rocket launchers were positioned on Dekyi Nub Lam, the major road leading west from the old city and running past the Potala Palace. The missiles were targeted on the Palace.' 'Rockets in the Barkor', *News Update*, TIN, London, June 7, 1989.

17. A standard English-language guide to Tibet, produced by the Chinese Government in 1988 and apparently aimed at tourists, makes no mention of the Monlam festival or any religious ceremony and does not report that Tibet's major religious festival had been restored, unlike pre-1987 publications of this kind. It gives a list of 'the most important festivals', all of which are entirely secular: 'The Tibetans have many festivals, the most important being the New Year festival, the Lingka festival, the Muyu [bathing] festival, Ong-kor [harvest] festival and Yaji festival.' Heyu, *A General Survey of Tibet*, Beijing: New World Press, 1988, pp. 98–9.

18. This attempt to reconstruct a tradition has a more visible parallel in the concrete re-building of the city of Lhasa itself, so that Chinese-style buildings now cover an area twenty times greater than the portion of the city that is still Tibetan in its architecture or history. The greater part of the rebuilding of Lhasa has been in the west of the old city, in the vicinity of the Norbulingka, so that the Summer Palace is no longer outside the capital, as it was in 1959, but a part of it. The change is sometimes referred to as a symbol of progress in official propaganda, as in this quotation from a Tibetan member of the Chinese People's Political Consultative Conference: 'When I returned to new Tibet a few years ago, I saw earth-shaking changes in Tibet with my own eyes. In the past in Lhasa, we had only a small winding path linking (?Luobulinka) [the Norbulingka] to (?Wajiao) [the Barkor]. Now this small path has been replaced by a smooth asphalt road.' Radio Lhasa, 13 December, 1988, in SWB, FE/0337 B2/1 17 December, 1988. Queries added by SWB monitors.

19. 'Over the past few days, major organisations and masses in Lhasa's urban areas have taken an active part in doing thorough cleaning and vying for non-staple food to make preparations for the National Day celebrations in a joyous atmosphere . . . Some of the residents have hung amulets symbolising good luck on their doors and are ready to celebrate the National Day happily.' Amulets and cleaning are traditional characteristics of New Year celebrations. The National Day events are referred to throughout as a 'festival' and the broadcast ended with a warning that there would be no leniency for any splittists who 'take advantage of the festival'. 'Lhasa Public Prepares for National Day', Radio Lhasa, September 29, 1988, in SWB, FE/0273 B2/8, October 4, 1988.

20. 'Under the care and concern of the Party Central Bommittee [*sic*], the People's Government of the Tibet Autonomous Region has decided to reopen the Grand Prayer Ceremony Festival, which has been closed for 20 years since the beginning of the 'Cultural Revolution.' *The Grand Buddhist Prayer Ceremony Festival in Lhasa (Lha ldan cho-'phrul smon-lam chen-mo)*, undated, no author or publisher, apparently the souvenir book of the 1986 Monlam celebrations produced in Tibet.

21. As part of this process the state–church relationship was traditionally inverted during the festival, so that the secular officials voluntarily relinquished power to the monks. 'For three weeks two Provosts of Drepung rule the city assisted by a number of monk "police" armed with whips', as Spencer Chapman described the Monlam in 1937, adding that some 30,000 monks had 'taken control of Lhasa' (F. Spencer Chapman, *Lhasa: The Holy City*, 1938, repr. Delhi: Cosmo Publishing, 1989, pp. 322, 316). Harrer describes the last day of the feast when 'the four Cabinet Ministers exchange their costly head-dresses for the red-fringed hats of their servants in order to show for a moment their equality with the people', Heinrich Harrer, *Seven Years in Tibet*, London: Hart-Davies, 1953, p. 154.

22. The releases appear to have been part of an arrangement with the Panchen

Lama whereby the monks would agree to hold the Monlam in return for the prisoners being released. 'Namgyal, a responsible person of the Lhasa City Public Security and Judicial Department, said . . . [that] during his recent inspection tour in Xizang, Vice Chairman Banqen proposed that lenient treatment be given to rioters as much as possible. Considering his proposal, the Public Security and Judicial Departments, after studying the cases, decided according to law to give lenient treatment to 59 rioters.' The released prisoners, probably all monks or nuns, were 'urged . . . to be monks and nuns who love the country and the religion'. 'Xizang Rioters Accorded Lenient Treatment', NCNA, January 21, 1988, in FBIS, CHI-88-014, January 22, 1988.

23. According to some sources, Yulu Dawa Tsering, the first and still the most important dissident to be arrested by the Chinese apart from those caught in demonstrations, was detained in December 1987 after he failed or refused to dissuade monks at Ganden monastery from their planned boycott of the 1988 Monlam. The police video of the protest on March 5, 1988, shows clearly that the incident began when monks demanded that lay officials release Yulu Tulku. See note 7.

24. Disregard by Chinese officials of the political symbolism of the Monlam had led to major unrest in the past. Tibetans staged demonstrations against Chinese officials in Lhasa in 1895 after three of them insisted on watching the Monlam procession from an upstairs window, a breach of etiquette which implied that they were superior to the Dalai Lama (who would have been sitting below them) as well as to the images of the Buddha being paraded. There were similar protests in 1911 when people threw 'mud and dropped old socks' on to the Amban and the Panchen Lama when they emulated the Dalai Lama by taking part in the Monlam procession. W.D. Shakabpa, *Tibet; Political History*, New York: Potala, 1984, pp. 195, 237. Harrer was able to watch the 1946 Monlam from an upstairs window, but only because he hid behind the curtains on the second floor of the Chinese legation. Harrer, *op. cit.*, p. 151.

25. Shakabpa gives earlier examples of the political significance of attending the Monlam, notably in the period from 1498 to 1517, when Gelugpa monks were forbidden to attend the festival by Donyo Dorje, who then ruled Lhasa and was a supporter of the Karmapa, head of the Kagyupa school. Shakabpa, *op. cit.*, p. 88.

26. The main leaders inside the room were Tibetans, not ethnic Chinese. The most senior official was Raidi (Rakti), a deputy secretary of the TAR Party Committee.

27. The only exception to this had been a demonstration in the Norbulingka by nine nuns on September 2, 1989. The nuns disrupted a Tibetan folk opera being performed during the Shoton festival to an audience that included Chinese officials.

28. 'Local Buddhist associations and monasteries have decided that the religious festivals Monlam Genmo, or the Grand Summons ceremony, will not be held in Lhasa this year.' The announcement declared that this decision was reached by the 'majority of lamas' and had nothing to do with the government. 'The Communist Party's policies on the freedom of religious belief will be unswervingly carried out and normal religious activities will be protected' despite the lamas' decision to cancel the festival, it said. NCNA, (Xinhua) February 5, 1989, in SWB, FE/0379 B2/2, February 8, 1989.

29. See for example Yang Shangkun on the subject: 'To speed up the economic development and to do work well among the religious believers are the major tasks for Tibet, Chinese President Yang said here today . . . Religion and lamaseries occupy a special position there and . . . special attention [has been]

given to the freedom of religious belief.' 'Yang Shangkun Discusses Tibet with NPC Deputies', NCNA (Xinhua), March 31, 1989, in SWB, FE/0425 C1/5, April 4, 1989.

30. The official, named in *pinyin* as 'Lamu Renjiu Weishe', probably Lhamu Wangchuk Geshe, was perhaps trying to protect the religious concessions from erosion by hardliners. He prefaced his remark by saying, 'However, we make it clear that respecting the masses' freedom of religious belief and protecting normal religious activities has been a consistent policy of the Party and the government and this will remain unchanged.' 'Lhasa's Vice-Mayor Warns Trouble-Maker', Radio Lhasa, September 30, 1988, in SWB, FE/0273 B2/8, October 4, 1988.

31. 'Tibet: Government Threatens to Shoot Demonstrators, say Tibetans', TIN, *News Update*, London, March 6, 1990.

32. There were a number of arrests of people in the Jokhang area that week, but it is not known if they were throwing *tsampa* or shouting pro-independence slogans. Two laywomen, Kelsang Drolkar and Tsichoe, were detained for shouting 'reactionary' slogans in the Barkor on October 14, 1989. Four nuns (Tenzin Wangmo, Tenzin Seldron, Kelsang Wangmo, Tenzin Choekyi), all from Michungri nunnery, were detained after 'staging an illegal demonstration' in central Lhasa on the same day (*Xizang Ribao* [*Tibet Daily*], Lhasa, October 18, 1989, in FBIS, November 1, 1989). Two other nuns (Lobsang Drolma and Ngawang Tsultrim) were detained for chanting reactionary slogans in central Lhasa on October 15, 1989. All were sentenced to two or three years re-education through labour, except for two (Phuntsog Palmo and Phuntsog Nyidron) who were sentenced respectively to eight and nine years in prison (Asia Watch, TIN).

33. The injunction against *tsampa*-throwing was repeated in neighbourhood meetings in Lhasa before the anniversaries of December 10, 1989 and March 5, 1990, when the authorities expected further protests. See note 25.

34. The Chinese Constitution permits only the freedom to practise 'normal religious activities'. 'No-one may use a religion to carry out activities that disrupt the public order, harm the physical health of the citizens, or undermine the state's education system' (1982 Constitution, Article 36). No definition of 'normal activities' is given. Heberer has a useful chapter on this, and comments on the constitutional provisions: 'Elastic paragraphs such as these enable the bureaucracy to drastically restrict religious freedom in political ideological campaigns such as the campaign against "spiritual pollution" (1983) or against "bourgeois liberation" [*sic*] (1987)'. Thomas Heberer, *China and its National Minorities – Autonomy or Assimilation?* Armonk, NY: M.E. Sharpe, 1989.

THE ROLE OF NUNS IN
CONTEMPORARY TIBET

Hanna Havnevik

In most of the demonstrations that have taken place in Tibet since the autumn of 1987 young nuns have been very active. About half have been organised by nuns alone. In a detailed report on the role of nuns in Tibetan protest, Robert Barnett writes that there are usually between five and thirty nuns demonstrating. In one case he describes more than 200 nuns who were planning a demonstration but were stopped by the police. The nuns gather in small numbers, and circumambulate the Jokhang while they shout pro-independence slogans. Then they disperse. After periods of unrest and riots, the Chinese enforce strong police control, but after each period of 'relative peace', which usually lasts for a few months, political unrest and demonstrations are again stirred up by nuns.

Barnett suggests that about 50 per cent of the demonstrating nuns since 1987 have been arrested. Nuns have been imprisoned without trial and many have undergone severe torture. Particularly brutal torture seems to be meted out to nuns, including the use of dogs, lighted cigarettes, stripping them naked and the use of electrical batons on sensitive parts of the body such as the eyes, mouth, soles of the feet and the vagina. Some have been sentenced to several years of reform through labour. However, they seem very resilient in the face of pressure.

Why do young nuns, aged between eighteen and thirty, take on leading roles in demonstrations and seem to be particularly active in the opposition against the Chinese? It would be impossible to clarify such questions through fieldwork in Tibet at the moment, and data concerning nuns in contemporary Tibet is scanty. On the basis of reports available we will outline possible ways of analysing the present socio-cultural position, particularly the political activity of young Tibetan nuns.

A survey carried out by the Council for Religious and Cultural Affairs of His Holiness the Dalai Lama (1984) estimates that there were 818 nunneries and about 27,000 nuns in Tibet before 1959. Most belonged to the Gelugpa school, followed by the Nyingmapa and Kagyupa schools, while the Sakyapa school had only about 1,000 nuns. Although there are differences of opinion as to how many nuns there were in Tibet before 1959, there is no doubt that there were always far fewer nuns than monks.

259

Most nunneries were destroyed during the Cultural Revolution, and the number of nuns was drastically reduced. The Kagyupa nunnery of Chedo in Nyemo, for instance, was totally destroyed by the Chinese. Of a total of thirty-three nuns belonging to the nunnery before 1959, four escaped to India and of the remaining twenty-nine, only three were nuns in 1984. They lived in their homes, as the nunnery had not been reconstructed. Lama Paltul Jampal Lodö maintains that 410 nuns were affiliated to the Nyingmapa Shungseb nunnery (south of Lhasa) before 1959. Today there are thirty to forty nuns. In Nechungri nunnery (sometimes called Michungri), north-east of Lhasa, there were ninety-five nuns in 1959. The nunnery re-opened in early 1988 and there are now five nuns. In Tsangkhung nunnery in Lhasa there used to be between seventy and eighty nuns. The nunnery was completely destroyed, but today there are forty nuns. In Gari nunnery, northwest of Lhasa, there used to be fifty to sixty nuns; at present there are thirty. In Chubsang nunnery to the north of Lhasa, there used to be some twenty-five nuns, while today there are ten. The last four of these nunneries belonged to the Gelugpa school, and nuns there and in the Nyingmapa nunnery of Shungseb have been active in the demonstrations that began in the autumn of 1987.

The Kagyupa Galo or Kaglo nunnery was also destroyed. This was situated in the village of Yangpachen, west of Lhasa, and used to be one of the most famous nunneries in Tibet. One informant maintained that there were 500 nuns there before the Chinese occupation. The Chinese made the nuns live in labour camps, where they were subjected to intensive re-education.

In 1985, fifty nuns were affiliated to the Yangpachen nunnery, which was then being reconstructed with the support of local people. Most of the nuns stayed in their homes as there was no room for them in the nunnery. The leader was an elderly nun, a *yogini*, while the other nuns were mostly young. Only five nuns owned religious texts, and during prayers they recited them while the others chanted mantras. The prayers they recited were incomplete, and they needed help with making offering cakes and with reciting properly. There was no one to give them religious instruction and they had made several unsuccessful attempts to invite lamas to teach there. In 1985 there was a steady recruitment of young nuns to the nunnery.

Today, without Chinese help, some nunneries are being reconstructed, and there seems to be an increasing number of young women joining the order. A learned lama (*dge-bshes*) from Kham asserted that it was his definite impression that young women are particularly eager to enter the order. In his opinion they serve as models for young men who do not show the same interest in religion. The lama visited Lhasa in 1984 and wherever he and his companion moved, they were approached by young women who asked if they could take vows or religious teachings from the lama. A Swedish nun, Britt Lindhe, and Lama Ngawang from the Tibetan Buddhist Centre in Stockholm visited Tibet in 1985 and reported that young nuns continually prostrated themselves before them, asking for religious instruction.

There is also a steady flow of young Tibetan women (and nuns) who walk all the way from Tibet to India in order to be ordained nuns or to obtain religious teachings; they give the impression of having very strong religious conviction. In 1984 two nuns from Tibet joined others from the Kagyupa nunnery, Karma Drubgyu Targye Ling, in Tilokpur. Soon after their arrival they started a three-year retreat in Sherab Ling. Another young woman from Tibet, Pema Dechen, came to Dolanji in northern India in February 1984 in order to be ordained a Bonpo nun by Sangye Tendzin, the abbot of the Bonpo monastery established in exile. While in Dolanji, Pema could be observed every morning doing full prostrations around the monastery, and after her ordination she set out on a pilgrimage to Mount Kailash.

Traditionally, becoming a nun did not bring all the advantages that accrue from becoming a monk. In Tibet before 1959 and presumably also today, monks more easily obtained education, financial support and social prestige. Generally nunneries were poor, insignificant institutions, and nuns had an elementary level of education. Nunneries were usually sub-branches of important monasteries and monks or yogis were often abbots in nunneries. There were hardly any official positions in the ecclesiastical or lay hierarchies for nuns to fill, and they had no important religious functions to carry out for lay people. A few nuns have made an impact in Tibetan history as famous *yoginis*, as administrators and as freedom-fighters. Most, however, neither pursued advanced philosophical studies nor undertook elaborate *yoga* practices, but mainly spent their time on what is considered elementary religious practice such as performing rituals and reciting prayers. Nuns in the Tibetan tradition are novices (*dge-tshul-ma*), and there seems to be no evidence from textual or oral sources that the full ordination (*dge-slong-ma*) ever existed for them in Tibet.

Without doubting the religious motives of young Tibetan nuns today, one can believe that more than religion is involved when they choose to embrace monastic life, which is more than a commitment to religion; it is also a commitment to the survival of the Tibetan people and culture.

The traditional Tibetan way of life has been brutally disrupted for the last forty years. Tibetans are deprived of even the most elementary human rights, and mass immigration of Chinese to Tibet threatens to make them a minority in their own country. The Chinese are actively trying to assimilate Tibetans and transform Tibetan culture. The brutal killings and disrespect for Tibetan customs, language and religion have created a situation where great psychological stress and disorder exist. Traditional norms and values lose their social foundation, the traditional ideological charts are out of harmony with social reality and Tibetans have problems in creating a meaningful existence. The growing interest in religion among young Tibetan women may be understood as part of a revitalising process.

Anthony Wallace defines revitalisation as 'deliberate, conscious, organised efforts by members of a society to construct a more satisfying culture' (Wallace, p. 279). According to him, revitalising movements are characteristic of societies in radical and rapid change, often encountered by another and dominant culture where a high degree of social and cultural stress exists. In her discussion of revitalisation, which she prefers to call 'millenarism', Annemarie de Waal Malefijt stresses that such movements provide ways in which people can consolidate their feelings and take a united stand against the impact of the new conditions (Malefijt, p. 333). Malefijt defines millenarism as 'any religious movement that expects a change in social conditions here on earth' (*ibid.*, p. 331). She maintains that these movements usually demand intense commitment and unconditional faith and loyalty from their followers, that they often involve active struggles for greater political participation or independence, and that they are generally action-oriented (*ibid.*, pp. 339–40). Wallace's definition needs to be modified since the revitalising process in Tibet is not always conscious, but it will be illuminating to analyse the political activity of young Tibetan nuns in this perspective.

Melvyn Goldstein argues that cultural revitalisation in Tibet is due to the reform policy of the Chinese in the early 1980s (Goldstein, pp. 146–56). However, he fails to explain why, in the face of strong police control and martial law following the demonstrations which started in 1987, religious revitalisation seems to have increased.

In Tibet today, there is strong cultural and economic pressure from the majority culture, and one option for young Tibetans is to become assimilated. However, 'becoming Chinese' is no real alternative, as Tibetans who do this still remain second-class citizens in Chinese eyes and are seen as collaborators and traitors by other Tibetans. In their everyday encounters with Chinese, Tibetans experience role conflicts. They are treated as second-rate citizens, and therefore Tibetan identity has to be underplayed in these encounters. Tibetan customs, ways of behaving and language are irrelevant means of communication. The social rules are made by the Chinese, and Tibetans have to play along with them. Hence, living a lay life and taking part in everyday social and economic activity involves many compromises, and by suppressing their own identity Tibetans experience a high degree of frustration.

Choosing to become nuns or monks today may represent a solution to the role-dilemmas. By so doing, young Tibetans stress their Tibetan cultural and religious identity and seek to make it relevant in social life. They choose what the Norwegian anthropologist Ingrid Rudie calls 'role-blockage', that is, they make alternative choices of roles impossible; they are creating cultural barriers that are meant to defend Tibetan identity. When the choice to become a nun or a monk is made, there is often a spiralling effect, where the novices invest more and more energy and time in their new identity in order to legitimise and give meaning to this alternative choice of role and worldview. Clifford Geertz and Peter Berger both stress the fact that people tend to avoid chaos and seek order. Religion creates the world for the individual, legitimises and explains action, gives meaning and keeps chaos at a distance (Berger 1967, Geertz 1973). The process of revitalisation must thus be analysed not only as an internal process within an ethnic group, a religious group or both, but also as part of a communication between such groups, with the creation of cultural barriers as a part of this communication.

There are numerous examples of revitalising processes all over the world, either ethnically or religiously based, or both. A Norwegian anthropologist, Berit Thorbjørnsrud, has recently studied Coptic nuns in Egypt. Today many well-educated young Coptic women, often with university education, undertake ordination. The nunneries are overcrowded and there are long waiting-lists. Thorbjørnsrud's hypothesis is that they choose to become nuns partly in order to minimise role conflicts in their encounters with the Muslim majority culture, where they have to suppress their own identity.

In Buddhism, the opportunity to become nuns and monks is as old as the religion itself. For centuries Tibetan Buddhism has been the core of Tibetan culture, and Buddhism has become integrated in the society to such a degree that it is impossible to talk of Tibetan culture without reference to Tibetan Buddhism. Tibetan literature, painting, philosophy and medicine originated

Nun being interrogated after a demonstration in March 1989. (*TIN/ Hainan Bao, 1989*)

Two nuns from Michungri (Ne'u-chung-ri) nunnery photographed in the Barkor Square, Lhasa 1993. (*TIN*)

and were maintained in the monasteries. By their choice to become nuns, young women are thus copying ancient traditions, and choosing what for centuries has been the most highly respected role in Tibet.

But in all Buddhist traditions male monasticism has been dominant; in traditional Tibet, too, nuns in several respects had a marginal existence. Today, with even the nunneries in ruins, young nuns have somehow to create their own roles as nuns. They copy tradition, but they also transform it by combining it with new elements called for in a situation of critical urgency: they become political nuns.

There are several nuns and laywomen with whom Tibetan nuns today can identify. On March 12, 1959, Tibetan women arranged a large demonstration against the Chinese and several nuns were among the leaders, among them Galingshar Ani and Tsangkhung Ani Yonten. Nuns were also involved in actively fighting the Chinese during the Cultural Revolution. Of Thinley Choedon from Nyemoru nunnery it is said that she had a network of contacts stretching from Mount Kailash to Kham, and that she organised a guerrilla movement which killed many Chinese. Along with several other nuns, she was executed in 1969. In the persecution that followed, many nunneries were ruined.

Young nuns in Tibet today seem very serious religious practitioners, and undertaking ordination is a conscious choice. As they look back to tradition they learn from female role models who made an historical impact in Tibet as advanced religious practitioners, political activists or both. An attempt is now being made to combine these two roles.

The Chinese occupation of Tibet and the enforced communication with the Chinese on Chinese terms are external factors creating change. Rules and regulations are enforced by military power and Tibetans react with counter-action, thus becoming traditional and political activists. But there are also factors within the Tibetan religious tradition that may help to explain why nuns in particular become political activists.

Change generally comes about when there is incongruity between real life and the symbolic image of it. Fredrik Barth emphasises the role of entrepreneurs as instigators of socio-cultural change. The agents of change, who are often marginal in the traditional system, manipulate ambiguous values, and perhaps it is illuminating to see the political activities of young Tibetan nuns in this perspective.

In Tibetan Buddhism different layers of ideas co-exist, monastic Buddhism being combined with Tantric practices. It thus provides scope and models for different types of religious practitioners: the monastics and the Tantric adepts. While the ordinary Tibetan nuns have to adjust to the monastic structure and ideology which serve and perpetuate male talent, the Tantric path gives a more positive image of women and greater possibilities for them to advance spiritually. The ordinary nun has a rather low status while the *yogini* is highly revered. One might expect that the praise bestowed by Tantric ideology on the female principle would have consequences for the position of all female religious specialists and for women in general. However, the ordinary nun does not profit from this positive ideology. Tibetan nuns are thus subjected to a triple subordination: first, they are discriminated against by the Chinese; second, they are women within a patriarchal society; and third, they have to adjust to a monastic structure made by monks for monks. Thus the potential exists for change, with nuns as the main actors.

REFERENCES

Barnett, Robert, *The Role of Nuns in Tibetan Protest – Preliminary Notes*. TIN, London, October 17, 1989.

—, TIN, *News Update*, London, November 17, 1989.

—, *Tension Rises in Tibet: Monks Close Down Major Monastery*, an 'Urgent News Report' issued by TIN, London, April 22, 1990; later included in TIN, *News Update*, April 30, 1990.

Barth, Fredrik, *Models of Social Organisation*, Occasional Paper no. 23, Royal Anthropological Institute, London, 1966.

Berger, Peter L., *The Social Reality of Religion*, London: Faber and Faber, 1967.

Dowman, Keith, *The Power-Places of Central Tibet*, London: Wisdom Publications, 1988.

Geertz, Clifford, *The Interpretation of Cultures*, New York: Basic Books, 1973.

Goldstein, Melvyn and Cynthia Beall, *Nomads of Western Tibet*, London: Serindia, 1990.

Havnevik, Hanna, *Tibetan Buddhist Nuns: History, Cultural Norms and Social Reality*, Oslo: Universitetsforlaget, 1989.

Malefijt, Annemarie de Waal, *Religion and Culture*, New York, 1968.

Thorbjørnsrud, Berit, 'Messias piker. En analyse av koptisk ortodoks revitalisering i et identitets-perspektiv', unpubl. thesis, University of Oslo, 1989.

Wallace, Anthony, 'Revitalisation Movements', *American Anthropologist*, vol. 58 (1956), pp. 264–81.

THE RHETORIC OF DISSENT
TIBETAN PAMPHLETEERS

Elliot Sperling

The questions this paper addresses are essentially simple, one might even say basic, ones: what do Tibetan dissidents want, and what are they thinking? Yet they have not been dealt with as thoroughly as we might imagine. This has not inhibited many people from offering opinions on the subject, and this paper has to a certain degree been conceived with some of the more provocative of these in mind. In a letter to the editor of the *New York Times* in the summer of 1988, headlined 'In Spirit, Tibet's Lamas Resemble Iran's Mullahs', a reader wrote:

> [I have] just returned from a trip to Tibet and China. During my days in Tibet I saw street lights that had been pulled down by Tibetan lama-led protestors; many broken windows were also in evidence. The same demonstrators showed their distaste for Chinese-assisted housing construction. The introduction of electricity, sanitation and literacy is seen by many of the backward lamas and monks as a threat to their authority . . .
>
> Near the entrance to the Potala, the stench coming from the monks' own living quarters speaks eloquently about the level of their development. The monks are free to be literate and to bathe, democratic rights that they choose not to exercise.[1]

Not long afterwards A. Tom Grunfeld offered his explanation of the motivations of Tibetan protesters:

> In dozens of interviews with Tibetans of all social strata there was a consensus that a majority of those who participated in the disturbances did so, not to protest a lack of independence and religious freedom, but to express their anger at Public Security Bureau officials, the police and party cadres.
>
> When the issues of independence and religious freedom were raised, there was less interest in them than anticipated. Independence is an abstract notion which most Tibetans do not seem to think about very much while others, especially the educated, believe it to be totally unrealistic. Similarly, religious restrictions have little effect on the majority of the population . . .

Grunfeld did make a concession to the conclusions of most observers (and in the process contradicted himself somewhat):

> To be sure, independence and religious freedom are emotional issues and Tibetans invariably express their support for a theocratic Tibetan nation state.[2]

Such comments call upon us to ask whether there are any intellectual considerations being made by Tibetan protesters, or whether
what we have been witnessing all this time has simply been an emotional and irrational reaction; one precipitated by the siren song of
secular and religious nationalism. Similarly, we should attempt
to gauge the contours of this nationalism, with a view to understanding why it has succeeded as much as it has.

Manifestations of nationalism in Tibet appear within a context that
at times seems quite ambiguous. Clearly, the words and actions of
some of Tibet's 20th-century leaders do not always accord with
what one would expect from a strongly nationalistic party or
state – for example, the approval by the Retring (*Rwa-sgreng*)
regime of the payment of Chinese governmental salaries to their
representatives in Nanjing[3] and, more recently, revelations that
the Dalai Lama's former representative in Tokyo (and one assumes
others in the exile Tibetan government) had been receiving pay-
ments from the Kuomintang government in Taiwan.[4] Better
known is the Dalai Lama's renunciation of Tibet's independence as
a condition for reaching an agreement between his exile government and the government of China.

There are a number of possible reasons that could explain the
lack of a consistently clear 'nationalist' position encompassing
the congruity of a nation and its territory, and the explicit control
of the former over the latter. Certainly one can speculate about
the absence in Tibet, until quite recently, of certain commonplace
facets of modern life, an absence characterised by Tibet's distance
from the industrialised and industrialising world for most of the
20th century (and the bureaucratic and social order engendered
by it), and the lack of access to the European intellectual tradition
that has played a role in much of the nationalistic sentiment of
the post-war world. We should, of course, draw a line between
the expressions of nationalism by Tibetans in exile – most of whom
left Tibet at a time when these factors were largely unknown in
the country – and Tibetans in Tibet. While the former have
developed a 'diaspora nationalism', the latter have been drawn
into the orbit of an industrialised China and exposed to elements
of the Western intellectual tradition as refracted through the lens
of Chinese Leninist and Maoist education. It is the Tibetans in
Tibet with whom we are concerned here, and in particular with
their expressions of nationalist dissent (as opposed to mere discontent with a government's policies, however widespread and violent).
This is not to ignore the contact that has existed between the

exile community and Tibetans in Tibet, for we see clear evidence of familiarity with information and materials originating with exile Tibetans within dissident circles in Tibet; but there has obviously been some picking and choosing of ideas and influences. Thus, for example, the Dalai Lama's statements renouncing Tibetan independence, or the Tibetan exile view that the late Panchen Lama was a suppressed Tibetan nationalist, have been more or less ignored in dissident pronouncements, while dissident rhetoric has clearly made use of exile materials dealing with the question of human rights.

The notion that modern nationalism (with the ideas of majority rule and self-determination that form important parts of its intellectual milieu) draws its roots from Western traditions is hardly novel, whether one is discussing 19th-century Europe or the post-war Third World. In the latter case, as described by Kenneth Minogue (with imagery reminiscent of Lenin), 'modern Europeans carried with them the boot that would eventually send them packing'.[5] This intellectual element was not conspicuously present in Tibet before its incorporation into the People's Republic of China, although there was an awakening interest in nationalism and some knowledge of the idea. We have recently begun to flesh out our understanding of intellectual developments in 20th-century Tibet, beyond clear-cut issues of Buddhist philosophy. Heather Stoddard's biography of Dge-'dun chos-'phel (Gendun Choephel),[6] in particular, has revealed a Tibet in which people were taking up questions of the country's political future in a manner far removed from Western stereotypical notions of Tibetan other-worldliness.[7]

As to the educational factor in the development of intellectual elements associated with nationalistic thinking, there are two lines to which we should point, each playing a different role in the development of nationalist concepts. The first is the introduction of a Marxist-oriented Chinese educational system that for the first time, and in a systematic manner, imparted European ideas about nations and nationalisms to a Tibetan élite.[8] Even before the growth of Chinese education in Tibet in the 1980s, official pronouncements and policy statements often contained a measure of rhetoric about such subjects as nationality distinctions and the inevitable course of history that bound the Tibetan and Chinese peoples. Systematic Marxist education and the concomitant circulation of Marxist ideas about nations inevitably raised the question of Tibetan identity in the minds of intellectuals, students and others in a new way. While these ideas (and associated notions of people's collective will, and so forth, as filtered through a Maoist lens) were not carried into Tibet by Europeans, their injection into the intellectual picture does in some way represent a variant of the situation described by Minogue; and, as in the anti-colonial cases to which he referred, the results were not exactly those that the bearers of the ideas in question had anticipated. This is reflected in accounts of the imprisonment of *Dge-bshes* Blo-bzang dbang-phyug (Geshe Lobsang Wangchuk), who is said to have authored a work showing that Mao Zedong's writings on the question of national liberation substantiate the case for Tibetan independence.[9] In the same light we must also note the presence of Tibetan students in demonstrations in Lhasa and other points on the Tibetan Plateau, as well as in Beijing. In essence, then, China has consistently explained its presence in Tibet in the context of a theory of nationality; thus Chinese policies and pronouncements, whether benign or oppressive, have effectively affirmed a Tibetan national identity. To put it more bluntly, although harsh Chinese policies, particularly before 1980, undoubtedly exacerbated the conflict and fostered a legacy of deep resentments, even a history of benign rule would most likely have produced some sort of broadly felt nationalist movement.

The second educational factor is of more specifically social significance. This is the existence of a Buddhist clergy which, by representing a traditional intellectual class (though, by virtue of its size, hardly a thoroughly scholarly group), fills a role akin to that described by Ernest Gellner, wherein a high (that is, 'literate') culture comes to serve as the focal point of an identity that crystallises around the discontents of an ethnic group, particularly in the potent time when 'the high cultures which survive the period of transition [from an agrarian to an industrial society] cease to be the medium and hallmark of a clerisy or a court and become instead the medium and emblem of a "nation" . . .'[10] As will be seen below, in recent years the Buddhist clergy have played a pivotal role in the formulation and propagation of dissident thought in Tibet. Socially, they have come to represent the epitome of Tibetan culture, to the point where Tibetans can easily see in official restrictions and attacks on the clergy *ipso facto* anti-Tibetan measures.

Having touched on some of the conditions that help make a dissident nationalist movement in Tibet possible, we approach our primary subject: the thinking behind the movement as it has manifested itself intellectually in Tibet (and most visibly in Lhasa) during the last few years. There are some clear constraints in our approach: obviously we cannot conduct in-depth interviews and research among large numbers of Tibetan activists and demonstrators, and even if we could, it is questionable whether the circumstances would be conducive to frankness.[11] It is possible, nevertheless, to go beyond the subjective observations quoted above and deal at least with actual Tibetan expositions.

The rest of this paper examines what Tibetans are thinking and what they want, on the basis of their own utterances – specifically, some fifteen documents produced in Tibet and meant for circulation there (and in some cases abroad).[12] Excluded are handwritten pen and ink materials, although these have been fairly plentiful and easy enough to come across, as many visitors to Lhasa have found, in favour of mechanically reproduced documents on the principle that these can represent or inform opinion that is more likely to derive from or relate to group thinking. Of course this too is a problematic approach, for reasons already mentioned and, for example, because polemical and non-polemical expressions of an individual on the same topic can obviously diverge in a number of ways. Nevertheless, under the present circumstances an examination of such documents can at least allow us to make a preliminary approach to the intellectual setting of dissident activity in Tibet.

Several currents of thinking are noticeable in these documents. Perhaps most striking is the absence of reference to specific, relevant Buddhist principles. This is not to say that the authors of these documents are anti-Buddhist; on the contrary, in many cases the authors, distributors or both are members of the clergy. Furthermore, they do speak of defending Buddhist doctrine, and some describe the Chinese broadly as 'enemies of the doctrine' (*bstan-dgra Rgya-dmar*, for the most part). But there is no particular appeal, in terms of scriptural argumentation or similar methods, to Buddhist principles as such. What we do notice, immediately, are numerous references to the concepts of rights and legality.

Not unexpectedly the term 'human rights' is mentioned quite prominently in these instances. The notion of human rights has a relatively short history, as is well known, having developed in the 18th century into the form that we would most easily recognise (that is, one which sets down dictates as to the bounds beyond which state authority may not intrude with regard to the individual).[13] The concept is furthermore a development within the Western philosophical and political tradition that has come into its own as a major political consideration in the post-war world. The appearance of notions of human rights in dissident rhetoric illustrates the movement of European concepts into Tibet as part of the package of ideas influencing the growth of nationalism. In this case these ideas have been circulated by the Chinese authorities themselves, often in a negative light. The latter have gone to pains, particularly in the post-Tiananmen atmosphere, to draw a line between the economic rights of the collective, which China believes it and other Third World and socialist countries guarantee for their citizens, and the bourgeois individual rights emphasised by liberal Western democracies.[14] Nevertheless, a clearly responsive chord has been struck among Tibetan dissidents when they see their circumstances in the light of China's deprecatory attitude towards liberal human rights.

A second source of dissident information on human rights clearly comes from the Tibetan exile community. A copy of the Universal Declaration of Human Rights was circulating in Lhasa up to at least January 1989, which on examination turns out to be nothing less than a hand-written, word-for-word copy of the translation of the declaration produced in Dharamsala in June 1970, minus the introduction and colophon.[15] A miniature version produced in Dharamsala specifically for circulation in Tibet was only published later in 1989.

As if to underscore the point that there are areas of contact between exile materials and what we find being produced in Tibet, another document, with a title page dated 1989 and proclaiming 'This World News Is Circulated by the Independence Uprising Committee' (*'dzam-gling gsar-'gyur de rang-btsan ger-langs tshogs-chung-nas bsgril-bsgrags-zhus*), details a US Congress bill, introduced in April 1988 into the State Department Authorisation Act, which is highly critical of China's human rights record in Tibet. The document is copied again, word for word, from an article in the 'World News' (*'Dzam-gling gsar-'gyur*) section of the Tibetan exile magazine *Shes-bya* of June 1988.[16]

The awareness of human rights as a relevant concept takes several forms. Two of the available documents were produced in connection with the demonstration in Lhasa on December 10, 1988, International Human Rights Day, to commemorate the anniversary of the adoption of the Universal Declaration of Human Rights. The relevance of human rights thinking to the Tibetan situation is expressed by a Tibetan in the following terms:

Because today is a day of remembrance for the struggle for human rights, we, the Tibetan people, remember, and we call upon the United Nations and friendly countries [to do so], in order that our just rights will be restored. Currently the World Organisation and many countries are taking human rights as their highest priority, and we, all the people of Tibet, lay and clergy, suffering under Chinese oppression, thank you with both happiness and sadness . . .[17]

Left: Tibetans reading a pro-independence poster pasted up on a wall in Lhasa, August 1988. *Right:* the text of the poster: 'Tibet is independent! May the victorious Tenzin Gyatso [the Dalai Lama] live for 10,000 years! May the victorious Tenzin Gyatso return home.' All the Tibetan people are members of one family and of the same flesh and blood. The Chinese have seized [our country] but we are never disheartened. The Chinese have killed Tibetans but we have determination and are not disheartened. 13 August 1988.' *(Both pictures: Anders Anderson/Tibet Image Bank, 1988)*

The second document simply calls upon everyone to 'remember the human rights [proclaimed by] the World Organisation!' (*'dzam-gling rgyal-tshogs-kyi 'gro-ba mi'i thob-thang-la dran-gso zhu*).[18] But within the documents I have dealt with there are further elaborations on the question of human rights, most noticeably the firm assessment that the right to self-determination and the right to Tibetan independence are basic components of the human rights that Tibetans are entitled to enjoy. Thus we find one of our pamphleteers stating:

. . . [We] have protected the Tibetans' very own country and protected the Tibetan people, and are determined to fight for a future in which the human rights of the Tibetans are restored and then, through the exercise of national self-determination, here in Tibet the 'independent country of Tibet' is established.[19]

And further along in the same document:

The goal of our interwoven violent and peaceful 30-year-long struggle against the Red Chinese aggressors is the human right that we had for several thousand years previously: [the right to an] 'independent country of Tibet' . . .[20]

Perhaps the most interesting exposition on the question of human rights, however, is to be found in a pamphlet to which the Tibet Information Network has already called attention, entitled *Essentials of the Precious Tibetan Democratic Constitution* (*Bod-kyi dmangs-gtso'i rtsa-khrims rin-po-che'i dgongs-don*). This document is a commentary on the constitution proclaimed by the Dalai Lama in 1963, a copy of which was obviously in the possession of the group that produced it.[21] Although this group was a monastic one, there is little reference to specific points of Buddhist doctrine beyond general remarks to the effect that the constitution derives from 'the ideals of the holy *Dharma*, well enunciated by the fully perfected Buddha' (*yang-dag-pa rdzogs-pa'i sangs-rgyas-kyis legs-par gsung-pa'i dam-pa'i chos*), and that representative democracy is in accord with the 'Buddhist position' (*sangs-rgyas-pa'i lta-spyod*). Of course, a respect for Buddhism is clear when the authors allude to Tibet's traditional concept of intertwined religious and secular authority, saying 'There can be no doubt about our ability to enjoy the glory of full religious and secular independence via the principle of self-determination encompassed in international legal tradition.'[22] On the subject of rights this commentary continues:

[The constitution] is founded on the proclaimed principles of internationally practised human rights and on the right of self-determination and the right to exercise self-determination . . . [The constitution] clearly proclaims for all Tibetans the equal rights of or to thought and opinion, religious affiliation, assembly, life, the vote, travel, freedom of speech, the establishment of political parties and organisations, and the free pursuit of an occupation; and it is by this method of [ensuring] freedom and liberty for the people that a great, expansive democratic future with the potential for social growth and development is begun and established . . . In the shade of the tradition of a democratic constitution different individuals having different methodological views, using their democratic prerogatives, need not be fearful, deceitful, or secretive, and can, in fact, practise their prerogatives in thought and in word.[23]

However, there is also this caveat:

In implementing democratic rights and equal freedoms one must clearly understand the essence of basic democracy; yet what is called 'democracy' is absolutely not without beginning or end, with one being allowed to do whatever one likes. Therefore, it is not proper to lie about democratic rights while not having to fulfil any democratic duties whatever.[24]

Thus questions concerning the ideals and concepts of democracy and human rights have to some extent occupied the thoughts of polemicists in the Tibetan dissident movement. These notions are also part of a milieu of nationalist dissent that has partaken intellectually of the international development of human rights thinking via Chinese references to these rights and, indirectly, via Western views of them.

The desire for a democratic future expressed by our polemicists here is counterbalanced by remarks on Tibet's past. The same commentary on the Tibetan constitution refers to considerations that Tibet's previous political structure was a feudal one:

Just as we have fully discarded the faulty aspects of the customs of the old society, [the Dalai Lama] has taken into consideration the need [in] the future Tibet for a democratic religious and secular government, different from the previous conditions of the old tradition of governmental administration, and without a restoration of serfdom or the continuity of feudal monastic estates and official posts on the basis of family inheritance . . .[25]

Another pamphlet, entitled *The Naga Cry of the Just Cause at the Dawn of the Seventeenth Rab-byung (Rab-byung bcu-bdun 'char-kha'i bden-don klu-sgra)*, goes further:

Since September 2, 1960, and the beginning of the democratic Tibetan state, feudalism has been expelled and a system like that of the rest of the world shines. Fraternal peoples have no doubts! Again the enemies are linking things that are unconnected, falsifying history and saying that Tibet belongs to them. They say feudalism will return [that is, if Tibet is separated from China].[26]

Elsewhere, the same document provides a view of the Tibetan past which is rather idyllic, to say the least:

> From the first Tibetan king, Gnya'-khri btsan-po [Nyatri Tsenpo], and the founding of the Tibetan nation, for more than 2,000 years on the roof of the world [Tibet] shone like a golden pinnacle, known to all the world. Gradually the tradition of Dga'-ldan pho-brang [Ganden Podrang] developed, and a firmly politically free people of this world, making use of the wise among them; these people enjoyed happiness in the land of Tibet. But in the 1950s Red Chinese imperialism, using military strategies, surrounded the Land of Snows with modern weapons and invaded it . . .[27]

There is an obvious contradiction inherent in the views expressed by the authors of this document about the nature of the Tibetan past. The exemplary society described in the last extract hardly squares with the acknowledgement of a 'feudal' past mentioned in the former one, or with the reference acknowledging both feudalism and serfdom in the earlier passage from the document discussing the Tibetan constitution. That passage, with its references to feudal estates and inherited positions, shows a familiarity with concepts of feudalism transmitted through Chinese analyses of the Tibetan past. The authors of *The Naga Cry of the Just Cause at the Dawn of the Seventeenth Rab-byung*, however, seem to use the term simply as a negative characterisation of something undesirable in traditional Tibetan society.[28] The choice, in that document, of September 2, 1960, as the date for the termination of feudalism and the beginning of a 'democratic Tibetan state' is interesting because that is the date on which the Dalai Lama inaugurated the Assembly of Tibetan People's Deputies (*Bod mi-mang spyi-'thus lhan-tshogs*),[29] an exile assembly whose establishment had no direct relation to a dismantling of what might be termed 'feudalism', unless this is understood as a broad term encompassing Tibet's previous society and political culture in general. Judging from quotations alluding to the possibility of its restoration, feudalism is an issue for most pamphleteers largely insofar as it has been used as an argument for Tibet's incorporation into the People's Republic of China. The authors are concerned to deny its validity as such, but not to deny that feudalism and serfdom existed in Tibet. And while there is an undoubted sense that social conditions in pre-1959/60 Tibet were, by present-day measures at least, inequitable, there also seems to be a strong desire on the part of pamphleteers, such as the authors of *The Naga Cry of the Just Cause at the Dawn of the Seventeenth Rab-byung*, to see the previous religiously oriented Tibetan state as an ideal with which to contrast conditions there since that state's incorporation into China. Thus this document presents us with clearly contradictory images of Tibet's past, indicating an area where a largely emotional impulse has come to the fore.

Considerations of Tibetan history by pamphleteers in and around Lhasa are understandably the most transparent conduit for the introduction of broad nationalist expositions, and we find in such writings an insistence on the distinction between Chinese and Tibetan characteristics that we can term 'national'. Of course, with regard to what was said earlier about the development of nationalism and nationalistic sentiments, the perception evinced by our documents of the unity of those who partake of Tibetan characteristics should be as striking to us as a perception of division between Tibetans and Chinese. After all, up to a generation ago most Tibetans had little, if any, substantial contact with Chinese; regional differences among Tibetans themselves were undoubtedly the distinctions most commonly called to mind by them. One of the documents prepared for the demonstration to mark International Human Rights Day on December 10, 1988, asserts:

Our Tibet has a long and verifiable history. We Tibetans have origins that are absolutely different from those of any other people. Our character, language, customs and clothing are unlike those of other people. If today we talk briefly of Tibet's history it will be something to make the Red Chinese aggressors ashamed and embarrassed. The Red Chinese aggressors must return to their own country. The masters of Tibet are the Tibetans. [Our] secular and religious king is His Holiness the Dalai Lama.[30]

When nationalistic distinctions are drawn between what is Tibetan and what is not, we find religion, not surprisingly, mentioned several times. We have already noted Gellner's ideas about the circumstances in which a clerical group representing a nation's or people's high culture becomes linked to the evolving national identity, often to the point where it is wholly secularised as such, whatever its previous religious and sacral role.[31] References to religion in our documents take for granted a clear link between Tibetan Buddhism and the Tibetan national identity, as expressed, for example, in one pamphlet:

There is no way for the enemies of the doctrine to be in harmony with the Tibetan people. If the enemies of the doctrine are too harmonious with the Tibetan people, it is like welcoming a leader from outside [one's group]. How can one be impassioned for another people? That only comes directly from one's origins; it only comes directly from [common] food, clothing, customs.[32]

When adopting a nationalistic tone, our authors often use rhetoric that is part óf a vocabulary common to both Chinese Marxism and anti-colonial movements in general. Thus, they routinely use the term 'imperialist' to describe China (usually 'imperialist Red China' – *btsan-rgyal Rgya-dmar*), a term admittedly also found in much of the writing produced by Tibetan exiles. A clearer reliance on Chinese-derived rhetoric is shown, however, by one comment on Tibet's Chinese rulers: 'Outwardly they say that they are anti-fascist, but in actuality the Red Chinese themselves practise unlimited fascism.'[33] The precise understanding of the term 'fascism' on the part of this document's authors might be called into question – for example, whether the authors are imputing to China the practice of harsh dictatorial rule over Tibet or, more precisely, aligning Chinese rule with Marxist concepts of class and of nation-oriented fascism. In any event, it is clear that the term used, *hu-shi-si'i lam-lugs*, is derived from Chinese writings and not from exile works.[34]

Other usages and references indicate the use of information derived from non-PRC sources beyond those we have already mentioned. In another pamphlet, put out in 1987 and essentially meant as a missive to the members of the US Congress, it is recounted that Tibetans had learned that in 1985 a number of congressmen and senators had signed a letter addressed to visiting Chinese President Li Xiannian expressing concern about conditions in Tibet. The pamphlet goes on to say that in October 1986 a Voice of America broadcast had noted that a US bank bill had listed Tibet as a 'free and independent' (*rang-dbang rang-btsan*) country.[35] This did of course happen, and the US Government subsequently notified China that America in no way considered Tibet as anything other than Chinese territory; this is probably what is alluded to when the pamphlet notes that President Reagan 'abandoned what was just' (*bden-don blos-gtong*).[36] The spellings of Reagan's name (*Ri-ghan* and *Ri-ghin*) indicate that the information probably did not come via Chinese sources (that is, through the Chinese-language service of the VOA, in which case it would probably have been rendered in a manner somewhat similar to the Chinese *Ligen*) but through Tibetan ones – no doubt materials produced by Tibetan exiles in India.

A further point of interest in our documents is the fact that, contrary to more stereotypical views of the Tibetan approach to protest, one document at least does advocate a certain level of violence. This is *The Naga Cry of the Just Cause at the Dawn of the Seventeenth Rab-byung*. Though written in verse, it is in some ways the most unpolished of the documents under discussion. Its spelling is in many places idiosyncratic (for example, *mkhe-dbang* for *mkhas-dbang*, etc.), and its call to arms rather blunt and unforgiving:

. . . the people's heroes carry natural weapons and fight. The natural weapons will face up to machine-guns. Don't stop the people's struggle! [As we] protect today what was established long ago, if the father dies then the son fights [in his place].[37]

A note explains that the 'natural weapons' are meant to be stones, without which the Tibetans have no weapons, according to the author or authors. The document then advocates that stones, as a symbol of the Tibetan struggle, be newly accorded a ritual place in the celebrations of the New Year beginning with the Earth Dragon Year (1988–9).[38]

In a similar (though non-violent) vein, another text describes, as a symbolic protest tactic, the offering of prayer flags and the burning of *bsangs* or incense every Wednesday, specifically to obtain long life for the Dalai Lama, long reach for his actions, and independence for Tibet and the expulsion of the Chinese. This form of protest, which is carried on without obvious outward symbols but with a common awareness by Tibetans in Lhasa, is said in our pamphlet to have occurred every Wednesday since 1959, with a break of three years during the Cultural Revolution; this makes for a total of 1,277 Wednesdays. Moreover, the author describes the offerings on March 10, 1987, as having constituted a massive day of this sort of disguised protest.[39]

We have seen several ideas, not always in accord with each other, on human rights, Tibetan society, democracy, and so forth, propounded by the authors of our pamphlets. Among these writings, some are contradictory and some present a rather erroneous view of Tibet's history, but they are clear evidence of active consideration and thinking going on within a stratum of those involved in the dissident movement in Lhasa. As we have seen, commentators can easily advance various ideas about the motives and goals of the protests, but to understand these, it is better to grasp the ideas expressed by Tibetans themselves and to this end to examine the documents produced by Tibetan dissidents.

All the documents referred to in this paper demand essentially one thing, namely the independence of Tibet. For these pamphleteers independence is not 'an abstract notion which most Tibetans do not seem to talk about very much'.[40] According to one of the documents,

[If, under China] Tibet were built up, the livelihood of the Tibetan people improved, [so that] their lives surpassed those of human beings as lives of happiness that made the deities of the Divine Realm of the Thirty-Three embarrassed; if we really and truly had this given to us, even then we Tibetans wouldn't want it. We absolutely would not want it.[41]

Nothing but independence will do.

NOTES

1. Michele Hoffman, 'In Spirit, Tibet's Lamas Resemble Iran's Mullahs', *New York Times*, August 27, 1988.
2. A. Tom Grunfeld, 'Independence is second to Dalai Lama's return', *Far Eastern Economic Review*, October 13, 1988, p. 26. In reference to Grunfeld's 'dozens of interviews', one cannot fail to note that his published work on Tibet to date evinces no evidence that he has any facility with either the Tibetan or Chinese language. Additionally, while general literature on Tibet often uses the term 'theocratic', it is actually quite misleading, not to say erroneous, in the Tibetan context. See the more unambiguous use of the term 'hierocracy' in Turrell V. Wylie, 'Lama Tribute in the Ming Dynasty' in Michael Aris and Aung San Suu Kyi (eds), *Tibetan Studies in Honour of Hugh Richardson*, Warminster, 1980, p. 335.
3. See Thub-bstan sangs-rgyas (Thubten Sangye), *Rgya-nag-du Bod-kyi sku-tshab don-gcod skabs dang-gnyis tshugs-stangs skor-gyi lo-rgyus thabs-bral zur-lam*, Dharamsala, 1982, pp. 46–53. The exile Tibetan Government reacted to the publication of this account by suppressing the volume for several years, even though it was a publication of the Government's own Library of Tibetan Works and Archives and had already been distributed to a small number of people and institutions (including libraries in the West).
4. See 'Dharamsala Severs All Ties with Taiwan', *Tibetan Review*, February 1990, pp. 4–5. Nothing approaching a full account of this affair has yet been published.
5. Kenneth Minogue, *Nationalism*, New York, 1967, p. 81.
6. Heather Stoddard, *Le mendiant de l'Amdo*, Paris, 1986.
7. *Ibid.*, pp. 69–94.
8. This is of course in an indirect way: through the filter of Chinese Marxism. We may note the earlier and equally indirect introduction of Western ideas about nations and nationalism to a much smaller number of Tibetans via an unsystematic exposure to the thinking of Sun Yat-sen. Stoddard, *op. cit.*, pp. 82–6.
9. *Dge-bshes* Blo-bzang dbang-phyug (Geshe Lobsang Wangchuk) died in prison in November 1987, having spent numerous years in confinement on a variety of charges (see TIN Docs T5(H), T1(YB)). His last period of imprisonment began in 1982, when he was arrested for the composition and circulation of writings advocating Tibetan independence. The story of his having based his arguments in part on works by Mao Zedong might well be apocryphal; no copy of the work has found its way out of Tibet. Nevertheless, the story itself is indicative of a school of Tibetan thinking that sees Chinese Marxist theory itself, if impartially applied, as sustaining the case for independence.
10. Ernest Gellner, *Nations and Nationalism*, Ithaca, NY, 1983, pp. 77, 73–81.

Gellner further states (pp. 77–8) that high cultures that survive this transition are further transformed: 'When they were carried by a court or courtly stratum or a clerisy, they tended to be trans-ethnic and even trans-political, and were easily exportable to wherever that court was emulated or that clerisy respected and employed . . . [But after the transition] the price these high cultures pay for becoming the idiom of entire territorial nations, instead of appertaining to a clerkly stratum only, is that they become secularized.' It is easy to see the 'trans-ethnic' aspect of Tibetan Buddhism in its presence and growth among Mongols and Manchus from the 17th to the 20th centuries; however the revival in Mongolia of interest, albeit nationalistic, in Tibetan Buddhism would give us pause to be flexible in speculating about an end to that aspect of Tibetan Buddhism. It is also clear, both in Tibet and among Tibetan exiles, that Tibetan society is noticeably more secular, in terms of the decreased participation of clerics and monasteries in political administration, than was previously the case. We may also note that this comes at a time when Tibet has gone from being an 'agrarian' society to an 'industrial' one, broadly speaking, if we allow our understanding to encompass Tibet's pastoralism as part of what would be termed Tibet's agrarian society; and also if we see Tibet as industrial in the sense that it has been politically and economically bound to the larger industrial entity of China. Such broader definitions do not, I believe, go beyond the margins of what Gellner describes.

11. This question is not all that simple. Vaclav Havel has eloquently spoken of the double personae that people living under coercive and repressive regimes adopt with regard to their intellectual, social and political behaviour; see Timothy Garton Ash, 'Eastern Europe: The Year of Truth', *New York Review of Books*, February 15, 1990, p. 18. It is this forced adjustment to coercion that led observers so far astray in predicting popular sentiment in a number of places (perhaps most notably the outcome of Nicaragua's 1990 election). Put bluntly, a state that penalises people for holding 'wrong' opinions is ill equipped to take an accurate reading of those opinions, and may likely poison the atmosphere for such investigations. In 1979 the Chinese authorities were stunned by the overwhelming emotional reception accorded the Dalai Lama's emissaries when they arrived in Lhasa. So too, the authorities appear to have actually believed, at some level, that only a 'handful' of Tibetans supported 'separatism', until the depth of the problem forced the authorities to take repressive measures well beyond a basic restoration of order.

12. Some have been in my possession for some time. Many (in fact most) were kindly supplied to me by Robbie Barnett and the Tibet Information Network.

13. On the development of human rights thinking see Kenneth Minogue, 'The History of the Idea of Human Rights' in Walter Laqueur and Barry Rubin (eds), *The Human Rights Reader*, New York, 1990, pp. 3–17.

14. Regarding this position see, for example, Yi Ding, 'Opposing Interference in Other Countries' Internal Affairs Through Human Rights', *Beijing Review*, November 6–12, 1989, pp. 14–16.

15. *Yongs-khyab gsal-bsgrags 'gro-ba mi'i thob-thang*, Dharamsala, 1970.

16. 'A-ri'i Gros-tshogs 'og-ma'i thog 7 snyan-seng zhus-pa'i gros-char', *Shes-bya*, June 1988, pp. 16–22, copied over in TIN Doc. 3(R). Documents obtained from the Tibet Information Network are cited in this paper by the document numbers TIN has assigned to them, preceded by 'TIN'. Where relevant, page numbers are given. Note the orthographic error in the title of the 1989 document (more correctly titled: *'Dzam-gling gsar-'gyur de rang-btsan [s]ger-langs tshogs-chung-nas bsgril-bsgrags-zhus*). I have generally left the wording of

documents quoted in this paper untouched; orthographic or grammatical irregularities should mostly be clear from my translations.

17. TIN Doc. 23(Q) (A): *//de-ring ni 'gro-ba mi-'i thob-thang-la rtsod-len byed-pa'i dran-gso'i nyin-mo zhig yin dir-rten nga-'tsho Bod-mi-rnams-nas // rang-re'i bden-pa'i thob-thang slar-gso yong-ched 'dzam-gling mnyam-sbrel rgyal-tshogs dang / de-bzhin mthun-phyogs yul-khag-rnams-la re-'bod dang bcas-te dran-gso gso-byed-rgyu yin / deng-skabs 'gro-ba mi'i thob-thang-la 'dzam-gling rgyal-tshogs dang rgyal-khab mang-po zhig-gi thugs-'gan che-shos gnang-ba dang / nga-tsho Rgya-ma'i btsan-gnon 'og-du sdug-bsngal myong-bzhin-pa'i Bod-mi ser-skya yongs-nas dga'-skyo dga'-gnyis-ldan ngang thugs-rje-che zhu-rgyu . . .*

18. TIN Doc. 24(Q).

19. Pha (This document seems to be one in a series. It has a cover sheet with '3–10' (that is, March 10) emblazoned on it and dated the tenth day of the first month of the Tibetan Royal Year 2114. The first page of text has the letter 'pha' (indicating that it is part of a series) and the date 1987 at the top, and two lines below the common date of March 10. Another document in the same hand-writing has the letter 'ma' and the date April 10, 1987 at the top.), p. 3: *Bod-mi rang-nyid-kyi rgyal-khab-la srung-skyobs dang Bod mi-rigs-la srung-skyobs bcas byas-nas ma-'ong Bod-mi rnams 'gro-ba mi'i thob-thang bskyar-gso byung-nas Bod-ljongs 'dir mi-rigs rang-nyid-kyis rang-thag rang-gcod-kyi slar-yang 'Bod rang-btsan rgyal-khab' gcig bskrun rgyur brtsod-len bya-rgyu'i sems thag-gcad-pa red/.*

20. Pha, pp. 7–8: *nga-tsho lo-ngo sum-cu tsam-gyi ring-la Rgya-dmar btsan-'dzul-par zhi-drag bzung-'brel-gyi 'thab-rtsod byed-pa'i migs-yul ni nga-tshor lo-ngo stong-phrag kha-shas-kyi sngon-nas yod-bzhin-pa'i 'gro-ba mi'i rigs-kyi thob-thang 'Bod rang-btsan rgyal-khab' yin . . .*

21. That is, the well known 'Bras-spungs (Drepung) group whose members were given very heavy prison sentences in 1989 for producing counter-revolutionary propaganda. The group and their activities have been described in TIN, *News Update*, December 27, 1989, pp. 3–5.

22. TIN Doc. 6(J), pp. 1r–1v: *. . . rgyal-spyi'i khrims-srol rang-thag rang-gcod-kyi thob-thang yod-pa'i sgo-nas chos-srid rang-dbang gtsang-ma'i dpal-pa spyod thub-rgyur the-tshom med.*

23. TIN Doc. 6(J), pp. 2r, 2v–3r, and 3v: *'dzam-gling rgyal-spyi'i 'gro-ba mi'i kun-spyod thob-thang dang rang-thag rang-gcod-kyi thob-thang   rang-thag rang-gcod-kyi thob-dbang gsal-bsgrags-kyi rtsa-don gzhi-rtsar bzung-ba zhig red . . .   Bod-mi rer bsam-blo rnam-dpyod dang   chos-lugs 'du-tshogs lus-srog 'os-bsdu   'gro-skyod   gtam-brjod 'dod-dbang   skyid-sdug dang tshogs-pa   'dzugs-pa rang-rang 'dod-mos las-rigs-la gzhug-pa'i rang-dbang dang 'dra-mnyam-gyi thob-thang-rnams kyang gsal-por 'khod-pa bcas mi-dmangs-kyi rang-dbang dang 'dod-mos-kyi thabs-shes brgyud-de spyi-tshogs yar-rgyas gong-'phel 'gro thub-pa'i dmangs-gtso'i mdun-lam yangs-shing rgya-che-ba zhig gsar-gtod gtan-'bebs gnang-yod   . . . dmangs-gtso'i rtsa-khrims-kyi lam-srol grib-bsil 'og nang-gses rang-rang so-so'i thabs-lam-gyi lta-ba 'dra-min yod-pa-rnams dmangs-gtso'i khe-dbang bed-spyod-kyis 'jigs-dngangs dang ngo-lkog sbas-gsang ma dgos-par bsam-pa dang   bshad-pa lag-len bstar chog-pa zhig-kyang red . . .*

24. TIN Doc. 6(J), pp. 5r–5v: *dmangs-gtso'i thob-thang dang rang-dbang 'dra-mnyam bcas bed-spyod byed-pa-la gzhi-rtsa dmangs-gtso'i ngo-bo gsal-po shes dgos-yang dmangs-gtso zhes-pa 'go-mjug gang-yang med-par rang-snang gang-dran byed chog-pa zhig-kyang gtan-nas ma-yin   de-bzhin dmangs-gtso'i las-*

'gan gang-yang sgrub mi-dgos-par dmangs-gtso'i thob-thang ham-rtsod byed-pa de-yang ma-'grig-pa red.

25. TIN Doc. 6(J), p. 1v: *spyi-tshogs rnying-pa'i lam-srol skyon-cha yod-rigs yongs-su dor-zin-pa bzhin ma-'ongs-pa'i Bod-de zhing-bran-gyi lam-lugs bskyar-gso byed-pa'am   yang-na bkas-bkod rgyud-'dzin-pa pha-bu brgyud-'dzin-gyis chos-gzhis dang dpon-khungs zer-ba'i rnying-lugs srid-'dzin lta-bu'i sngar-gyi gnas-stangs ltar ma-yin-par chos-srid gnyis-ldan dmangs-gtso'i gzhung zhig dgos-par dgongs . . .*

26. TIN Doc. 2(R), p. 3: *spyi-lo 1960 tham-pa zla 9 tshes 2-gyi nyin   Bod-ljongs dmangs-gtso rgyal-khab dbu-brnyis-nas bkas-bkod rgyud-'dzin ring-lugs pha-mthar bkrad   'dzam-gling lam-phyogs gcig-mtshungs 'od-stong 'phro spun-zla mi-rigs the-tshom ma-byed-cig   slar-yang dgra-bos ma-'dus lhu-'grigs-kyis mnga'-khong yin-zhis lo-rgyus mdzun-bzo byas   bkas-bkod rgyus-'dzin phyir-log sleb-yong-zhes.* Note that the seventeenth *rab-byung* cycle referred to in the document's title began in 1987. This document, written in verse, is a rather rough piece and is filled with all sorts of orthographic mistakes. Note that only basic translations are provided of those passages, forgoing English versification.

27. TIN Doc. 2(R), p. 1: *Bod-rgyal thog-ma gnya'-khri btsan-po nas   Bod-kyi rgyal-khab dbu-brnyes lo-ngo ni nyi-stong lhag-tsam 'dzam-gling rtse-mo-ru gser-rtog star-brjid 'jig-rten kun-kyi shes   rgyas-ba rim-byon Dga'-ldan pho-brang-gi lugs zung chab-srid rang-dbang btsan-po-yi   'jigs-rten mi'i-rigs mkhe-dbang bid-spyad-nas   Bod-ljongs mi-rigs dga'-bder rol-bzhin-kyang   dus-rabs nyi-shu'i lo-rabs lnga-bcu'i nang   Rgya-dmar btsan-rgyal ring-lugs dmag-shes-kyis Kha-ba'ı-ljongs   dır deng-dus mtshon-chas bakor btsan-'dzul byas . . .* The 'tradition of *Dga'-ldan pho-brang*' refers, of course, to the government of the Dalai Lamas.

28. Note that while Western journalists often use the term to convey impressions of Tibetan 'backwardness', Western Tibetologists generally find the term technically inappropriate.

29. See Tshe-dbang phun-tshogs (Tsewang Phuntsog) *et al.*, *Rgyun-mkho'i Bod-gnas lag-deb*, New Delhi, 1987, p. 33.

30. TIN Doc. 23(Q)(B): *nga-tsho'i Bod-'di ni lo-rgyus yun-ring-la khungs-btsan-pa zhig yin   nga-tsho Bod-mi-rnams-kyi 'byung-khungs ni mi-rigs gzhan dang brtan-nas 'dra-gi med nga-tsho Bod-mi-rnams kyi gshis-rgyud dang skad-yig lugs-srol cha-lugs sogs mi-rigs gzhan dang 'dra-gi med   de-ring ni lo-rgyus 'dor-bsdus tsam-zhig brjod-nas Rgya-dmar btsan-'dzul-pa-tsho ngo-tsha kha-skyeng dgos-pa bzo-rgyu yin Rgya-dmar btsan-'dzul-pa rnams rang-yul-du log-dgos   Bod-kyi bdag-po Bod-mi yin   chos-srid gnyis-ldan-gyi rgyal-po ni skyabs-mgon Tā-la'i bla-ma yin   .*

31. We might also mention in this context George Orwell's musings about religions as forms of nationalism. See his 'Notes on Nationalism' in Sonia Orwell and Ian Angus (eds), *The Collected Essays, Journalism and Letters of George Orwell*, New York, 1968, vol. III, p. 363.

32. TIN Doc. 2(R), p. 2: *bstan-dgra Bod mi'i rigs dang mthun 'thabs med   bstan-dgra Bod mi'i rigs dang mthun drag-na   rang-gi mgo-dpon phyi-nas bsus dang mtshungs   gzhan-gyi mi-la sha-tsha byed-don ji   mi-rigs byung-khung kho-na thad red   za-mgyon gom-gshis tshang-ma tha-dad red.*

33. TIN Doc. 1(P), p. 2: *kho-pas phyi-tshul-nas hu-shi-si'i lam-lugs ngo-rgol zer-ba dang   don-dngos thogs Rgya-dmar rang-nyid-gi hu-shi-si lam-lugs lag-bstar byed-pa ni tshad-las bsgal-yod.*

34. See the Tibetan definition/transcription of the term in *Zang–Han duizhao*

cihui (= *Rgya–Bod shan-sbyar-gi tshig-mdzod*), Beijing, 1976, p. 222 ('*Hpha-shi-si ring-lugs*', for the Chinese '*faxisizhuyi*'); and in Gdong-thog Bstan-pa'i rgyal-mtshan (T.G. Dhongthog), *Dbyin–Bod shan-sbyar-gyi tshig-mdzod snang-ba gsar-pa* (= *The New Light English-Tibetan Dictionary*), Dharamsala, 1973, p. 154 ('*I-ṭa-li'i dmar-po'i phyogs 'gal tshogs-pa'i rtsa-'dzugs dang sgrig-lam*').

35. Ma, p. 2.
36. *Ibid.*, p. 5.
37. TIN Doc. 2(R), p. 2: *mi-rigs dpa'-bo-tshos   rang-byung mtshon-cha 'khyer-nas 'thab-rtsod byed ṭarang-byung mtshon-chas 'khrul-mda'i kha-gtad bcag   mi-rigs 'thab-brtsod mtshams-'jogs ma-byed-cig   gna'-'dzugs deng-srung pha-shis bu-brtsod byed.*
38. TIN Doc. 2(R), p. 4.
39. Pha, pp. 5–6.
40. Grunfeld, *op. cit.*
41. Pha, pp. 8–9: *Bod-ljongs 'dzugs-bskrun dang   Bod-mi'i tsho-ba yar-rgyas btang-nas 'gro-ba mi'i rigs-kyi tsho-ba-las 'gal-ba'i lha-gnas sum-cu-rtsa-gsum-gyi lha-rnams-kyang kha-bskyeng dgos-pa'i bde-skyid-kyi tsho-ba zhig kha-yod-lag-yod-kyi nga-tshor sprad-kyang nga-tsho Bod-mir mi-dgos   rtsa-ba-nas mi-dgos.*

On the 'Divine Realm of the Thirty-Three' and the thirty-three deities associated with it, see He Wenxuan and Dou Cunqi (= Ha'o Wun-Zhon and To'u Tshun-chi), *Zang–Han duizhao changyong hechengci cidian* (= *Bod-Rgya shan-sbyar-gyi shes-bya'i rnam-grangs kun-btus tshig-mdzod*), Xining, 1987, pp. 786–7.

POSTSCRIPT

I

HU YAOBANG'S VISIT TO TIBET, MAY 22–31, 1980

AN IMPORTANT DEVELOPMENT IN THE CHINESE GOVERNMENT'S TIBET POLICY

Wang Yao

During the week from May 22 to May 31, 1980, Hu Yaobang led a Working Group of the Party Central Committee (PCC) to visit and inspect Tibet. This event was watched with great interest by those, both at home and abroad, who were concerned with Tibetan society, and it can be said that this event marked the beginning of a new era for the PCC's Tibet policy

In the ten years that followed that visit history marched on with its strong steps, leaving behind impressive footprints: amongst them, indisputably, the open door, a revitalised economy, changes in the social structure and an improvement in people's lives. As for Hu Yaobang himself, he experienced his ups and downs with officialdom and left the world with his ambitions unfulfilled on April 15, 1989. The great honours that were paid to him at his funeral could not make up for the regrets during his life. But the past has passed. According to Chinese custom, final judgement can only be passed on Hu when the lid is placed on his coffin, and this note is a reflection on the historical significance of Hu's visit to Tibet, as a mark of respect to him and as a way of cherishing the memory of a great man.

The Composition and Timing of the Working Group

The importance of the Central Committee's Working Group can be judged from Wan Li's description of it: 'This is the first working group to be formed since Comrade Hu Yaobang became the General Secretary after the new secretariat was formed at the Fifth Plenary Session of the Eleventh Central Committee.' The Working Group was composed principally of five people: Hu

Yaobang, the General Secretary of the Central Committee and a member of the Standing Committee of the Politburo of the Central Committee; Wan Li, member of the Central Committee and Vice-Premier of the State Council; Ahpeiahwangjinmei [Ngapo Ngawang Jigme], the Vice-Chairman of the National People's Congress; Yang Jingren, member of the Central Committee and the Head of the State Commission of Nationalities Affairs, and Zhao Zhengqing, Vice-Minister of the Organisation Department of the PCC. There were several other staff members, amongst whom I was the only one who was not a government official.

Edgar Snow, as an old friend of the Party leadership who knew their working style quite well, once said, 'Nothing carried out in public by the leaders of the Central Committee is ever casual or without significance.' This was true of the date chosen for the visit, and there were at least three reasons which led the Working Group to select May 22 as the date when it should arrive in Lhasa.

First, the date indicated that the Central Government's policy on Tibet was based on the 'Seventeen-Point Agreement'. This was the agreement (entitled in full, 'Seventeen Points for the Peaceful Liberation of Tibet') signed in the Qinzheng Hall in Zhongnanhai, Beijing, on May 23, 1951, after a long period of discussion and consultation, by the delegation of the Central People's Government, headed by its plenipotentiary Li Weihan, and the delegation of the Tibetan Regional Government, headed by plenipotentiary Ahpeiahwangjinmei. That agreement marked the first time since its victory in the domestic revolution that the Chinese Communist Party had found a point of convergence with the Tibetan regional government; it was also the first agreement, based on compromise and harmony, which was acceptable to all the political forces in Tibet. It thus became the governing principle in Tibetan work and policy for a long period.

Secondly, the choice of date pointed out that the Central Government was willing to settle matters through consultation with the local people. Thirdly, it aimed to show the Central Government's wish to restore the harmonious atmosphere of cooperation which had prevailed in the early 1950s.

The Working Group arrived at Gong Ga [Gongkar] airport near Lhasa at 10 a.m. on May 22, and two hours later had reached Lhasa and begun its meetings with the Tibetan leaders. Hu Yaobang came straight to the point by asking Paba-la [Phagpa-la Gelek Namgyal] a question: 'Comrade Paba-la, what is tomorrow?' This summed up the feelings and intentions of the Group. At the cocktail party held on May 23 to celebrate the 39th anniversary of the Seventeen-Point Agreement, Wan Li held the hands of

Street scenes in modern Lhasa. The banner reads 'Everyone has the responsibility to pay taxes'. (*Jirina Simajchlova, 1991*)

Sangpodunzhengdunzhu (Sampho Tenzin Dundrup[1]) and said: 'You have rendered an outstanding service to history! Thank you!' Apart from Ahpeiahwangjinmei, Sangpodunzhengdunzhu was the only surviving member of the delegation sent by the Tibetan government who had signed the Agreement. He had just been released after nearly twenty years in labour camps.

The Speech

On May 29 Hu Yaobang made a very sincere and passionate political speech at a gathering of 5,000 cadres in Lhasa. The slogan put forward in the speech was 'Strive to build a united, prosperous and civilised new Tibet' ('*Wei jianshe tuanjie, fuyu, wenmingde, xin Xizang xiang nuli douzheng*'). In the speech Hu listed six tasks facing Tibet:

1. To exercise nationality autonomy in the region fully – that is to say, to let Tibetans really be the masters of their own lives.
2. A commitment by the Central Government to relieve and reduce burdens on the people, exempting them from agricultural and animal husbandry tax over the next three to five years in order to allow the Tibetan people a chance to recover.

3. To adopt a special policy to revive the Tibetan economy, including the adoption of a system of private economy in line with Tibetan circumstances. Nationwide this initiative was developed into the economic (household) responsibility system.

4. To make great efforts to develop agriculture and animal husbandry as well as the manufacture of consumer goods, in order to promote economic prosperity and enrich people's lives.

5. To make efforts to develop Tibetan science, culture and education, and to prepare for the establishing of the University of Tibet.

6. To implement the policy on minority nationality cadres correctly, to strengthen the unity between the Han and Tibetan cadres, and to transfer a large quantity of Chinese cadres who had worked in Tibet for many years back to the interior.

Naturally, these six tasks were endorsed and supported by the Tibetan people. The atmosphere was very lively both inside and outside the meeting. Hu Yaobang was an excellent orator and his address was received with waves of warm applause, especially when he admitted very frankly:

'Our present situation is less than wonderful because the Tibetan people's lives have not been much improved. There are some improvements in some parts, but in general, Tibetans still live in relative poverty. In some areas the living standards have even gone down. We comrades in the Central Committee, Chairman Hua as well as several vice-chairmen, were very upset when we heard about this situation. We feel that our party has let the Tibetan people down. We feel very bad! The sole purpose of our Communist Party is to work for the happiness of people, to do good things for them. We have worked nearly thirty years, but the life of the Tibetan people has not been notably improved. Are we not to blame? If we don't make this clear, people won't let us off the hook; party members won't let us get away with it!'

What he said touched people's hearts. They admired him for his statesmanship and his broad-mindedness as a true Communist. He was open and honest, dared to act, dared to face reality and dared to bear responsibility. Ten years later Hu Yaobang's words still ring out forcefully. To this day, the Tibetan people still keep his likeness in their hearts, referring to him affectionately as '*sku-zhabs* Hu' [Gentleman Hu].

The Two Cordial Conversations

In the first of the Two Cordial Conversations, Hu Yaobang invited three leading Tibetan cadres, Duojiecaidan [Dorje Tseten], Luosangsicheng [Lobsang Tsultrim], and Pengcuozhaxi [Phuntsog

Tashi], to the hotel in which he was staying in Lhasa. Hu, in his sitting room, opened his hearts to them and said:

'You are all exemplary Tibetans. You are leaders as well as communists; the Tibetan cause relies on you. I hope that you will make further contributions towards the construction of a united, prosperous and civilised new Tibet. I did not know you before, but now we have become friends. Tibetan affairs will rely on you. You can directly come to see me if there are any problems.'

These three men were later appointed to important positions. Duojicaidan became Director of the TAR Department of Education, First Secretary of the Lhasa Party Committee, and Chairman of the TAR People's Government. Now he is the Director of the China Tibetology Centre in Beijing. Luosangsicheng was appointed as the Director of the TAR Party Committee's Department of Organisation, and as the vice-Chairman of the Standing Committee of the Tibetan People's Congress. Unfortunately, he died of a heart attack shortly afterwards. Pengcuozhaxi became at various times in his career the Director of Publications for the Tibetan Administration, the vice-Chairman of the Tibetan People's Congress and the vice-Chairman of the Social Science Academy. Now he is the vice-Director of the China Tibetology Centre.

In the second of the Two Cordial Conversations, Hu invited two leading figures of the Old Tibet to talk with him. Xuekangtudengnima (Sholkhang Thubten Nyima)' and Qiabagesangwangdui (Chapei Kelsang Wangdu) were old acquaintances of Hu, who as members of the Chinese Youth Delegation had been to visit Moscow and Bucharest with him in the 1950s. Hu did not forget his old friends although thirty years had passed. Hu held their hands and chatted delightedly. He looked back over their past friendship and hoped that they would guide the patriotic leading figures of the old Tibet to strive together to construct a new Tibet. Before long, Xuekangtudengnima was appointed as the vice-Director of the Tibetan Cultural Department and the vice-Chairman of the People's Political Consultative Conference of the TAR, and Qiabagesangwangdui later became the Director of the People's Bank of the TAR.

NOTES

1. Sampho Tenzin Dundrup left Tibet and went to live in India in 1982. [Editor's note]

II

THE DISPUTE BETWEEN THE TIBETANS AND THE HAN: WHEN WILL IT BE SOLVED?

Wang Xiaoqiang*

The dispute between the Zang, or Tibetan, people, and the Han, as we call the majority ethnic group in China, is a kind of cultural conflict which goes beyond political or economic interests.

In Yunnan and Guizhou provinces there are several minority ethnic groups which still keep their traditions and customs separate from the Han nationality. Perhaps because they live in such scattered groups, or for other reasons, their cultures have hardly evolved into complete systems and often lack languages or other social apparatus. Therefore, these ethnic groups rely more or less on Han culture to make up for their deficiencies. Generally they get along well with the Han on the cultural level. This phenomenon is similar to some scattered cultures in Africa which have integrated with Western culture. In other words, 'incomplete' equals 'open'.

Tibetan culture is completely different. Tibetan Buddhism incorporates astronomy, geology, the calendar, philosophy, literature, art, architecture, medicine, politics, economics, religion, history, ethics, morality . . . everything that one can expect to find. Like any mature culture, Tibetan culture has independently evolved into a complete system with a history almost as old as the Han, and has developed simultaneously with Han culture in China. Just as it is not possible to replace Indian culture with British culture, or to subsume China into the 'Asian Co-Prosperity Sphere', Tibetan culture cannot be taken over by any outside culture. Subjugation? Look at one simple fact – until now, not one single generation of non-Tibetans can multiply healthily on the 'roof of the world'.

In 1984 Bai Nanfeng and I went to the Tibet Autonomous Region for a field study.[2] One day we stopped at a '*Jian xie*', an ancient folk festival, where a group of actors dressed in ancient costume were dancing on the grassland. To the beat of a drum an old white-haired man sang a desolate and sonorous song: 'Where do the mountains come from? Where do the rivers come from? Which came first, the chicken or the egg?' We were deeply moved

---

* Wang Xiaoqiang was invited to contribute this chapter on the basis of his book on the economic development of China's western regions, *The Poverty of Plenty*.[1]

by the strength of this ancient culture. The Tibetan *Legend of Gesar* is the longest epic in the world, even exceeding the *Odyssey*, the *Iliad* and *Arabian Nights*. Anyone who has been to Tibet is easily convinced that Tibetan culture is immortal, like Han culture.

The dispute between the Zang and the Han is in substance a cultural conflict. The adjustment of economic and political interests cannot solve the problem. Since 1978, China's religious and nationalities policies have been relaxed along with the readjustment of policies in other fields. In Tibet we have reduced the number of Han cadres, increased central government support and removed the ban on freedom of religious worship. Nevertheless, what has been done is a kind of 'returning to the period of the 1950s', that is, reversing the policies of the Cultural Revolution. This is believed to be good enough. As a matter of fact, we are only attempting to set to right the things that are in disorder; but there is no creativity in the spirit of reform.

One inevitable outcome is that 'a lot of money has been spent but still [we] do not get any favourable comments'. Many Han cadres are confused: 'Why are we blamed and criticised by Tibetans when we have invested so much without any attempt to benefit ourselves from Tibet?' The interesting thing is that usually discontented Tibetans cannot give you a clear answer to explain why they nurse a grievance. What is the answer? In 1987 when former Party Secretary Wu Jinghua, himself from the Yi ethnic minority in Sichuan, appeared in Tibetan costume at the anniversary celebration of the Tibet Autonomous Region, he was hailed enthusiastically and applanded by all the Tibetans. This symbolic behaviour had much greater impact than huge amounts of money.

Cultural conflicts are often reflected in national dignity. In the framework of China's former 'philosophy of struggle', however, there is simply no legal space for national dignity. Communism has two basic principles: party members are expected to be atheists, and religion is seen as the 'tool of the ruling classes and the opium of the people'. Until now, Tibetans have not forced their Han compatriots to be lamas. But the view that religion is a 'tool of the ruling classes and the opium of the people' has long been imposed, and still sounds like advice to stop smoking. Unfortunately, Tibetan culture integrates not only politics but *everything* with religion, including astronomy, the calendar, medicine, architecture, literature, the arts and so on. If religion were opium, then Tibetan culture would be entirely negated. Although the Marxist-based theory of religion is no longer talked about, the Chinese Government does not yet have anything new to say about it.

The essence of national dignity is to seek equality, to sit as equals at the same table. In administration, Tibet is a local region of the central government, yet in the relations between nationalities, all should be on an equal footing. This creates a problem. The Party has its two principles on religion, but there is no officially recognised position on religion in Tibet. Obviously, the readjusted religion and nationalities policies are only intended to return to those outlined in the period before the 'Cultural Revolution', which, as already mentioned, is totally inadequate. Wu Jinghua proposed a 'Reinvigorated Tibet and an Enlarged Culture', and this inspired the people. Unfortunately, soon after the 'Battle on the Octagonal Street' [Barkor] in Lhasa in 1988, this proposal was labelled as a sign of 'right deviation'. Wu, a rare leader who deeply understood the emotions of minority nationalities, returned to Beijing on unclear charges.

What does 'the Kingdom of the Snow Lion and the Snow Mountains' mean? Tibetan independence has the following three characteristics, which differentiate it from other areas of China seeking independence, such as Taiwan.

First, from the point of view of the Mainland Chinese, Taiwan has a large population and much wealth, in spite of being an island. The sparsely populated territory of Tibet is vast. Just counting the existing administrative Tibetan areas, we can see that, in addition to the Tibet Autonomous Region, there are the Tibetan autonomous districts of Haibei, Hainan, Huangnan, Yushu and Golok, as well as the Haixi Mongol-Tibetan-Kazakh Autonomous Prefecture in Qinghai, which covers almost the entire province. Then there is the Aba Tibetan Autonomous Prefecture and the Ganze Tibetan Autonomous Prefecture in Sichuan, which covers about half the area of the province, the Deqen Tibetan Autonomous Prefecture in Yunnan, and the Gannan Tibetan Autonomous Prefecture and the Tianzhu Tibetan Autonomous County in Gansu. Geographically over a quarter of China's territory would be removed if Tibet became independent. In addition, we should not forget that the religion of the Mongolians is entirely controlled by the Yellow-Hat School of Tibetan Buddhism. In addition, the Uighur Autonomous Region, Xinjiang, may still remind people of the historical plan for the kingdom of 'East Turkestan'. Therefore, it is not difficult to imagine that once the flag of the 'Snow Lion and the Snow Mountains' is raised, what might follow initially would not be cultural prosperity but endless boundary conflict.

Secondly, from the point of view of the Tibetans, Taiwan has been independent in fact for the last forty years. During its early years it had an advantageous position in the world, even holding a seat in the UN Security Council for nearly three decades. Today it is rich and appears triumphant. In contrast, since 1950, Tibet has been increasingly economically and socially dependent on 'blood transfusions' from inland China. In the 1980s, the revenue of the regional government of the TAR was marked by deficits every year. Expenditure on all social and economic facilities is subsidised by financial appropriations from the Central Government, including all levels of government: schools, hospitals, post offices, public security bureaux, civil administration organs, social relief facilities, the transport, trade and industry sectors, and so on. Moreover, over 90 per cent of the goods traded in the autonomous region are provided and transferred by the Central Government at administrative low prices. These goods include food, commodities, fuel, and materials for building and industry. Except for its culture, Tibet has remained totally dependent on the Central Government for a long time. It is safe to say that the day Tibet gains its independence will be the day when it will immediately collapse. Tibet might try to find other forms of 'external circulation' such as dollars, pounds or rupees, but, as Chairman Mao said, 'There is absolutely no such thing in the world as love or hatred without reason or cause.' When spending someone else's money, please watch out for a replay of the battle against the British at Jiangzi [Gyantse] in a new form.

And thirdly, the reason for 'Taiwan independence' is either economic or political. The economic and political conditions are easy to change, especially in today's changing world. Today, become independent; tomorrow, re-unify with the Mainland – it is not absolutely impossible. There is no conflict whatsoever at the deep level of culture between Taiwan and the Mainland. Nurtured by the same culture and the same ethnic origins, the people of Taiwan are still Chinese, even though they are separated. In comparison, if the reason for 'Tibetan independence' lies at the deep level of culture, it is hard for it to be retrieved by one or two Chinese princesses marrying Tibetan kings.

National dignity is, in the final analysis, dependent on economic development and social improvement. If society is left far behind both socially and economically, there is no real dignity to speak of.

The basic reason for the underdevelopment of the Tibetan economy is the poor ability of people in using resources. In *The Poverty of Plenty* we listed many facts in support of this point. For instance, the introduction of the production responsibility system has won an unprecedented development in coastal areas, while in Tibet it has produced no response. The peasants and herdsmen who sincerely believe in Buddhism often spend all their money travelling to the Potala palace to perform prostrations or give their money directly to the temple as alms, while they themselves live in utter destitution without any complaint. There are few '10,000 yuan families' in Tibet. The money that Tibetans have earned through hard work has been used to compete in repairing temples. Most peasants and herdsmen are satisfied with their poor life and show little interest in making money. As a result, many peasants from Zhejiang have gone to Tibet and made fortunes.

Change in people's views is a strong lever for the modernisation of society. But the comprehensiveness of Tibetan religion and the existing level of Tibetan culture have seriously inhibited social progress. If we want to rejuvenate and expand Tibetan culture, religious reform becomes an essential historical task. After our study tour in 1984, we suggested helping Tibetan compatriots to start this reform. Of course, it is a dream, although historically the Mongolian cavalrymen helped the Tibetans establish the Yellow-Hat School of Buddhism as the leading religious force. Nobody knows how to 'trigger off' a religious reform, or where the 'trigger' is. Nevertheless, as history has claimed the necessity of reform, the following three principles can be said to be needed if that is to come about.

First, the external environment should be relaxed. Thirty years of 'leftist' rule in Tibet proved that when pressure is stronger, believers become more united. Strong pressure easily forces people to save every bit of their tradition indiscriminately without bothering to distinguish the 'gold' from the 'dross'. On the other hand, in the last few years since religious policies were relaxed, the different views and interests of the different temples have been exposed and have grown quickly.

Secondly, the need for reform by the meritocratic class should be acknowledged. During our study tour, we found that the peasants and herdsmen at the grassroots level are quiet and gentle and hold themselves aloof from the world, while the cadres trained by the government in Beijing or Chengdu have a stronger national sense. They often complain about and resent the backward reality and are highly motivated by the desire for national rejuvenation; they have seen developments outside and thus realise their own backwardness. This feeling is probably also true òf Tibetans who have been educated abroad. On many occasions, Bai Nanfeng discussed the Buddhist scriptures with the religious upper circles and found that many high lamas have all along seen some of the evil concomitants of religion. Many of them have already recognised the necessity of reform.

And lastly, one should seek the presence of a religious leader who has great wisdom and courage, and a spirit of dedication like the legendary 14th-century Tibetan reformers Zong Gaba (Tsongkhapa). Perhaps he will be a reformer in a top position like Gorbachev and Yeltsin, or maybe just a regular believer like Martin Luther. Unfortunately the Panchen Lama died early, but even if he were still alive he would be far less influential than the Dalai Lama, who is respected by everyone in Tibet, and who, as a spiritual leader, can make an overall examination of Tibetan culture, discard the 'dross' and expand the 'gold', thus establishing the spiritual foundation for a new Tibet. This would be a charitable and pious deed, and of boundless benefit to Tibetan history.

NOTES

1. Bai Nanfeng and Wang Xiaoqiang, *The Poverty of Plenty*, Angela Knox (trans), London: Macmillan, 1991.
2. At the conference in 1990, Wang said: 'I only wish my co-author, Bai Nanfeng, could be here with me. Unfortunately he was detained in Beijing last year. We have worked together for ten years, and our book reveals Bai's boundless loyalty to China and his enthusiasm for its development. I hope the government will also see his patriotic faith and let him return home.'

PROVINCIAL-LEVEL LEADERS IN TIBETAN AREAS SINCE 1950

(pre-1979 names are given in Wade-Giles transliteration)

Tibet Autonomous Region: Party Leaders

November 1951–August 1965. Zhang Jingwu (Chang Ching-wu). First Secretary of the Tibet Work Committee of the CCP.

November 1960–September 1965. Tan Guansan (T'an Kuan-san). May have been acting First Party Secretary or a high ranking Deputy Secretary. First Political Commissar of the Tibet Military Region, February 1952 to July 1967.

September 1965–September 1967. Zhang Guohua (Chang Kuo-hua). Party Secretary of the TAR. Commander of the Tibet Military Region, October 1951 to September 1967. Acting Party Secretary on the Tibet Work Committee in early 1956. Deputy Chairman of the Preparatory Committee for the Autonomous Region of Tibet (PCART) from its inauguration in 1956 until its disbanding in September 1965. Party Secretary, Sichuan, August 1971–1973.

September 1968–August 1971. Zeng Yongya (Tseng Yung-ya). Chairman of the Tibet Revolutionary Committee. Commander of the Tibet Military Region from February 1964 until January 1968.

August 1971–May 1980. Ren Rong (Jen Jung). TAR Party. Secretary and Chairman of the Tibet Revolutionary Committee. Political Commissar of the Tibet Military Region and Vice-Chairman of the TAR Revolutionary Committee from 1968. Deputy Political Commissar of the Tibet Military Region and of the Tibet Military District from September 1963 (the region was reduced to the status of a Military District in 1971). Held the rank of Major General from 1955.

May 1980–1985. Yin Fatang. Political Commissar of the Tibet Military District and Party Secretary of the TAR. With a PLA unit in Tibet 1950-67.

1985–July 1988. Wu Jinghua (Yi nationality). Party Secretary of the TAR. Returned to Beijing because of 'ill health'; reportedly sacked for 'right deviationism'.

December 1988–1992. Hu Jintao. Party Secretary of the TAR. October 1990: returned to Beijing because of 'ill health'. October 1992: promoted to the Standing Committee of the Politburu of the PCC.

December 1992–? Chen Kuiyuan. Party Secretary of the TAR. Vice-Governor of the Inner Mongolian Autonomous Region in 1991. Member of the Party Committee of the Inner Mongolian Autonomous Region, responsible for higher education, from 1989.

Apparent Acting Party Leaders during Hu Jintao's Absence

March 1989. Zhang Shaosong. Political Commissar during martial law (March 1989–May 1990); apparently the effective leader of the TAR Party Committee to July 1990.

July 1991. Raidi (Tibetan: Rakti). Described as Executive Deputy Party Secretary in July 1991; subsequently described as Deputy Party Secretary but listed before others until March 1992 (see Chen Kuiyuan).

August 1991–1992. Zhang Xuezhong. Apparently the leading Deputy Party Secretary to March 1992.

March–December 1992. Chen Kuiyuan. Apparently leading Deputy Party Secretary, listed before Raidi and before the Governor of the TAR, Gyaltsen Norbu.

TAR Heads of the Government

1951-9. Dalai Lama (Ta-lai La-ma). Head of Local Government, April 1951 to April 1956; Chairman of the Preparatory Committee for the TAR (PCART), April 1956 to March 1959.

1959-64. Panchen Lama (Banqen Erdeni/Pan-ch'an E-erh Te-ni). Acting Director of the PCART, March 1959 to December 1964. Deputy Director, May 1956 to March 1959.

March 1965–September 1967. Ngapo Ngawang Jigme (A-p'ei A-wang Chin-mei). Acting Director of the PCART, March to September 1965. First Chairman of the TAR from its foundation in September 1965 to September 1967. Deputy Chairman of PCART, March 1959 to March 1965. First Deputy Commander of the Tibet Military Region, September 1954 to March 1959. Deputy Commander, March 1959 to June 1964.

September 1986–August 1971. Zeng Yongya (Tseng Yung-ya). Chairman of the Tibet Revolutionary Committee. Commander of the Tibet Military Region, February 1964 until January 1968.

June 1971–August 1979. Ren Rong (Jen Jung). Chairman of the Revolutionary Committee Party Secretary.

September 1979–February 1981. Tian Bao (T'ien Pao) alias Sangye Yeshe. Chairman of the TAR. Vice-Governor of Xikang (Sikang), November 1950 to January 1953. Vice-Governor of Sichuan, December 1955 to May 1967. Vice-Chairman of the Tibet Revolutionary Committee, 1968 to 1969. Deputy Party Secretary of the TAR, August 1971 to August 1978. Deputy Political Commissar of the Tibet Military Region, May 1970 to June 1971. Second Political Commissar of the Tibet Military District, 1973 to February 1981. Deputy Party Secretary in Sichuan, 1981-2.

April 1981–August 1982. Ngapo Ngawang Jigme. Second term as Chairman of the TAR. Remained Chairman of the TAR People's Congress; later became a Vice-Chairman of the Standing Committee of the National People's Congress. Was First Deputy Commander of the Tibet Military District in 1979.

April 1983–1985. Dorje Tseten. Chairman of the TAR. Deputy Party Secretary, March 1983 to June 1985. Director of the China Institute of

Tibetology, Beijing from 1985. Vice-Chairman of the TAR People's Congress for six months in 1981.
1985–April 1990. Dorje Tsering. Chairman of the TAR.
May 1990–? Gyaltsen Norbu. Chairman of the TAR; Deputy Party Secretary.

Qinghai: Party Leaders

October 1949–August 1954. Zhang Zhongliang (Chang Chong-liang). Party Secretary of Qinghai and Governor of Qinghai, November 1952 to December 1954.
August 1954–October 1961. Gao Feng (Kao Feng). Party Secretary of Qinghai.
November 1961–May 1962. Wang Zhao (Wang Zhao). Acting First Party Secretary of the Qinghai Party Committee. Governor of Qinghai, 1963; Deputy Political Commissar of the Qinghai Military Region, 1965 to August 1967.
May 1962–October 1966. Yang Zhilin (Yang Chih-lin). Party Secretary in Qinghai. First Political Commissar of the Qinghai Military Region, July 1964 to July 1965. Previously Governor of Suiyuan (since disbanded), late 1949; demoted to Vice-Governor of Suiyuan, December 1949 to December 1952. Deputy Party Secretary of Inner Mongolia, July 1952 to May 1962.
March 1971–September 1976. Liu Xianquan (Liu Hsien-Chu'uan). Party Secretary of Qinghai; Chairman of the Qinghai Revolutionary Committee, August 1967 to March 1974. Commander of the PLA in Qinghai, December 1964–February 1968. Commander of the Inner Mongolia Military Region for three months in 1967. Deputy Commander of the Lanzhou Military Region for nine months in 1968.
March 1977–January 1980. Tan Qilong (T'an Ch'i-lung). Party Secretary of Qinghai. First Political Commissar of the Qinghai Military District, March 1977–September 1978. Deputy Party Secretary of Zhejiang from 1949; First Party Secretary and Governor of Zhejiang, 1952–4. Governor of Shandong, 1954–5, and 1958–63. Party Secretary of Shandong, 1961–7. Deputy Chairman of the Revolutionary Committee in Fujian, 1970–2. Chairman of the Revolutionary Committee of Zhejiang, 1972–7.
January 1980–January 1983. Liang Buting. Party Secretary. First Political Commissar of the Qinghai Military District, February 1980–May 1982.
April 1983–July 1985. Zhao Haifeng. Party Secretary of Qinghai. Vice-Governor of Qinghai in October 1981. First Political Commissar of the Qinghai Military District, February 1980 to January 1984. Vice-Chairman of the Qinghai Revolutionary Committee, 1977 to 1978.
July 1985–? Yin Kesheng. Party Secretary of Qinghai. Vice-Governor of Qinghai, March 1983 to August 1984.

Qinghai: Heads of the Government

October 1949–November 1952. Zhao Shoushan (Chao Shou-shan). Governor of Qinghai.

November 1952–December 1954. Zhang Zhongliang (Chang Chung-liang). Governor and Party Secretary of Qinghai.
December 1954–June 1958. Sun Zoubin (Sun Tso-pin). Governor of Qinghai. Deputy Party Secretary of Gansu, 1949 to 1953.
June–July 1958. Sun Junyi (Sun Chun-i). Acting Governor of Qinghai.
June 1958–October 1962. Yuan Renyuan (Yuan Jen-yuan). Governor of Qinghai. Vice-Governor of Hunan, 1949 to 1955.
October 1962–March 1967. Wang Zhao (Wang Chao). Acting Governor of Qinghai to December 1963; then Governor. Deputy Political Commissar of the Qinghai Military Region, July 1965 to August 1967. Acting First Party Secretary, November 1961 to May 1962.
August 1967–March 1974. Liu Xianquan (Liu Hsien-Chu'uan). Chairman of the Qinghai Revolutionary Committee. Party Secretary of Qinghai, March 1971 to September 1976.
March 1977–September 1979. Tan Qilong (T'an Ch'i-long). Chairman of the Qinghai Revolutionary Committee and Party Secretary of Qinghai.
September 1979–December 1982. Zhang Guosheng. Governor of Qinghai. Party Secretary, probably at Deputy level, of the Qinghai Party Committee, March 1957 to October 1965.
December 1982–August 1985. Huang Jingbo. Acting Governor of Qinghai to April 1983, then Governor. Vice-Governor in Shaanxi, 1958 to 1963. Vice-Chairman of the Guangdong (Canton) Revolutionary Committee, 1978 to 1981; Vice-Governor of Guangdong from 1981.
August 1985. Song Ruixiang, Governor of Qinghai.

Xikang (Kham)

March 1950–July 1955. Liao Zhigao (Liao Chih-Kao). Governor and Party Secretary of Xikang.
The Province of Xikang (Sikang) was disbanded and absorbed into Sichuan in 1955, when the Tibetan areas were split up into 'autonomous prefectures' or counties.

INDEX